THE CINEMA OF
GOSHO HEINOSUKE

THE CINEMA
OF
Gosho Heinosuke

Laughter through Tears

ARTHUR NOLLETTI, JR.

INDIANA UNIVERSITY PRESS

Bloomington & Indianapolis

This book is a publication of

Indiana University Press
601 North Morton Street
Bloomington, IN 47404-3797 USA

http://iupress.indiana.edu

Telephone orders   800-842-6796
Fax orders   812-855-7931
Orders by e-mail   iuporder@indiana.edu

The paper used in this publication meets the minimum
requirements of American National Standard for Information Sciences—
Permanence of Paper for Printed Library Materials,
ANSI Z39.48-1984.

Manufactured in the United States of America

Library of Congress Cataloging-in-Publication Data

Nolletti, Arthur, date-
The cinema of Gosho Heinosuke : laughter through tears / Arthur Nolletti, Jr.
p. cm.
Includes bibliographical references and index.
ISBN 0-253-34484-0 (alk. paper) — ISBN 0-253-21725-3 (pbk. : alk. paper)
1. Gosho, Heinosuke, 1902-1981—Criticism and interpretation. I. Title.
PN1998.3.G67N66 2005
791.4302'33'092—dc22

                                    2004017026

1 2 3 4 5 10 09 08 07 06 05

To the memory of my mother,
Vera,
who taught me to love the movies

CONTENTS

ACKNOWLEDGMENTS

This book began innocently enough. I knew that Gosho Heinosuke was celebrated for his work in the *shomin-geki,* the drama of ordinary people, but I had never seen any of his films. This situation changed in the winter of 1985. In January I saw the first of five Gosho films that were included in the retrospective "Before *Rashomon*: Japanese Film Treasures of the 30's and 40's" at the Japan Society of New York and the Boston Museum of Fine Arts. (For the record, these films were *The Bride Talks in Her Sleep, The Groom Talks in His Sleep, L'Amour, Burden of Life,* and *Woman of the Mist.*) After that, I read whatever I could find on the director in English and French (there is precious little), and planned my first research trip to Japan. In April 1985 I spent two weeks in Tokyo, saw eight more films, and met with a variety of film people, including critic Sato Tadao and screenwriter Uekusa Keinosuke, who kindly granted me interviews. In July of that year, thanks to a grant from the Northeast Asia Council, I traveled to the Pacific Film Archive where I saw two more films. Soon after, I found myself writing an article on *Where Chimneys Are Seen* and serving as a consultant (of sorts) for a Gosho retrospective in London. In December of 1989, I delivered the opening night talk at the Gosho retrospective in New York. By then I was committed to writing this book, the first such study in English on the director. For the next fourteen years, I spent my life researching and studying Gosho, trying to learn some Japanese, traveling back to Japan, and seeing as many films as I could, while collecting whatever Gosho I could find on video—all in all, not a bad life. My hope is that this book not only offers a worthy introduction to this Japanese master but also stimulates further study of his work.

As has been said many times, anyone who writes on Japanese film owes a profound and lasting debt to Donald Richie. His expertise is exceeded only by his friendship, generosity, and wonderful humor. Indeed, what other Japanologist can hold forth on the oeuvre of the American 50s film star, Dewey Martin?

At Indiana University Press, thanks must go to the following people for their vital assistance: the manuscript reviewers; Richard Higgins, assistant sponsoring editor; and Matt Williamson, jacket designer. Thanks, too, to copy editor Karen Kodner for her keen, yet sympathetic critical eye; managing editor Jane Lyle for her graciousness and moral support; and project editor Dawn Ollila for her inspiration, good counsel, and impressive command of Japanese. Above all, my deepest gratitude to Michael Lundell, my editor, for his friendship, subtle but firm guidance, and belief in this book from the start.

I also wish to thank Framingham State College for supporting my research with professional development money and granting me a sabbatical leave at a crucial stage in the writing. In addition, I am grateful to the college's library staff, which located even the most obscure articles I requested; to my students, who responded to Japanese films with sensitivity, intelligence, and enthusiasm; and, last but not least, to Teresa Pagliuca of Technology Services. A marvel with the computer, she reproduced the video images that make up the greater portion of the stills in this book. Thanks to these images and her steadfast dedication to the project, specific points I analyze are brought to life and greatly enriched.

Along the way, I have benefited from the support and encouragement of friends and colleagues: Linda Ehrlich, Kathe Geist, Peter Grilli, Leger Grindon, Sumiko Higashi, Iwamoto Kenji, Kakehi Chieko, Keiko McDonald, Lloyd Michaels (thanks for those Saturday morning phone calls!), Donna Paruti, James Quandt, Janet A. Walker, and Lois Ziegelman. Thanks, too, to David Desser, boon companion, erudite scholar, and trusty gourmand, who accompanied me to Sagamihara in the summer of 1992 to see some Gosho films; to David Bordwell and Dennis Washburn, who came to my rescue with essential illustrations; to Komatsu Hiroshi, who gave me a copy of *An Inn at Osaka;* and to Stephen Prince, whose friendship, passion for film, and unfailingly cogent advice helped keep me sane throughout my work on this book.

Numerous individuals in various film organizations also have been most generous: the staff of the International House of Japan (*Kokusai bunka kaikan*), especially Shimamura Naoka for translating material; Lee Amazonas and Nancy Goldman of the Pacific Film Archive; Kyoko Hirano and Tochigi Akira of the Japan Society of New York; Professor Vladimir Petric of Harvard University; Victor Kobayashi of the University of Hawaii at Manoa; Hayashi Kanako, Wachi Yukiko, and the late Shimizu Akira of the Kawakita Memorial Film Institute; and Sadamu Maruo, Saeki Tomonori, Ohba Masatoshi, Okajima Hisashi, and the staff at the National Film Center of the Museum of Modern Art in Tokyo. The latter two organizations arranged screenings, set up interviews, and provided me with invaluable research material. I also must acknowledge the special kindness of several individuals. The late Shimizu Akira not only took time to discuss Gosho at great length with me, but also sat beside me during a screening of *The Valley between Love and Death* to give me the benefit of his translation. Ohba Masatoshi and Okajima Hisashi, film curators at the National Film Center, shared their tremendous knowledge of film, allowed me to witness firsthand the important archival work they were doing, and, at the end of a very long, busy day, treated me to dinner.

This project would not have been possible without the superb help I received from Tacey Miller, Ryu Yukiko, and Sachiko Fujii Beck. Talented translators, they gave me access to information, which proved instrumental in shaping a number of my most important arguments. Deserving additional and very special thanks is Sachiko Beck, my friend and colleague at Framingham State College. Working with me from the project's inception, she not only translated numerous articles and carried out correspondence for me in Japanese, but also did research on her own, usually to decode an impossibly difficult family name. On top of this, she scoured video stores in Tokyo, tracking down Gosho films, and even had family and friends do the same.

In May 1990 I met two of Gosho's longtime friends and associates: Horie Hideo and the late Kakehi Masanori. Both have written eloquent, insightful essays on the director, which constitute essential reading. A filmmaker in his own right, Kakehi was Gosho's assistant director on *Once More* and *A Visage to Remember;* Horie was one of Gosho's key scenarists in the last decades of his career. In 1992, at the invitation of Kakehi and his lovely wife, Chieko, I spent a memorable Sunday afternoon at their home. By then, Kakehi was failing with terminal cancer; nevertheless, he seemed invigorated by the visit and by the chance to talk about a man he so clearly loved and admired. At one point Kakehi rose from the dinner table and left the room, returning with a copy of Gosho's autobiography, which he signed and gave to me. To this day, I believe this was his way of expressing gratitude for my interest in Gosho, as well as urging me to write the best book I could. One of the Kakehis' guests that day was their good friend, Horie Hideo. While in Tokyo, I spent some time with Horie; but it was only when I returned to the United States and began corresponding with him that I got to know him. An astute chronicler, who does not shy away from revealing Gosho's faults, Horie generously answered my many questions and made sure that I obtained whatever essays and information I needed. To Horie, Kakehi, and Chieko, who has become a close friend, my heartfelt thanks.

Finally, thanks to those people whose love and inspiration is the mainstay of any project I undertake. My father, Arthur, taught me the value of hard work, family loyalty, and rooting for the underdog; he also likes a good Western. Mitchell Fields, a lifelong friend and dedicated film teacher, listened to large chunks of the book (often on the phone), commenting on what he heard with good humor, kindness, and perception. My daughter, Alexandra, is proof that the apple does not fall far from the tree. Her love of Gosho is surpassed only by her love of the Beatles and of film itself, both of which are an indissoluble part of her life. And to Diana, my wife, I owe more than I can say. She is my most demanding critic and enduring supporter. For her, no detail is too small or insignificant; no task—technological or otherwise—is too big or daunting. Her contribution to this book is present on every page.

The still of Gosho Heinosuke is reproduced by permission of Kawakita Memorial Film Institute. The cover page of the program for the 1989–90 Gosho retrospective, which was sponsored by the Japan Society and the Museum of Modern Art, is reprinted by permission of the Japan Society.

I also wish to express thanks to the following sources for permission to reprint two of my articles. "*Once More* and Gosho's Romanticism in the Early Occupation Period" originally appeared in *Word and Image in Japanese Cinema,* ed. Dennis Washburn and Carole Cavanaugh (Cambridge University Press, 2001). "*Woman of the Mist* and Gosho in the 1930s" appeared in slightly different form in *Reframing Japanese Cinema: Authorship, Genre, History,* ed. Arthur Nolletti, Jr. and David Desser (Indiana University Press, 1992).

Note: Japanese names are presented in standard Japanese form: family name first, given name second; however, when a Japanese author has published in English, his or her name appears in Western order.

THE CINEMA OF
GOSHO HEINOSUKE

Gosho Heinosuke. Photo courtesy of Kawakita Memorial Film Institute.

Introduction

F ew of Gosho Heinosuke's films have been seen in the West.[1] It is no small wonder, then, that the brief references to the director in various encyclopedias and histories are not just incomplete, but often misleading and inaccurate. Thus, even the unfailingly astute David Thomson, in *A Biographical Dictionary of Film*, erroneously claims that the immense popular success of *Madamu to nyobo* (*The Neighbor's Wife and Mine*, 1931) "launched Gosho on carefully acted film adaptations of plays and novels" and that he belongs to the "school" of Mizoguchi.[2] If the first statement is at best a half-truth, the latter is simply wrong. The *Oxford Companion to Film* makes an even more damaging error when it notes that Gosho "confine[d] himself to the *shomin-geki*, the drama of the common people."[3] This error is a common misconception, which has led to pigeonholing Gosho and unintentionally denying him his true achievement. As if to make up for this mistake, the *Oxford Companion* credits Gosho with fifty more films than he actually made.[4] The fullest and most accurate discussions of the director in English are to be found in Anderson and Richie's *The Japanese Film*, their 1956 essay in *Sight and Sound*, and the anonymous profile in Wakeman's *World Film Directors: Volume One—1890–1945*. However, these are not intended to be much more than extended introductions to the filmmaker's work.

No understanding of Japanese film history can be complete without acknowledging the contribution of Gosho (1902–81). In Japan, Gosho is generally regarded, along with Ozu, Mizoguchi, Tasaka Tomotaka, Shimazu Yasujiro, Kumagai Hisatora, and Toyoda Shiro, as one of the key figures in the first Golden Age of Japanese Cinema in the 1930s.[5] He also was a prominent figure in the postwar era, reaching his peak in a series of films in the 1950s that included *Entotsu no mieru basho* (*Where Chimneys Are Seen*, 1953), *Osaka no yado* (*An Inn at Osaka*, 1954), and *Takekurabe* (*Growing Up*, 1955). Gosho's long and distinguished career spanned forty-three years, beginning in the silent era with the 1925 love story, *Nanto no haru* (*Spring in Southern Islands*), and ending with the 1968 feature-length puppet film, *Meiji haru aki* (*Seasons of the Meiji/A Girl of the Meiji Period*).[6]

During that time, he made nearly one hundred films, of which little more than a third survive.[7] While it is true that he was a major exponent of the *shomin-geki,* it is equally important to recognize that he worked in a wide range of genres, including *nansensu* (nonsense or slapstick) comedy, *sarariman* (salaryman) comedy, romance, melodrama, family drama, social drama, and the *jidai-geki* (period film).[8] As one of the most committed humanists of Japanese cinema, Gosho believed that a director's task was to describe life as it is lived around him, to confront the issues and concerns of his society, and, above all, to express the true and most authentic feelings of human beings. Throughout his life Gosho remained true to this credo. Indeed, his commitment to these beliefs doubtless led him to retain the *shomin-geki* as the base of his work, even when he ventured into other genres. In Gosho, one finds none of Kurosawa's nihilism, Mizoguchi's determinism, or Naruse's pessimism. Instead, one finds an indissoluble compassion and affection for character, which reminds one of Ozu, albeit with an occasional sentimentality that Ozu never allowed. Audiences and critics were quick to recognize the special, often lyrical mood of Gosho's films, "the warm, subtle, and sentimental depiction of likable people,"[9] the mixture of pathos and humor that makes one want to laugh and cry at the same time. Reminiscent of Chaplin and De Sica at their best, this mood has come to be known simply as "Goshoism."

Although Gosho's career was long and distinguished, it was by no means untroubled. Projects unsuited to him and two protracted bouts of tuberculosis took their toll. So, too, did the establishment of "national policy" films during the war, which morally and temperamentally he could not make. Finally, there were various conflicts with the studios. Of these, the most serious and bitter was his support of the union in the Toho labor strikes of the late 1940s. These troubles notwithstanding, his work not only survived but flowered, and in 1947 he returned to form with *Ima hitotabino* (*Once More*), an opulently mounted love story that captured the hopes and aspirations of postwar Japan.

Among Gosho's many accomplishments, the following stand out: he directed the first successful Japanese "talkie," *The Neighbor's Wife and Mine;* helped to launch the *junbungaku* ("pure literature") movement, which brought classical Japanese literature to the screen; founded one of the first independent production companies in Japan, Studio Eight; made one of the best and most beloved of all *shomin-geki, Where Chimneys Are Seen;* and represented Japan at film festivals in the 1950s, carrying home prizes. Throughout his career, he also received numerous other honors and awards, including the selection of eleven of his films by the prestigious *Kinema Jumpo* as among the "Best Ten" of the year.

Gosho's work in the 1920s clearly paved the way for his even finer achievements to come in the 1930s. It was during the 20s that he found what was to be his characteristic theme: illuminating the lives of the common people in all their beauty and sorrow. Moreover, his visual style—which would remain consistent throughout his career—had already begun to take shape in his second film, *Sora wa haretari* (*The Sky Is Clear,* 1925). With his fourteenth film, *Sabishiki ranbomono* (*The Lonely Roughneck*) in 1927, Gosho established himself as an up-and-coming director. Two years later he made *Shinjoseikan* (*A New Kind of Woman,* 1929), which not only criticized "that golden calf with hoofs of clay—capitalism" but also captured the mood of a country suffering from an ongoing recession.[10] However, his greatest success of the decade was *Mura no hanayome* (*The Village Bride,* 1928), a tale of a crippled young woman who is replaced at the altar by her healthy sister. (Unfortunately, like all his films of the 20s, it is no longer extant.[11]) Dealing with common people, it not only attacked feudal values (specifically the attitude toward the physically handicapped), but also demonstrated his sympathy for the oppressed. The film's critical and commercial success seemed to promise a continued string of successes for Gosho, but this was not the case. When a beloved younger brother contracted polio and lost the use of one leg, Gosho fell into a deep depression and turned out a series of films that were preoccupied with suffering, disease, and physical infirmity. Not surprisingly, these films failed utterly at the box office. Gosho had temporarily lost his way. He, therefore, was in no position to refuse when Shochiku insisted that he direct the company's first talking picture, an assignment that many other directors had rejected.

The result was a personal triumph for Gosho and the beginning of his first sustained creative period. Between 1931 and 1937, beginning with *The Neighbor's Wife and Mine* and ending with *Hanakago no uta* (*The Song of the Flower Basket,* 1937), a comedy set in a small Ginza restaurant, he produced a series of often brilliant films, which ranged from lighthearted comedies to works of social criticism. It was a decade in which he experimented—with sound, with narrative structure, with various thematic material, with adapting literature to film, and perhaps, as one of his assistant directors suggests, with the limits of expression offered by film itself.[12] But most of all, it was a decade in which he made significant developments in his art.

Throughout the seventy-nine years of his life, Gosho retained a youthful vigor and curiosity, and never stopped searching for new challenges. On his seventieth birthday, he wrote:

> I still want to study and explore all that I can, and there is much I am willing to risk my life to learn. Although some may say that I have too many desires,

the desire to learn something new and master it, and the ability to always a have a sense of wonder is what keeps me young. This is my inexhaustible youth.[13]

Thus, in the postwar period Gosho rethought and reconfigured his beloved *shomin-geki* to better describe the life and times of common people. He also tried his hand at new genres, such as the *jidai-geki,* experimented with color, and sought to deepen his study of human relationships by appropriating elements of the European art film. Eager to tackle new ideas, he even collaborated with novelists, such as Shiina Rinzo or Inoue Yasushi, who, on the face of it, were temperamentally and even ideologically incompatible with him. Sometimes these collaborations succeeded admirably; sometimes they failed miserably. Either way, they kept Gosho alive to his art and his society. Gosho's striking out in new directions, however, did not mean the renunciation of the old, but rather a combining of the old and the new. The results of this rich synthesis are especially evident in the 1950s. His period of greatest achievement, it also saw him gain international recognition. *Where Chimneys Are Seen* (1953), his most celebrated film and "one of the really important postwar Japanese films,"[14] is a moving examination of the struggles of two tenement couples; *An Inn at Osaka* (1954) is a superb study of the relationships between staff and residents in a small hotel; *Growing Up* (1955) is a sensitive adaptation of Higuchi Ichiyo's classic story of a young girl fated for a life of prostitution; and *Banka* (*Elegy of the North,* 1957) is an exploration of the tragic relationship between a handicapped young woman, a married middle-aged architect, and his alienated wife. During the late 50s, he also made two notable, if uneven, works: *Kiiroi karasu* (*Yellow Crow,* 1957), his first film in color, and *Hotarubi* (*The Fireflies,* 1958), a *jidai-geki* (period film) set in the turbulent 1860s.

In the 1960s, his last decade as an active director, Gosho demonstrated his continued mastery of the medium in films like *Ryoju* (*Hunting Rifle,* 1961), *Osorezan no onna* (*An Innocent Witch,* 1965), and *Utage* (*Rebellion of Japan,* 1967). Unfortunately, like other veteran directors, Gosho found himself struggling to survive in the new atmosphere of rampant commercialism. Consequently, his work suffered and was decidedly uneven. Still, his best films were as intelligent and meticulously made as ever, and he used the widescreen process to particularly good effect in underscoring the psychological relations between people. He also continued to explore the major themes that had preoccupied him throughout his career: the nature of male-female relationships, the situation of the oppressed, and the plight of women. Indeed, along with his empathy for the ups and downs of his characters' lives, Gosho's sensitivity to the social and psychological pressures exerted upon his female protagonists is the single most important concern of his work as a whole. Finally, Gosho was a consummate director of actors.

Scholars generally agree that there were three major influences on Gosho: his mentor at Shochiku Studio, Shimazu Yasujiro; haiku; and Ernst Lubitsch. A pioneer of the *shomin-geki,* Shimazu Yasujiro brought to the mode a "realism, warmth, and humor [that] left their mark on the work of all his pupils," including Gosho.[15] Shimazu's comedy, *Tonari no Yae-chan* (*Our Neighbor, Miss Yae,* 1934), arguably his most famous film, provides an excellent example of his work. It deals with two next-door neighbors who are too shy to admit their attraction to each other: Keitaro (Ohinata Den), a college student, and Miss Yae (Aizome Yumeko), a high-school student. Shimazu's emphasis is on the ordinariness of daily life in all its sweet banality: neighbors chatting, brothers playing pitch and catch (and accidentally breaking a neighbor's window), people simply going about their business. In a key scene Keitaro, bored with his studies at Tokyo University, stops by to see Miss Yae. But she isn't home, so he waits. Hungry, he asks her mother (Iida Choko) for something to eat. She kindly obliges. In a series of comic accidents that follow, he spills tea on one of the pillows on the floor. When Miss Yae and a school friend (Takasugi Sanae) show up, the latter immediately senses the attraction between the two neighbors, which Miss Yae, of course, denies. But her treatment of Keitaro suggests otherwise. Seeing the holes in his socks, she instructs him to take them off. "I love mending," she exclaims. However, as soon as she smells the socks, she immediately tosses them aside. Next, she pulls the pillow he is sitting on out from under him. "This is only for guests," she says, puzzled that it is wet. Very little "happens" in this seven-minute scene, yet typical of Shimazu's work, it makes viewers "laugh with and not at the characters."[16] More important, it makes them *feel,* thanks to Shimazu's ability to reveal these lives as meaningful.[17] The easy affection and low dramatic register of such a scene could not have gone unnoticed by Gosho. Nor could Shimazu's visual style, which, as has been often noted, was influenced by Hollywood codes of *découpage.*[18] One example of this influence will suffice: Shimazu's use of inserted close-ups. Shimazu includes three such shots for emphasis—one of the holes in the heels of Keitaro's socks, a second of his dirty feet, and a third of the tea-stained pillow. In this way Shimazu conveys not only the two girls' surprise and amusement, but also Keitaro's understandable embarrassment. More crucially, Shimazu gets to the heart of the scene, teasing out the characters' naiveté and innocence, something that all of us can recognize as part of being human. Quite clearly, Gosho took to heart the lessons Shimazu taught him. He also was receptive to other influences, as well.

Known as the director who "uses three shots where others use one," Gosho attributed his visual style to two sources: haiku and Ernst Lubitsch. A haiku poet, as well as a filmmaker, Gosho began studying this three-line form (which usually consists of seventeen syllables) when he was seventeen, and he published in the form throughout his life. From haiku, he—like other Japanese directors—learned abbreviation, association, and a sensitivity to nature and the seasons. This influence, in part, led to Gosho's fondness for *suikyo* settings (locations near water) and shooting on location. Unlike Ozu or Mizoguchi, Gosho would even change his shooting schedule if he saw a composition of clouds, mist, or a beautiful sunset that could crystallize or express a particular feeling or emotion of a scene. Similarly, during an editing session, he would replace scenes or parts of scenes that failed to work with shots of nature.[19] Yet this kind of lyricism is only one form that haiku takes in Gosho's films, and as the poet Azumi Atsushi has said, it perhaps is not even the most profound or important form.[20] By this, Azumi means that Gosho's films themselves are haiku, in that they are made up of compressed, evocative images which invariably suggest more than they show. In this respect, Gosho's films are not unlike the haiku of Basho, which are divided into two parts, representing "a tension between the evanescent and the eternal."[21]

From Ernst Lubitsch, whose *Marriage Circle* (1924) he had seen over twenty times and "which he credited as the greatest foreign influence on his work, along with Chaplin's *A Woman of Paris* (1923),"[22] Gosho learned analytical (or piecemeal) editing—the breakdown of a scene into brief, individual shots to capture even the most minuscule nuances of character and emotion. In his hands, close-ups in particular privileged character psychology to a degree that went far beyond Shimazu's use of this strategy. In fact, Gosho built on Lubitsch's style, making it very much his own, while also deploying the moving camera to underscore social and psychological connections between people and to give added depth to his images.[23] Even when Gosho filmed in widescreen, he never abandoned Lubitsch's style, but rather modified it. While there is no question that Gosho's editing style depends on Western notions of *découpage,* his style as a whole represents an assimilation of Western and indigenous norms, what Richie aptly calls a "double aesthetic heritage."[24] Hence, to cite one example, while using Western-style editing, Gosho frequently resorts to sudden reverse shots (*donden*), which clearly deviate from classical Hollywood norms by cutting across the 180-degree axis. This strategy is very much in keeping with Japanese norms. We will examine it more closely in chapter 5 when we discuss *Where Chimneys Are Seen.*

Finally, Gosho's art, like his values and attitudes, was almost certainly shaped by his childhood and upbringing. Born in 1902 in the Shitamachi (old downtown) section of Tokyo, Gosho was an illegitimate child. His father, a prosperous tobacco merchant, never married his mother, a geisha of great beauty; but when Gosho was five years old, his father's legitimate son died, and Gosho's life changed forever. Taken by his father to come and live in Osaka, he was named heir and groomed for a position in the family business. He was also told by someone in his father's household, "From now on, you no longer have a natural mother." After that, Gosho uttered the word "mother" only once: to his natural mother when she was on her deathbed.[25] Yet, as he himself later said, he was genuinely loved by his father and grandfather, and had a happy and full childhood. While this is doubtless true, it is probably no less true that he always remained very sensitive to the complex nature of his circumstances, and even felt guilty. There was, on the one hand, the situation of his mother, whose life was far from easy. By contrast, his life was filled with every conceivable advantage. In fact, as part of his informal education, his grandfather introduced him to the arts, and his father took him along to the tearooms, restaurants, and geisha houses that he loved to frequent—a milieu that Gosho would later depict with great affection in films like *Oboroyo no onna* (*Woman of the Mist,* 1936).

What Gosho could not help but appreciate, in short, were the contradictions in life—and the fact that nothing was black or white. He saw the plight of his mother, and the deaths of four of his five younger brothers. But he also saw the goodness and generosity of his father and grandfather, and so he could not cast them in the roles of his mother's oppressors. Indeed, he couldn't even identify them as the principal cause of her suffering. What Gosho came to realize was that no one was to blame.[26] It is this knowledge, this unerring sense of life's injustices, contradictions, and complexities, that lies at the heart of Gosho's films, giving them an expansiveness, generosity of spirit, and wisdom.[27]

By now it should be clear that even though Gosho worked primarily within the studio system—and mostly at Shochiku—his films are characterized by a distinct style and set of themes that give unity and coherence to his career as a whole. Indeed, besides directing, Gosho often wrote or co-wrote many of his scripts. He also took an active role in every phase of production. Reputedly, he even personally polished the wooden floor of one of the sets for *Growing Up* to get the "requisite sheen."[28] Gosho's films, however, were products of collaboration. In fact, a number of his collaborators worked alongside him throughout much of his career; many others joined him frequently, their participation in a half-dozen or more films not uncommon. Among these key collaborators were cinematographers Ohara Joji and Miura Mitsuo; scriptwriters Fushimi Akira, Kogo Noda, Kitamura Komatsu, Yasumi Toshio, Hasebe Keiji, and Horie Hideo; musical composer Akutagawa Yasushi; and the following actors and actresses: Yakumo

Emiko, Tanaka Kinuyo, Iida Choko, Sano Shuji, Saito Tatsuo, Kobayashi Tokuji, and Yoshikawa Mitsuko, to name just a few. All of these individuals were united in one common purpose: to bring "Goshoism" to the screen. In other words, it was Gosho's themes, concerns, and attitudes—his vision, if you will—that provided the *raison d'être* for the collaborative process in the first place. Throughout this study, important contributions by collaborators are acknowledged. But there can be no doubt that Gosho was the author of his films.

The Cinema of Gosho Heinosuke: Laughter through Tears is the first book in English to examine the work of this renowned director. A developmental study, it traces the relationship between Gosho's visual and narrative style and the specific thematic and ideological concerns to which he is committed. By and large chronologically organized, it provides close readings of individual films, paying particular attention to the cultural, historical, and industrial conditions that influenced these films and, in turn, are reflected in them. This study concerns itself with how Gosho shapes his *shomin-geki,* how at times he reformulates it and breathes new life into it, how he frequently blends and reconfigures it with other genres, and how he occasionally diverges from it altogether. In short, this study does not confine itself to the *shomin-geki,* but focuses on other modes as well, namely, literary adaptations, melodrama, and psychological drama. In so doing, it not only explores the critical issues that are germane to an understanding of Gosho's work, but also reveals the diversity and coherence within that work. Thus, while Gosho's films are best known for their warm and gentle affection, and their evocation of laughter through tears, some of his most important films depart from this model. Far from being exceptions in his body of work, they represent yet another example of its range and depth. However, even when Gosho does not ask for laughter and tears, even when he shifts the focus from common people to the middle class, his films remain linked by the overarching theme of compassion and respect for human beings. That said, his emphasis on human nature does not mean that he neglects larger cultural or political concerns. On the contrary, throughout his career Gosho was engaged in an ongoing dialogue with social issues, among them the impact of World War II, the implications of democratization, the persistence of feudal values, and the dehumanizing effect of Japan's materialism. He also remained a champion of individual rights. Although this study's overall goal is to investigate Gosho's themes and cinematic forms, the specific issues and stylistic strategies that are treated in each chapter differ, depending on the film (or films) being discussed. Finally, in examining Gosho's achievement, this study hopes to provide insights into Japanese cinema as well.

Since many of Gosho's films no longer survive, we must obviously proceed with caution in tracing his development. After all, we are unable to see the films that established his reputation in the 1920s. Nor will we probably ever know whether some of the films of that decade, unheralded at the time, may have proved to be seminal or significant in retrospect. Still, as John Gillett has said, "Fortunately, enough survives to place his work in the 30s, 50s and 60s into some sort of perspective from silence to sound, from black and white 'Scope to gorgeous colour."[29] In fact, we have nine of Gosho's most important films of the 1930s (out of a total of thirty-six), five of his six films of the 1940s, plus parts of the missing one, *Shinsetsu* (*New Snow*, 1942), and all of the films from the 1950s and 1960s. All told, there are forty extant films—enough to give us the most complete picture of his career that we are likely to have until hopefully other lost films are discovered.[30]

Needless to say, it would be impossible to analyze all of Gosho's extant films. Thus, in this study I have chosen to concentrate on those films that are most representative of his achievement and most important historically. As it happens, these films—nineteen in all—are also among his best known and highly regarded.

Chapter 1, "Gosho and *Shomin* Comedy in the 1930s," examines the nature, origins, and scope of Gosho's early *shomin* comedy. The first section, "'Nonsense' Comedies," provides a close analysis of three farces, which today are regarded as classics: *The Neighbor's Wife and Mine, Hanayome no negoto* (*The Bride Talks in Her Sleep*, 1933), and *Hanamuko no negoto* (*The Groom Talks in His Sleep*, 1935). Partly inspired by American silent comedy, these films taught Gosho how to blend comedy, farce, and drama into a special mood of laughter. They also allowed him to explore themes that would preoccupy him throughout his career, including the plight of women and the nature of male-female relationships. The second section, "'Slice-of-Life' Comedy," investigates two notable features of Gosho's development, as seen in *Jinsei no onimotsu* (*Burden of Life*, 1935): his incorporation of "irrelevant events" in the narrative, and his use of the *shomin-geki* as a vehicle for character study.

Chapter 2, "*Dancing Girl of Izu* (1933) and the *Junbungaku* Movement," focuses on a film that holds a prominent place in Gosho's career and in Japanese film history. One of the first works in the *junbungaku* ("pure literature") movement, which thrived between 1935 and 1941, it enabled Gosho and the industry to bring more ambitious fare to the screen. It also gave him the opportunity to portray people more realistically than he had done. Based on Kawabata Yasunari's acclaimed novella, *Izu no odoriko* (*Dancing Girl of Izu*) is about the doomed love between a young itinerant dancer and a college student on summer vacation. This chapter examines how Gosho adapts his source, achieves the mood of laughter through tears, and adds a subplot to Kawabata, which gives the story greater resonance by showing the effect of the Great Depression on Japan.

Chapter 3, "*Woman of the Mist* (1936): Blending the *Shomin-geki, Shitamachi,* and Romantic Melodrama," focuses on arguably the most accomplished film by Gosho in the 1930s. An outstanding example of the *shitamachi,* a subgenre of the *shomin-geki,* the film is set in an area that Gosho knew intimately and loved, the Shitamachi, the old downtown neighborhoods of pre–World War II Tokyo. Here goodhearted people relied on humor and bantering to see them through life's vicissitudes. Gosho depicts this now-lost world as he tells the story of an ill-fated love affair between a young barmaid and a student. True to romantic melodrama, the film deals with the domestic sphere, romantic love, and a heroine whose desires clash with society. True to the *shomin-geki,* the film presents its milieu in a documentary-like style. Made when the military movement was at its height, *Woman of the Mist* is ultimately an indictment of the treatment of women and the repression of individuality.

Chapter 4, "*Once More* (1947) and Gosho's Romanticism in the Early Occupation Period," examines Gosho's first film after the war. A work of considerable historical and aesthetic importance, it is a love story set against the backdrop of World War II, beginning with Japan's invasion of Manchuria and ending with its defeat fifteen years later. In focusing on how the film exemplifies Gosho's "romanticism," this chapter situates the film in its historical context, paying special attention to the Toho labor strikes of the late 1940s. It also considers the film's relationship to the "democratization" films of the day, its troubled production history, and its indebtedness to foreign and Japanese films. At the center of this chapter are a detailed discussion of Gosho's concept of romanticism, which he outlined in an article that he wrote for the journal *Eiga Tenbo* (*Film Review*), and an in-depth analysis of the film, which illustrates the forms that Gosho's romanticism takes thematically and stylistically.

Chapter 5, "*Where Chimneys Are Seen* (1953): A New Kind of *Shomin-geki,*" focuses on how this landmark film constitutes a turning point in Gosho's career. Always interested in new themes and approaches, Gosho sought a new kind of *shomin-geki* to reflect the vast changes Japan had undergone since the war, in particular the new humor and sorrow of common people struggling for survival. He found what he was looking for in Shiina Rinzo's novel, *Mujakina hitobito* (*The Good People*). This chapter shows that the film is not so much a break from Gosho's earlier *shomin-geki* as a reimagining and reshaping of many of the genre's basic ingredients. Gosho's themes remain much the same, but unlike the 30s comedies, there is none of the physical comedy and a much greater degree of narrative causality, a more intricate structure, and the use of the chimneys themselves as a recurring motif. Still, the film possesses a playfulness, a lightness of tone and gentle pathos, that tempers the mood of uncertainty with a sense of optimism.

Chapter 6, "*An Inn at Osaka* (1954): "Money, Democracy, and Limited Knowledge," explores Gosho's continued reinvigoration of the *shomin-geki*. The film depicts Japan on the brink of the "economic miracle," and has to do with the efforts of a young, idealistic insurance man to help those around him, especially three maids who work at the small inn where he resides. Although the film is not devoid of Gosho's characteristic blend of laughter and tears, its tone is unusually sad and melancholy—appropriately so, given the uncompromising depiction of postwar Japan where money controls every aspect of people's lives. This chapter has a double focus. First, it explores the complex and often surprising mix of moods, which range from slapstick to tragedy. Second, it examines the no-less-complex narrational structure and strategies, and how they problematize the central protagonist's well-meaning but flawed desire to do good. A deeply felt film, *An Inn at Osaka* is one of Gosho's most progressive works.

Chapter 7, "*Growing Up* (1955): Adapting the *Meiji-mono*, Reconfiguring the *Shomin-geki*," focuses on Gosho's adaptation of Higuchi Ichiyo's classic novella about adolescents living in the Yoshiwara red-light district of Tokyo in the 1890s. First, this chapter discusses how Gosho alters Ichiyo's story, so that it centers not just on the young heroine destined for a life of prostitution, but also on a group of women who are already trapped in that life. Second, it examines the narrative and visual strategies that Gosho uses to compare and contrast the lives of these women. It also teases out the film's main themes: the loss of innocence, society's dehumanizing obsession with money, and the dissolution of the Japanese family. Finally, it shows how Gosho blends the *shomin-geki* with an important subgenre, the *Meiji-mono*, films set in the Meiji period (1868–1912). In doing so, he not only captures the texture of common people's lives, but also foregrounds the fact that postwar Japan has not changed all that much from the Japan of the Meiji period.

Chapter 8, "The Late 1950s: New Challenges and the Quest to Create," concentrates on Gosho's work in the late 1950s, demonstrating how he extended his range and conducted formal experiments, while once again combining the old and the new. In *Yellow Crow*, a characteristic *shomin-geki*, Gosho films in color for the first time, using color to investigate the psychological state of a troubled young boy. In *The Fireflies*, he directs one of his rare *jidai-geki* (period films), blending the mode with his *shomin-geki* to examine a well-known historic incident through the eyes of common people, in particular a woman innkeeper. The greater part of the chapter, however, concentrates on *Elegy of the North,* one of Gosho's most fully realized studies of adult relationships and one in which he departs from his usual mood of laughter through tears. Modeled in part on European art films, it constitutes a bold attempt to refashion romantic melodrama. Emphasis in this chapter is on Gosho's deviations from conventional melodrama, his use of theatre as a metaphor to structure the narrative, and the role of *mise-en-scène* and analytical editing to convey the theme of alienation.

Chapter 9, "Gosho in the 1960s: Changing Times, Undiminished Mastery," focuses on the last decade of Gosho's career. It opens with a brief description of the changing climate—the rapid spread of television, the drop in movie attendance, the emergence of the "new wave" Japanese directors, and increasing commercialization—noting the impact that this climate had on Gosho. It then analyzes three of his most accomplished melodramas: *Hunting Rifle, An Innocent Witch,* and *Rebellion of Japan.* The discussion of the first two films centers on how Gosho's use of widescreen reinforces his themes and relates to his analytical editing style. Consideration is also given to the unusually harsh tone of *An Innocent Witch,* a tone that is atypical of the director. The examination of *Rebellion of Japan,* a film that is often cited as Gosho's last representative work, concentrates on the relationship between the love story and the political theme. This chapter concludes with some final remarks on Gosho's signature mood of laughter through tears and on his significance in cinema history and Japanese film history.

An appendix focuses on three notable films, which have been mentioned elsewhere in this study and which merit fuller consideration: *L'Amour* (*Ramuru/ Aibu/ Caress/ Love,* 1933), a richly observed melodrama, which is especially important for its narrative structure; *Omokage* (*A Visage to Remember,* 1948), an atmospheric chamber piece, which is indebted to the European art film; and *Wakare-gumo* (*Dispersing Clouds,* 1951), a psychological drama whose headstrong young heroine and theme of spiritual health anticipate *Elegy of the North.*

A filmography provides vital information heretofore unavailable in English, and a selected bibliography lists sources I have used, along with works of special interest for further reading.

ONE

Gosho and Shomin *Comedy in the 1930s*

As stated in the Introduction, the *shomin-geki,* the drama of the everyday lives of the lower-middle classes, was the base from which Gosho worked throughout his career. At Shochiku, where Gosho worked exclusively from 1925 to 1941, studio head Kido Shiro made the genre one of the company's specialties. To a certain degree, then, Gosho's subjects, themes, and dramaturgical choices can be seen as variations and transformations on a genre defined and developed by studio policy.[1] Yet we must not forget that the *shomin-geki* was a broad, all-encompassing mode that could accommodate a disparate range of moods (all the way from farce to serious drama) and mix various genres and subgenres (including melodrama, romance, salaryman comedies, home dramas, and nonsense comedies). Throughout the long history of the *shomin-geki*—its golden years were from the 1920s to the early 1960s—it attracted an impressive number of directors, many of whom excelled in it. These included, besides Gosho and Shimazu Yasujiro, Ozu Yasujiro, Naruse Mikio, Shimizu Hiroshi, Toyoda Shiro, Kinoshita Keisuke, and Yamada Yoji, to cite only a few. As a genre, the *shomin-geki* was unusual in that it allowed for a wide range of different visual styles —Gosho's analytical montage, Ozu's rigorous formalism, and Naruse's minimalism being only three of these styles. Nonetheless, as Noël Burch has observed, it was "a remarkably unified genre" with "extraordinary homogeneity."[2] It was characterized by simple plots; a de-emphasis of the dramatic; a privileging of the "ups and downs" of life; an attention to character, mood, and milieu; a mix of humor and sentiment; an often documentary-like feel; at times, a near-tragic intensity; and, at its best, a subtle cadence of emotion.

The *shomin-geki* had its origins in a variety of sources, both foreign and domestic. There were the dramas of Chekhov, Ibsen, and Shaw. These found their way to Japan around 1900 and introduced Western ideas of realism, helping to shape the *shingeki* (new Japanese theatre) of the 1920s, which espoused that "life must be presented as it appears."[3] There were the American comedies of the period (especially influential were Chaplin and Lloyd) and Universal's now-forgotten Bluebird movies of the 1910s and 1920s, with their simple stories, heartfelt idealism, and bucolic settings. There also was the emerging realist tendency of Japanese cinema itself, as evidenced in such landmark films as *Rojo no reikon* (*Souls on the Road*, 1921).[4] In effect, there was a confluence of influences and a shared notion of "realism" as the look and feel of quotidian reality. In actual practice, however, what shaped this "common people" genre was the work of individual practitioners. Shimazu, for example, in films like *Chichi* (*Father*, 1923), took his cue in part from American comedy, but "relied more on character and mood than upon plot and slapstick."[5] The result was light comedy, something that the *shomin-geki* lent itself to quite naturally. In fact, inherent in the very scope and nature of the genre was the possibility for a different emphasis, a different mix—for example, more slapstick and less characterization, or vice versa, depending on what a scriptwriter or director wanted. Consequently, subgenres gradually emerged: the *sarariman* (salaryman or "white collar") film of the early 1920s and the *nansensu* (nonsense) film of the late 1920s.

Ideologically, the *shomin-geki* was a highly protean genre. It could serve traditional values by celebrating the strength, courage, and resilience of common people in the face of pain and hardship. For many scholars, this aspect of the genre is epitomized by the phrase *mono no aware,* an awareness of the transitory nature of life, which is rooted in Zen Buddhism and urges acceptance rather than resistance.[6] Bittersweet in mood, *mono no aware* is something "between grief and nostalgia, the coming of autumn, the echo of what has passed and was loved."[7] In Japanese film, this mood finds visual expression in the unfolding of the seasons and the perception that human existence is part of the cycle of nature. Seen in this way, the *shomin-geki* becomes a kind of allegory that privileges quotidian reality and those at one with that reality. But there is another way to see the genre's emphasis on acceptance. Indeed, some critics have argued that the *shomin-geki* was a conservative genre that "served quite directly the interests of the reactionary forces at work in Japan" in the 1930s.[8]

However this may be, the genre was equally capable of taking a progressive stance. In fact, by showing the loosening of the role of the patriarch and the changing relationships among family members, by focusing on the oppression of women, and by presenting the family "in a tense confrontation with society,"[9] it not only proved to be a vehicle for protest, albeit implied protest, but it also managed to convey Western concepts of liberalism and democracy.[10] Thus, in the hands of Gosho and others as well, the genre valorized individualism, a central concern in Gosho's work. In the postwar period, when the *shomin-geki* became increasingly preoccupied with the disturbing currents of society, the need for individuality became an even more pronounced concern, as did the tension between the traditional and the progressive. In truth, the genre could only speak to this tension; it could not resolve it. But in doing so, it presupposed an immutable value system, a belief that the nobility of people was as fixed and certain as the world is evanescent and ever changing, and that in this nobility lay the possibility for a better, more equitable society. Put differently, these values might seem to change, and might even be confused with the often-overwhelming external changes taking place in society. Nevertheless, they remained valid and were there to be seen, almost as incontrovertible facts, in the documentary-like aspects of the genre and its slice-of-life approach, both of which downplayed the dramatic and had the effect of celebrating not only people "like you and me" but also life as it is lived, unmediated.

So attractive is this view of the genre as a slice-of-life, as a discursive, simple recording of events, that it has led some scholars virtually to define the entire genre in these terms. Thus, for Burch, the *shomin-geki* was at its best when its "unaffected approach" conveyed the "flow of life."[11] It achieved this quality when it opted for a relatively loose narrative causality that privileged subplots over a single story line and allowed for many "irrelevant events."[12] Given this preference, Burch praises Gosho's slice-of-life approach in the 1935 comedy *Burden of Life:* "If ever the ideology of the 'slice of life' were realized in cinema," he rhapsodizes, "it is in such films as this."[13] Burch's enthusiasm for this approach becomes problematic, however, when it prevents him from recognizing the validity of other approaches. Hence Burch finds fault with Gosho's 1953 *Where Chimneys Are Seen* because its use of the central symbol of the chimneys and its emphasis on dramatic conflict seem to deny an "unaffected approach." Besides not seeming to realize that the "unaffected approach" is at best a matter of degree, Burch also seems unwilling to allow the genre to change and evolve. In so doing, he ends up insisting upon an ultimately ahistorical mode.

It is imperative to understand the problem with Burch's position because Gosho's discursive slice-of-life approach in *Burden of Life*—as undeniably central to his *shomin-geki* as it is—represents only one of the two major modes in which the director worked in the 1930s. The other was "nonsense" comedy. Both forms were apropos of a particular time and place, stepping stones or building blocks, as it were, in Gosho's career, and must be recognized as such. And both forms are equally important. As Sato Tadao has argued, Gosho's work cannot be properly understood without taking into consideration the integral role that these early comedies had in his development.[14] Indeed, like many directors working at Shochiku Studio—even Ozu—Gosho was required by Kido Shiro to hone his craft in these comedies.[15]

To be sure, any study of the *shomin-geki* is complicated by the fact that the genre spawned a variety of subgenres and also that there was a great deal of overlapping between these subgenres. Thus, while *Madamu to nyobo* (*The Neighbor's Wife and Mine,* 1931), *Hanayome no negoto* (*The Bride Talks in Her Sleep,* 1933), and *Hanamuko no negoto* (*The Groom Talks in His Sleep,* 1935) may be effectively grouped as nonsense comedies, each has a somewhat different emphasis and generic mix. *The Neighbor's Wife and Mine* has elements in common with family drama, social drama, and light comedy; *The Bride Talks in Her Sleep* has affinities with social drama and yet another subgenre, the "college" or "student" film; and *The Groom Talks in His Sleep* borrows from both family drama and social drama. By contrast, *Jinsei no onimotsu* (*Burden of Life,* 1935), with its predominant slice-of-life approach, is at once a "salaryman" film, a family drama, and a social drama.

"NONSENSE" COMEDIES

Let us now turn to the three nonsense comedies. Anderson and Richie have explained the importance of these comedies as follows: "The excesses of the typical nonsense film had taught him [Gosho] the value of lightness, of underplayed, understated humor: the *shomin-geki* gave his films their solidarity and depth."[16] Put differently, nonsense comedy gave Gosho the opportunity to learn how to temper and modulate the emotional tone of his material so as to create "realistic studies with comic overtones."[17] In essence, it marked the beginning of "Goshoism," that is, making one want to laugh and cry at the same time.

Regarded in their day simply as entertainments, *The Neighbor's Wife and Mine, The Bride Talks in Her Sleep,* and *The Groom Talks in His Sleep* today are considered classics.[18] Virtually plotless, and feeling more like comic sketches than fully developed stories, these three light comedies, or farces, take a wholly trivial matter (often a socially embarrassing situation) and use it as a springboard for a succession of gags. These gags almost always build to a climax in which the major characters resolve any and all problems. Rarely is there an explicit statement of theme, or even a suggestion that any theme is intended. And the tone invariably is gentle, warm, affectionate, and of course—apropos of farce—zany, even silly. Gosho invites us to laugh as much with his characters as at them. He saves his occasional ridicule for those most deserving of it—the envious, the incorrigible, or both—who are most ripe for comic comeuppance.

Partly inspired by American silent comedy,[19] these comedies were enormously popular with Japanese audiences, who doubtless found them both entertaining and liberating. Indeed, these films not only captured the spirit of the neighborhood and community, emphasizing an underlying solidarity among people and showing the simple joy in living, they also spoofed the social and familial pressures brought to bear on individuals. In many respects these films are "westward looking." That is, they try to incorporate a living style of the West that advocates freedom, individual expression, and energy itself—the very qualities that the Japanese most envied and emulated,[20] even as the country moved away from the liberalism of the 1920s and toward the reactionary politics of the 1930s, which would plunge it into war. Seen today, these nonsense comedies retain their freshness and fun, having acquired perhaps a certain nostalgia value as evidence of more innocent times.[21] But they also tend to evoke a less favorable response. French scholar Max Tessier, for example, sees these comedies not only as "amateurish" and "naive" but contends that *The Neighbor's Wife and Mine* offers an unreliable version of the Japanese middle class of the day.[22] No doubt Tessier is correct about this last point, but one wonders if Gosho's film is any more deficient in this respect than American silent comedy of the day and its depiction of the American middle class. Perhaps the best response to Tessier comes from famed comedian Harold Lloyd, who wrote: "Exaggeration is the breath of picture comedies, and obviously they cannot be true to life, but they can be recognizably related to life."[23]

The Neighbor's Wife and Mine, The Bride Talks in Her Sleep, and *The Groom Talks in His Sleep* all poke gentle, affectionate fun at modern pretensions. All three capture the mixture of exasperation, exhilaration, and affection that we feel for family and friends; and all three show that to be human is to be by turns silly, grand, caring, callous, and terribly curious about the private lives of others. Taking their cue from American films in yet another way, they convey the high spirits of youth and tend to tell their stories in quick, deft strokes, favoring gags above all else. In *Bride* and *Groom,* true to the underlying premise of the genre—to focus on human response in exaggerated, extreme, even absurd situations—Gosho takes a matter of singular unimportance and teases comedy out of the fact that to his characters, this matter assumes an earth-shattering significance. In short, a bride's and groom's sleeping habits become the all-consuming obsession of family, friends, and acquaintances. In *Neighbor's Wife,* writer's block—though arguably more serious—is treated no less comically. Yet in all of these comedies, in which nonsense reigns supreme, Gosho also manages to offer some apt insights into the human condition. At the same time, he demonstrates how early on he could blend various kinds of elements, both serious and comic.

The earliest Gosho film that survives—his thirty-ninth!—*The Neighbor's Wife and Mine* occupies a prominent place in Japanese film history as the first technically and commercially successful talkie. Discussion understandably has focused on Gosho's solutions to the problems involved with sound. Iwamoto Kenji offers an especially appreciative analysis of Gosho's use of off-screen dialogue and sound, and how he avoided making the kind of static film dominated by talking heads that characterized Hollywood's early sound efforts.[24] Other scholars have detailed how Gosho employed several cameras simultaneously, thereby covering different angles and ensuring the possibility of editing and cinematic flow, and how he recorded music directly with a live orchestra kept off-camera, at times even stashed away among trees and bushes.[25] The film was a triumph, and was named "Best One" in the 1931 *Kinema Jumpo* poll.

Recently, however, serious attention has begun to be paid to the role of the film in Gosho's development. A playful tribute to Western influences, *The Neighbor's Wife and Mine* has to do with Shinsaku (Watanabe Atsushi), a playwright suffering from writer's block. To meet his deadline, which is fast approaching (in five days, in fact), Shinsaku packs up his family and rents a house in a Western-style Tokyo suburb that appears to be a colony of artists. To motivate himself, he writes memos to himself: "Don't talk about it—do it!" "Time is money," "Five hundred yen—don't forget!"[26] But this ploy doesn't work. Nor does it help that he is an inveterate procrastinator, who at one point plays mahjongg late into the night with friends. When he finally does hunker down to do some serious work, he is distracted by a succession of noises: mice scampering around in the attic, a stray cat screeching outside his window, his baby squalling, his daughter (Seki Tokio) whining that she needs to be taken to the toilet, and finally a noisy jazz band rehearsing next door. (These noises, of course, provide Gosho with ample opportunity to have fun exploiting sound.) As Shinsaku becomes more frustrated, and his wife (Tanaka Kinuyo) more worried that the family will end up penniless, he decides to go next door and put a stop to the noise of the jazz band. Once there, he is unable to voice his complaint and ends up staying for the rehearsal and partying with Madame (Date Satoko) and her band. He even gets drunk. All of this is naturally played for laughs as Gosho and gagman Fushimi Akira poke fun at the foibles of human nature. Meanwhile, his wife, anxiously waiting his return, becomes convinced that he has succumbed to the charms of Madame.

The long-suffering wife (Tanaka Kinuyo) worries while her husband (Watanabe Atsushi) struggles with writer's block. *The Neighbor's Wife and Mine* (1931).

The film's title represents the playwright's point of view and implies a comparison between his traditional Japanese wife and Madame. A *moga* (modern-day woman), Madame dresses, postures, and acts like a Western-style vamp, presumably modeling herself on Ruth Chatterton's *Madame X* (1929). (She even has a poster of this "all talking" American film prominently displayed on her wall.) But very little is made of the implied comparison. And since Madame has no designs on the playwright, the supposed triangle is more imagined than real, especially on the part of the wife. Madame, in fact, is less important as a woman or rival than as the site of rapprochement between Japanese and Western (American) values. Thus, while she clearly is caught up with things Western and even sprinkles her speech with English ("cheerio" is an especially favorite word), she remains very much "Japanese" in her effort to promote caring, neighborly relationships. Indeed, there is no small irony that it is she, rather than Shinsaku's wife, who gives the playwright the inspiration to write. Madame, it turns out, only *looks* like a vamp.

Consisting of a series of loosely connected vignettes, the film derives as much comedy as possible from Shinsaku's predicament. Structured in four

Madame (Date Satoko) inspires the writer-husband. *The Neighbor's Wife and Mine* (1931).

parts, the film opens with a comic confrontation between Shinsaku and a none-too-talented artist trying to paint scenery (Yokoo Dekao). That the two men bear an uncanny resemblance to Laurel and Hardy only serves to add to the fun. Although this opening scene may be irrelevant to the main story, it sets the tone of the comedy and has the merit of introducing the playwright and, later, Madame herself. (This scene also makes clear that Gosho used his "unaffected approach" outside of the slice-of-life mode.) The scuffle begins when the two men childishly insult each other and end up taking offense. The painter (wearing requisite painterly attire, a French beret) is irritated that the playwright doesn't appreciate his art, while the playwright is outraged that the painter doesn't know who he is. Soon they are flinging paint at each other, hurling more insults, and chasing each other through a nearby field. Only Madame's arrival puts an end to the silliness. This scene, while clearly slapstick (and not unlike the incorrigibly infantile shenanigans of Laurel and Hardy themselves), is set in an actual suburban residential area, according to Sato, probably one around Kamata.[27] Interestingly, Gosho calls attention to this setting, first by opening the scene with a panning shot of the neighborhood and then by having two bickering artists point out one of the houses in their brief chat about art versus reality. In one sense their dialogue, like the scene itself, is "irrelevant" (indeed the painter never reappears in the film), yet it serves a deeper purpose. In emphasizing the setting as real, the effect is to put in perspective the would-be pretensions of both artists as extravagant and out of place.

The two central sections of the film detail the playwright's unsuccessful efforts to write and the problems this creates between him and his long-suffering wife. Primarily light in tone, these sections allow occasional suggestions of something darker. At one point, for example, a creepy salesman (Himori Shinichi), who looks like a character out of a German Expressionist film, discombobulates the wife. Insisting that Shinsaku deal with the intruder, she watches from a safe distance, occasionally stealing a peek at what is going on. But her husband is no better able to deal with the salesman than she is. In fact, the salesman flatters him into buying some of his wares. Clearly, the suburbs, even select little artistic communities like this one, are not immune to real life in its various guises. Nor is Shinsaku quite as sophisticated as he may believe himself to be.

Even more incisive are those observations that have to do with the couple's marital relationship. Although Shinsaku and his wife love each other, the stress they are under fuels an endless cycle of bickering. When she tries to cajole him into working, he accuses her of being a scold; when they argue about money, he gets defensive. They even argue about the children. Hence when he complains that it is her responsibility to keep the baby from crying so that he can write, he adds insult to injury by lecturing her. "Having babies is serious," he insists. "Well, it's your responsibility, too," she rejoins. One thing leads to another, and soon he protests that she is not the bashful, polite woman he married. She counters that he has changed too, and in an example of Gosho's use of quick and incisive insert shots, Shinsaku turns over a photo of her in exasperation: "That was then," he says, with finality. Although he is by and large genial and good-natured, he repeatedly indulges in infantile behavior. Thus, in order to block out the noise from next door, he goes through a series of antics: covering himself with a blanket, plugging his ears, and finally hiding inside a large wooden trunk.

The comedy is perhaps at its richest and most suggestive in its delineation of the wife. She is by no means perfect; nonetheless, she is hardworking, nurturing (especially to her children), and unfailing practical. When she finds a coin, she immediately scoops it up, since money is at a premium. Forever urging her husband to get to work, she is understandably distraught when he plays mahjongg, continually procrastinates, and stays on to party next door. The party next door poses an additional threat. Feeling that she cannot compete with the sophisticated charms of Madame, she fears for her marriage. When Shinsaku finally returns home, she lets her feelings be known, calling Madame "a sex delinquent 100%." Only in the film's fourth and final section, after her husband has delivered a successful play and the family is out of harm's way, does she recant, admitting that Madame is actually pretty nice after all. To be sure, she has overreacted to Shinsaku's "dalliance," and has been jealous and insecure in the bargain. Hence the reason why she asks him to buy her some Western-style clothes.

Still, Gosho treats her feelings with understanding and sympathy. In one particularly notable shot—yet another example of the kind of inserted close-up that shows his Lubitsch-like attention to psychological detail—he conveys the anxiety she feels by having her take the large ornamental pin from her hair (*kanzashi*) and bend it in the palm of her hand. In yet another shot, we see her alone at work in the kitchen, feeling abandoned and singing a plaintive song. In keeping with the mood of *shomin-geki* comedy, however, Gosho only develops her character so much and no more. Mostly, he hints at her strengths, weaknesses, and vulnerability. But that is enough to give the comedy a degree of gravity and realism that it would otherwise lack. In addition, it makes the happy ending all the more sweet and satisfying.

True to the genre, a happy ending has been virtually guaranteed from the beginning. But Gosho, gagman Fushimi, and scenarist Kitamura Komatsu take nothing for granted; they earn the right to have such an ending. Thus, Shinsaku is so inspired by the song Madame sings, "Speed Up," which also happens to be a salute to the modern age, that he takes it up as his new motto and rushes home. Shortly after, Gosho introduces the only intertitle in the film: "After that, Shinsaku wasted no time. He really speeded up." In short, Shinsaku is not only "unblocked," he also effectively becomes a new man.

In the final scene the entire family takes a stroll down a neighborhood road on their way home from shopping. Shinsaku pushes their baby carriage; his wife, reflecting his newfound success, has a new permanent and kimono and carries an assortment of packages (perhaps one of which contains Western-style clothing); and their little girl holds a balloon. Hearing an airplane, everyone looks up. The little girl says she would like to go on a trip to Osaka; the wife remarks, "What a beautiful blue sky." Soon the wife and husband are reminiscing. This idyll, however, is interrupted when the little girl announces that she has to pee. The call to nature taken care of, Shinsaku and his wife and daughter resume their walk. In the background, the tune "My Blue Heaven" can be heard, which the threesome begin humming. Suddenly, Shinsaku realizes that they have left behind the baby. Hurrying to retrieve their charge, who seems to have taken its abandonment in stride, they continue on their way home: the wife wheeling the carriage, Shinsaku holding his little girl's hand, and all three joining in to sing "My Blue Heaven." The family is safe and secure, and the idyll has been restored. But it has also been tempered by the call to duty—precisely the right note on which to conclude this charming comic reflection.

Even more typical of nonsense comedy is *The Bride Talks in Her Sleep,* which was Shochiku's New Year's release for 1933. It has virtually no plot to speak of, contains a profusion of gags, is fast-paced, and has a minimum of characterization. Basically, it deals with four school chums, one of whom, Komura (Kobayashi Tokuji), is a recently married salaryman. When Komura's friends (Egawa Ureo, Oyama Kenji, and Tani Reiko) learn that his bride, Haruko (Tanaka Kinuyo), talks in her sleep, they descend upon her while he is away, eager to hear her firsthand. "Where do you sleep?" they ask, after barely introducing themselves. Although they are rude and off-putting, and freeloaders in the bargain, Haruko tries to do the polite thing and entertain them. Still, she is understandably puzzled and uncomfortable. She even checks her husband's class photos to make sure that these three boors are his friends.

The bulk of the film's fifty-five-minute running time is devoted to one long sequence, an all-night party. In this sequence Gosho develops the comic possibilities inherent in the situation, leaving it up to viewers to formulate the theme for themselves. Thus, when Komura arrives home and is met with open arms by Haruko, who is clearly relieved to be rescued, the friends are not chastened in the least. Instead, they begin imposing themselves even more on the couple. They insist that Komura send his wife to bed, and she willingly goes just to get away from them. (Of course, neither Komura nor Haruko knows what his friends are up to.) Komura then joins his buddies drinking and playing a round of games.

In the opening scene of the film, we learned that Komura and his friends made a vow not only to graduate at the same time but also to get married at the same time. In short, they pledged never to betray their friendship. In their eyes, Komura has broken this vow not once but twice. First, he has actually graduated while they flunked out ("Komura's our pal, but by mistake he graduated first," remarks one of them). Second, he has married and become a successful salaryman. Worst of all, he has made an effort to grow up. Not surprisingly, then, there is an edge to their comic antics at the party, which goes beyond mere mindless fun; in fact, there is a suggestion that they are envious without quite realizing it. Their behavior gives Gosho the opportunity to make some apt observations about the world of adolescent males—and male bonding—even within the supposedly unassuming *nansensu* mode.

Consider, for example, the friends' insistence that Komura perform his special monkey imitation as part of their drinking and games. This is a parody of what the Japanese call *kakushi gei* ("hidden talent"), which allows an individual to demonstrate a particular skill or aptitude that he or she doesn't normally have the chance to show.[28] Here, however, it represents a way for Komura's buddies to reassert their claim on him, to bring him in line—however foolishly or misguidedly. Unfortunately, the noise caused by Komura's carrying on like a monkey awakens Haruko, who has been asleep in the next room. Seeing him with a cord tied to his neck like a leash and stripped down to his underpants, she is stunned and humiliated. "To me you act like a gentleman," she rebukes him, "but you're only a two-faced chimpanzee." She is dismayed not only by his adolescent behavior, but also by the fact that he has lied to her, claiming that he never touches drink. Now she learns that not only does he like spirits but also—even worse—he likes to drink while eating sausages! While Komura and Haruko have their first spat, the friends—still intent on hearing her nocturnal mutterings—chant, "Go to sleep."

As Gosho's comedy moves toward the conclusion, Komura asks Haruko's forgiveness and the couple leaves their apartment to the three friends while they go to another friend's apartment to get some sleep. Komura's decision to make up with his wife reaffirms his determination to grow up, yet Gosho's comedy does not quite end here. When Haruko falls asleep, the only thing she says is, "Don't deceive me," an utterance obviously directed toward her husband. In fact, as it turns out, Haruko talks less in her sleep than do the three friends, who, sleeping overnight at the couple's apartment, babble on about money and clothes. Indeed, the film's title is a deliberate misnomer. With this revelation, Gosho pokes fun at the friends (and perhaps viewers as well), but his most pointed satire is yet to come. When Komura and Haruko return to their apartment the next morning, they find the three friends tied up by a burglar who broke in and stole their clothes. The only things left for them to wear are Haruko's kimonos. Thus, in what is the final (and perhaps funniest) sight gag in the film, the friends rush out from the apartment in kimonos, but not before Komura takes full advantage of having the upper hand. To rub in their embarrassment and give them some good parting advice, he says, "Stop doting on sleep-talking and study hard so that you won't have to wear these [clothes] again." And with that Komura and Haruko are free to live their lives—at least for the rest of the day.

The Bride Talks in Her Sleep is a simple (some might even say "simple-minded") farce, and not meant to be taken seriously. Yet its implications are not trivial. Given its target audience of the lower-middle classes (and one imagines students as well), its affirmation of traditional values is to be expected. Thus, Komura's friends are satirized not so much for their bad manners or feelings of envy as for their hopeless immaturity. To be sure, nonsense comedy as a genre celebrates freedom of spirit, but Gosho's inflection of the mode ups the ante by implying that such freedom ultimately is to be found in assuming responsibility and growing up. In this respect Komura's friends are sorely lacking. By contrast, it is here that Haruko shows her mettle. Traditional Japanese wife that she is, she takes her weak husband in hand and demands that he be concerned with his own self-respect and dignity. In the face of adolescent silliness and excess she is the voice of reason. She is also, of course, Komura's truest friend. Hence it comes as no surprise that Gosho asserts the claim of Komura and Haruko's marriage over that of friendship. But he doesn't stop at that. On the contrary, he wittily suggests the two pitfalls that the married couple must avoid. The first is the easy cynicism of the couple next door (as expressed most vividly in the wife's assertion that "obeying my husband gives him a swelled head"). The second is the failure of a husband and a wife to be honest with each other. Very simply, there are lessons for everyone to learn.

Earlier we said that Gosho's style was greatly influenced by Lubitsch's analytical (or piecemeal) editing. Donald Richie has rightly described this style as a succession of shots that constitutes "perhaps the most direct method for registering reaction, and certainly best suggests the subtle interplay that occurs during any conversation."[29] Although one might not necessarily expect "subtle interplay" in nonsense comedy, there is certainly a need, at least occasionally, for "registering reaction" as directly as possible. This is no less true of *The Bride Talks in Her Sleep*. Take, for example, Gosho's use of Komura and Haruko's wedding picture. During the extended party sequence, Gosho cuts to this photo at particularly telling moments. The first time occurs when Haruko happens upon Komura's monkey act and, deeply hurt and disappointed by what she sees, chides him. Quite clearly, this is not the man in the photograph. Later in the sequence, Gosho cuts twice more to this photo, but in both instances the shot is motivated by Haruko's or Komura's glance. In the first instance Haruko turns to the photo as evidence of their once-idyllic happiness after Komura— much to her amazement—gives her an order, presumably something he has never done before. In the second instance Komura looks at the photo when Haruko weepingly tells him that she does not want to stay in their apartment so long as his friends remain. Here the photo not only reminds him of his love for Haruko but also of where his responsibility lies. Typical of Gosho, the entire episode is imbued with a mixture of pathos and humor. In other words, we are amused by what amounts to little more than much ado about nothing at one level, even as we are touched by what we know to be far from trivial: the purity and innocence of Komura and Haruko's love. In this regard Gosho's comedy is anything but nonsense.

The success of *The Bride Talks in Her Sleep* prompted a companion piece two years later, *The Groom Talks in His Sleep*. Like its predecessor, it centers on a wholly inconsequential matter and blows it out of proportion. Unlike its predecessor, it gently parodies Japanese bourgeois life and values, is more inventively plotted, and puts somewhat more emphasis on character. However, the single most important difference between these two nonsense comedies is that while *Bride* leans heavily on "student comedy," *Groom* has much in common with family drama. Indeed, the film's middle-class setting and focus on family life help to give it a feel of everyday life. This quality also results from Gosho's inclusion of an outsider in this setting, a con man who poses as a spiritualist/mesmerist (Saito Tatsuo) in order to dupe those people in the neighborhood suffering from "light diseases." No matter that he proves so inept at this trade that he cannot tell the difference between a napping woman and a sick one. In the opening scene, at least, he seems authentic and downtrodden as he teams up with a young boy (Kozo Tokkan), who sells fermented beans. This scene, in fact, has a documentary flavor that Gosho later dispenses with when these characters become involved in the comic action. Even so, their presence gives the comedy a feel of everyday Japanese life in the 1930s that it otherwise would have lacked.

Groom's plot has to do with two newlyweds who are head over heels in love, Komine Yasuo and Yukiko (Hayashi Chojiro and Kawasaki Hiroko respectively), and the complications that arise when husband, family, and friends discover that Yukiko takes a nap in mid-morning—an act that in the world of nonsense comedy is an affront to middle-class mores and common decency. Indeed, it is an affront that makes infidelity pale by comparison. When Yasuo confronts Yukiko about her scandalous habit, he learns the whole truth. It is a saga and then some. It turns out that she takes a nap because he used to mention the names of old girlfriends in his sleep, keeping her awake. But now that he is cured of this habit, she is unable to sleep at night because she misses his talk. To make matters worse, she suffers from insomnia! So enchanted is Yasuo by his wife's explanation that he apologizes profusely. As far as he is concerned, the matter is closed. This, however, does not prevent family and friends from descending on the couple to solve an already solved problem. On the contrary, in the penultimate scene Yasuo's mother (Takamatsu Eiko), Yukiko's father (Mizushima Ryotaro), and Tamura and Kiyo, the couple next door (Kobayashi Tokuji and Shinobu Setsuko, respectively), insist on seeing for themselves whether

Yasuo actually talks in his sleep. They also enlist the aid of the spiritualist and his boy assistant to facilitate matters by hypnotizing Yasuo on the spot. In the end the understandably fed-up groom turns the tables on everyone. He and Yukiko then resume their happy married life.

Stylistically, one of the film's most striking features is Gosho's blocking and composition. Hence the scene in which Yasuo's mother and Yukiko's father arrive unexpectedly to resolve the already resolved napping problem. At first the newlyweds try to hide from their interfering parents. When this does not work, Yasuo has Yukiko conceal herself in one room, while he deals with their parents in the adjoining one. His aim is to protect Yukiko, but neither character makes a serious effort to keep her hidden, even though Gosho's composition puts the maximum amount of space between Yukiko and the parents. Specifically, Gosho positions the parents in the foreground corners of the frame—Yasuo's mother on the left, Yukiko's father on the right—and Yukiko in the background. Appropriately, Yasuo is in the middle. What makes this shot comic is that Yukiko, who sits demurely behind a shoji screen, is both removed and not removed from the other three characters, for she has opened the screen just enough to peer out and see what is happening. And, of course, she can be seen as well. At one point Yasuo even turns to talk with her, while the parents watch, in effect being temporarily put on hold. Most interestingly, in this four-way interaction, the parents go along with the idea that Yukiko is "not present"; therefore, they speak only to Yasuo, who is the self-appointed buffer between them and his bride. Gosho's delightful staging implies an altogether different social dynamic at work than what appears to be. That is, while the parents protest and demand, they also seem willing to abide by the wishes of their children. Even so, this does not prevent them from making their feelings known. Sensing all of this, the audience can sit back, enjoy, and relax. There is every reason to believe that all will end well.

Like many of Gosho's films, *The Groom Talks in His Sleep* combines genial, lighthearted humor with witty observations on human nature. Take, for example, Yasuo's mother. Seizing the opportunity to regain control over her son, she no sooner hears about her daughter-in-law's napping than she urges him to get an immediate divorce from that "awful woman."[30] When Yasuo, about to be hypnotized, protests that he is unable to sleep on demand, especially in broad daylight, she handily reminds him of his duty as a good son. "Your late father's name is at stake," she declares. Not to be outdone, Yukiko's father adds, "Do this for your mom before she dies"—proving that fathers can be equally adept at emotional blackmail. Still, there are precious few villains in Gosho—and none in nonsense comedy. Consequently, when Yasuo's mom realizes that he is only pretending to be asleep under hypnosis so that he can tell his meddling family and friends to mind their own business, she allows him to think that he has fooled her, too. Thus, she graciously steps aside to let the couple live their own life. After all, what she really wants most is her son's happiness.

Although Gosho's humor has various functions throughout the film, its primary task is to help characterize Yasuo and Yukiko and shape our response to them. These two protagonists are never quite three-dimensional, but they are drawn with such affection that it is impossible not to root for them, even when they go overboard in their ardor for each other. When we first meet them, Yasuo—a salaryman—is getting dressed for work. But his dilatory manner makes it obvious that he is having trouble tearing himself away from his bride. "The tie you chose for me is best after all," he tells Yukiko, who is dressed in the kimono he has just picked for her to wear. Even after he makes it out the door, he and Yukiko cannot quite manage to separate themselves. She follows him—he is barely a stone's throw away from the house—they say more "good-byes," and he implores her to stay inside because it is a cold day. Then, suddenly inspired, he decides that it is imperative for them to take a photograph of each other right then and there. She promptly goes and gets the camera. Several scenes later, we see that the newlyweds are, if anything, even more in love. Eager to please her husband, Yukiko remarks that she has a new hairdo. She then proceeds to model it for him in such a coy way that we half expect her to announce that he is going to become a father. She makes no such announcement, but Yasuo reacts as if she does. "Wonderful!" he exclaims, and with that he rushes off to get—no surprise—the camera. No matter that there isn't enough light. He is bound and determined to preserve her hairdo for posterity. Indeed, Yasuo's snapping of Yukiko's picture—any time, any place, and for any reason—becomes one of the film's most endearing running gags. This gag reaches a climax in the scene in which Yasuo confronts Yukiko about her napping. At one point Yasuo angrily tells her that they are through. To prove that he means business, he storms out of the room and returns with a large box, dumping its contents unceremoniously on the floor. There, in a heap, are the seemingly hundreds of photos he has taken of Yukiko in the few short weeks that they've been married. It is a hilarious moment that offers irrefutable proof that Yasuo's anger of the moment is no match for the love he feels for her. In short, thanks to Gosho's special blend of humor and sentiment, we know that the quarrel will be patched up—indeed, it is already, for all practical purposes.

Still, were it not for Gosho's humor, Yasuo and Yukiko would be insufferable, and we would soon be laughing at them rather than with them. To make sure this doesn't happen, Gosho introduces the character of Tamura,

Yasuo's friend and co-worker. In the scene in which the newlyweds have trouble parting, Tamura not only grows understandably impatient as he waits for Yasuo to accompany him to work, but he becomes positively disgusted by the spectacle of marital bliss that he witnesses. Although we can appreciate Tamura's attitude, and even share it to some degree, we quickly reject it because we recognize that it is rooted in envy. Specifically, Tamura envies Yasuo for having an adoring wife and marrying into a wealthy family. In fact, the only thing that he does not seem to envy Yasuo for is his taste in ties, which he dismisses as "lousy."

Tamura also finds Yasuo and Yukiko's marital bliss irksome because of his own marriage, which is characterized by an altogether different dynamic between husband and wife. Actually, he has a fine, upstanding wife in Kiyo, but whereas Yukiko is sweet and accommodating, Kiyo is tart and strong-willed. She will not let Tamura get away with anything. Thus, when he peels too many onions for supper—apparently they share household duties—she tells him that he will have to eat some of them for lunch, a prospect that hardly pleases him. Even worse (from his point of view), she keeps him on such a tight budget that he feels compelled to borrow money from friends. That Tamura is henpecked, however, seems poetic justice, given his constant whining about what Yasuo has and his refusal to make the best of his lot—which is far from bad. In fact, this is the very lesson that Kiyo tries to teach him when she warns him not to be envious but to be thankful that, unlike Yukiko, she does not come from a rich family. Otherwise, he might look stupid like some other husbands. This lesson is lost on him.

A hopeless milquetoast and incorrigible busybody, Tamura is never malicious or scheming, but, as Yasuo says, he is "thoughtless." It is he who first informs Yasuo about Yukiko's naps. It is he who starts the entire imbroglio in the first place by telling Yukiko that Yasuo mentions the names of former girlfriends in his sleep. When Yasuo finds out the extent of his friend's meddling, he takes sweet revenge when he is "hypnotized." First, he deliberately praises Yukiko to the skies, leading a thoroughly disgusted Tamura to proclaim, "He even talks this way in his sleep!" Second, he reveals that Tamura has borrowed money from him, but deliberately kept it a secret from Kiyo. He then carefully directs her to check Tamura's inside vest pocket. The last time we see Tamura and Kiyo, she has stripped him down to his underclothes to make sure he isn't hiding any more cash. Thus, in the last analysis, it is the meddlesome, envious Tamura who becomes the chief butt of Gosho's humor, not the overly ardent newlyweds.

Despite its lightness of tone, *The Groom Talks in His Sleep* is not without serious implications. These can best be summed up by what the Japanese call *giri* and *ninjo. Giri* refers to the powerful sense of obligation, responsibility, or duty that one feels toward society; *ninjo* refers to the satisfying of one's personal desires and inclinations, and often connotes the indulgence of one's ego at the expense of *giri*. It is a commonplace that much of Japanese film and literature is characterized by the conflict between these two concepts. That said, Gosho and his writers give this conflict something of a new twist. *Giri* is clearly spoofed when family and friends treat Yukiko's napping as a betrayal of her marital vows, but it figures most prominently in the various conflicts that Yasuo has, especially the one with himself. Thus, when he confronts Yukiko over her napping, he behaves the way he thinks a wronged husband should, barking out accusations, putting Yukiko on the defensive, and asserting his patriarchal privilege. However, it is apparent from the start that his heart is not in this posturing. In fact, each time Yukiko expresses hurt or questions him, he forgets himself. At one point he even unconsciously fondles her scarf, only to catch himself. His resolve to suppress any expression of tenderness—and act as he thinks society expects—provides an amusing example of *ninjo* under fire.

Yet, ironically enough, by following the dictates of his heart in the end—that is, making up with Yukiko and putting all the meddlers in their place—Yasuo is not so much rejecting *giri* for *ninjo* as meeting the demands of both. For in his case both are equally concerned with protecting the sacred bonds of matrimony. Granted, this harmonious reconciliation of the demands of *giri* and *ninjo* may be possible only in the world of comedy. Nevertheless, it is gratifying to see, for it manages to affirm both traditional values and individualism. Moreover, when one stops to consider that, at the time *The Groom Talks in His Sleep* was made, the Home Ministry regarded the concept of individualism as an undesirable American *and* democratic influence,[31] the fact that Gosho and his colleagues pulled off this feat in the least didactic and most unthreatening way possible was in itself an achievement. But then again, who would have thought to look for political implications in nonsense comedy?

"SLICE-OF-LIFE" COMEDY

Rooted in "salaryman" comedy and family drama, *Burden of Life* represents a marked advance over Gosho's previous three *shomin* comedies. It placed sixth in the 1935 *Kinema Jumpo* polling, and has been praised by Burch for its seriousness and slice-of-life quality. Concurring with this judgment, John Gillett finds the film "imbued with a naturalistic tone and 'lived in' visual texture quite beyond American and European cinema."[32] David Owens is similarly enthusiastic, adding, "As is typical of the best Japanese directors, Gosho concentrates on developing characters rather than plot.

Each of the family members is carefully drawn and each grows before us as an individual, surpassing the sort of character typing that was usual for family melodramas."[33] These comments effectively sum up the film's most notable achievement. However, they do not specifically address what must be our first concern in this section: How does *Burden of Life* fit into Gosho's development?

This question is by no means easy to answer. First of all, we must remember that Gosho made *Burden of Life* and *The Groom Talks in His Sleep* in the same year, and that while both are *shomin-geki* comedies, they are quite different in theme, mood, and emphasis. The difference, of course, lies in part in the material itself, but mostly it has to do with the treatment of that material by Gosho and screenwriter Fushimi Akira. In other words, the development of Gosho's work in the *shomin-geki* was not a matter of clearly defined or demarcated stages, in which he used one particular approach or subgenre at a time, then moved on to the next approach or subgenre. Instead, it was, as in the case of *Groom* and *Burden of Life,* a case of working in various modes more or less at the same time. Nevertheless, by the mid- to late 1930s, Gosho for all practical purposes had effectively said farewell to nonsense comedies and light *shomin-geki* comedies. From that time on, his films, regardless of genre, would give precedence to the kind of emotional makeup and texture—the slice-of-life quality, the emphasis on character—that constitutes the special richness of *Burden of Life.*

That said, there is a second difficulty involved in assessing the place of *Burden of Life* in Gosho's development: it probably was not the first Gosho film to venture into the "slice-of-life " mode, or even to incorporate aspects of it. *L'Amour (Ramuru/Aibu/Caress/Love),* Gosho's 1933 character study of a small-town doctor and his two adult children, also is preoccupied with recreating the feeling of everyday life and, like *Burden of Life,* "delays" the central story. (See the Appendix for a discussion of this film.) Moreover, given the fact that all thirty-eight of the films that Gosho made before *The Neighbor's Wife and Mine* are lost, who is to say that he might not have worked in this mode even earlier, perhaps as early as the 1920s? Likewise, given his enormous productivity in the 1930s (he averaged four films a year), it seems reasonable to assume that the shaping of his unique blend of pathos and comedy depended not just on comic subgenres within the *shomin-geki,* but also on genres outside the *shomin-geki,* such as melodrama and literary adaptations. Be that as it may, one thing is certain: *Burden of Life's* critical and commercial success encouraged Gosho to continue with more serious, character-centered work.

Burden of Life is deliberately, anecdotally slight. As such, it does not actually focus on the central dramatic action, the "burden" of the title, until well into the narrative. This burden has to do with the resentment that fifty-nine-year-old salaryman Fukushima (Saito Tatsuo) feels toward his nine-year-old son, Kanichi (Hayama Masao), whom he never wanted. Therefore, he treats the boy with disdain, when he doesn't ignore him altogether. The boy acts accordingly, doing his best to keep out of his father's way. The demands and responsibilities of life have left Fukushima exhausted, especially the heavy price he has paid to get his daughters married. When the film opens, he is in the process of marrying off his third and last daughter, Machiko (Mizushima Mitsuyo). To come up with her dowry, he has been forced to sell off family rentals. No sooner is the wedding over than he informs his wife Tamako (Yoshikawa Mitsuko) that he will not pay for Kanichi's education and insists that the boy be sent to work. This angers Tamako, and in the row that follows Fukushima throws her and the boy out. They go to live with one of the daughters. Meanwhile he decides to treat himself to some of the things in life he thinks he has missed, taking in a few bars and restaurants. This proves to be a hollow, depressing experience. A boy selling flowers reminds him of Kanichi; even worse, a barmaid calls him "father." When he asks her age, she confides that she is nineteen years old. He realizes that he is completely out of place. One day, Kanichi, forgetting that he no longer lives at home, ends up walking there after school by force of habit. Genuinely happy to see his son, Fukushima treats him to a meal of his favorite food, and the two have a real conversation for the first time. When Tamako hears about Fukushima's change of heart toward Kanichi, she rushes home.

Burch has said of *Burden of Life:* "It is not that there is no dramatic conflict or underlying narrative movement. . . . It is simply that the fundamental diegetic economy is not centred around a plot-line or character of privileged 'density' in any way comparable to the dominant Western model. There are, in particular, many 'irrelevant' events which are offered as being equal in importance to those articulated to the 'main theme,' and the diegetic space-time of the film as a whole is offered as being of no more importance than what 'preceded' or 'will follow' in the family's life-stream."[34] While basically in agreement with Burch, I would qualify his statement in this way: the film has two interrelated narratives, with the main action (or "theme," as he calls it) gradually emerging out of the loose, casual flow of events of the other narrative and eventually taking center stage. The key phrase here is "gradually emerging." Indeed, it must be pointed out in this regard that Fukushima, the character most central to the main action, does not even appear until twenty-five minutes into the film, which altogether runs a mere sixty-six minutes. It's as if Gosho is saying, "There's no need to rush or get to the main action immediately. Let's just spend a day with the Fukushima family and get to know them."

This is precisely what happens in the first twenty-five minutes. Dramatic incidents as such are banished or downplayed in favor of human interest for its own sake. Even the most unusual activity—the preparations for Machiko's wedding—is simply one of many activities taking place on this particular day. Thus, this part of the film proceeds by "indirection," immersing us in the texture of the Fukushima family's life and moving from one event to another, from one group of characters to another. True to the slice-of-life approach, this movement feels casual, loose, even at times random, giving the film room to breathe and allowing characters to talk, act, and interact at leisure. Some critics have complained that Gosho relies too much on dialogue,[35] but when the dialogue is good and the characters interestingly drawn, why complain?

In this part of the film, thanks to the slice-of-life approach, Gosho has time to offer concise, flavorsome character sketches of all the members of the family—except, of course, Fukushima. First, we are introduced to Itsuko, the Fukushimas' second daughter (Tanaka Kinuyo, looking especially trim and chic in a series of Western-style outfits), and her husband Kurita (Kobayashi Tokuji), a painter of sorts, who dresses for the part in beret, sweater, and scarf. They live in a modern, Western-style house, enjoy the good life, and constantly borrow money from Itsuko's parents. When Kurita—who is neither prone to hard work nor driven by fiery ambition—has to postpone his show, Itsuko asks for money once again, and is advised by her mother to "live economically." However, once Itsuko gets the money, she ignores this advice and takes Kurita out to a restaurant. Next we meet Takako, the eldest daughter (Tsubouchi Yoshiko), a pampered, kimono-clad beauty, and her doctor-husband Komiyama Tetsuo (Oyama Kenji). When the film opens, they have had one of their habitual fights—over a "trifle," as they themselves readily admit. And as usual, they have involved the entire family. Hence Takako rushes off to her mother, while Komiyama enlists Itsuko and Kurita to help patch things up. The last daughter we meet is Machiko. About to be married in two days, she seems rather young and naive for her years. This impression is reinforced not only by her inability to see Takako and Komiyama's spat for what it is but also by her getting into an unnecessary scrap with her little brother. Clearly, she has some growing up to do.

Finally, we are introduced to Tamako, Nami, and Kanichi (nicknamed "Kan-chan"). Tamako is the family anchor, overseeing wedding arrangements, contending with her two married daughters, acting as both mom

Kan-chan (Hayama Masao): both "a good boy" and the "burden" of the title.
Burden of Life (1935).

and dad to Kan-chan—and dropping everything on the spot to provide a
meal and companionship for Fukushima when he gets home from the office. Assisting her is Nami (Rokugo Kiyoko), the family maid. She has a
special rapport with Kan-chan and does something no other member of the
family does, not even Tamako: she actually talks with the lad. As a result,
she has come to know him. Kan-chan, for his part, is basically like most
boys his age. He prefers playing to doing his homework, and couldn't care
less about such things as babies ("I'm a boy, not an uncle," he tells Itsuko
when she tries to interest him in hers). Even so, at times he is wise beyond
his years. He knows, for example, that his father dislikes him. Yet when
Nami asks if he dislikes his father, he replies, "I don't dislike him, but I
don't like him, either." It is an honest answer that shows him to be surprisingly mature, at least in this respect. As Kurita (to his credit) says about
Kan-chan, "He's a good boy."

Interestingly, while Tamako and Kan-chan figure prominently both in
this early slice-of-life section of the film and in the main action to come,
most of the other family members fade from the scene. Replacing them is a
new set of characters, including first and foremost Fukushima. Before that

happens, however, Gosho uses these family members to underscore the kind of social and psychological observations that characteristically permeate his work.

As might be expected, in the first third of the film most of these observations simply exist as part of the texture of everyday life. Take, for example, Komiyama's attraction to Itsuko. In the scene where he and Kurita while away the afternoon in the latter's studio, drinking, eating peanuts, and trying to decide what to do for fun, he cannot keep his eyes off the semi-nude portrait of Itsuko that Kurita has painted. Realizing this, Kurita turns the painting around. Although nothing comes of Komiyama's interest in his sister-in-law, it adds to his characterization and is exactly the kind of "irrelevant" detail that is redolent of the slice-of-life approach. The same is true of Itsuko's patronizing attitude toward her older sister, Takako. Gosho foregrounds this attitude in frequent, isolated shots of her looking skeptical or bemused. Hence, when Takako complains that Komiyama wants to do all the buying for her (the reason for their latest argument), Itsuko purposely takes his side as the quickest way to end the quarrel and get her sister back home. Likewise, Itsuko can barely contain her laughter when the well-meaning but tactless Takako tells their mother that she plans to make her a present of hormonal skin lotion because it "restores youth." Clearly, Itsuko feels superior to Takako, but after this scene, Gosho does nothing more with this matter. Nor does Takako reappear in the film. In short, this scene, like the one with Komiyama and Kurita, exists to add richness, texture, and characterization to the film. As such, it provides yet another example of Burch's "irrelevant events."

Be that as it may, most of the social and psychological observations bear directly on one of the film's most resonant themes: the failure of family members to understand each other. In what amounts to something of a roundelay, one character after another picks up on this theme. We hear that husbands don't understand wives, wives don't understand husbands, men don't understand women, and sisters don't understand sisters. Added to this is Kan-chan's particular problem. "Adults are hard to handle," he remarks at one point; at another, he throws up his hands in confusion. "I don't get grownups," he says. "Why do they drink?" That Kan-chan cannot fully understand the adults around him is to be expected. That these adults cannot understand him is another matter entirely—especially when one of them is his father.

Fukushima's lack of understanding—indeed, his cruel neglect—of Kan-chan provides the catalyst for the main action of the film. This action by and large can be seen as the journey toward understanding that Fukushima must make, a journey that is completed only when he comes to see the error of his ways and admits that he, not Kan-chan, is "the one who's probably to be pitied." As a well-known Japanese proverb says, "*Kunshi hyohen*" ("A wise man changes his mind"). Unfortunately, before Fukushima does so, he ends up subjecting himself, his wife, and his son to no small amount of pain and suffering.

In the first scene in which he appears, Fukushima makes no bones about his attitude toward Kan-chan. "Having him was a total mistake," he says bluntly. Nor does he care if the boy, who is in the next room, hears him. With this scene, Gosho signals the shift in emphasis from the slice-of-life mode of the first twenty-five minutes to the dramatically inflected mode of the last forty-one minutes. Apropos of this shift, Gosho compresses or elides certain story elements, a typical strategy of dramatic modes. Machiko's wedding is thus treated very much in shorthand. We see a single shot of a procession of cars, followed by a shot inside one of these cars as Tamako adjusts Machiko's gown. The wedding ceremony is deleted altogether. Instead Gosho cuts directly to the end of the reception, providing a quick glimpse of the bride and groom as they leave for their honeymoon.[36] Then he gets to the heart of the scene: Fukushima's joyous reaction at seeing the couple drive off. Fukushima thinks he is now "unburdened" of further responsibility, but the obnoxious ramblings of a drunken wedding guest intimate otherwise. So does what happens in the next scene.

The film's most powerful and psychologically complex scene, it is an extended conversation between Fukushima and Tamako, which ends with Tamako's taking her son and leaving. Running twelve minutes and fifteen seconds, and consisting of fifty-seven shots, this scene not only demonstrates that Gosho "has the eye of a dramatist,"[37] but also that he is a skilled practitioner when it comes to blending drama and the slice-of-life mode. Here he charts in exacting, documentary-like detail the step-by-step process by which the Fukushimas move from being a tired but happy couple on their return home from the wedding to an estranged couple who end up barely speaking to each other. Sober in mood, decidedly unsentimental, and nearly devoid of Gosho's characteristic humor, the scene is a beautifully rendered delineation of each character's feelings, spoken and unspoken. In addition, it constitutes virtually a textbook example of how a director can use camera, editing, and blocking in a dialogue scene that is set in a confined space—in this case, a single room—and still maintain visual interest.

Stylistically, the scene is and is not typical of Gosho. To be sure, Gosho uses analytical montage in combination with the moving camera, but with some striking differences. First, he moves his camera sparingly, in fact, no more than several times. Second, the overall rhythm of the scene is slower, more pronounced, and more modulated than scenes in previous *shomin* comedies. And while Gosho holds some of his shots no more than 2 seconds, what is striking about this scene, which has an average shot length of 12.8 seconds, is the number of shots that are held 25 seconds or longer. One shot even runs 60 seconds. The effect here is not only to render the sense and texture of "real time," but also to expose feelings barely held in check beneath well-laid surfaces. Hence, while Tamako is seemingly absorbed with external activities (putting away Fukushima's robe, serving him sake, making him tea, and so forth), in truth her attention is riveted on his complaints about having to support Kan-chan. Nor is Fukushima as absorbed in his activities (drinking sake, reading a newspaper, and so forth) as he pretends to be. Primarily, his intent is to let Tamako know his mind and that he will brook no opposition. Gosho's main strategy for revealing what is going on beneath the surface—a revelation to which only the viewer is privy—is the quick, short shot. Almost always a close-up, it privileges the gestures, actions, and reactions of the two characters. It also creates undeniable tension, for surfaces, no matter how well laid they may be, are just that: surfaces. Sooner or later they must give way.

The scene can be divided into three parts. In the first part, eighteen shots in all, the couple arrives home, tired after a long day and eager to relax. Their ease with one another bespeaks a mutual affection. Gosho even gives them a shared physical gesture that not only illustrates that affection but also provides the only hint of humor in the scene. In one shot Fukushima massages his shoulder; in the matching shot that directly follows, Tamako does the same. What better way to convey how much of a couple the Fukushimas are? And how poignant these shots become in retrospect as the scene progresses and the couple has their falling out. Before that happens, however, the Fukushimas sit and chat, and even joke that the only thing they have left to their name after paying for Machiko's wedding is the leftover food. But the mood begins to change when Fukushima says, "I got rid of our burden," meaning that he has married off all three daughters. Tamako lets this remark pass, or rather she tries to deflect it by suggesting that he go to a spa for some much-needed relaxation. But when she says that she will stay home to take care of Kan-chan, Fukushima is suddenly reminded that only three-fourths of the burden has been lifted from his shoulders. In the most dramatic shot in the entire film—a fast dolly-in to Kan-chan, who is sleeping in the next room—Gosho uses a subjective camera to communicate the rush of feelings that overwhelms this exhausted, resentful salaryman. "Boys are even harder to get rid of," he says. "With his looks, it'll be even harder to get him a bride." Gosho then repeats the dolly-in shot of Kan-chan, not only reinforcing Fukushima's feelings but also heightening what already is a dramatically heightened scene. Indeed, Gosho's camera strategy, like the scene itself, is as far from "uninflected" as one can imagine.

The second part of the scene (shots nineteen through thirty-nine) begins with a close-up of the pained look on Tamako's face. Knowing that Fukushima fully intends to ship the boy out somewhere to work rather than educate him, she asks, "Don't you love him?" He rebuffs her. "No time for love," he declares. "It's not a matter of love." From this point on, Tamako uses every ounce of tact and diplomacy she has to give Fukushima his say and not risk challenging him or angering him. Caught between her husband and son, she also constantly steals glances toward Kan-chan's room, anxious that he may wake up and overhear the discussion. At the same time she holds her tongue and keeps ministering to Fukushima, as if doing so will somehow lead him to soften and change his mind. At one point, to give herself time to think and find the best possible way to appeal to him, she rises and goes to the door. Then, moving into his space, she joins him at the *kotatsu* (warmer), sitting down and sharing a blanket with him. She knows that she must be the conciliatory one.

This shot of the couple seated at the kotatsu (shot forty) begins the last part of the scene. At sixty seconds, it is the longest shot in the scene. By the time it is over, Tamako has, more unintentionally than not, given expression to her feelings of anger. She has been sympathetic to Fukushima for as long as possible, but overcome with pity for Kan-chan, and knowing that his welfare lies in her hands, she accuses Fukushima of not loving their son. She also calls him irresponsible. As their confrontation heats up, Fukushima tells her, "Love him your way all you want, but don't involve me." This is too much for her to bear, and she erupts, catching Fukushima off guard. He is so astounded by her boldness and intensity of feeling that he backs away from her, as if afraid she is about to strike him. They have reached an impasse. Staring at each other in stony silence, neither one is willing to give an inch. Gosho underscores this impasse with a series of three quick alternating shots: Fukushima/Tamako/Fukushima. Three to four seconds in duration, these shots feel like quick jabs or punches—all the more so because they represent a decided break in the rhythm of shots, which have generally ranged from twenty-five to thirty-five seconds. These three staccato shots are followed by a resolution shot in which Fukushima is too stunned even to bluster. He has been defeated, and he knows it. Seeking refuge in his futon, he wraps a blanket around his shoulders, and sulks. "I'm insulted," he declares. But Tamako pays him no mind. She remains seated, her back turned to him. Nevertheless, he casts frequent, pleading glances her way, as if checking for signs of acquiescence on her part. No such signs forthcoming, he rouses himself to full patriarchal indignation and orders her and Kan-chan to leave his house. Her immediate reaction is to rise, cross to the opposite end of the room, and position herself outside of Kan-chan's door in a show of solidarity. Moments later, Fukushima rises, walks toward her, and pauses, towering over her. Now it is she who backs away, as if expecting a blow. However, he merely reaches for his bottle of sake. Left alone in the frame, she says, "The way we are now, I feel sorry for him." The scene ends with a shot of Kan-chan. He has slept through the entire altercation.

In addition to the combination of moving camera and analytical editing, the scene makes notable use of shallow focus, blocking, and composition. Gosho and cameraman Ohara Joji use shallow focus particularly in the early part of the scene to privilege Fukushima and Tamako's closeness as a couple by de-emphasizing the space around them. Yet the filmmakers also use shallow focus to achieve an altogether opposite meaning: the growing distance between the couple. In other words, shallow focus functions as a push-pull dynamic, serving to dramatize the ever-shifting nature of the couple's interaction. Complementing this use of shallow focus is Gosho's blocking and composition. Throughout the scene, Tamako is almost constantly in motion, as befits her efforts to placate and persuade her husband, minimizing the physical and emotional distance between them. By contrast, Fukushima, seemingly secure in his position as patriarch, mostly remains seated. As tempers flare, however, Tamako literally moves further away from him until there is nothing more to say and no room for compromise.

This complex scene is also remarkable for its delineation of character. Indeed, in many respects it is an actor's scene, and Saito Tatsuo and Yoshikawa Mitsuko deliver felt, nuanced performances, demonstrating that Gosho is a fine director of actors. Yoshikawa's Tamako is far more than a dutiful, traditional wife or mother. Respectful as she is of her husband's position, she has no recourse but to challenge him when he puts her in the untenable position of having to defend her son. Yoshikawa shows us the conflicted emotions, the pain and anxiety, that the traditional Japanese wife is rarely permitted to express. She also hints at something even deeper: Fukushima's treatment of her is a blow to her self-esteem as a wife, mother, and human being that she simply cannot allow. If Tamako ultimately emerges as the stronger of the two characters, it is Fukushima who is more intricately drawn. Gosho neither sentimentalizes nor demonizes him, but presents him as a man who has allowed life to coarsen him. Implicit in Fukushima's resentment of his son and his desire to be unburdened of responsibility is a capsule history of what it meant to be a salaryman in the 1930s. Sandbagged all too often by a system that stressed conformity and required one to keep one's nose resolutely to the grindstone, these white-collar workers lived in constant fear of unemployment,[38] a fear that became even more exacerbated as one got older. Thus, for Fukushima, being a salaryman has meant a muted but ongoing bludgeoning of the spirit. Saito's stooped shoulders go a long way toward chronicling this bludgeoning, showing how at fifty-nine Fukushima seems to have lost the core of his humanity.[39] Or so it would seem in his argument with Tamako. In actuality, however, he means only to stave off further demands from his wife and family, insisting that they ask or expect nothing more. After a lifetime of responsibilities, he is weary, but has allowed self-pity to get the best of him. And yet even as he lays down the law to Tamako, his sad-sack looks and sidelong glances are tip-offs that he is unhappy playing the tyrannical paterfamilias. Most of all, he does not like hurting his wife. He is in a double bind. Having announced that he will not support Kan-chan, he is in effect hoist on his own petard. He waits for Tamako, as the traditionally dutiful wife, to feel sorry for him and apologize, thereby relieving him of the guilt he doubtless feels. But she adamantly refuses, and so he hardens his position, blanching with indignation, his hackles raised. Gosho and Saito enable us to understand Fukushima's conflicted feelings, and even to sympathize with him to a degree, while also realizing what he does not: that denying his son and estranging his wife is not what he truly wants. By allowing us to see Tamako's and Fukushima's sides of the situation, the actors not only prevent the scene from collapsing into melodrama, but make it all the more authentic and moving. Perfectly pitched, its predominant tone is that of unsentimental pathos.

However, *Burden of Life* would not be a Gosho film without his trademark blend of humor and pathos—and without the resolution of the Fukushimas' seemingly intractable problem. Hence in the next scene Fukushima pays a visit to the Abes (Arai Jun and Iida Choko), the go-betweens who arranged his marriage. His mission is simple: he wants them to persuade Tamako to return home—but without his son. "He's a failure and a headache of a boy," he explains. Needless to say, the Abes realize that no mother would ever agree to such a condition. Therefore, they try to use gentle persuasion on Fukushima, remarking that their son is a failure, too, by which they mean that parents must accept their children as they are. At first the Abes are genuinely pleased to see Fukushima, but the more he explains what he believes to be a perfectly reasonable request, the more bemused, bewildered, and discomforted they become. And therein lies the humor of the scene. The Abes find themselves trapped by the demands of etiquette and politeness. Nonetheless, they agree that Fukushima should have his wife back, so they end up interceding on his behalf—but with no

The reconciliation of Kan-chan and his father (Saito Tatsuo). *Burden of Life*
(1935).

success. The only person who can solve Fukushima's problem is Fukushima
himself. Thus, almost in spite of himself, he comes to feel a loss in his life,
missing not only his wife but also his son. And in the climax of the film
when he and Kan-chan reconcile, all the troubles and fears that formerly
weighed him down are dismissed and forgotten. He has rediscovered a
sense of family. In the last scene, an ecstatic, relieved Tamako hurries home
in a taxicab, urging the driver to "go faster, faster." It is the perfect Gosho
ending—both touching and funny at the same time. It is touching because
it provides us with the happy ending we want and funny because it makes
clear that when it comes to her family, Tamako is indisputably in the driver's seat.

By now it should be apparent that *Burden of Life* represents an advance
in Gosho's *shomin-geki* in its seriousness of tone, depth of characterization,
and use of slice-of-life elements. In closing, however, we need to consider
the thematic implication of the delay of Fukushima's entrance into the
film. Stated directly, by keeping Fukushima off-camera for the first twenty-
five minutes, Gosho implies that this patriarch does not play a central role
in his family's life. This impression is further underscored by the exclusive
attention devoted to slice-of-life elements, which show life going on around
him in various and sundry forms: marital squabbles, money problems,

knotty interpersonal relationships. In all these matters, which on the whole are routine, Fukushima is at best only marginally involved. This, of course, is fine with him, for he still remains a powerful figure, as proved by the central dramatic action—and the family crisis he precipitates. Yet his power is not what it seems. If Fukushima is not quite the pathetic salaryman of some of Ozu's 1930s films—he is mercifully spared, for instance, the humiliation that the father suffers in *Umarete wa mita keredo* (*I Was Born, but . . .*, 1932)—he comes close enough, suggesting that what his family (presumably like most Japanese families of the period) seems to want in a father is someone who doesn't have *all* the power. Indeed, Fukushima comes to understand that he retains his power by using it sparingly, instead of exercising it like a dictator.

Fukushima's changing role as patriarch must be viewed in light of an even deeper and more fundamental change taking place in 1930s Japan: the renovation of the family from within by ordinary human beings who were simply caught up in the process of living their lives. Obviously, this change was also affected from without, by the influx of Western values and increasing urbanization and industrialization. However, Gosho does not foreground or detail this change as such; rather, it forms the Zeitgeist, the here-and-now, which the Fukushimas by turn embrace, accept, or barely notice. In either case, Gosho's film shows the redefining of interpersonal relationships within the family unit and the pulling in opposite directions, which at times accompanies that redefining. In certain instances, this "redefining and pulling"—as in the case of Itsuko's relationship with Takako—is basically meaningless; in other instances—as in the breach between husband, wife, and son—it strikes at the very heart of the family as a social institution and threatens to destroy it. Nevertheless, like all of Gosho's *shomin-geki, Burden of Life* posits the notion that no change, however threatening, must necessarily be destructive, nor must life's problems remain insolvable. Indeed, the first step in solving a problem is the willingness to adapt, just as Fukushima adapts. And in adapting, Fukushima finds the worst part of his burden lifted from his shoulders—the emotional, psychological burden. Gosho is too much the realist to suggest that Fukushima has somehow been miraculously freed from the financial burden. Quite the contrary, he still is obligated to pay for Kan-chan's education, and so he must keep his nose to the grindstone a few more years. But the difference is that he no longer sees his son as an obligation, a "burden." And that difference makes all the difference. Like all of Gosho's *shomin-geki, Burden of Life* defines what it is to be human.

TWO

Dancing Girl of Izu *(1933)* *and the* Junbungaku *Movement*

Years before receiving the 1968 Nobel Prize for literature, Kawabata Yasunari told Gosho that he would probably be remembered only as the author of *Izu no odoriko* (*Dancing Girl of Izu*).[1] If the renowned author was lamenting the vagaries of fame, he was also complimenting Gosho on the enormous popularity of his film adaptation.[2] The first of six film adaptations of Kawabata's classic novella, and in the view of many still the best,[3] *Dancing Girl of Izu* is one of Gosho's masterpieces during the silent era. It also holds a prominent place in Japanese film history as one of the seminal films in the *junbungaku,* or "pure literature" movement.

Published in 1926, Kawabata's novella tells the simple story of the ill-fated love between a Tokyo college student and the thirteen-year-old itinerant dancer he meets while on a walking tour of Izu. Told in the first person by the student himself (he is given no name),[4] Kawabata's tale deals with one of the author's central themes—the search for beauty—what Makoto Ueda sees as striving after an ideal, "a pure life."[5] In his quest the student takes up with a troupe of traveling players and finds himself attracted to the purity and innocence of Kaoru, the young Izu dancer. However, in the end, as in most of Kawabata's works, the lovers must separate.[6] In Gosho's film, the student, now named Mizuhara, may be less psychologically complex than his counterpart in the novella, but he still is a seeker of beauty and an idealist who is blessed with a gentle, unpretentious nature and sympathy for others.

Clearly, Kawabata's theme had considerable appeal for Gosho. Indeed, the notion of romantic love as a thing of beauty, a search for self, a striving after an ideal, as well as ultimately a metaphor for the pervasive sadness and evanescence of life, preoccupied Gosho throughout his career. It was the central theme of his first film, *Nanto no haru* (*Spring in Southern Islands,* 1925), which also is a love story between a Tokyo student and a native girl. Thereafter, it found bittersweet treatment, most notably in the plights of the law student and barmaid of *Oboroyo no onna* (*Woman of the Mist*, 1936), the idealistic doctor and middle-class woman of *Ima hitotabino* (*Once More*, 1947), the young Buddhist acolyte and girl forced into prostitution of *Takekurabe* (*Growing Up*, 1955), the married architect and disabled drama student of *Banka* (*Elegy of the North*, 1957), and the army officer and married woman of *Utage* (*Rebellion of Japan*, 1967).

Kawabata's story appealed to Gosho for an equally compelling reason: it focuses on the lives of common people and the theme of social oppression, concerns Gosho first treated with distinction in *Mura no hanayome* (*The Village Bride*, 1928). In fact, the year before he made *Dancing Girl of Izu*, Gosho combined the themes of romance and social oppression in the now-lost *Tengoku ni musubu koi* (*Love Requited in Heaven*, 1932), about two lovers who commit suicide rather than be separated by class barriers. So successful was the film at the box office that it spawned a series of love suicides at the same location where the film lovers killed themselves—hardly the response Gosho could have wanted.[7] In *Dancing Girl of Izu*, class differences are inextricably linked with prejudice against the traveling players, and in the end prove insurmountable for the student and the dancer. Indeed, if the student ever felt such prejudice, he has worked through it. "I felt no condescension toward them," he explains in Kawabata's novella. "Indeed, I was no longer conscious that they belonged to that low order, traveling performers."[8] Others, however, do not share this sentiment. When he asks an old woman where the players will stay that night, her answer says it all: "People like that, how can you tell where they'll stay? If they find someone who will pay them, that's where it will be. . . ."[9] For her, they are lowlifes pure and simple. Later, the student relates observing signs on the outskirts of villages: "Vagrant performers keep out."[10] As we shall see, Gosho makes much of this particular detail.

In his excellent study, *The Flash of Capital*, Eric Cazdyn examines the *junbungaku*, or "pure literature" movement of the 1930s, as the first important stage in the history of Japanese film adaptations (*eiga-ka*). *Junbungaku* referred to serious or classical literature, as opposed to "popular" literature, which stressed action and a less complex handling of romance.[11] According to Cazdyn, the *junbungaku* movement privileged fidelity to the original source. It presented the story in linear fashion, "literally (and cinematically) granted center stage, or center frame" to the plot, and refrained from cutting or adding content to the narrative.[12]

In adapting Kawabata's novella, Gosho and screenwriter Fushimi Akira clearly have sought to capture the spirit of this classic work. They also can be seen as adhering to two of the characteristics that Cazdyn describes above (linear structure, foregrounding the plot). However, they diverge dramatically from the third and last-named characteristic in that they not only embellish the love story, but also add a subplot and new characters. In fact, the story that Gosho and Fushimi tell is more complicated than the original. Thus, soon after Mizuhara (Ohinata Den) joins up with the traveling players, he learns that Kaoru's brother, Eikichi (Kobayashi Tokuji), once owned a gold mine, but lost it because of his profligate ways. As a result, Eikichi and Kaoru have been forced to become traveling performers to avoid poverty. When Mizuhara and the troupe stop over at the hot springs village where the mine is located, they hear that gold has been discovered. Also staying at the village is Kubota (Kawamura Reikichi), a mining engineer who quit just before gold was struck. Determined to get a share of the wealth, he tries unsuccessfully to blackmail the present owner, Zenbei (Arai Jun), now a successful innkeeper. Bent on revenge, Kubota persuades Eikichi that he and his sister were cheated out of the mine by Zenbei. In the complications that ensue, Mizuhara learns that Zenbei not only has been putting aside money from the mine for Kaoru but also plans for her to marry his son, Ryuichi (Takeuchi Ryoichi). Mizuhara realizes that he has misjudged the innkeeper. He also realizes that his and Kaoru's love can never be. At the Shimoda dock, about to board a ship to take him back to Tokyo, he tells her about Zenbei's plans for her. He also confesses that he truly loves her. Weeping, Kaoru bids him farewell and watches as his ship disappears from view.

As Cazdyn points out, there is a connection between the *eiga-ka* of any given period and the predominant national discourse.[13] In Gosho's film, it is the addition of the subplot that makes this connection possible. Thanks to this subplot, Gosho is able to relate Kawabata's story to the historical moment—specifically, Japan's social unrest and shattered economy, both of which were exacerbated by the Great Depression and the war abroad.

That said, aesthetic and ideological considerations were not the only factors that played a part in the making of *Dancing Girl of Izu*. Gosho also had to meet studio demands. Capitalizing on his hugely successful "talkie," *The Neighbor's Wife and Mine,* he planned to make *Dancing Girl of Izu* as a sound film, but Shochiku refused because of financial considerations. Nor was this refusal the only obstacle Gosho faced.[14] In an era when light comedies were the dominant mode in Japanese film, "there was considerable prejudice against making such an overtly 'arty' film."[15] However, offsetting this prejudice was the industry's need for more ambitious fare to ensure continued growth. In the end, Shochiku gave the go-ahead for the film, but sought to minimize the risk by making it as a silent.

All told, *junbungaku* literature proved a boon for Gosho and the film industry. As canonical literature, it was generally able to circumvent war-time censorship. It also had the distinct advantage of a ready-made audience, and as it appealed to the norms of high culture, it could be marketed as prestige cinema. In addition, it provided filmmakers with the opportunity to "get closer to ordinary people whose lives they could portray realistically."[16] For Gosho, of course, this was nothing new. He had already been doing as much with his work in the *shomin-geki*. But now he could wed the high-brow pedigree of the *junbungaku* with a "popular" or mainstream approach, be it the *shomin-geki* or Shochiku's staple, melodrama, which catered to a predominantly female audience. Simply put, *Dancing Girl of Izu* represents an artful accommodation, not only of Gosho's beloved *shomin-geki* and Kawabata's novella but also of melodrama. As Keiko McDonald has aptly pointed out, Gosho and Fushimi mined "the melodramatic vein in Kawabata's tale."[17] They did this in two ways: by making explicit Kawabata's sentimentality and by adding a subplot strong on melodrama—what McDonald calls "the vengeance plot."[18]

If the main plot, the love story, has been faulted for introducing a "skein of sentimentality,"[19] the subplot, which has to do with intrigues surrounding the gold mine, has come in for even harsher criticism on the grounds that it is "extraneous" and "out of keeping with the tone of the original."[20] There is some merit in this charge. At first Kubota's plot to exact revenge on Zenbei seems far removed from the love story. Yet it soon has a ripple effect, resulting in a series of melodramatic plot devices—misinformation, misunderstandings, and withheld information, among others[21]—that ultimately involve the lovers and generate pathos for them, especially Kaoru. Indeed, the subplot broadens the implications of the love story by grounding it not only in the world of melodrama, in which good and evil and generosity and greed are pitted against each other, but also in the materialist world of 1930s Japan.

When Gosho's film came out in 1933, Japan was suffering from a downturn in the economy that had been exacerbated by the worldwide Depression of 1929 and "the drop in silk and rice prices that devastated the rural sector by 1931." These conditions "would hold until 1934."[22] With these conditions in mind, Gosho introduces the dissension over the gold mine and the constant talk of money that preoccupies most of the characters and even intrudes upon Mizuhara and Kaoru's happiness. "Do you need money?" a distraught Kaoru asks Eikichi at one point. At another Mizuhara ruefully admits to Zenbei that he knows money matters. Indeed, money proves to be the undoing of Eikichi, a basically good man, but an incorrigible spendthrift who threw away his inheritance. The world of *Dancing Girl of Izu,* then, is not simply one of romance but one in which money and materialistic success matter. This particular theme was not new to Gosho. According to Donald Richie, it was the concern of his now-lost 1929 film, *Shinjoseikan* (*A New Kind of Woman*), which was a protest against a money-obsessed upper class during the height of the Depression.[23] In short, in Kawabata's story, Gosho saw a tendency toward social commentary that in no way was incompatible with the love story.

Still, viewers familiar with Kawabata's novella must have been puzzled by the first two scenes of the film, which focus entirely on the subplot, introduce the theme of materialism, and present a new set of characters, most importantly, Kubota and Zenbei. In the opening scene, a policeman from the small rural village of Yukawaro asks two workers if they have seen a geisha. She has run away without paying her debts. Overhearing this conversation is Kubota, "a notorious engineer." The workmen tell him that the village is in the midst of a boom, and that he left his job at the mine just before gold was discovered. Wearing his perpetual scowl, Kubota remarks that he is not about to overlook a gold mine. If this first scene introduces the villain of the piece (one of Gosho's few villains), the next scene introduces his foil, Zenbei. The employer of the missing geisha, and a wealthy man, thanks to the boom, he instructs an old and loyal servant to tell the police to call off the search. True to his name, Zenbei, which means "Goodheart,"[24] is concerned only with the missing geisha's well-being. He is not so stingy or blind as to be bothered by what he euphemistically calls "a small loan." Moreover, he doesn't wish to disturb the other guests at his inn by pressing charges. In a world in which money and wealth is on everyone's mind, Zenbei's generosity of character is as welcome as it is exemplary. It will be even more welcome and exemplary later in the film.

Scenes three and four draw their inspiration from a few lines in Kawabata that we alluded to earlier: "Now and then, on the outskirts of a village, we [the student and the traveling players] would see a sign: 'Vagrant performers keep out.'"[25] Both scenes are pure Gosho. In scene three, a transitional scene, a wandering Buddhist priest, wearing a *tengai* (a large straw hat covering the entire head) comes upon a sign that prohibits beggars and itinerant artists from entering the village. He tosses the sign in a ditch. Realizing that two boys have seen him, he frightens them away, then nonchalantly enters the village.

The stage is now set for scene four and the introduction of the main characters. In it, Gosho not only reveals the plight of the players but also expands upon the theme of social prejudice, situates the dramatic action in the *shomin-geki* mode, and develops the characters of Mizuhara and Kaoru, establishing his attraction to her. He manages to accomplish all of this in five minutes and ten seconds and with ninety shots. The scene opens with a deceptively simple moving-camera shot, which begins with a close-up of the tossed-aside sign and ends with a long shot of the players as they approach the village. In this manner Gosho makes an immediate connection between the sign and the players, who are, in effect, innocents walking into a trap. That they also are poor and down on their luck is evident when Eikichi and his mother, Otatsu (Takamatsu Eiko), are forced to share the same cigarette. While Otatsu, Eikichi, his wife, Chiyoko (Wakamizu Kinuko), and Yuriko (Hyodo Shizue) stop to catch their breath, Kaoru discovers the sign and calls it to her brother's attention. "No good," she tells him, meaning that they must move on. How different her reaction is from the priest's! He refused to be cowed; she, on the other hand, wants to avoid trouble, and has accepted prejudice simply as a fact of life. The same is true of Eikichi. Later in the film, he tells Mizuhara that it is not proper for him to stay with the troupe at their inn; he needs to lodge at an inn that caters to a better class of people.

Ironically, Eikichi and the troupe find themselves in trouble, even though they have no intention of entering the village. No sooner does Eikichi pick up the sign than he is confronted by a local who grabs him, demanding to know what he is doing. Eikichi and Kaoru try to explain that they found the sign tossed in a ditch, but to no avail. Soon a second villager joins the scuffle to help the first one drag Eikichi off to the police. However, they must also contend with Kaoru, who remains steadfastly at her brother's side. If the scene dramatizes the social prejudice directed against itinerant actors, it also establishes Kaoru's pluck and spirit. She does not hesitate to get involved, unlike the other women, who remain helpless bystanders until the scuffle begins to escalate. Just as it seems that the two villagers will succeed in taking Eikichi away, a new character appears in the distance: Mizuhara. He is passing through the village, but when he sees what is happening, he stops, a decision that Gosho presents in a close-up of his *geta* (wooden sandals), a short, quick shot that is typical of the director's piecemeal cutting style. In the next shot Mizuhara is in the thick of things, breaking up the fracas and mediating. Whereas most of the shots in the scene are in the medium range, those in which Kaoru tearfully pleads her case to Mizuhara grant close-ups to both characters (shots fifty-eight through sixty). Clearly, Gosho is preparing the way for the love story. That said, Mizuhara—despite his good intentions—can only stop the quarrel, he cannot resolve it. Enter the person who can: one of the village lads who saw the vagabond priest pull up the sign. His story saves the day. Grateful and relieved, Kaoru wipes her eyes and even manages a smile. Mizuhara insists that the two villagers apologize.

True to its origins in the *shomin-geki,* the scene ends with a blend of comedy and pathos. The comedy is of a piece with the broad humor one finds in *The Bride Talks in Her Sleep* and *The Groom Talks in His Sleep.* Annoyed at being forced to apologize, the two villagers take out their anger on the boy. One bops him on the head; the other knocks him down. Bursting into tears, the boy protests: "I told the truth, as I was taught in school." While we laugh in disbelief at the villagers' outrageous behavior, we cannot help but be touched and amused by the boy's comeback—a passionate declaration of morality that puts the two bumpkins in their place. Feeling for him and perhaps recognizing that his words echo her own protestation earlier in the scene—"We never lie"—Kaoru soothes his hurt pride with some candy. Mizuhara watches admiringly. It is at this moment that he begins to have feelings for the young dancer. The scene closes with an important variation on the opening shot. Again, Gosho's camera moves from the sign to the players, but now they are *leaving* the village, and with them is their new friend, Mizuhara.

Dancing Girl of Izu cannot be properly understood without recognizing the informing sense of place and the impact that place has on the lovers. Ably assisted by cinematographer Ohara Joji, who photographs nearly every scene in bright sunlight, Gosho captures the beauty and feel of the rural setting of South Izu—the Amagi mountains, small villages, winding roads, bustling harbor, and open expanse of sea—without ever succumbing to picture-postcard prettiness. He also effortlessly conveys the rhythm of everyday life—a policeman on his beat, people taking time to chat, old friends renewing friendships. To be sure, as the scene discussed above illustrates, not everything is idyllic, and conflict and tensions abound. Yet the setting encourages one to imagine another time, another place—a world in which the appearance of an occasional car or bus almost seems an anachronism. Admittedly an unabashedly romantic view, it was nevertheless one that many Japanese of the 1930s wanted to believe in. Indeed, as Christena Turner reminds us, in the 1930s the Japanese spirit was thought to be found, not in the urban culture of Tokyo, but in the countryside, in just such a place as South Izu.[26]

Mizuhara and Kaoru embody that spirit. For them, nature and the rural countryside constitute a space in which social position can be minimized and even, for a time, ignored. On the open road, they enjoy the freedom to grow closer. And in their innocence and purity of heart, they take pleasure in simple things. During one of the troupe's first stops, Mizuhara shows Kaoru how far he can toss a stone. He means to impress her; needless to say, she is impressed. Several scenes later she can barely contain her pleasure when she learns that he will remain with the troupe until they reach the port at Shimoda. Too shy to say anything or even to look at him, she unconsciously bites down on the stem of a flower she is holding, her feelings made explicit by one of the many "song" intertitles that appear throughout the film: "I am a floating leaf / Guided by waves. / The prime of youth is spent / On an endless journey. / Awake or sleep wherever I am / My love will bloom."[27] Of course, this intertitle could also apply to Mizuhara, who is no less shy or able to look at her. Sentimental? Undoubtedly so, but for Gosho feelings and ideas are rarely at odds. If youth, like life, is fleeting, then love must be celebrated unashamedly.

For a time the celebration continues. Indeed, when the troupe first arrives at the village of Yukawaro, the lovers are as carefree as they were on the road. In one especially delightful scene Kaoru, who now makes little effort to conceal her fondness for Mizuhara, gives full expression to the childlike, winsome side of her character. Mizuhara is about to leave for his inn, accompanied by Eikichi. When he tries to take his briefcase and cap from Kaoru, who has playfully snatched them away, she returns only his cap. Then, dashing across the room, she stops suddenly, looks back, and performs a mock bow. What better way to make clear that she refuses to surrender the briefcase until she is good and ready? What better way to announce her intentions of tagging along with him and her brother? Eikichi is amused; Mizuhara, shy as ever, is completely captivated. She has worked her magic on him. In a gleeful surge of confidence and energy, she races ahead of the two men, leading the way. Finally, at the top of the steps outside Mizuhara's inn, she stops, checks her hair for any renegade strands, and waits impatiently for the slowpokes to catch up. When they do, she dutifully turns over the briefcase and rushes back to the inn, thoroughly pleased. Things couldn't be better. Back at the inn, she joins her mother, sister-in-law, and Yuriko at the bathhouse. When Yuriko teases her about Mizuhara, she waves away the suggestion that she likes him. However, she is so absorbed in her reveries that she fails to notice that the three women have gone off to bathe without her.

Yet even before this scene, there are intimations that the lovers' happiness cannot last. Specifically, Gosho's use of crosscutting between Mizuhara and Kaoru on the road and Kubota in Yukawaro suggests that the lovers' fate and the unscrupulous engineer's machinations are somehow linked. Gosho does not disclose the full nature of this linkage until Mizuhara and Kaoru's final farewell. Instead he has Kubota set in motion a chain of events that progressively and irrevocably involves not only the lovers but Eikichi, Zenbei, and Ryuichi as well. These events take the form of five confrontations.

In the first confrontation, Kubota tries to blackmail Zenbei, only to be checked by Ryuichi, who is standing in for his father. "Who ran away when father was short of funds?" the young man asks, bringing Kubota up short. Irate, Kubota insists on speaking directly to Zenbei, and begins shouting.

Zenbei (Arai Jun) and his son Ryuichi (Takeuchi Ryoichi) dismiss "notorious engineer" Kubota (Kawamura Reikichi) in the subplot of *Dancing Girl of Izu* **(1933).**

This attracts the attention of some of the guests at the inn, as well as Zenbei's trusted servant, Kisaku (Aono Kiyoshi), who bursts into the room and threatens Kubota with a gun. Ryuichi quickly disarms the servant, but a terrified Kubota collapses to the floor in what appears to be an epileptic seizure—a curious moment in the film and the only time that the engineer seems remotely human. Finally, Zenbei appears, and dismisses Kubota with some money. The outmaneuvered, humiliated engineer sneeringly refers to the obviously small sum as "railway fare," but pockets it anyway and storms off. Now he is even more bent on revenge.

How exactly does this first confrontation affect Kaoru and Mizuhara? By introducing us to a character who will play a central role in their relationship: Ryuichi, the innkeeper's son. Only later when Zenbei tells Mizuhara that he intends Kaoru for Ryuichi's wife will we appreciate how important Ryuichi's role is. To prepare us for this, Gosho establishes Ryuichi as a man of courage and integrity; in subsequent scenes, Gosho also shows him to be a good friend to Mizuhara, who is his junior at the same university. In short, Ryuichi may not be Mizuhara, but if he is to marry Kaoru, he must be worthy of her.

In the second confrontation Kubota seizes the opportunity for revenge by ingratiating himself with Eikichi, plying him with liquor, and telling him a boldfaced lie: that Zenbei knew there was gold in Eikichi's mine when he bought it. Taking the bait, an indignant Eikichi decides to pay Zenbei a visit and demand his fair share of the profits. Kaoru tries to dissuade her brother from this rash act, knowing that Kubota is not to be trusted. But Eikichi will not listen. He heads off for what is to be the third confrontation scene. As for Kubota, having sown the seeds of discontent, he disappears from the film, apparently satisfied.

Not surprisingly, Eikichi's meeting with Zenbei proves a disaster. Zenbei advises him to come back when he is sober, or, if he must have money, to send Kaoru to him. Imagining the worst, Eikichi sinks to the floor, reduced to picking apart a tatami mat in frustration. What follows is the fourth confrontation scene. One of the most powerful scenes in the film, and one of the few that takes place at night, it finds the normally kind and loving Eikichi irrationally turning on his sister, an act that is made all the more disturbing by Ohara's *noir*-like lighting and the deserted street setting. On his way back to the inn, Eikichi runs into Mizuhara and explains that he has never been so angry. Moments later, the two men are joined by Kaoru, who has been worried about her brother. He tells her that he feels sorry for her, then orders her to go to Zenbei. Shaken by his strange mood, she clings to his arm and tries to placate him. "Do you need money?" she asks. When he answers that he plans to retaliate against Zenbei, she tells him she doesn't like it, and pleads with him: "I bore this job because I am with you," she declares. "If I can't work with you, I'll go to Tokyo with this student." But her words fall on deaf ears. He insists he must have money and repeats his determination to be revenged. Weeping, she pulls away from him, but he races after her and grabs her, demanding that she obey him. Mizuhara can remain silent no longer. Stepping in to prevent Eikichi from striking Kaoru, he shames him with a simple utterance: "To raise money by selling your sister!" The confrontation over, the three walk off in silence. The scene fades out.

By contrast, the next scene, which takes place the following morning, is the most sublime in the film. An interlude before the fifth and final confrontation scene, it shows Kaoru and Mizuhara experiencing their happiest moment together. As the scene opens, however, Kaoru is alone on the second-floor balcony of her inn, staring forlornly into the distance, like a fairy-tale princess waiting to be rescued. An intertitle describes her feelings. It speaks of cloudy skies that bring rain like tears, autumn winds that vanish like memories. Suddenly, her mood changes. She sees Mizuhara walking below, and running as fast as she can, catches up with him. He explains that he is taking a stroll, but actually he is on his way to see Zenbei and demand justice for her and Eikichi. Even so, he cannot pass up the chance to be with her.

Stopping at a bridge, he invites her to sit beside him. But she is too elated to remain seated, and begins tossing pebbles into the river below, as if to remind him of what they shared on the road. So far Mizuhara has been smiling, but a thought occurs to him, and he asks: "How's your brother?" Explaining that Eikichi feels bad about how he treated her, she says, "He's thoroughly blue," adding, "He's weak-minded, but becomes worse when tipsy." However, she says no more, not wanting to spoil the mood. Taking Mizuhara by the arm, she leads him to the river. There he promises to help her, if ever she needs him. Gosho cuts to a shot of the water, shimmering in the sunlight—a pause in the action that gives Kaoru time to think. Then he cuts back to the couple. All Kaoru can say is, "I . . . I'm glad." If words prove inadequate, her little "dance" of sorts does not. First, she impulsively embraces one of the wood beams of the bridge—a gesture that almost never fails to get a laugh from audiences. Clearly, her feelings for Mizuhara are not platonic. Then she scoots along another beam, with Mizuhara by her side to make sure she doesn't lose her balance. Next she lies back on a large boulder and stretches, leaps to her feet, and waves her arms to and fro in mock exercise. When Mizuhara puts his arm around her—at once a welcome and long-overdue move—she is beside herself with happiness, and scurries off to splash her feet in the water. Now it is Mizuhara's turn to act. Taking out his handkerchief, he tenderly dries her feet, an undeniably erotic act (anticipating Gosho's later film *Rebellion of Japan* [1967], in which a young army officer wipes the snow from the feet of the woman he loves but can never have). The scene comes to a close with Kaoru being summoned back to the inn and Mizuhara continuing on his way.

It is a remarkable scene. Here, as elsewhere in the film, Gosho is especially sensitive to the emotional currents of his characters, his intuitive understanding of people infusing the dramatic action with a sense of psychological reality. That said, the scene is inconceivable without the visual delicacy of Ohara's photography, which creates exactly what is needed: the mood of an enchanted idyll. For although the lovers have not left the village, they have managed to transform it into a space as natural and lovely as any they experienced on the road. Indeed, the river, with its translucent, diaphanous glow, becomes virtually a third character in the scene, providing Kaoru and Mizuhara with the space they have secretly longed for. In this space, this natural setting, they are free from the constraints of society and at one with their true selves and desires. Here they may even dare to hope for a future together.

An enchanted idyll: Mizuhara (Ohinata Den) and Kaoru (Tanaka Kinuyo) at the river. *Dancing Girl of Izu* (1933).

Unfortunately, these hopes are dashed in the fifth and final confrontation scene. It is here that Zenbei informs Mizuhara of his plans for Kaoru, news that comes as a blow and changes everything. Mizuhara can say nothing, not even to Ryuichi, who appears at the end of the scene. Ryuichi, of course, has no idea what his father and Mizuhara have been discussing. Nor is it clear if he knows anything about his father's marriage plans for him. Indeed, we cannot help but wonder if he and Kaoru have even met; they certainly have no contact in the film. Not that this would be unusual in the case of an arranged marriage. Still, these matters puzzle and perplex.

However that may be, Mizuhara and Ryuichi's encounter is also notable for the way that Gosho has chosen to film it. Instead of breaking it down into separate shots—his usual strategy—Gosho positions the two men in profile and holds this two-shot for the duration of the scene. As a result, we see very little of what we want to see most: the expression on Mizuhara's face. In addition, Gosho has Ryuichi dominate the scene with expansive gestures: patting Mizuhara on the shoulder, playfully swapping caps with Mizuhara, and so forth. Yet we are never really in doubt about Mizuhara's feeling. He is affecting good cheer for the benefit of his friend and out of his own sense of pride. The brilliance of Gosho's strategy is that it manages to make us empathize with Mizuhara in a way that we have not done before. In a film that primarily evokes pathos for the heroine, here we feel that same emotion for the hero. He has come face-to-face with his own powerlessness, his inability to do anything to change Kaoru's lot. The role of money as a deterministic force has been brought painfully home to him. And this knowledge has so stunned him that from this point on, he begins to pull away from Kaoru and her brother, stepping aside for a man who has the money and means to give Kaoru a new life. Announcing that he must return to Tokyo, he leaves Kaoru and Eikichi upset and confused, thinking that they have somehow offended him. Not until the final scene does he realize that he can in fact do something for Kaoru.

Thus, for a time Mizuhara falls victim to *akirame,* "the resignation which is taken for granted in the face of an inescapable destiny."[28]

However, as Gosho makes clear, Mizuhara's "inescapable destiny" is not really in the hands of Zenbei and Ryuichi. Nor for that matter are these two characters the main obstacles to Mizuhara and Kaoru's union. The real obstacle is social class. Mizuhara does everything in his power to overcome or minimize it. In fact, he even endearingly, if rather naively, replaces his student cap with a hunting cap in order to fit in with the players.[29] But egalitarianism is not so easily achieved.

Indeed, Gosho never allows the audience to forget that social barriers also make Mizuhara himself an outsider. To this end Gosho once again relies on crosscutting. Thus, while Kaoru and the other players entertain at a banquet, Mizuhara sits alone in his room at the inn until another guest drops by and invites him to a game of Go, a complicated game somewhat reminiscent of chess. Gosho's crosscutting underscores not just Kaoru's and Mizuhara's different activities—which are a necessity for the former, a way to pass the time for the latter—but also the different worlds that she and he occupy, even while in the same village. Just as social class dictates that he lodge in a different inn, the fact that he is neither a member of the troupe nor one of the invited guests effectively excludes him from the banquet. Later that evening—the same evening that he witnesses Eikichi and Kaoru's quarrel—he stops while on a walk and gazes longingly in the direction of Kaoru's inn. This moment is rendered all the more dramatic by Gosho's stylistic flourish and use of subjective camera, which work in concert to make us experience Mizuhara's feelings as directly as possible.[30] First we see a shot of the inn, which slowly goes out of focus; then a medium close-up of Kaoru, smiling demurely; and finally, a shot of the inn, which returns to sharp focus. The fantasy is over; the longing and separation remains, and with it the irrefutable fact that not only are Mizuhara and Kaoru each outsiders in their own way, but that their parting, as we have always known, is inevitable.

We are now ready to examine the final scene. Justly famous, it lasts for twelve minutes and fifty-five seconds, consisting of 164 shots, and it takes place at the Shimoda dock where Mizuhara is about to depart for Tokyo. As might be expected, here, more than elsewhere in the film, Gosho's visual style is coded for melodramatic intensity. Close-ups capture the lovers' every emotion and gesture; composition, camera angle, and camera distance underscore the psychological shifts and turns of their interaction; long shots and insert shots, especially of sky and water, transform the *mise-en-scène* into the landscape of the lovers' souls. Typical of melodrama, Gosho foregrounds his heroine's emotional state, in essence fetishizing her suffering in tearful close-ups and her sometimes near-hysterical body language in medium and long shots. (On one occasion, she spins around and collapses in a move worthy of Lillian Gish.) It is she whom the camera concentrates on in the closing shots, though it must be said that prior to this point Mizuhara is given nearly equal screen time. Gosho understands full well that excess is the lifeblood of melodrama—"excess of emotion, sentiment, affect, empathy."[31] Therefore he shapes the scene accordingly. Building it detail by detail, he extends it, heightens it, and even prolongs it, so as to achieve the feel of real time and to make the lovers' pain palpable and the climax moving. Needless to say, the scene is also highly sentimental—too much so, in the opinion of some critics.

The scene can be divided into three sections. In the first section (shots one through twenty-five), Kaoru, Mizuhara, and Eikichi arrive at the pier. An opening intertitle describes the mood and warns of the futility of lamenting or weeping: "Tears cannot help. There comes no tomorrow." Tears, however, will be unavoidable. Pensive, Kaoru goes off by herself, leaving the two men to say their goodbyes. Eikichi thanks Mizuhara for his kindness. In turn, Mizuhara makes Eikichi a present of his hunting cap and dons his student cap, "signaling the end of youthful freedom and a return to his allotted, and confining, place in life."[32] In the first and last piece of humor in the scene, one indebted to *shomin-geki* comedy, Eikichi promptly checks out his new hat from every conceivable angle, using a nearby window for a mirror. Interestingly, Gosho devotes a half-dozen shots to this bit of business, including a reaction shot of an amused Mizuhara. For a moment the two friends have forgotten the sadness of the occasion. But only for a moment, only until Eikichi glances in Kaoru's direction. As always, sympathetic to the lovers, he offers to buy Mizuhara's ticket for him, so that Kaoru and he may have more time together. For the rest of the scene, he stands at a distance, respecting their privacy.[33]

The second, and largest, section of the scene (shots 26 through 127) painstakingly details the lovers' parting. At first, Kaoru still clings to the hope that she and Mizuhara can be together. By contrast, he is deeply torn between his feelings for her, his innate kindness, and the knowledge that her future lies elsewhere. His struggle is to find the courage to give her up forever, while persuading her to marry another man—not an easy thing to do. Understandably, he is no more able to hide his feelings or suppress his tears than she is. In fact, he makes his affection for her quite clear from the start when he asks for her hair comb (*kanzashi*) as a memento. Here, typical of the scene as a whole, Gosho extends the dramatic action for maximum emotional and psychological effect. Thus, Mizuhara asks for the comb in shot thirty-five, but it is not until shot forty-three that she gives it to him. In the eight shots in between, Gosho uses shot/reaction shots to register the lovers' gradations of thought and feeling, and medium two-shots to situate the lovers against the ocean background—an echo of the scene at the river when they were at their happiest. He also uses one very striking long shot. In it, he deliberately slows down the tempo and creates a lingering sense of sadness by fixing his camera on an expanse of empty space and waiting for the lovers to enter—precisely the kind of thing that Antonioni would do twenty-six years later in *L'Avventura.* Then, in a poignant series of shots (forty-three through forty-five), Kaoru gives Mizuhara her comb. Holding it in her hand, she looks at it tenderly, as if it were precious or sacred. And in a sense it is, for in Japanese culture, as Keiko McDonald reminds us, this comb is an object that a woman "would give to a departing husband or lover."³⁴ Kaoru, of course, knows this. Handing Mizuhara the comb, she manages a faint smile, but is quickly overcome with emotion and bursts into tears. Sitting beside him, she struggles to regain her composure. Then she asks if she may write him. He does not answer. She asks again; he rises and takes a few steps away from her. A series of close-ups follow. In the first shot she watches soulfully as he tries to fend off tears; then she turns away, staring into space. Gosho cuts to a shot of water from her point of view, then returns to her. Raising her head slowly, she looks at Mizuhara once more, but still he says nothing. He has given her his answer.

Although Mizuhara cannot bring himself to tell Kaoru that they will never see each other again, he is determined to leave her with something, to give her hope. Now he reveals the information he has been withholding. "You aren't destined for the life of a vagabond," he says. "Happiness is in store for you." For the first time her face lights up. "Happiness?" she asks, "Please tell me." He pauses, searching for the right words. "Your brother thinks ill of the inn owner at Yukawaro," he explains, "but he's wrong. He will ask you to marry his son." A close-up conveys her disappointment. "Is this the happiness you mean?" she asks. Unable to look at her, he nods "yes." Then, suddenly, she swings around violently, falling to the ground.

He helps her up, pleading with her to take to heart what he has said. He even appeals to her selfless nature, explaining that she will help not only herself but also Eikichi. "Encourage your brother to find a purpose in his life," he says. But she is too upset to listen. Clinging to him and weeping uncontrollably, she says, "Now all my hopes are gone." Gosho then cuts to Eikichi, who is visibly moved by the scene he has witnessed. A few shots later the boatman announces that it is time to board. At this point Mizuhara and Kaoru's farewell would seem to be over. Indeed, this is the impression Gosho means to create. In a long shot Mizuhara hurries to the boat; in the following long shot Kaoru makes her way slowly in the opposite direction. The farewell, however, is not over. Racing back to Kaoru for one last moment together, Mizuhara finally dares to speak from his heart: "Kaoru . . . I truly love you," he declares. Needless to say, only close-ups will do to capture this new rush of emotion and to showcase Mizuhara's fervor, Kaoru's tears, and the memento he gives her, his pen. In the closing shot Mizuhara leaves her, this time for good; she glances at the pen in her hand, looks in his direction, then starts to follow after him. But after only a few steps, she stops.

In the third and final section (shots 128 through 164), Gosho evokes every ounce of pathos possible from the lovers' separation, crosscutting between Mizuhara on the boat and Kaoru on the shore. His primary focus, however, is on Kaoru. Her grief is total, and in Gosho's hands, her plight assumes near-tragic proportions. Indeed, he makes us feel that she has been abandoned. Although the section ultimately builds to a fever pitch, it opens on a relatively restrained note. Chiyoko, Yuriko, and Otatsu arrive to see Mizuhara off, but they are too late. Upset, they don't even seem to notice Kaoru, who, in one particular shot, is barely visible in the left background of the frame. Yet if this shot implies that they overlook her, it also implies that she is equally oblivious of them. Clutching Mizuhara's pen to her chest and staring out to sea, she is in her own world. In shots 139 and 140 Gosho's camera, representing Mizuhara's point of view from on deck, pans across the water, dissolving to a close-up of Kaoru on shore, weeping. Admittedly sentimental, these shots are nevertheless affecting, for while they suggest that the lovers' thoughts bridge the distance between them, they also make painfully clear that this distance continues to widen. Realizing that she will never see Mizuhara again, Kaoru runs frantically along the shore to catch one last glimpse of him. A cut to Mizuhara shows him in tears; a cut back to Kaoru shows her tripping and falling, then picking herself up and continuing to run, all the while waving her handkerchief. Even after the boat disappears from sight, she keeps on waving. Gosho momentarily cuts away to a shot of Otatsu and Chiyoko, who have been observing

Kaoru's last glimpse of Mizuhara. *Dancing Girl of Izu* (1933).

the scene and acknowledge that Kaoru "loved the student after all"—a decided understatement, given the circumstances. As the film comes to a close, Gosho focuses exclusively on Kaoru's tumultuous emotional state, intercutting shots of her with shots of waves crashing against the rocks. In the penultimate shot, an extreme close-up, she presses the pen to her cheek and looks directly into the camera, as if to make a direct appeal to the viewer. A dissolve yields to the final shot—a long shot of her sinking slowly to her knees, all emotion spent.

One commentator has noted that this final scene is saved from "cloying excess" by cutaway shots from the lovers to other characters, primarily Eikichi and the boatman.[35] To some extent this is true. Nevertheless, for Gosho, excess and sentimentality go hand-in-hand, and he embraces both without apology. He even departs from Kawabata to embrace these qualities more. Therefore, he not only has his lovers make their feelings explicit; he also gives them a second farewell. And why not? His narrative requires no less, for in a love story, especially one with an unhappy ending, it is virtually *de rigueur* that the lovers find some way to give themselves to each other. Hence Mizuhara's parting memento to Kaoru. Indeed, Gosho makes us feel that this is the only gift that matters, for it is personal, intimate, and speaks directly to what the world of the film values most: purity of emotion. In short, when Mizuhara places the pen in Kaoru's hand, he gives her himself in the same way that she has given herself with the comb. Small wonder that this act takes on a reality more meaningful than anything else in the scene.

And yet another point needs to be made. Given the sentimentality of this final scene, it is easy to overlook the fact that Gosho is also suggesting ambiguities and contradictions. This point seems to have been lost on most of his critics. Specifically, two questions persist: What are we to make of Zenbei's plan for Kaoru, which promises her future happiness? And why does this plan fail to satisfy us? On the surface, the answer would seem obvious: it cannot give her the one thing she truly wants. Instead it offers her an arranged marriage, albeit to a fine, upstanding young man. This answer, however, does not explain away our lingering uneasiness. Stated baldly, Zenbei's plan seems to deny Kaoru any say in her own life. Equally unsettling, it cannot possibly address, let alone alleviate, her overwhelming sense of loss. And here is where the ambiguities and contradictions take hold. Despite its best intentions, Zenbei's plan can offer only the illusion of happiness. Hence Gosho prompts his audience to ask the above questions and others as well. (McDonald, for example, wonders: "Will Kaoru be adopted by Zenbei's family?"[36]) In short, to ask these questions is to recognize that the ending elicits a far from simple or sentimental response.

Be that as it may, from the standpoint of material advantage, Kaoru must be considered lucky. In a period when the Japanese economy could help few people, and rescue even fewer from poverty or misfortune, Kaoru's good fortune would seem to be a fantasy come true, complete with an actual gold mine. She has become rich, while remaining above the corruption and money-madness that took place at the height of the Depression. Viewers could vicariously experience her good fortune, yet still weep for her, for after all, money isn't everything. In this respect Gosho's film serves as a balm of sorts, even as it implicitly enters a protest against existing economic conditions. Put differently, Gosho's audience knew better than to expect economic rescue anytime soon; for this reason alone the film's materialist theme could not help but have resonance for them. No less resonant was the issue of class. Here, too, Gosho's treatment is not as simple or straightforward as it may appear. Specifically, while class differences prove an impediment for Kaoru and Mizuhara, they do not for Kaoru and Ryuichi, thanks to Zenbei's money and largesse. This might tempt us to imagine that perhaps class differences are not all that rigid after all, that they can be swept aside by the democratizing power of money. But is this actually the case? In Kawabata's story, Kaoru and Eikichi come from humble origins (read: lower class); in Gosho's film, they are children of a prospector and members either of the middle or the lower-middle class (hence: *shomin*) who have fallen on hard times. This being the case, Zenbei is not so much raising Kaoru from one class to another as restoring her to her rightful place in society. At the same time he is in no way challenging social strictures on class. To be sure, he is not required to put aside money for Kaoru any more than he is obligated to marry her to his son. That is entirely his choice. Yet, how many Japanese during the Depression could expect to find a benefactor? Which brings us to the heart of the matter. Viewed one way, Gosho and Fushimi's change of Kaoru and Eikichi's class might seem to be a case of backpedaling on the part of the filmmakers. Viewed another way, this change carries a decided sting, implying that nothing short of a miracle—which is exactly what Zenbei is performing—could make inroads on social strictures regarding class. In other words, Kaoru's case is the exception that proves the rule. Yet, once again, Gosho makes manifest that Zenbei's largesse cannot alleviate Kaoru's real plight, which has everything to do with her loss of Mizuhara and very little to do with her lowly status as a traveling player. Perhaps saddest of all, even the man she loves believes that Zenbei offers her the only chance for happiness.

Throughout this chapter, we have noted the important contributions of Gosho's scriptwriter Fushimi Akira and cinematographer Ohara Joji. Here we need to acknowledge the equally important contribution of Tanaka Kinuyo.[37] The success of any adaptation of *Dancing Girl of Izu* depends in large part upon the ability of the leading actress. In fact, it is said in Japan that anyone who wants to be a star must play the dancing girl.[38] Although five others have done the role, Tanaka's performance remains the most acclaimed and famous. Needless to say, the temptation is to play Kaoru as cute, coy, and girlish. Tanaka avoids this trap admirably. She finds shading in the character and by the end of the film her young dancer has become a woman "who suffers hidden agonies that give her an almost tragic stature."[39] Put differently, for all her young years and cheerful disposition, Tanaka's Kaoru is filled with a world-weariness that is never far from the surface. In the banquet scene Kaoru sings this plaintive song: "With powder and rouge on cheeks / I lead a sorrowful life." Indeed, the banquet illustrates as much, for it is about the discomfort, humiliation, and even hostility that she and the other players must endure. Thus, when a drunken guest (Sakamoto Takeshi) becomes boorish and unruly, she can only stand by helplessly, trapped as she is in her double role of woman and performer. It comes as no surprise, then, when she tells Eikichi, "I bore this sort of job as I am with you." Nor does it come as a surprise when the chance for love comes her way and she grabs onto it like a lifeline. For, indeed, it is a lifeline: it holds out the promise not simply of romance but also of the fulfillment of her hopes and dreams. Tanaka manages to convey these various facets of Kaoru's character with such naturalness and emotional clarity that when she and Mizuhara part, the feeling of loss is undeniable. Without this feeling, no adaptation of Kawabata's novella can be deemed a success.

Dancing Girl of Izu may not be a flawless film, but on the whole it constitutes a harmonious collaboration between Gosho and Kawabata. Interested in literature throughout his life and buoyed by the film's critical and commercial success, Gosho would go on to make other literary adaptations. Some of these would be regarded as among his best works, including his adaptation of Shiina Rinzo's novel *Mujakina hitobito,* which became *Entotsu no mieru basho* (*Where Chimneys Are Seen,* 1953), and Higuchi Ichiyo's *Takekurabe* (*Growing Up*), which became the 1955 film of the same name. Other adaptations would be less successful. Indeed, at times Gosho's warm and sympathetic treatment, as well as his penchant for melodrama, clashed with the darker or more detached tone of the literature he was adapting. In *Dancing Girl of Izu,* however, this was not the case. Here his combination of melodrama, warmth, and sympathy served him well. It also served his audience, Shochiku Studio, Kawabata, and—last but not least—the new movement that he helped to launch, the *junbungaku.*

THREE

Woman of the Mist *(1936)*: *Blending the* Shomin-geki, Shitamachi, *and Romantic Melodrama*

D uring the 1930s, beginning with *The Neighbor's Wife and Mine* in 1931 and ending with *Hanakago no uta* (*The Song of the Flower Basket*) in 1937, Gosho developed his *shomin-geki* into a richly supple and expressive mode. He also brought sound to Japanese film, helped to create the *junbungaku* movement, and continued to hone his narrative and visual style. He did this within the span of six short years in films that we examined in previous chapters and in such key works as *L'Amour* (*Ramuru/Aibu/Caress/Love*, 1933), *Ikitoshi ikerumono* (*Everything That Lives*, 1934), and, most importantly, *Oboroyo no onna* (*Woman of the Mist*, 1936). A personal favorite of Gosho's, *L'Amour* is a psychological study of a small-town doctor's relationship with his two grown children, and is noteworthy for its narrative structure and blending of genres. (See the Appendix for a discussion of the film.) An even more remarkable achievement, *Everything That Lives* ranked third in the *Kinema Jumpo* "Best Ten" poll of 1934, and is considered by Anderson and Richie to be one of the finest films Gosho ever made.[1] Unfortunately, the film no longer survives. Based on a celebrated novel by Yamamoto Yuzo, it dealt with a salaryman who embezzles company money and a young female office worker who is blamed for his crime. An examination of social injustice, it dared to criticize "the rigid bureaucracy of Japanese law enforcement."[2] Fortunately, its screenplay was preserved and has been published.[3]

Even so, the full extent of Gosho's achievement in the 1930s may never be known, for only slightly more than a half-dozen of the thirty-six films he made are extant. The only consolation we have—and it is not a small one—is that the surviving films are among his most popular and critically acclaimed of the day. Thus we can feel reasonably confident that they provide an accurate picture of Gosho's themes and style, even if that picture is ultimately incomplete.

Of Gosho's extant films of the 30s, none is more representative of his style, themes, and concerns than *Oboroyo no onna* (*Woman of the Mist*, 1936).[4] Arguably his most mature work of the period, it is, first of all, an outstanding example of the *shitamachi* film, yet another subgenre of the *shomin-geki* that Shochiku specialized in.

The *shitamachi* genre was named for the Shitamachi district, the eastern part of pre–World War II Tokyo, the old downtown neighborhoods consisting of merchants, craftsmen, and other members of the bourgeois class. It was an area that Gosho knew intimately, one that he and other Shochiku directors depicted as a place where "warm people help each other along while wittily bantering among themselves."[5] Of these directors, none more so than Gosho

> excelled at expressing the delicately refined humanity of the families and relatives of the cities and the local societies. They hated grandiosely moralistic themes. They preferred casual humor and pathos. Excluding wildly theatrical conflicts as boorish, they were charmed by the kind of story in which a slight misunderstanding between well-intentioned people gives rise to a conflict which is then skillfully resolved by a wise person.[6]

This description fits *Woman of the Mist* except for one important detail: its central conflict is the result of something far more serious than "a slight misunderstanding." Indeed, as we shall see, the casual and often affectionate observations of daily life that characterize the *shomin-geki* and *shitamachi* films are gradually tempered by the pathos and tragedy of romantic melodrama, thereby resulting in an especially rich and moving drama. In fact, it is Gosho's blending of these three modes that makes *Woman of the Mist* one of his most formally accomplished works of the 30s.

Based on an original story idea by Gosho himself,[7] the film focuses on two families: Bunkichi (Sakamoto Takeshi) and his wife, Okiyo (Yoshikawa Mitsuko), a childless, middle-aged couple who runs a dry-cleaning shop in downtown Tokyo; and Otoku (Iida Choko), Bunkichi's widowed sister, and her only child, Seiichi (Tokudaiji Shin), a law student. Otoku works as a maidservant in order to send her son to school, his success being her greatest goal in life. She becomes distraught, however, when she learns that he is reading novels instead of concentrating on his studies. Thus she asks her brother to speak to him. Sympathetic to mother and son alike, Bunkichi tells his nephew that there is nothing wrong with reading novels so long as he does his studies, too. Seiichi takes this advice to heart, but shortly afterward, he falls in love with Teruko (Iizuka Toshiko), a delicate bar hostess, and she becomes pregnant. Not knowing what to do, Seiichi turns to his uncle for help.

Like Gosho's best *shomin-geki, Woman of the Mist* is essentially a character study. At first the central protagonists seem like stock types in domestic comedy: the henpecked husband, the shrewish wife, and the profligate son, among others. But this is exactly the initial impression Gosho wants to create, for he means to reveal his characters, in all their contradictions and complexities, little by little. Thus, we cannot safely assume that we know them until the very end.

Of the five major characters, the most developed—and the most different from what he first appears to be—is Bunkichi. Initially, he strikes us as something of a bumpkin—a naive, henpecked little man susceptible to flattery. In fact, in the opening scene, we see him pretty much through his wife's eyes as he allows the local synod to talk him into canvassing the neighborhood to raise funds. "Isn't this a bit beyond you?" Okiyo asks at one point, making her feelings unmistakably clear. Yet, while Bunkichi frequently looks her way for approval—an act underscored by Gosho's connecting pan shots between husband and wife—he simply cannot resist being flattered. "I'm the only one who can do it," he boasts. But far from convinced, she asks, "Are you sure?" After the synod has gone, he meekly tries to defend himself by explaining, "I'm being counted on." But Okiyo will have none of this. She reminds him about the last time he volunteered for the group, and how it ended in disaster. Then she scoffs, "Aren't you easy!"

Gosho not only gradually qualifies our first impression of Bunkichi, but in time totally reverses it. This process gets underway in the next scene when Otoku asks him to speak to Seiichi about neglecting his studies. "He's in your hands," she later tells Bunkichi, a directive that acquires even greater meaning in the course of the narrative as Bunkichi becomes surrogate father and good angel to his nephew. As such, we see another side to him: his warmth, sensitivity, common sense, and, above all, wisdom. Consequently, when he first speaks with his nephew, he doesn't reproach him or insist on anything. Rather he acknowledges two equal obligations: the one Seiichi owes his hard-working mother (*giri*) and the one he owes himself, namely the right to seek more out of life than what is offered in his studies (*ninjo*).

Recognizing the need to find a balance between the demands of *giri* and *ninjo,* Bunkichi is the advocate of the middle path, the proverbial golden mean (*chuyo*). This is the path he takes when he intervenes to save Seiichi and Teruko from ruining their lives when she becomes pregnant. He thus devises a bold plan in which he not only claims to be the father of Teruko's child but also insists that Okiyo and he adopt it, an act that puts his marriage at considerable risk. In resolving this delicate problem, he clearly reveals his true nature to be courageous, selfless, and caring. Yet, in order to keep the entire matter and his pivotal role in it a secret, he masks most of his true nature and plays the unapt fellow that the world takes him to be.

Even so, Bunkichi is not all goodness and nobility. On the contrary, away from his wife's vigilant eye, he quickly finds his way to restaurants and tearooms where he is not averse to getting drunk. There is also a bit of the con man in him. Thus, while he genuinely loves his nephew, he is not above using him to get money from his wife and his sister. (On one occasion, he even interrupts Otoku while she's giving a singing lesson—a source of extra income—and bluntly demands, "Give me all the money you've got!" on the pretext that Seiichi's teacher is eating and drinking with them.) Far from damning Bunkichi in our eyes, these flaws—actually, peccadilloes—endear him to us all the more, for they prove that he is thoroughly human. Moreover, they flesh out the portrait of a man that only Seiichi, Teruko, and we the viewers are privileged to see.

Although less individualized than Bunkichi, the other main characters still manage to surprise us, thanks to the subtle shading and depth that Gosho gives them. On the face of it, Seiichi seems a rather conventional young man. Yet he is also an idealist and something of a quester who is trying to fulfill that part of himself that his law studies deny. It is this desire that leads him to literature, and to make the claim, "Only in novels are there really humane things," a claim that his uncle tells him is simply wrong. It is in part this same desire that leads to his romance with Teruko, for after all, what better affirmation of one's humanity is there than love? "A good boy," as he is described in the film, Seiichi is basically decent and honorable. But when Teruko becomes pregnant, he discovers that he is wholly unprepared to deal with the situation. Until now he has gone through life untested. Thus, in an important sense, the film is about Seiichi's rite of passage from youth to manhood—a rite that proves both painful and inescapable.

Throughout the film, however, the qualities that make Seiichi particularly interesting as a character are his shyness, indecision, and lack of social graces. These qualities illustrate not only his youthful innocence but also his vulnerability and confusion. Even at the synod meeting, where—at his uncle's request—he gives the group much-needed legal advice, he becomes ill at ease, self-consciously rubbing the back of his neck and stammering when the members thank and compliment him. He is even more uncomfortable when he first meets Teruko, and finds himself seated alone with her at the restaurant in which she works. In fact, though he is attracted to her, he can barely make conversation. Far from being put off by his behavior, however, she does everything in her power to make him more comfortable. Indeed, she understands him almost immediately.

Ultimately a conventional figure of womanly self-sacrifice, Teruko is like a devoted heroine on the *shimpa* (popular melodrama) stage, giving up her life to benefit the career of the man she loves while feeling, to some degree, unworthy of him. Typical of such heroines, she even takes upon herself any and all blame when she becomes pregnant and sees herself as a burden. "I'm a bad woman," she tells Seiichi. And though it is true that she has seduced him, it is no less true that he loves her and has acted, albeit reluctantly at times, of his own free will.

Interestingly enough, before her sacrifice is required by the drama, Teruko is carefully individualized and even somewhat unconventional. Once a geisha, but now determined to make it on her own, she is independent-minded and worldly wise (though not hardened or cynical in the least). That she is drawn to Seiichi in the first place suggests her own purity of heart and innocence; and the fact that she takes the initiative in their relationship by telling him outright that she likes him and arranging to meet him again indicates the extent to which she is her own person.

Yet, despite her specific qualities as an individual, she remains throughout the film "the woman of the mist," a woman forever destined to be an outsider. Her lack of a real place in the world is underscored by the fact that her very identity is tentative and uncertain. Hence she is known by two different names. To Bunkichi, she is Kotaro, the name she had as a geisha when he first knew her (and when, it is suggested, they may have been lovers). To Seiichi, however, she is Teruko, the name she now goes by in her work as a bar hostess—the name that she has chosen in order to begin a new life. A creature of considerable pathos, Teruko is admirable not only because she possesses delicate and inexpressible feelings but also because she comes to accept transitory happiness as her fate. Nevertheless, as we shall see, there is a certain ambiguity in the sacrifice she makes for Seiichi and the very pathos it generates, just as there is ambiguity in Seiichi's career being saved.

Okiyo and Otoku, the last of the main characters, are in certain respects alike. Okiyo at first seems shrewish, even downright stingy, for besides trying to monitor Bunkichi's behavior (especially his drinking), she holds the family purse strings and is frugal when it comes to giving him spending money. Yet she does give him money, even though she knows that soon he will be broke and ask for more. She also knows that she will not refuse him. In fact, despite appearances, Okiyo and Bunkichi are happily married, their playful banter and acceptance of certain roles—wife/mother; husband/child—evidence of a warm, comfortable relationship. Okiyo's good-hearted and generous nature, however, is perhaps best seen in her relationship with Teruko, who she thinks is the mother of Bunkichi's child. Indeed, it is a tribute to her character that when Teruko dies, she faults herself for not having been even kinder to the young woman! This is the *shitamachi* spirit at its best. True, Okiyo has to be flattered and cajoled by Otoku into forgiving her husband and adopting the baby. But her anger and hurt are perfectly understandable, especially when we stop to consider that she has been unable to give Bunkichi children and that she forgave him for infidelity in the past on the condition that it never happen again.

Like Okiyo, Otoku is basically good-natured and warm-hearted. But in her determination to see Seiichi become a success, she is often stubborn and forever trying to control him. In his words, she's "nosey and noisy." When he understandably "rebels" by reading novels, she overreacts and is even comical in her moaning and complaining. Her best qualities emerge in her dealings with other people. When a student patron at the restaurant where she works asks her to ignore his large, unpaid bill and bring him more food, she gently scolds him, but serves him anyway. When Okiyo threatens to divorce Bunkichi, she does a remarkable job soothing her sister-in-law's feelings; indeed, she proves herself a veritable expert on human nature. Finally, when she befriends Teruko, she tends to her every need. She even chastises Bunkichi for failing to give the young woman a waist-warmer, apparently a necessity for expectant mothers. No matter that she believes Teruko is bearing her brother's child. If she knew the truth, chances are she would have been just as kind, just as pragmatic—eventually.

No less important than characterization in *Woman of the Mist* is the way in which Gosho blends the *shomin-geki* and the romantic melodrama. Like *Burden of Life*, the early scenes of *Woman of the Mist* in particular treat the customs, interactions, and unhurried lives of its characters with a casualness and documentary-like feel—what Noël Burch calls, in discussing another of Gosho's films, an "unaffected approach."[8] Here gentle comedy and irony predominate, and certain actions seem merely to portray details in the ups and downs of family life. The most significant example of this is Otoku's request that Bunkichi talk to her son. Only later do we realize that this detail functions as a vital plot thread in the skillfully woven fabric of the finished film. Indeed, the film seems to be virtually plotless until midway through, when (in the twenty-second of the film's forty-one scenes) Gosho introduces the catalyst to the dramatic action, Teruko's pregnancy. From this point on, *Woman of the Mist*'s narrative becomes far more conventional, and the predominant tone shifts to one of seriousness and pathos. Still, Gosho retains enough of the earlier comedy to temper the increasingly tragic mood, and to underscore the fact that despite the hardships they suffer, his characters manage—as always—to prevail.

Besides being characterized by a blending of different genres and moods, Gosho's narrative is organized as a series of interrelated personal sacrifices, beginning with Otoku's years of hard work to put Seiichi through school and ending with a sacrifice that preserves and protects all those that have gone before it: Seiichi's decision to abide by Teruko's will and not reveal that he is the father of her child. In between these opening and closing sacrifices, there are four others: Bunkichi's naming of himself as Teruko's lover; Teruko and Seiichi's promise to Bunkichi never to see each other again; Okiyo's forgiveness of Bunkichi's "infidelity" and acceptance of Teruko's child; and Teruko's final rejection of Seiichi.

Within this overall structure, Gosho—like all filmmakers—uses various forms of parallelism and repetition to unify his film and develop and intensify the dramatic conflicts. Among the most important of these forms are recurring motifs and compositions, recycling of principal locales and settings, and a form that often incorporates both of these: the double scene. Situated at different points in the narrative, each of these two scenes treats the same characters in the same setting in much the same situation. As the word "much" suggests, the duplication is not exact, but that is precisely what Gosho wants, for ultimately the progression and development of his narrative depends upon the principle of contrast and differentiation, and our recognition of this principle. Gosho's double scenes, then, are in effect mirror images of one another, in which he relies not only on narrative form but also on visual strategies by echoing specific camera angles, movements, and compositions.

Take, for instance, the double scene in which Otoku and Seiichi confront each other in their home. The first of these scenes—scene five—occurs early in the film; the second—scene twenty-four—comes in the middle, and serves as a catalyst for the rest of the dramatic action. Both scenes deal with the nature of Otoku and Seiichi's relationship, and the struggle for power in that relationship. In the first scene, there is never any question that Otoku remains in control. It is Sunday morning. She is in the kitchen, preparing breakfast; he is upstairs in his room, surrounded by books and reading (probably surreptitiously). On this particular morning, Otoku has arranged for Bunkichi to drop by to talk with Seiichi. Expecting him any minute, she thus hurries Seiichi along so that he will be dressed and finished eating. In the process we are given a clear and accurate view of their relationship as a contest of wills in which each is locked into a fixed role. Wanting the best for her son, but troubled by his behavior, she ends up constantly ordering him around in an effort to retain control. Thus, no sooner does she see him than she greets him with a rapid succession of comments: "Not washing?" "That's terrible," "You look filthy," and "Make it quick." In turn he mostly tries to ignore her, but before long he obediently goes off to wash, gargle, and do what he is told.

As might be expected, Gosho visually reinforces Otoku's domination of Seiichi. Thus, in the final shot of the scene, as they are seated for breakfast, Gosho privileges her in the frame by locating her in the center and by giving us a full view of her face. By contrast, Seiichi is seated in the lower left-hand corner, his back turned to us. Gosho also relies on other visual strategies to bring depth and nuance to the relationship. When Otoku first calls Seiichi for breakfast, the camera—representing her point of view—pans to the bottom of the stairs. That it stops there instead of moving any higher suggests her realization that Seiichi's room is his domain, a place where she has no power. As he descends the stairs, however, he knowingly enters his mother's domain. What he sees and how he feels is conveyed by Gosho's subjective camera, which now assumes the young man's point of view. Thus, not only do we observe Otoku toiling and rushing around (perhaps more than is necessary) to get the breakfast just right for her son but also we get a sense of how harassed and smothered he sometimes feels living under her roof.

Nothing is exactly resolved in this scene. In fact, Gosho trusts that his viewers have the sensitivity and intelligence—and experience—to know that the young man loves his mother, appearances notwithstanding, and that no matter how painful the conflict between them may be, it is an inevitable part of life. The son must find his own way and grow up to be independent; the mother must gradually let go.

By the time of the second scene, much has happened. Two scenes earlier, Seiichi has learned from Teruko that she is pregnant, and loving her, he means to do right by her. In the scene that follows, however, his situation becomes even more complicated when a well-meaning co-worker tells Otoku that she has seen Seiichi with a woman, a remark that sends Otoku rushing home immediately in order to confront him. During the course of this confrontation, which occupies the last scene of this double scene, we see Otoku's domination of Seiichi come to an end. We also see Seiichi deliberately throw away the chance to assert himself, for not only is he shackled by feelings of fear and guilt over his involvement with Teruko, but he cannot bring himself to add to his mother's grief by telling her the truth.

At first Otoku seems in control as usual. Repeatedly asking if he is seeing a woman, she does most of the talking, while he says little, looks visibly uncomfortable, and seems more or less trapped at the small table where he is seated. At one point he adjusts his collar; at another, he even picks up a book, as if he intends to read. But, determined to have answers, she quickly pulls it out of his hand and tosses it aside. "Who is she? I'd like to meet her," she says, half-pleading, half-demanding.

Seiichi, however, is far from indifferent to his mother's pleas and demands. This becomes evident when she bursts into tears, upbraiding him with, "And I trusted you! Have I worked so hard for this?" Here Gosho cuts to a close-up of his face. On it we see shame and guilt, feelings that are exacerbated by his knowledge that she also worked hard and sacrificed to help his father become a lawyer—an effort that went for naught. Thus, Seiichi lies, telling her what she wants to hear: that there is no woman in his life. Given his body language here and throughout the scene—the pained expressions, the constant fidgeting with his clothing, the frequent avoidance of eye contact, and, perhaps most telling of all, the fact that he covers his face—it is difficult to believe that Otoku would be taken in for a second. Yet, taken in she is, no doubt because she so desperately needs to be. Grateful and relieved, she weeps, calls him "a good boy," and apologizes for being foolish. Moments later, she is once again immersed in the comforting rituals and routines of daily life.

This scene is particularly enriched by the way that Gosho reworks visual strategies and elements of *mise-en-scène* from the first scene. Hence his use of the stairs setting. About halfway through this second scene, Seiichi finds himself standing face-to-face with Otoku and being forced to repeat his lie. So repugnant is his own behavior to him, and so great his feelings of shame, that he moves away from her at the first opportunity. He cannot look her in the eye. Yet, rather than escape to his room, though no escape is possible, he sits at the bottom of the stairs. From this safe distance, it is somewhat easier to lie.

In the first scene Gosho used a subjective moving camera to communicate Seiichi's point of view as he came down the stairs. In this scene, however, Gosho does not follow Seiichi's movement with even so much as a functional pan. Rather, he gives us a single shot in which Seiichi simply walks into the frame and sits down: as blunt and objective a recording of the action as one can imagine. Quite clearly, then, Gosho does not wish us to empathize with the young man, as we did before. Instead he seems to be asking us to watch, to consider, and to understand the gravity of the situation.

Doubtless the most striking instance of Gosho's repetition of visual strategies is to be found in the closing shot. Like the closing shot of the first scene, it is a two-shot of Seiichi and Otoku. But, as we might suspect, this time it is not Otoku who visually dominates the frame. Praying at the family altar, she is located in the left background, while Seiichi—seated once more at the table—is in the right foreground, and is therefore the larger figure. Even so, his visual dominance is subtly qualified by the empty space at the center of the frame and by his own behavior. Thus, after watching his mother briefly, he turns away and lowers his head, wiping away a tear. She has touched him deeply, and he has spared her. But in doing so, he has betrayed Teruko and his love for her. Caught in a clash of conflicting loyalties, he is not strong enough to solve the dilemma he is in, and he knows it. Consequently, in the very next scene, he pays his uncle a visit. "I'm in a bind," he says, asking for help.

In discussing Gosho's narrative structure and use of double scenes, we have examined many of the most salient characteristics of his style, including some of his visual strategies. Now we need to concentrate on the two principal influences on his style—the haiku and Lubitschian *découpage*—and how they function in the film. Nowhere are these forms more strikingly used than in the montage sequence that traces the development of Seiichi and Teruko's love affair. Exacting forms, they both make use of omission, condensation, and suggestion; but, as we shall see, Gosho calls upon each form for a somewhat different task.

Because of its very brevity, the haiku—most often a poem of seventeen syllables—can render only the outline of its subject, the essence of what the poet sees and feels: in short, the high moments. Left to the reader is the task (and pleasure) of filling in the details, making the connections and associations necessary to complete the poem.[9] Consider, for example, one of Gosho's own haiku, in fact the very last that he wrote:

Hana oboro	Along, the misty, flower-strewn road,
Hotoke izanau	Buddha beckons—
Sanpomichi	Come stroll along.[10]

These lines, which very nearly say outright that the poet expects to die soon, offer a series of concrete, serene images: "misty flower-strewn road," "Buddha beckons," and finally, an invitation that is all the more inviting because of its casual and informal tone, "Come stroll along." Like all haiku, this poem is simple, and elegant in its simplicity. It requires the reader to see and feel in these particular images the sense of calm and peace, the promise of tranquility that emerges only after one passes through the austerity of life itself. As such, it is at one and the same time highly concrete in its images and thoroughly allusive and suggestive in its meaning.

In *Woman of the Mist* the montage sequence functions as visual haiku in two distinct ways. Structurally, it relies on the principles of omission, condensation, and suggestion, providing viewers with "high moments" only and expecting them to fill in the rest. Tonally, it creates a specific mood and atmosphere in its depiction of the physical settings and environment. Situated halfway through the narrative, this sequence is made up of the following seven scenes (scenes sixteen through twenty-two):

16. Seiichi receives a letter, which he tells Otoku is from a friend at a rival school. She remarks that lately this friend has been writing often.

17. In the privacy of his room, Seiichi reads the letter. From Teruko, it asks him to meet her the next day at the same place.

18. One evening as Seiichi and Teruko walk together, they discuss what will happen if his mother and uncle find out that they are seeing each other. Teruko also asks Seiichi to walk her home.

19. Outside her apartment building, she invites him in. Not yet ready to accept her invitation, he hesitates.

20. Seiichi, his face filled with uncertainty, follows Teruko down the hallway to her apartment, only to leave after a few minutes.

21. Sitting alone on a bench overlooking the city, Seiichi is deep in thought, presumably about his relationship with Teruko.

22. Teruko tells Seiichi that she is pregnant; he promises to stand by her and accept his responsibility.

As this outline suggests, Gosho's structure of the couple's evolving relationship is marked by ellipsis. Certain information is withheld; specific actions are omitted. Even the period of time covered is hard to determine. Is it a matter of weeks, a few months, or possibly longer? To be sure, scenes eighteen through twenty seem mostly straightforward. The events they cover are confined to a single evening, their chronology is relatively clear, and their basic point is unambiguous—that is, Seiichi and Teruko have not yet become lovers. Nevertheless, even these scenes are characterized by ellipsis. Between scenes nineteen and twenty, for example, Seiichi obviously changes his mind. No less important is the way in which Gosho manages to keep one step ahead of us when it comes to the exact stage of Seiichi and Teruko's relationship. Thus, in scene seventeen we are surprised to learn from Teruko's letter that the relationship is already underway—having begun, as it were, between scenes, off-camera. And in the next scene we are once again surprised when we discover that Teruko and Seiichi's relationship has already turned serious.

This montage sequence, however, is at its most elliptical in the last two scenes. In scene twenty-one we see Seiichi alone, but have no way of knowing whether this scene immediately follows scene twenty. If it does, then perhaps he is trying to decide whether or not to return to Teruko's apartment, which he has left rather abruptly. At any rate, Gosho deliberately keeps us in the dark until scene twenty-two, the closing scene. Then we see Seiichi reading a book inside Teruko's apartment, and suddenly learn that she is pregnant. In short, the haiku-like gaps and omissions in this sequence

Ill-fated lovers Teruko (Iizuka Toshiko) and Seiichi (Tokudaiji Shin). *Woman of the Mist* (1936).

have the effect of moving forward the relationship from one major stage to another, imparting a strong determinism to the story and making it seem as if events are beyond anyone's control. Thus, Seiichi and Teruko's love seems doomed from the start.

Gosho's treatment of the physical environment to evoke atmosphere and mood and to comment upon the dramatic action also shows the influence of haiku. This is particularly true of scenes eighteen through twenty, in which Seiichi and Teruko meet. It is evening. We see them walk along a crowded, brightly lit street, then turn off onto a quiet side street where they sit at a park bench for a few minutes. Although they are alone and although he gives her a gift—cosmetics, which she accepts with more politeness than enthusiasm—the mood is neither romantic nor carefree. On the contrary, it is one of uncertainty and anxiety, in which he tries to assure her (and perhaps himself, as well) that he can handle the situation if his family finds out about them. As they continue walking, now to Teruko's apartment, the streets are dark and empty, and suddenly it seems very late. A heaviness and gloom hangs over the couple, and in the background the muted sound of a train adds a note of melancholy. This mood intensifies as they reach

Teruko's apartment. "It's a humble building," she says, apologetically. "Sort of," he answers, sensing, and fearing, that she is about to invite him in. Gosho never actually shows Seiichi accept her invitation, but he does show him follow her very tentatively down the long, gray hallway that leads to her apartment—a passageway completely devoid of design or decoration. And that is enough, for the very blandness of this setting, along with the small, cramped quarters of the apartment, serves to underscore the pervasive feeling that what Seiichi and Teruko are doing is, at one level, wrong.

Indeed, from the very beginning, the lovers never seem to experience any real joy or happiness. Seiichi is forever vacillating, claiming in one scene that he does not care what others think of his relationship with Teruko, only to contradict himself in the next scene. Teruko, on the other hand, sees in Seiichi her last chance for happiness; and though she knows that to take advantage of his naiveté, his uncertainty, and his genuine love for her is neither wise nor wholly right, she does so anyway. It is, in a real sense, her last chance to bring beauty into her life.

So far we have spoken of the influence of haiku on this montage sequence in terms of structure and tone. But perhaps there is a third type of influence, as well—what might be termed *metaphoric.* Hence in scene twenty, the moment Seiichi arrives at Teruko's apartment, he sets down a bonsai plant that he has been carrying for her since scene eighteen. This plant plays no further role in the scene; indeed, it is never subsequently seen or mentioned. Why, then, has Gosho bothered introducing it in the first place? One reason may be that its presence in scenes eighteen through twenty helps make it clear that the time covered is a single evening. Yet, the real reason for its presence, I think, lies in the special meaning and resonance that this plant has for Japanese audiences. A tree of enduring interest and beauty, the bonsai is said to teach the meaning of patience and humility to the owner in the five, ten, fifteen, or twenty years that it takes to grow. Similarly, in contemplating a single leaf one can find peace and harmony in the quiet rhythms of nature itself. As one writer has said, "It is not what we do to these plants that is important, but what they do to us. The need for patience, humility, and peace is universal. So too is the power of the bonsai."[11] Quite clearly, we should not attempt to "explain" what was intended to be oblique, evocative, and suggestive. Suffice it to say that in the image of the bonsai Gosho conveys all our hopes and fears, and all our deepest feelings for these young lovers. Such is haiku.

Lubitschian *découpage,* the other major influence on Gosho's style, is best exemplified by the last scene of this montage, particularly in its use of close-ups of props and other details to reveal the psychology and often complex feelings of the characters. Like Lubitsch, Gosho employs a piecemeal editing style that often locates these props and details ("plastic material") in cutaway shots.¹² But unlike the Lubitsch of *The Marriage Circle*— the Lubitsch that influenced him most—Gosho also relies on a mobile camera (most often in the form of a pan) to underscore the relationship between any given character and the prop or detail being isolated.

In this scene, in which Teruko tells Seiichi that she is pregnant, there are four especially significant close shots of plastic material. The first of these shots, an insert of a miniature Buddha, takes place soon after she returns to her apartment, where Seiichi is waiting. Understandably trying to delay giving him the news, she warms her hands and asks if he has waited long. But there is only one thing on his mind. "How was the hospital?" he asks obliquely. She does not answer, but walks over to a chest of drawers, on top of which sits the miniature, glass-encased Buddha. In close-up we see her hand lightly rub it, a gesture that suggests not only her continued reluctance to answer but also her silent plea for strength and support. "Relax," she says quietly, perhaps as much to herself as to Seiichi. Then, after bowing before the Buddha, she declares, "I don't want to be your burden." When he replies that she is not, she says—almost apologetically—"Don't worry. I'll raise your child."¹³

What weighs on Teruko's mind is not just the pregnancy, but her complicated feelings regarding Seiichi. Put simply, she wants to relieve him of any responsibility at the same time as she needs him to take responsibility—and, in fact, desperately wants him to do so. But she will ask or hope for nothing. Rather, she will put herself in the hands of Buddha.

Throughout the scene, Gosho emphasizes the sense of confusion, the gnawing fear, and the undeniable pain that both Seiichi and Teruko experience and often try to keep to themselves. Having revealed Teruko's feelings in the first close-up, in the second Gosho focuses on those of Seiichi. Hence, immediately following Teruko's announcement that she is prepared to rear the child on her own, Gosho gives us an insert shot of Seiichi's school cap, which is casually tossed on the floor and almost completely covers the book it rests on. The meaning is unmistakable: now Seiichi suddenly realizes that what he has formerly treated with indifference—his career in law, for which the cap and the book are metonyms—is probably lost to him forever. Acutely aware of what he is thinking, Teruko insists that she can work a little and that she can even emigrate to China.¹⁴ She then glances at a photograph on the wall, a picture of herself as a geisha.

The third significant example of a Lubitschian close-up, this shot of the photograph parallels that of Seiichi's looking at his cap and book. Here too there is a sudden and undiluted confrontation with stark reality; here too there is the sense of seeing oneself as if for the first time. Thus, Teruko realizes, with painful clarity, what trying to take up the life of a geisha again will mean for her: not just hardship and struggle, but almost certainly prostitution. Perhaps Seiichi understands all of this as well, for he addresses her tenderly as "Teru" for the first time in the film. He also seems more genuinely selfless than he has ever been before. "Let me think about this a bit more," he says. Then he adds, "I'll be a full grown man shortly. I'm ready to be a father." Teruko thanks him for his kindness, but still cannot bring herself to ask for anything.

Even so, at the close of the scene Seiichi takes his most decisive action yet. Placing his hand affectionately on her shoulder, he rubs it gently, thereby not only comforting her but implicitly making a vow to stand by her. He then reinforces this vow with a simple and eloquent action that is captured in the fourth and last insert shot. Thus, he picks up a hinged picture frame containing a photograph of her in geisha dress, and slowly closes it. With this act, he in effect promises that she will never have to return to her past life because her life is now with him. Overwhelmed with gratitude and deeply relieved, Teruko no longer resists Seiichi's offer to assume responsibility, but now rushes to his side and embraces him. Weeping, she says, "I really worry." And once again she apologizes: "I'm a bad woman."

The scene, however, is not quite over. In fact, although the lovers seem united, it ends on a disturbing note, for instead of returning Teruko's embrace, Seiichi stands stiffly, allowing himself to be embraced. It is as if, in spite of his best intentions, he still remains indecisive. And, indeed, such is the case.

Although Gosho is indebted to Lubitsch for his cutting style and use of plastic material, in the last analysis his visual style is very much his own: an artful orchestration of hundreds of static shots and numerous moving-camera shots. In fact, in the scene just discussed, Gosho's combination of close shots and the mobile camera has a richness and range that we have barely touched on. Take, for example, the close shot of Seiichi's discarded cap and book. It is preceded by the following two shots: (1) a pan shot that assumes Seiichi's actual point of view as he quickly looks away from one of Teruko's dolls (clearly a symbol of their child) to Teruko herself; and (2) a close (objective) shot of Seiichi himself. Together these three shots function as a succinctly expressive unit that conveys Seiichi's feeling of panic, of being simultaneously trapped, overwhelmed, and powerless. Indeed, in this example and throughout the film as a whole, Gosho uses a panning camera to connect characters, to show the emotional and psychological ties that bind them—as here where Seiichi recognizes the inexorable ties between Teruko and himself. But in addition, in this present scene the orchestration of cuts, close-ups, and moving-camera shots has the effect of visually bringing Teruko and Seiichi together in the frame only to separate them time and again—an expression of their imperiled, tentative relationship. Hence this provides another reason why we find little comfort in their closing embrace.

Earlier in this essay I said that what ultimately emerges as the dominant mood in the last half of *Woman of the Mist* is pathos: the privileging of passion, sentiment, and emotionalism that is characteristic of melodrama. This pathos mainly results from the increasing emphasis on Teruko's plight. However, interwoven with this pathos and counterbalancing it—if only for a short time—is the comic, casual, and documentary-like flavor of the *shomin-geki*. How does Gosho shape and use these two moods, alone and in conjunction with each other? And to what purpose? In answering these questions, we will arrive at a fuller understanding not only of the film's specific themes and concerns but also of "Goshoism" itself.

Gosho relies on the *shomin-geki* to help dramatize Teruko's plight and make it as poignant as possible. He does this by contrasting it with Bunkichi and Okiyo's marital problem, which serves as the central interest for three scenes. Although the first of these scenes is as tense and dramatic as any in the film—it is here that Bunkichi tells Okiyo about his affair and illegitimate child—the two scenes that follow are characterized by gentle, ironic comedy.

This is especially true of the scene in which Otoku convinces her understandably hurt and angry sister-in-law not to divorce Bunkichi. In this scene—the wittiest and perhaps most psychologically incisive in the film—Otoku assumes the role of mediator to patch up the breach as quickly as possible. By turns she cajoles, soothes, flatters, scolds, and counsels Okiyo, finally getting her to agree that it is in her best interest to take Bunkichi back *and* to adopt the child. (It helps, of course, that to some extent Okiyo wants to be talked into doing both.) At one point, Otoku even produces a handy photograph of Seiichi—as a baby, no less!—to help persuade Okiyo of the joys of motherhood. Thus, when Bunkichi shows up unexpectedly, Otoku has little to do but put the finishing touches on a job well done. Scolding him in private, she ushers him into the room where Okiyo is sitting. He tells Okiyo that he has been worried about her; she asks, "Really?" clearly wanting to hear more; and Otoku—recognizing that the moment is propitious—invites her to join Bunkichi and her for a drink of sake. In short, the couple is "remarried," harmony is restored, and in the next scene —just as Otoku predicted—Okiyo ends up as the talk of the town for being an extraordinarily open-minded and forgiving wife.

As we have said, these scenes serve to moderate and offset the pathos inherent in Teruko's situation. They do this in part because of their good-natured and warm-hearted humor, which is characteristic of the *shomin-geki* and the *shitamachi* modes. But they also do this because of their cunning location in the narrative. Following the scene in which Teruko informs Seiichi about her pregnancy, and preceding the one in which she banishes him from her life, these scenes temporarily draw us away from her, in effect demonstrating that life is not only tragedy and suffering.

And yet, in the long run, these same scenes—far from muting or minimizing Teruko's plight—only serve to deepen it, for the more we see the bonds and community that the other characters share, the more we come to realize what she has been permanently denied. Indeed, there is no small irony in the fact that only by rejecting Seiichi can she become a member of his family and enjoy a sense of community, if only until the baby is born. This irony is never more striking than when Otoku, completely ignorant of the baby's paternity, visits her, and treats her as if she is in fact a beloved daughter-in-law.

Having established this particular irony, for the remainder of the film Gosho reinforces and intensifies the pathetic element and with it the mood of melodrama. Stylistically, he achieves this in a number of ways. Thus, in the scene in which she banishes Seiichi from her life, Gosho expresses her feelings of longing, isolation, and despair through a combination of *mise-en-scène,* editing, shot distance, and performance gestures. Seiichi, in spite of his promise to his uncle never to see Teruko again, appears at her apartment to plead with her to marry him. "I must have lost my mind," he declares, referring to his failure to come forward as the father of her child. But she implores him to accept what must be and sends him away. As he leaves, Gosho keeps his camera close on her: "Seiichan, I am sorry," she says, urging him to "study hard." In the next shot, Gosho subtly dollies back to capture the look of anguish on her face and the tension in her body as she hears Seiichi close the sliding door behind him. A cutaway shot reveals what she sees in her mind's eye: Seiichi walking away dejectedly. A medium shot follows in which she watches him from a window. Gosho holds this shot briefly, then cuts to the closing shot—a long one in which she is swallowed up in the space of the nearly empty room. Finally yielding completely to her feelings, she bends over, prostrate with grief. She has done what she felt had to be done.

Gosho also reinforces and intensifies pathos by concentrating almost entirely on the drama of separation, self-denial, and repression that is central to the mode of melodrama. In particular in two of the film's last scenes—Teruko's deathbed scene and the confrontation between Seiichi and Bunkichi at her wake—Gosho's narrative posits one obstacle after another in order to show the impossible gap that exists between his characters' personal desires and the chances of realizing those desires. Thus, even on her deathbed, when Bunkichi offers to bring Seiichi to her, Teruko refuses. "Tell him to study hard and be a great man," she says, in effect displacing her desires onto Seiichi, and leading Bunkichi to weep. But although Teruko is unquestionably the figure of greatest pathos in the film, she is by no means the only one. There is also Seiichi. Obviously having been advised not to attend the wake, he nonetheless shows up, filled with guilt and remorse about Teruko, and insisting on telling the truth about their relationship. Yet once more he is prevented from doing so by Bunkichi, who urges him to respect the "purity" of Teruko's love and sacrifice—and do what will be of benefit to others. Seiichi reluctantly obeys, but seems a broken young man. In both of these scenes, the pathos deepens not only because Teruko and Seiichi are denied their own desires but also because they too deny those desires, an act that is admirably selfless and undeniably sad.

The final scene of the film once more weds the worlds of the *shomingeki* and melodrama. Decidedly bittersweet, it is set in the student bar/restaurant where Otoku works. But now there are no customers singing and drinking, no litany of orders being shouted out by the waitresses, for the restaurant is closed. In long shot we see Otoku go to one of the tables to clear away the dirty dishes and stack them on a tray. Joined by two co-workers, she refers to Teruko, saying, "We're in mourning." They offer condolences. "It's a pity," one says, ruefully. "The good die young," adds the other. They then leave her to finish her work. In the closing shot, as she heads to the kitchen, Gosho's camera dollies out, a movement that serves to put everything in perspective: life goes on.

Even though there are only a few occasions in the last third of *Woman of the Mist* when we are led to laugh and cry at the same time, Goshoism is pervasive. However, it is a Goshoism that compels us not only to empathize with the sorrows, joys, and deeply human qualities of the characters but also to reflect on the disquieting ambiguity surrounding Seiichi and Teruko's fate.

At first glance, Gosho seems wholeheartedly to approve, even laud, Teruko's and Seiichi's personal sacrifices for the common good. In this respect he seems basically conservative, upholding the traditional values of loyalty and duty to family, emperor, and "the spirit of Old Japan" (*yamato-damashii*) that were being espoused by the military in order to check liberalism and Western ideas. Yet, as we shall see shortly, Gosho was fairly progressive for his day. In 1936, the year in which *Woman of the Mist* was made, the military movement was at its height,[15] and, like other artists, Gosho was forced to find ways to disguise any criticism he might have of the social system or political climate.

In *Woman of the Mist* Gosho outwardly conforms to the times by having Seiichi and Teruko submit to the will of their elders. Yet so sustained and intense is the emotion and sympathy he elicits for these two characters, denying themselves as they do, that the result is a deep and abiding ambiguity, in which their sacrifices come across as something less than ideal and good. How does Gosho achieve this ambiguity? Not surprisingly, by recourse to melodrama, which often disguises its social criticism by treating social crises in highly personal and emotional terms. Such is the case here. Indeed, we soon find ourselves asking a series of perhaps unanswerable questions: Although Seiichi's career and future have been saved, hasn't he in fact lost something even more valuable by not marrying Teruko, by not claiming his child? As for Teruko, hasn't she been punished far in excess of her "sin"? Indeed, what is her sin, apart from her sexual past (as a geisha) and her love for Seiichi, and why does its absolution require an act of "purity"—that is, her death?[16]

These questions, though they may be unanswerable, have one thing in common: they lead us to discover for ourselves one of Gosho's most important themes—the belief that "human individuality [is] the most precious thing in the world."[17] Seen in this light, Seiichi and Teruko become far more than doomed lovers; they represent the desires of those individuals who want something more than society is willing or able to give. Indeed, in their desire to marry for love, they anticipate a democratic (Western) value that even today remains in opposition to the long-standing practice of arranged marriages.

In defending the need for individuality, Gosho does not mean to suggest that traditional values of duty and loyalty are to be rejected. Rather, he means to imply, once more, that the claims of family and individuals, *giri* and *ninjo,* need to be constantly weighed and balanced. Bunkichi, Otoku, and Okiyo do the best they can, and while in the end they fall short, in their basic human decency, they represent society at its best. Like Bunkichi, Gosho advocates *chuyo,* the golden mean; but unlike him, Gosho acknowledges, with a single-mindedness of purpose and dedication, the need of the individual. Indeed, Gosho, ever sympathetic to the downtrodden, understands what it means to be a "woman of the mist," an individual on the periphery of society whose dreams and desires are unlikely to be realized.

In his last film of the decade, *The Song of the Flower Basket* (1937), Gosho would return to the Shitamachi district once again to tell the story of a young woman (Tanaka Kinuyo) and the three men who love her. Set in a small *tonkatsu* (pork cutlet) restaurant in a Ginza alley, this *shomin-geki* comedy bears Gosho's unmistakable signature and is a thoroughly enjoyable work. But it was never intended to be anything more than lighthearted entertainment,[18] and cannot compare with the richness or complexity of *Woman of the Mist.*

In conclusion, in its themes and concerns, its emphasis on character, its visual and narrational strategies, and its mixing of moods, *Woman of the Mist* is quintessential Gosho in the 1930s. In this film, the *shomin-geki,* the drama of the everyday life of common people, serves as the foundation for his work. Yet, as we have also seen, he draws on melodrama, and with it pathos, creating the mood of laughter through tears that is popularly known as "Goshoism." In *Woman of the Mist,* however, his blending of melodrama and the *shomin-geki* goes beyond the usual notion of "Goshoism," prompting us to deeper feeling and thought about the many contradictions—and injustices—that are part of life. Thus, *Woman of the Mist* is more than a character study or a melodrama or a *shomin-geki* drama. It not only sums up Gosho's work in the 30s but also effectively points the way for his work to come.

FOUR

Once More *(1947)*
and Gosho's Romanticism in the Early Occupation Period

A demobilized soldier in his early thirties stands on a street corner outside a Tokyo museum, waiting for someone. At his feet is a suitcase labeled with the name "Nogami Tetsuya." His face is tense, anxious. Suddenly, he sees a woman walking across the street, but she neither stops nor looks his way. Moments later he sees another woman, but she too passes by. Deep in thought, he paces back and forth for awhile. Then, from his breast pocket, he takes out a woman's wristwatch. Holding it tenderly, he thinks to himself, "I came back to the designated place. . . . I wanted to see her once again . . . but in vain." As his thoughts continue, the scene dissolves into another. Once again he waits at the same place. However, he is no longer in uniform, and the day, which before was sunny, is now rainy and dreary. "Did she forget her promise?" he wonders. "She said if she were alive, we'd meet again. Is she alive? Couldn't she survive the war?" Her words then come back to him: "Let's meet again," she says, almost pleadingly. "Remember, every Sunday at 10:00 in the morning."

Thus begins *Ima hitotabino* (*Once More,* 1947), the first film Gosho made after the war, and the first of two films he directed for Toho Studio. Based on the novel by Takami Jun and told in flashback, *Once More* is a sweet, unabashedly sentimental love story with political overtones. It focuses on the relationship between Nogami (Ryuzaki Ichiro), a doctor who devotes himself to caring for the poor, and Tozuki Akiko (Takamine Mieko), a sheltered woman from a wealthy bourgeois family who finds herself drawn to him and his humanitarian ideals. The couple first meet when Nogami goes to a play that is directed by his friend Kambara (Kitazawa Hyo), starring Akiko. Over a ten-year period, beginning in 1936 when Japan was at war in China, the couple continue to meet, only to be separated by various obstacles. These include their arrests because of their political beliefs and antiwar activities, Akiko's enforced marriage to a fiancé whom she no longer loves (Tanaka Haruo), and Nogami's conscription. Indeed, as fate would have it, Nogami receives his draft card the same night that Akiko and he have reunited after years of separation. Since he is ordered to depart the next day, they only have a few hours together. But during that time, they pledge to meet after the war at the same place and at the same time: Sunday morning at 10:00. Once again, circumstances intervene, but in the end they are reunited forever.

Although enormously popular and highly acclaimed in its day—it ranked third in the *Kinema Jumpo* "Best Ten" poll of 1947—*Once More* is all but forgotten today. This is unfortunate, for the film not only has undeniable historical and aesthetic significance but also is one of Gosho's major works. This chapter focuses on how the film exemplifies Gosho's "romanticism," a term that had particular relevance in the early years of the American Occupation. The first section, "Gosho during World War II," provides a brief overview of Gosho's career during the war period. The second section, "Democratization and the Toho Labor Strikes," situates the film in its historical context, paying special attention to the labor strikes of the late 1940s, which greatly affected it. The third section, "Romanticism and Moviemaking as an Art," explains Gosho's concept of romanticism in detail. And the final section, "The Love Story as Allegory," offers a close analysis of the film, in particular how it expresses Gosho's notion of romanticism both thematically and stylistically. This last section also comments on Gosho's collaboration with scriptwriter Uekusa Keinosuke, and on the film's relation to its source and its indebtedness to foreign and Japanese films.

GOSHO DURING WORLD WAR II

By the time Gosho made *Once More* in 1946, he had already directed seventy films and would go on to direct nearly thirty more. He never lost his passion for filmmaking, and never considered himself retired. Even when he was hospitalized in 1981 and anticipating his death, he was planning his next film, *Oku no hosomichi,* which is the title of one of Basho's poetic journals.[1]

As noted in previous chapters, Gosho's basic philosophy in life and art was a deep and unwavering belief in humanistic values. As he once said, "The purpose of a film director's life is to describe the real life around him and create works which express the true feelings of human beings. . . . All films, as all works of art, must touch the emotions of the audience and touch them deeply. . . . Only if we love our fellow human beings can we create. From this love of humanity streams all creativity."[2] Although this statement may sound banal, and although Gosho's films may occasionally slip into sentimentality, they are grounded in keenly focused observation and are as forceful in their moral acuity as they are compassionate in their understanding of the human heart. As Mark Le Fanu has observed, "Gosho knows what we are put here on earth for, and can communicate that knowledge transparently."[3] Gosho also knows, and shows time and again, that human individuality is the most precious thing in life and that when it is threatened the result is tragedy.[4]

Given Gosho's convictions, it is not surprising that he declined to make "national policy" films, which the authorities demanded during the war. In fact, under the Motion Picture Law (1939), which put the film industry under direct government control, not only were finished films subject to censorship, but all scripts prior to shooting were required to be submitted for "preproduction censorship."[5] Most of Gosho's scripts were rejected, and "those that were filmed were hardly to the liking of the Ministry of Information."[6] *Shinsetsu* (*New Snow,* 1942), which starred the popular Takarazuka actress Tsukioka Yumeji, emerged as a melodrama, its propaganda elements few and far between. Then there were his two works in the *junbungaku* movement. The first, *Bokuseki* (*Wooden Head,* 1940), from the novel by Funabashi Seiichi, was intended by the authorities as a *haha mono* ("mother film") with national policy overtones.[7] But in Gosho's hands it became a rich psychological study of an unmarried female doctor, whose life is dedicated to her work in viral medicine, and to her daughter, whom society believes is illegitimate. The doctor, nicknamed "Bokuseki" by her staff because she is stubborn—that is, strong-willed—is such an unusual woman character for the period that Sato Tadao considers the film to be about the emerging independence of women,[8] a theme that cannot have pleased the authorities. Gosho's second work in the movement was *Goju no to* (*The Five-Storied Pagoda,* 1944). Based on the classic novel by Koda Rohan, it tells the story of a brilliantly gifted journeyman carpenter who defies all odds to build a pagoda of unparalleled beauty and magnificence. Although the carpenter's determination and rectitude could be regarded as an example for the Japanese people to emulate, especially during the latter days of the war, Gosho's two principal themes—the glorification of individuality and the human will, and the belief in art as immortal and indestructible—are actually quite antithetical to the spirit of the time.

Gosho's resistance to making propaganda films, of course, came at a price. During the 1930s he had made over thirty-five films, but from 1940–45, when militaristic strictures were at their most severe, he completed only three films. A fourth, *Izu no musumetachi* (*The Girls of Izu,* 1945), he finished after the war. He was even replaced as the director on one film, *Kakute kamikaze wa fuku* (*Thus Blows the Divine Wind,* 1944), when the army found out that he intended to turn it into a love story.[9] To be sure, Gosho was not the only director whose output decreased during the war, a period in which the studios likewise experienced a decline in film production. Nevertheless, he made little or no attempt to conceal his resistance, and that in itself was sufficient to irk officialdom. What protected Gosho from censure or worse was poor health. He contracted tuberculosis in 1937 and nearly died. During the three years that it took for him to recover, he made no films, and for the rest of his life he suffered recurrent bouts of the disease.

DEMOCRATIZATION AND THE TOHO LABOR STRIKES

In October 1946 Gosho began filming *Once More* at Toho Studio. Japan had surrendered in August 1945, and now the American Occupation force was busy implementing its main goal for the country: democratization. As Kyoko Hirano has pointed out, this ironically meant that the film industry was once again subject to censorship.[10] Themes that were considered feudalistic, militaristic, or antisocial were forbidden, while those that dramatized the struggles of antiwar activists during the war or the new status of women (in keeping with Japan's 1947 Constitution) were approved and encouraged. As might be expected, the censors tended to see things from the American, not the Japanese, point of view, to say nothing of the fact that at times their objections could be petty, even absurd. For instance, in the case of *Once More,* they demanded the following changes: that the death of Akiko's artist-husband should be an accident instead of suicide, the latter presumably smacking of the kamikaze spirit; and that the lovers should rendezvous at a building with Western-style architecture, not Russian-style architecture, the latter being "communist-looking."[11] For the most part the Japanese film industry willingly complied with the recommendations of the Civil Information and Education (CIE) section of the Supreme Commander of Allied Powers (SCAP) and made "democratization films." At Toho these films were the staple product during the first few years of the postwar period, and were welcomed by a moviegoing public exhausted by fifteen years of war, beset by harsh economic times, and eager to sample the new democratic freedoms.[12]

Critics and historians alike have described the atmosphere of these days as complex, heady, and confusing. On the one hand, there was grinding poverty, rampant unemployment, and a feeling of numbness after Japan's defeat; on the other hand, there was a palpable sense of excitement and expectation regarding the prospect of freedom. Film historian Fujita Moto-hiko, for example, in describing the latter, writes: "People were able to see clearly and vividly a return to idealism . . . after a political period of suffo-cating fascism and war. . . . It was a rare period when people's single-minded devotion and purity were able to exist without any logical reason."[13]

The situation at Toho, which mirrored the national scene and was no less confusing, impacted the shooting of *Once More*. According to Kakehi Masanori, Gosho's first assistant director on the film, material shortages after the war left raw film in short supply; therefore, the amount of negative film a director could use was severely restricted. Since Gosho favored nu-merous short shots and the amount of raw film he had been allocated was far too little, Kakehi visited other production units and got them to donate a few feet of film.[14] This problem, however, was inconsequential next to the union strike, which closed down all productions.

As part of the democratic process, the Occupation authorities initially encouraged trade unions, but later changed their minds when they saw for-mer Marxist and Communist leaders assume leadership positions.[15] Be-tween March 1946 and August 1948 the labor union at Toho struck three times, gaining important concessions in the first and second strikes, such as salary hikes and a voice in the decision-making process.[16] (However, the union suffered defeat during the third and final strike.) It was during the second strike—which lasted fifty-one days from October through Decem-ber 1946—that shooting on *Once More* was brought to a halt until the fol-lowing year. Both Kakehi and Horie Hideo, one of the film's second assis-tant directors, give vivid accounts of what the shooting was like. According to Kakehi, the atmosphere was tense and emotional because cast and crew were sharply divided over whether to stay with the union or join those who now opposed the strike and left to form "Shin Toho" (New Toho). Under the circumstances, Kakehi came to see his task as trying to keep harmony on the set so that the film could be completed.[17] There was also, of course, no small irony in the fact that life was imitating art, that a film about polit-ical struggle and dissent was being made in precisely that environment. Horie relates yet another complication, one that occurred when production was resumed:

> Gosho pushed himself too hard in order to make up for lost time, and be-came ill. In order to get back on schedule, we were forced to work harder and to stay all night almost every day until the production was close to the end. Gosho's doctor advised him not to work but to have absolute rest; how-ever, he stubbornly continued to work. In fact, he asked us to bring a portable bed from studio storage, and then he directed from his bed. I re-

member vividly Hasebe [Keiji, the other second assistant director] shouting out directions while he translated Gosho's hand gestures. Since Gosho was not able to use his voice, he used hand gestures to give us directions. For example, he moved his right hand to show the position of props and his left hand to indicate the blocking of the actors.[18]

As ill as he was, Gosho refused to confine himself only to directing. He also was determined to fulfill his responsibilities as an active union member. Therefore, he not only attended meetings after work but also collected funds for the strike, even traveling to outlying districts to do some of the collecting.[19] During the third and final strike, he became even more involved in the union. "I couldn't stand seeing people who had faithfully helped me to make films get fired," he explained. "I was no communist, but I couldn't reject my friends' plight."[20] On August 19, 1948, he participated in the much-written-about sit-in that was broken up by the American military armed with tanks, machine guns, and even aircraft. The next day, a photograph of Gosho and other strikers appeared on the front page of the papers, with the caption, "The Red Fighters." Soon after, his contract at Toho was cancelled.

ROMANTICISM AND MOVIEMAKING AS AN ART

While filming *Once More,* Gosho wrote an article for the journal *Eiga Tenbo* (*Film Review*) entitled "Romanshugi no igi enshitsuka no tachibakara" ("The Significance of Romanticism in Movies—From the Director's Point of View"). In it he states that his purpose is to explore his thoughts on "romanticism." He also states that these thoughts are directly relevant to *Once More,* for in this film he means "to depict the value of 'affection' which exalts and uplifts the human mind."[21]

After declaring that he believes romanticism to be the foundation for moviemaking as an art, Gosho says, "I don't intend to write about the past at this moment, but no one can deny that one of the main thoughts of the literary arts in Japan has been romanticism, which has never faded away from the feelings of the Japanese people."[22] Here Gosho is referring to the specific literary movement in Japan that began around 1890, lasted for about fifteen years, and came to be chiefly associated with Kitamura Tokoku (1868–94).

The Japanese Romantics of the 1890s looked both to the Japanese past and to European literature, especially the poetry of Shelley, Wordsworth, Byron, and Keats. As Donald Keene has noted, "Not only was the emotional side of human feelings stressed, but the importance of the individual and of freedom was a prominent theme."[23] There was also "a special reverence for 'platonic' love, transcending desire, [which] was definitely not in the Japanese tradition."[24] In fact, in "Ensei shika to josei" ("The Pessimist-Poet and Womanhood," 1892), Tokoku began his essay by proclaiming the supreme importance of love: "Love is the secret key to life. Only after love came into being did human society exist. If love were taken away, what color or flavor would life possess?"[25] These words stirred Tokoku's readers greatly, for they enabled love "to be recognized as the motivating force behind much of life, and [to be] no longer mocked as a kind of malady that temporarily robs people of their senses."[26]

By now it should be apparent that this concept of romanticism is congruent with Gosho's own philosophy of art, life, and filmmaking. As such, it animates *Once More* and is the origin of and motivating force for Nogami's political activism and his love for Akiko. However, when he tries to explain to one of his friends that his love for her also causes him pain and suffering, the response he gets is not surprising: he is urged to cure himself, as if love were a malady. Nogami's friend, in fact, is guilty of the very thing that Gosho considers inimical to romantic belief: excessive intelligence, that is, an imbalance between reason and feeling. In this regard Gosho cites three novelists—Hori Tatsuo, Dazai Osamu, and Kawabata Yasunari—whose characters' search for peace of mind is exacerbated by this flaw. For Gosho these writers are proof positive not only that romanticism is still alive in the arts but also that all art is based on the expression of feelings. Hence he states unequivocally, "I want to advocate that artistic activity is based on the human being's fervent desire for nostalgia and growth."[27] While what he means by "nostalgia" is somewhat vague, its basic meaning seems clear enough: the attainment of love, the achievement of peace of mind.

Thus far in his essay, Gosho has spoken of romanticism pretty much as an end in itself. But he also sees it as a means to an end, as a way for film to give expression to something even more lofty and significant: "Humanitarianism is the main goal of film, and concerns all human nature and spirituality. Especially in this current social situation, to accomplish our mission we must reconstruct humanity and free ourselves from feudal mentality. Therefore, humanitarianism is an absolutely essential concept for contemporary society.[28]

As examples of films that successfully achieve this goal, Gosho cites Chaplin's *The Gold Rush* (1925), which looks at American society with a satiric but compassionate eye, and John Stahl's *The Keys of the Kingdom* (1944), which he had seen recently and about which he has this to say: "It plainly depicts that the hero [a missionary played by Gregory Peck] overcomes all hardships to attain philanthropy and belief in his own faith. This movie appeals very much to us because of its theme, the rediscovery of humanity."[29] Interestingly, Gosho's comments on Stahl's film might well serve to describe *Once More* and its two main characters.

In the latter half of the essay Gosho focuses on the question, "How should a director realize his concept of romanticism in a film?" His answer is that "the completion of an artistic and literary script is absolutely vital to successful filmmaking. Based on the scenario, a director is responsible for the synthesis of the six elements in filmmaking: scenario, camera techniques, setting, acting, music, and sound effects. Along with the results of this synthesis, a director composes the complete artistic effect and atmosphere, and creates a harmony between audience and film."[30] To illustrate this concept of romanticism, Gosho looks to French films of the 1930s, in particular Julien Duvivier's *Le Paquebot "Tenacity"* (*The Packet-Boat "Tenacity,"* 1933). He praises Duvivier for creating "a lyrical poem" in which the setting is not only "perfect" for the theme but also "glorifies" it, the theme having to do with an innocent, jobless couple who somehow manage to hold on to their belief in the future.[31] Gosho cites "the port harbor in Northern France, the cobblestone pavement in the backstreets, and the shabby hotel," singling out Duvivier's use of the whistle from a ship as "an important element in intensifying the romantic atmosphere of the love story."[32] But what doubtless impresses Gosho most of all in this and other French films (including René Clair's *Sous les toits de Paris* [*Under the Roofs of Paris,* 1929]) is that they are about the lives of ordinary people, yet the power of beauty emerges, thanks to the directors' romanticism.[33] In other words, their theme is that of humanitarianism, that is, the rediscovery of humanity. While, strictly speaking, Gosho is describing the above-mentioned films, in actuality he is also describing the one film that is certainly foremost in his mind at this time, *Once More.* In the next section of this chapter, we will examine how Gosho's romanticism manifests itself both thematically and stylistically. But first we need to comment on Gosho's collaboration with writer Uekusa Keinosuke, and on the film's relation to its source and to Kurosawa.

THE LOVE STORY
AS ALLEGORY

In his essay Gosho was sensitive to the fact that some readers might find talking about romanticism out of place, "especially after the war when towns were burnt to the ground."[34] He plainly knew that a love story, no matter how lyrical, tender, or touching, could not be simply a retreat into escapism or nostalgia. To be sure, it could eulogize the beauty of love, which indeed *Once More* does, but it must also tap into the mood of the time, the feeling of freedom and liberation mentioned earlier, to help the Japanese make the transition from the militaristic past to the postwar era.[35] In this respect, one of the primary reasons Gosho made the film was to correct the misconception held by young people that there had been no opposition to the militarists.[36] Gosho realized that the "black valley"—the term used by many Japanese writers to describe the period from the early 1930s to the end of the war—had to be confronted, understood, and come to terms with before the Japanese could rightly rediscover their humanity.

Knowing the unique importance that Gosho assigned a film's script, we can well understand that it was imperative for him to find a writer who shared his feelings about romanticism. In Uekusa Keinosuke, he found such a writer. Best known for his screenplays for Kurosawa's *Subarashiki nichiyobi* (*One Wonderful Sunday,* 1947) and *Yoidore tenshi* (*Drunken Angel,* 1948), Uekusa, like Gosho, had participated in the Toho strikes and was deeply pained by the union's eventual defeat. Nevertheless, as he explains in his memoir, *Keredo yoake ni: waga seishun no Kurosawa Akira* (*After Dawn: Memories of Kurosawa Akira in My Youth*), Uekusa also felt that the entire strike experience gave those who fought for their rights confidence and spiritual hope: "It was a period in which it seemed as if they could gain back their youth, which had been barren for fifteen years. The heart of youth came back to everyone. It was a new beginning, and it brought them back to human feelings."[37] It is precisely this kind of idealism, this romanticism, that Gosho and Uekusa sought to convey in *Once More* by means of the love story.

With this goal in mind, they made major changes in Takami Jun's novel, on which the film is based. Takami's novel was essentially political in theme and realistic in style, with the relationship between the hero and heroine underscoring the fact that life in totalitarian Japan was so intolerable that even an apolitical woman was prompted to join a leftist movement. Gosho and Uekusa retained this notion, but obviously "romanticized" the relationship. They also changed Nogami from a Marxist law student to a medical student in order to give concrete form to his commitment to socialist ideas and humanitarianism, and no doubt also to lend greater warmth to his character. Finally, they gave the lovers, and the audience, a happy ending. Takami, like many politically committed intellectuals, had been forced to recant his leftist beliefs during the war. Consequently, he wanted to emphasize not only the suffering and sense of frustration that he and others endured but also the continuing legacy of that experience even after the war. The way he sought to do this was to have Nogami return from the war alive, but then to have him forced to leave the woman he loves forever. Needless to say, when Takami saw Gosho's film, he felt, quite correctly, that it was entirely different from his novel.[38]

Takami's novel, however, was not the only important source that Gosho and Uekusa drew on. According to Fujita Motohiko, they were clearly influenced by Kurosawa's *Waga seishun ni kuinashi* (*No Regrets for Our Youth*, 1946), which Toho made the year before *Once More*.[39] First of all, the historical period and the narrative structure are much the same in both films. That is, both films begin in the present, right after the war, then flash back ten years earlier to portray the memories of their protagonists. Second, the atmosphere and the social and political conditions of the time, as well as the harassment that the characters suffer at the hands of the police, are conveyed mainly through the use of newspaper headlines. Third, both films deal not only with idealistic youth but also with a well-off bourgeois heroine who, seeking the meaning of life, falls in love with a man and follows him. Finally, both films tend to be vague about the political ideologies that their characters embrace.[40]

Three points need to be made. While Fujita is correct about the presence of a heroine who undergoes a personal and political transformation, Kurosawa's heroine, Yukie (Hara Setsuko), is clearly the central protagonist in the film, whereas Akiko, Gosho's heroine, is one of two main protagonists, the story arguably belonging more to Nogami than to her, since it is his memory. Also, Akiko is much more traditional than Yukie, whose characterization was fiercely attacked by critics as "extreme and unnatural."[41] Quite possibly, Gosho and Uekusa were aware of this criticism and wished to avoid it.

Fujita is also correct in claiming that *Once More* is vague when it comes to the exact nature of Nogami and Akiko's political beliefs. In fact, the most extended account of these beliefs is Nogami's lecture on socialism. "It's not just an idea," he explains. "We must face reality and tell the truth. Gaze into the face of poverty. Real society is filled with injustice. Just take a look at people around you and at the settlement. They are poor and unhappy." Clearly, these words are so general that they could be appropriated by any number of ideologies. But that is the point, for Gosho and Uekusa are not interested in political ideologies per se but in humanitarianism as the goal and motivating force of all ideologies.

Finally, although both *Once More* and *No Regrets for Our Youth* may be classified as melodramas, they are worlds apart in tone, mood, and style—the former is a sumptuously mounted love story, and the latter tells of a woman's rite of progress.

As mentioned at the outset of this chapter, *Once More* is a love story with political overtones. This is not to imply that the political theme is unimportant or merely tacked on as colorful historical background. Quite the contrary, it is an intricate part of the love story, for Nogami and Akiko's love for one another becomes political in that it compels them to search for the truth and take a stand against the oppressive military state.

Following the opening two scenes, in which Nogami waits for Akiko at the place that they have vowed to meet after the war, *Once More* moves into an extended flashback. The first scene of this flashback establishes Nogami's idealism and the political theme.

The time is 1936. The setting is Tokyo University. In the background the bells of the campus tower ring out, complemented by the sonorous voices of an unseen male choir—evocations of memory and halcyon college days. Nogami, who is soon to graduate, is talking with several classmates who ask why he has turned down the offer of a prestigious position at the university. When he says that he wants to work as a doctor at a settlement (i.e., a clinic) for the poor, one of his classmates scoffs, "Not that same old socialist doctrine." Only his two friends, Tanaka (Kono Akitake) and Kambara, respect his choice and share his political convictions. Later that afternoon, the three sit together on a hill directly beneath the bell tower, the sound of the male choir still filling the air. The setting may be idyllic, but it cannot prevent the three from being troubled by news that war in Manchuria is imminent. Agreeing to oppose the war, they also agree to serve the poor. As their discussion comes to an end, the bells ring out the hour. "Farewell to the campus trees, farewell to the town tower," Kambara remarks, half-playfully, half-ruefully. The time has come to put their ideals into practice. The carefree days of youth are over.

Throughout the film, Tanaka and Kambara serve as foils for Nogami. All three start out with strong convictions and the desire to change Japanese society, but each has a different opinion on how to bring about that change. Nogami, as we have seen, dedicates himself to serving the poor; Tanaka believes in political agitation leading to revolution; and Kambara puts his energies into theatre. Here he can help subsidize Tanaka's campaign to unite workers in Yokohama, stage classical and political works, and form study groups to educate his acting company about social conditions. At one point he even invites Nogami to deliver a lecture on the subject, a lecture that deeply affects Akiko, who is among the listeners. However, when the government begins crushing all political opposition, Tanaka and Kambara see that their beliefs have been compromised and have come to naught. Tanaka, like Nogami, is imprisoned; Kambara is defeated and demoralized. "The world has changed," Kambara tells Nogami, who has just been released from prison. "Tanaka predicted this war, and now we're fighting China. . . . All of our dreams are gone." Only Nogami manages to hold on to those dreams.

Also serving as a foil for Nogami is Sakon, Akiko's fiancé. Born of an aristocratic family, he plays Hamlet in Kambara's production and has aspirations as a painter. However, soon after his marriage to Akiko, he becomes obsessed by the idea that he is losing his talent as a painter and blames her. He knows that she was forced into marrying him, he knows that she tries to be a good wife, but he also knows that it is Nogami whom she loves. In short, he sees his inadequacies reflected in her eyes and he grows to hate her. Unlike Nogami, he has no inner resources on which to draw. Indeed, he is trapped by the imbalance between reason and feeling that Gosho sees as anathema to the artist. Concerned only with himself, Sakon cannot grow either as an artist or a human being. He is a product of his class, which is smug and complacent, and wholly uninterested in the world outside. Thus, when Akiko's birthday party is interrupted by a workers' strike at the factory that her brother owns, her guests' reaction is at first one of confusion, then of irritation. "I hate the poor," one of them blurts out. Their lack of compassion adds to the harshness and brutality of the time. Those among them, like Sakon—who have talent and under different circumstances might have made a contribution to society—are left defenseless and, in the end, believing in nothing.

What stands in greatest contrast to the harshness of the time is Nogami and Akiko's love. Their love in fact is the moral center of *Once More*, and everything that takes place is in relation to it. Indeed, their love not only represents a sublime faith and purity that ultimately transcends time and space, but it also underscores the theme that only through faith or belief in something outside oneself can one escape cynicism and despair in the world, and achieve a true sense of self. This is the lesson Nogami teaches Akiko as he awakens her soul; it is also the lesson she teaches him anew.

Nogami's commitment to love is as intense and complete as is his commitment to serving the poor. Having fallen in love with Akiko at first sight, he confides to Kambara that he is in agony because her wealthy background is an impossible barrier to overcome. When Kambara, somewhat cynically quoting Goethe, says that it is possible for a man to love ten women, Nogami replies, "I believe that true love means loving only one woman purely, spiritually, and totally."

There is no question that Akiko shares this feeling. Indeed, she is drawn to Nogami the first time she sees him, on the evening of the performance of *The Marriage of Ophelia*. Before the show, he accidentally enters her dressing room while she is going over her lines as Ophelia. After the performance, he waits in the auditorium for Kambara, who is on the stage with his cast to pose for a picture and to celebrate. All the while Akiko watches Nogami as he stands awkwardly, stiffly—like a pole, as she will later tell him. He does not know what to do with himself because he feels her eyes on him, and because he cannot help looking back. "Is that your friend?" she asks Kambara. "Won't he come on up?" "He's strange," Kambara answers. Still, she keeps looking his way. She almost certainly sees something that Nogami does that night in the auditorium, something that gives her a sense of his character. At one point a cleaning woman passes by him, dropping one of her rags. Although he has been watching Akiko as intently as she has been watching him, and is clearly smitten with her, he bends over to pick up the rag and hands it to the woman. Clearly not expecting such kindness, she bows gratefully in return. In one sense, of course, it is a purely insignificant act, this picking up of a cleaning woman's rag. But in another sense it is far from insignificant, for it shows his genuine concern for people, even at this intensely emotional moment in his life. Later, when everyone has gone, Nogami stays behind and secretly retrieves one of the white roses from Akiko's bouquet that was tossed aside during the celebration. Taking it back to the settlement as a keepsake, he feasts his eyes on its beauty. "I want to see her," he says.

Akiko, of course, sees none of this business with the rose, but she gets an even closer look at Nogami a few days later when Kambara formally introduces them. Once again, she sees his shyness and reserve and, more important, his selfless and compassionate nature. She steals a few quick glances at his clothes—his shirtsleeves, which are too long for his jacket, and his scuffed and worn shoes—and smiles gently. She knows this man.

She also trusts and respects him, and realizes that he is the one to help her overcome her feelings of guilt and emptiness due to living a privileged, sheltered life—a life that in her case directly exploits the poor. Thus, following the lecture that Nogami delivers to Kambara's acting troupe on socialism and the desperate situation of the poor in Japan, she goes off on her own to read as much as she can. Determined to pursue the idealism of the man she loves, she begins to take an activist position. When Kambara spends the profits from his show, which he promised Nogami for Tanaka's campaign, she takes money from her own pocket, allowing Nogami to think that it comes from Kambara. (To his credit, Kambara tells Nogami where the money really came from.) Shortly thereafter, she shows up at Nogami's settlement to see firsthand the nature of his work and to plead with him to help her understand the issues she is grappling with. "The rich and poor live in the same society," she says. "There are so many contradictions. Show me the way." At first Nogami does not want to love her because of her class, which he sees as callous and arrogant, and he tries to rebuff her. "This is not a place for a rich lady's curiosity," he says, his turmoil given requisite melodramatic expression by a raging rainstorm. But the combination of his love for her and her obvious sincerity leads him to soften. When he sees her off, he warns her about the danger of the political path she is about to take, but she is resolved. "Don't worry," she assures him, having found strength in his love and support, "now I can face anything that comes."

From this point on, the lovers experience increasingly difficult obstacles that test their love to the limit. Akiko becomes more involved in political activities (we hear about these but are not shown them). These include her work in the slums, which leads not only to her arrest but also to her being branded a "Red Lady" by the newspapers and being put under surveillance by the police after her release. When she flees from her estranged family to work in the country as a nurse, she writes Nogami and asks him to meet her, but he is arrested and imprisoned for several years. Alone and defenseless, Akiko is brought back to Tokyo by her family and forced to marry Sakon. However, Nogami remains in her thoughts, just as she remains in his—a fact that Gosho visualizes by superimposing images of her over Nogami's seated figure in prison. Having fallen back into her old life, she feels wholly unworthy of Nogami's love, a feeling that only intensifies when she sees him briefly after his release from prison. "I'm ashamed of myself. I was weak," she confesses. "I took the wrong way." Disappointed but determined to keep their love pure, Nogami urges her to be happy with Sakon, and leaves for a clinic at a dam site in northern Japan.

Their love, however, like all great loves, has a spiritual quality that defies even time and space; they cannot truly be separated. Thus, one night as Nogami stands at the dam, he reads a letter from Akiko, hearing her voice in his mind. Pausing, he shouts her name out longingly across the rushing waters, whereupon the scene cuts to a shot of her, as if she were only a few feet away. Later in the film, Gosho once again reaffirms this idea of mystic communion between the lovers. After Sakon's accidental death at the dam site, Akiko must come to the site to retrieve his belongings. (Half-mad because of his inability to paint, Sakon had visited the dam site to confront Nogami about Akiko.) Following a phone call from Nogami, who reports the news of what has happened, she prepares to leave. However, the sound of Nogami's voice continues over the visuals as he explains that out of respect for Sakon, it is better that they not see each other. As Nogami's voice carries over into the next scene, we see Akiko arrive. The implication is unmistakable: Nogami's words have been in her thoughts ever since he spoke to her. True to his word, he is nowhere to be found. But he has left her a white rose, the symbol of their love.

Although Nogami and Akiko preserve their love as a thing of beauty, doing so ironically denies them happiness. In fact, by this point in the film their very integrity has become a flaw—albeit a noble flaw. Kambara says as much when he brings them together one evening. "Let me give you a piece of advice," he tells them frankly. "Have more courage to be happy. Fight for it. Be hungry for it." These are exactly the words the audience wants to hear, for the couple's integrity has come to mean only continued self-sacrifice. Taking Kambara's words to heart, Nogami and Akiko finally talk openly in a way that they have never had the chance to do before. And the next day, even though Nogami has been drafted and must report for duty, the lovers enjoy their longest and happiest time together. Sharing a picnic lunch in the outer garden of the Meiji Shrine of the Museum of Fine Arts, they reminisce, talk of their future, and hope for the war to end soon. She even gently teases him about how stiffly he stood the first night they met. When it comes time for them to separate, she promises to commit herself once more to their shared political ideals. Finally, they exchange watches as keepsakes and vow to rendezvous at the same place on Sunday at 10:00 A.M., after the war ends.

On that first Sunday, she does not appear, but Nogami returns on each Sunday thereafter in the hope—and belief—that she cannot be lost to him. His faith is not in vain. He learns that during the war she worked as a nurse and that she has not met him because she is ill. Shortly after, they are poignantly reunited.

Takami's original ending notwithstanding, Nogami and Akiko's final, happy reunion is the only possible ending imaginable—at least in Gosho's world. Their reunion, however, is not simply the fulfillment of a vow, or even the triumph of love over all earthly adversities. Rather, it is a triumph over reason and credibility itself; as such, it is as incontrovertible and emotionally right as the reunion of two other lovers in screen history: Chico (Charles Farrell) and Diane (Janet Gaynor) in Frank Borzage's *Seventh Heaven* (1927). This time, however, unlike in Borzage's film, it is not the man who comes back from the dead, as it were, but the woman. Thus, in the final scene when Nogami awakens the sleeping Akiko, it is as if he were bringing her back to life—not just symbolically but literally—for she is barely able to speak, her strength is so depleted. What has earned the lovers this rebirth, this second chance, is their deep and abiding faith in love not just as a thing of flesh and blood but as a platonic ideal.

However, it is not just the lovers who believe—it is also, and preeminently, Gosho himself. To *Once More* he brings a total and unwavering belief in not only love but also melodrama itself—one that is without apology or condescension. It is easy to dismiss Gosho's conviction as naive, even quaint, and the film itself as sentimental, even banal melodrama, but that is to fall into the trap of the cynics and demoralized characters in the film and to miss the enormous skill and delicacy Gosho brings to the material. In the paragraph above I referred to Borzage's *Seventh Heaven*. There is no way of knowing if Gosho was influenced by the film, or even if he saw it. Nor does he mention it in his essay on romanticism. Even so, as Sato Tadao has pointed out, it was one of a half-dozen American films on which Japanese films were modeled until the late 1940s.[42] Certainly there are few films closer in theme and spirit to *Once More* than Borzage's.[43]

Although Gosho is deeply committed to the love story for its own sake, he is no less interested in it as a metaphor for Japan's postwar recovery. Specifically, he fervently believed that the country's recovery could not simply be political or economic in nature; it must also be moral and spiritual, entailing what he calls the "rediscovery of humanity." Thus regarded, *Once More* becomes an allegory, in which the two lovers serve as models for the new social and ethical order that Japan must establish, an order that is based on humanitarianism. Or, as Gosho himself said, in *Once More* he wanted "to depict the value of 'affection' which exalts and uplifts the human mind."

In the remainder of this discussion we will concentrate on the visual form of Gosho's romanticism, which depends on a synthesis of six elements: scenario, camera techniques, setting, acting, music, and sound effects. (For our purposes here, "camera techniques" will also include the editing by Nagazawa Yoshiki.) To examine this synthesis, we will focus on the sequence in which Nogami and Akiko first meet. Consisting of sixty-one shots in six minutes and nine seconds, this sequence is made up of four scenes:

1. Nogami's first sight of Akiko before the performance of *The Marriage of Ophelia* (forty-eight seconds; eleven shots).
2. The performance itself (two minutes, two seconds; twenty-three shots).
3. The cast party immediately afterward (two minutes, twenty-five seconds; twenty shots).
4. Nogami's return to the settlement (fifty-four seconds; seven shots).

The two stylistic elements that one immediately notices in the sequence—and in the film as a whole—are the editing and photography. Gosho's piecemeal editing makes for an often-fast tempo, one that keeps the narrative moving. Thus, while the average shot length in the sequence is

Nogami (Ryuzaki Ichiro) and Akiko (Takamine Mieko) meet for the first time. *Once More* (1947).

6.1 seconds, thirty-four of the sixty-one shots (i.e., 56 percent) are four seconds or less. This editing strategy has the distinct advantage of enabling Gosho to focus in tightly on emotion and achieve an intensity of effect by linking the audience to the two main characters' every gesture, mood, and response.

No less important is Miura Mitsuo's rich black-and-white photography. It not only captures the complete spectrum of shades but also uses both shallow-focus and deep-focus perspectives, along with a wide range of optical devices (including double exposures, rack focus, wipes, and dissolves). Miura was a longtime collaborator of Gosho—he shot his first film—and he gives the visuals a luminous glow befitting romantic love. (He is ably assisted by Onuma Masaki's lighting.) This was exactly the look Gosho wanted, for his aim was to make *Once More* sumptuous in every way so as to improve the quality of Japanese film, which he felt had been compromised by cheap and poorly made love stories since the end of the war.[44]

The first scene establishes the sequence's basic dramatic action—Nogami and Akiko's immediate attraction to each other—and its fundamental editing strategy, the shot/reaction shot. This strategy is used in six of the scene's eleven shots (shots three through nine), beginning with Nogami's stepping into Akiko's dressing room by mistake. In shot four Akiko, in cos-

Nogami is rapt by the vision of Akiko. *Once More* (1947).

tume as Ophelia, is seated at her dressing table, rehearsing her lines in front of the mirror and reflected in it. Shot five shows Nogami, frozen in place at the doorway, stunned by her beauty. Shot six offers a close-up of Akiko, whose sweet pleas for Hamlet's love are interrupted by the sight of Nogami in her mirror. Startled, she turns around. Nogami, however, seems wholly unaware that she has seen him, and in shot seven continues staring at her. In shot eight she rises, and in shot nine—the only two-shot in the scene—takes a few steps to get a better look at him. Clearly intrigued, she self-consciously touches her hair and waits for him to say something, but he stammers, attempting an apology, and rushes off.

Like most of the sequence, this scene privileges Nogami's point of view, allowing us to see Akiko through his eyes. However—albeit to a lesser degree—we also see Nogami through her eyes. Thus, while he gets a good first look at her, in return she gets a more than adequate first look at him, their faces appropriately laved by softly diffused light.

The second scene is in many ways not only the heart of the sequence but the richest example of Gosho's synthesis of formal elements. In this scene we see the opening of the play, Akiko's entrance, and, most important, her exchange of glances with Nogami, who is in the audience.

The scene begins with the camera tilting down from a close-up of the auditorium ceiling to a long shot of the stage as the curtain rises to the

Akiko on stage as Ophelia. *Once More* (1947).

sound of applause. At the same time we hear the first notes of the melody that plays throughout the scene and serves as Nogami and Akiko's love theme in the film. At first we assume that this melody is non-diegetic music, that it is simply part of Hattori Ryoichi's background score for the scene, but the last shot—a close-up of a phonograph record playing in the wings—shows that this is not the case. As it turns out, this is the first example of the playfulness that Gosho typically brings to the sequence as a whole.

After the introductory shot of the stage, the next two shots provide a closer look at Matsuyama Takashi's set. The perfect embodiment of idyllic love and romance, this tranquil garden setting is mounted on a platform two steps high, and it is decorated with arched trellises that are covered with white roses. The overhead and borders consist of netting strewn with leaves that have a silver sheen under the lights, and the cyclorama is painted in a pale hue to give the effect of a soft and gentle evening sky. Hamlet is seen dozing on what appears to be a Victorian love seat.

At this point Akiko enters in full costume, slowly crosses to center stage, and pauses momentarily. Illuminated by a pool of light, she looks directly out, as it were, into the house. Then she resumes walking, but more slowly and deliberately than before. A striking reverse shot in deep-focus shows her from behind as she moves from right to left, and beyond her we see the audience. All eyes are on her. Now the scene moves into a series of shot/reaction shots (shots eight through thirteen). The first of these is a medium shot of Nogami, who is completely rapt by the vision of Akiko and appropriately singled out in the audience by key lighting. The cut from this shot to the next, in which Akiko continues her walk across stage, bathed in soft-focus, is an eyeline match between Nogami and her. Although we cannot be perfectly sure that she is looking at him, and him alone, the effect of the match cut is to create just this impression—and, in the process, to suggest that the real drama at hand is not the public performance of Hamlet and Ophelia on stage but the private communion of Nogami and Akiko. At the end of this shot, Akiko lowers her eyes demurely, momentarily breaking the eyeline match. Shots ten and eleven resume these matches, and as she continues walking, the camera moves into an even closer view of her, revealing a lovely, but somewhat melancholic expression on her face.

It is not insignificant that Ophelia is the role Akiko plays. As Shakespearean scholar Elaine Showalter points out, Ophelia's behavior, appearance, gestures, costumes, and props are "freighted with emblematic significance, and for many generations of Shakespearean critics her part has seemed to be primarily iconographic. Ophelia's symbolic meanings, moreover, are specifically feminine."[45] That is to say, she represents the woman who feels too much and consequently is doomed to suffer disappointment in love—a victim of love-melancholy.[46] In Hazlitt's words, she is "almost too exquisitely touching to be dwelt upon."[47] Akiko's costume, props, and deportment clearly convey this image of Ophelia, which is as familiar as it is inherently pictorial. Thus, she is dressed in a long, flowing white gown with full sleeves, cinched waist, and pale-colored shoulder cape. A pearl necklace and earrings serve as accessories, and white roses adorn her hair and make up the wreath that she carries. For Akiko, however, Ophelia is less a role in a play than a means to define her own character: a woman who also feels too much and will suffer disappointments in love, but whose end will not be tragedy. If she is and is not Ophelia—if, in other words, she is enacting her own dream—she also embodies Nogami's dreams as a nonpareil of sensibility and loveliness. Indeed, this portion of the scene, in which she crosses the stage, even feels like a dream because of the look on her face, the soft-focus photography, and the gliding, floating motion of her walk.

By contrast, shot twelve seems at first a rather conventional, even gratuitous shot, as Gosho cuts to two women in the audience who remark on Akiko's beauty. But what justifies this shot and makes it highly unusual is that Gosho suddenly, unexpectedly pans from the women to Nogami, as if to reinforce the fact that he is the narrative's chief interest. Shot thirteen is a companion shot to shot twelve. In it, Akiko, who is seen in extreme long shot, no sooner completes her walk than Gosho once again quickly pans, this time from her to Nogami. Since it is by now unmistakably clear that Nogami is enamored of Akiko, these two back-to-back, moving-camera shots imply that Gosho is interested in more than simply telling the story. He means to reproduce the sense of exhilaration that Nogami feels—the cinematic equivalent of his rising heartbeat, the first excitement of falling in love. Still, one suspects that there is yet another reason for Gosho's moving-camera strategy: the sheer pleasure he takes in filmmaking itself. Indeed, the unexpected nature of the editing and camera movement in shots twelve and thirteen have a beauty and élan that remind one of what Robert Bresson once said about editing, that it is "a door through which the poetry enters."[48] Such is Gosho's poetry.

This poetry is no less evident in shots fourteen and fifteen, only here it is the use of sound that is noteworthy and playful. In shot fourteen, we are given a frontal, medium close-up shot of Nogami, who looks more mesmerized than ever. Several seconds into the shot we hear a sigh, "Oh," followed by a direct cut to shot fifteen, where the source of the sound is identified as Hamlet. Greeting Ophelia, he rhapsodizes: "Listen, Ophelia, I had a dream just now about our wedding. I was so happy. . . . Are you happy?" In these two shots the sound cut precedes the picture cut by some eight or nine frames. This practice is, of course, quite common today, but in 1947 it was not. What Gosho in effect does by using this sound bridge is to take advantage of the viewer's expectation established by synchronized sound. Simply put, Gosho gives voice to Nogami's feelings about Akiko by putting a "word" in his mouth, a strategy that is also witty since the voice actually belongs to Sakon, Nogami's rival for Akiko, and since Nogami is in no position at the moment to speak for himself.

Apart from the above example, sound in the scene is confined to the love theme, a few patches of dialogue, and a smattering of applause. This does not mean, however, that Gosho's use of sound elsewhere in the film is without interest. For instance, in the two opening scenes we see cars going by, rain striking the pavement, and people with umbrellas scurrying past Nogami, but there is a scrupulous avoidance of natural sounds. We hear only Nogami's thoughts in voiceover and through Hattori's musical score. Here the absence of expected diegetic sound constitutes a negation of external reality and a privileging of Nogami's subjectivity, that is, his and Akiko's world. Even when natural sounds are heard or are dominant—such as the raging water at the dam site—they frequently are pathetic fallacies in the world of romance, an externalization of the protagonists' emotions. In short, Gosho's use of sound is often complex.

Scene three of the sequence, which occurs immediately after the play, is almost totally devoted to Nogami and Akiko's interaction. It opens with yet another of Gosho's deliberately playful shots: a rack-focus shot that gradually comes into focus with its image inverted—which is to say that we are watching a picture being taken, in this instance, the cast picture. When this is done, while the cast celebrates—which we hear rather than see (a piano playing, the buzz of talking, occasional outbursts of laughter)—Gosho foregrounds the series of shot/reaction shots between Nogami and Akiko. Lit in lustrous high key, she is seated on the apron of the stage, looking directly into the house at Nogami, who is standing in the rear. Too shy to join the party, he waits for Kambara, but also feels the attraction of Akiko's unspoken invitation. Clearly, she wants him to come up on the stage. Gosho positions Akiko in close-up and situates the camera slightly below her face, underscoring her unapologetic staring. This is an Ophelia of a different order. By contrast, it is Nogami who is vulnerable and unsure of himself; indeed, he is touchingly boyish. Not only do the medium and long shots that Gosho gives him further this impression, so too does his body language. In shot four, he sways back and forth in place as he stands in the aisle; in shot seven, not knowing what to do with his hands, he twists the rim of his hat; in shot nine he sits on the armrest of the aisle seat, only to decide seconds later that he does not want to sit at all; then he takes out his cigarettes, which, in shot eleven, he decides he does not want; finally, in shot thirteen, he sits down again. During all of this, he tries not to look at Akiko, and at times even turns away, but not for long. As for her, she takes her eyes off him only for a moment or two at most, when she is handed a soft drink or asks Kambara who Nogami is. Of course, while Nogami is too shy to act on the attraction he feels, he is also unwilling to leave or stop looking. Realizing this, she does everything she can—short of taking the final, unthinkable step and actually speaking. It is at once a tender and amusing scene.

A word about the acting. As Nogami, Ryuzaki is appropriately stolid in a role that the Japanese call *tateyaku,* a man of honor, courage, strength, and purity of heart who typically is more comfortable with duty than with romantic love.[49] Hence Nogami's anguish and confusion, awkwardness and discomfort—he stands as stiffly as a pole, to quote Akiko. Ryuzaki conveys all of this splendidly, while also showing us the man Nogami truly is: one of sensitivity and feeling who even allows himself to weep, something no self-respecting *tateyaku* would ever do. Takamine brings to the part of Akiko a most poignant combination of strength and vulnerability. In this she is helped enormously by her remarkably expressive face and the look of sadness, pain, and yearning that almost always seems to be in her eyes. Indeed, Takamine's face becomes the site of the drama, and she expresses emotional shadings even when Akiko is unutterably happy and smiling radiantly.[50]

The fourth and final scene provides an apt coda for the sequence. As the sounds of the cast party fade, suggesting that it is over, the camera locates one white rose on the floor, then dollies to yet another one. As a hand enters the frame to claim this discarded rose, the love theme starts up softly. The shot dissolves to Nogami back at the settlement as he places the rose in a glass beaker and fills with water. He then sits down at his lab table and admires the rose. The next shot, representing his point of view, is quintessential Gosho in its sweetness and sentimentality: a close-up of the rose with a superimposed multiple image of Akiko dressed as Ophelia, looking up and smiling, before fading away very slowly. In strictly narrative terms, this elaborate shot is hardly necessary since both Nogami's thoughts and the association of the rose with Akiko are perfectly clear. But once again, Gosho's interest is not simply in telling a story but in delving into the texture of romance itself, and creating for the audience the secret emotional life—the fantasies, dreams, and desires—that each of has but often refuses to admit.

In concluding our discussion of the synthesis of cinematic elements necessary for Gosho's romanticism, we need to comment briefly on one last element: scenario. We have already talked about Uekusa's adaptation of Takami's novel. Here we wish to take note of the way in which Uekusa accommodates Gosho's visual style. The sequence just analyzed provides an excellent example. It not only depends almost entirely on visuals but also— as must be obvious by now—it makes its basic story point early on. Yet there is no feeling of attenuation or redundancy, in part because Nogami's and Akiko's characterizations deepen throughout the sequence, but also because the filmmaking itself is so fluid and elegant. To be sure, there are scenes in the film that rely as much on dialogue as on visuals. According to some critics, there are even scenes in the first half that are "didactic and stiff,"[51] presumably because the dialogue is burdened with political exposition. However that may be, Uekusa plainly understood that Gosho was the kind of director who "thought" through the formal elements of film and required his scriptwriter to do the same. In this respect Gosho clearly demonstrates his roots in silent film.

After the success of *Once More,* Gosho made a second film for Toho, *Omokage* (*A Visage to Remember,* 1948), about the relationships between an elderly professor, his young wife, and a friend and former student who is attracted to the wife. In it, Gosho retained some of the romantic elements of *Once More,* primarily in the photography and production values. But the theme and material were quite different, and with the film Gosho "made a decisive move in the direction of art cinema."⁵² (See the Appendix for a discussion of the film.)

Gosho would go on to make other love stories, his last being *Utage* (*Rebellion of Japan,* 1967), which deals with a married woman's frustrated love for an officer caught up in a coup d'état against the 1930s government. But never again would he make a film like *Once More.* Born out of a confluence of his personal vision, the tenor of the times, and the long-standing tradition of romanticism in Japanese literature, the film had a purity and innocence that could not be duplicated. On the surface, it was a paean to love—love as spiritual redemption—but underneath, it was an allegory about the need for postwar Japan to rediscover its humanity. In one sense this was the same humanistic theme that Gosho had adhered to from the outset of his career, but the war and the Occupation gave it new urgency and meaning. Like the American and French films that Gosho singles out for praise in his essay, *Once More* is a film whose themes are glorified by the power of beauty that the director brings to his images. But Gosho's romanticism is not merely a matter of style or theme; as we have seen, it is also a philosophy of art and life and a means to an even loftier and more noble end: humanitarianism. As the cornerstone of Gosho's cinema, humanitarianism gave his films a wisdom and sublimity, a warmth and compassion, which not only represented a new level of achievement but also enriched Japanese film as a whole.

FIVE

Where Chimneys Are Seen *(1953):*
A New Kind of Shomin-geki

The Toho strikes of the late 1940s and the labor problems that followed convinced Gosho that the major studios were in decline. Therefore, in October 1950 he founded Studio Eight Productions with cameraman Miura Mitsuo, director Toyoda Shiro, and writers Takami Jun, Kinoshita Junji, and Tanaka Sumie.[1] One of the first independent companies of the postwar era, its goal was to ensure the continuation of personal filmmaking, which Gosho saw as the lifeblood of Japanese cinema. He readily acknowledged that "no director is free of company policy," but he also saw "great danger" in making films that one does not believe in.[2] All told, he produced four films under the Studio Eight banner. The first film, *Wakare-gumo* (*Dispersing Clouds,* 1951), which was shot entirely on location, deals with a spoiled college girl from Tokyo, who falls ill during a walking holiday. A "'minor' film in certain ways, but perfect and harmonious,"[3] it was a critically acclaimed debut for Studio Eight and today is considered one of Gosho's more poetic works. (See the Appendix for a discussion of the film.) Unfortunately, it was only a moderate commercial success. Since Studio Eight never had a strong economic base, Gosho turned to a more commercial, although still personal, project for the company's second film, *Asa no hamon* (*Morning Conflicts,* 1952). Boasting a star-studded cast headed by Takamine Hideko, it is a romance set against the backdrop of the business world and offers "a refreshing portrayal of the life and manners of the period, which is Gosho Heinosuke's forte."[4] In the end Studio Eight lasted only four years; nevertheless, it was a godsend for Gosho, rekindling his creative energy and making possible his two most famous films: *Entotsu no mieru basho* (*Where Chimneys Are Seen*) and *Osaka no yado* (*An Inn at Osaka,* 1954). It also gave him the impetus he needed to produce other outstanding work in the 1950s, including *Takekurabe* (*Growing Up,* 1955) and *Banka* (*Elegy of the North,* 1957).

As longtime Gosho collaborator Hideo Horie has said, 1952 was the turning point in the filmmaker's career.[5] Since the success of *Ima hitotabino*

(*Once More*) in 1947, Gosho had been pigeonholed by critics as a director of sentimental romances, just as in the 1930s, after the success of *The Neighbor's Wife and Mine,* he had been pigeonholed as a director of light comedies. Frustrated at being typecast and always on the lookout for new challenges, Gosho sought a new kind of *shomin-geki,* one that reflected the impact of World War II and the vast changes Japan had undergone since the war. To be sure, he had dealt with this concern in *Once More.* But as one of the leading directors of the *shomin-geki,* he wanted to return to basics and examine the life of common people from a new angle. At the same time he also was "probably conscious of the fact that the genre had been worked out and needed to find a new orientation."[6] He found the opportunity he was looking for in Shiina Rinzo's *Mujakina hitobito* (*The Good People,* a.k.a. *The Innocent People*). As Gosho explained in his 1978 autobiography, *Waga seishun* (*My Youth*):

> When I finished reading Shiina Rinzo's *Mujakina hitobito* (*The Good People*), I felt as though I had discovered the feelings of the masses and the humor of everyday life, which I had somehow lost—no, forgotten—in my postwar work. Simultaneously a strong desire seized me to use this work as a basis for a new comedy. Of course this did not mean I intended to recreate the *shomin* comedies I made during my days at Shochiku Kamata Studio [in the 1930s], but to create a film which depicted the new humor and sorrow based on the lives of the people who were attempting to live earnestly in the present while bearing the burdens of the war.[7]

The result was Gosho's most celebrated film, *Where Chimneys Are Seen.* In this chapter we will examine the film not only as an example of his postwar *shomin-geki* but also as a significant part of the discourse of the day regarding democracy in Japan.

Winner of the International Peace Prize at the 1953 Berlin Film Festival and considered "one of the really important postwar Japanese films,"[8] *Where Chimneys Are Seen* focuses primarily on the interconnected lives of two couples in a lower-middle-class neighborhood in Senju, a poor industrial section of Tokyo. The narrative is structured as a series of juxtaposed scenes that dramatize this connection and show the cause and effect of events on the couples' lives. As part of this structure, there is the central motif of the chimneys and the kinds of "lyrical" interludes for which Gosho is famous. The story is simplicity itself: The Ogatas are a childless, married couple in their 40s, struggling to make ends meet. Ryukichi (Uehara Ken) sells *tabi* (socks worn with thonged clogs), while his wife, Hiroko (Tanaka Kinuyo), a widow whose first husband disappeared during the war,

An abandoned baby disrupts the life of the Ogatas (Uehara Ken and Tanaka Kinuyo). *Where Chimneys Are Seen* (1953).

secretly works at the bicycle races to bring in extra money—a secret she keeps from Ryukichi. The Ogatas have two renters in their twenties living on the second floor: Kenzo (Akutagawa Hiroshi), a shy, kind-hearted tax collector, and Senko (Takamine Hideko), a bargains announcer on the radio, who lodges next door. Kenzo is in love with Senko, but she is unsure of her feelings and treats him with equal parts affection, indifference, and condescension. One day a baby is left unexpectedly with the Ogatas. Its father is Tsukahara Chuji (Tanaka Haruo), Hiroko's husband, who is presumed to be dead. Not knowing Tsukahara's whereabouts and afraid to go to the police for fear of being accused of bigamy (in the postwar confusion Hiroko never thought to register under her second husband's name), the couple has no choice but to keep the baby. Its incessant crying soon puts a terrible strain on them and their upstairs renters. Exhausted and depressed, and convinced that Ryukichi means to leave her, Hiroko tries to commit suicide, but Kenzo saves her life and offers to find Tsukahara. After an initially unsuccessful search, he finds him living in abject poverty and estranged from Katsuko, the baby's mother (Hanai Ranko). By this time the Ogatas have grown accustomed to the baby and come to love it. When it falls gravely ill, they lovingly nurse it back to health, supported by Kenzo and Senko.

Upstairs renters Senko (Takamine Hideko) and Kenzo (Akutagawa Hiroshi).
Where Chimneys Are Seen (1953).

Shortly after, Katsuko comes to reclaim her baby. At first the Ogatas refuse
to give it up, but in the end they realize that it belongs with its mother, who
truly loves it. The Ogatas also come to another realization. They decide to
have a child now, rather than wait until they are more financially secure.
Thus, the baby serves as a regenerative force in their lives.[9] It also has a positive effect on Senko and Kenzo. They come to recognize each other's worth
as a person, and although they continue their verbal sparring—more out of
habit than anything else—it is clear that they will marry.

Sato Tadao calls *Where Chimneys Are Seen* a "comedy of the neighborhood" because of the sense of solidarity that unites the characters.[10] This
solidarity, however, is not at first apparent, especially in the case of two
neighboring families who seem to be little more than noisemaking nui-
sances. In one family, a Buddhist priestess (Miyoshi Eiko) and her husband
(Nakamura Zeko) spend most of the day chanting prayers at full volume;
in the other, a radio salesman (Ogura Shigeru) seems to play every radio in
his shop to keep his seven children occupied. Gosho uses this racket shrewd-
ly. Besides its obvious comic value, it has two significant purposes. First, it
shows that appearances can be misleading, for impervious and self-absorbed as the neighbors are, they also prove in the crunch to be caring and
considerate, and capable of extending themselves. Even more importantly,

this racket serves to demonstrate that in the scheme of things the Ogatas' problems prior to the baby's arrival are relatively small. Ryukichi worries that he doesn't really know his wife, but this doesn't prevent their relationship from having warmth and intimacy. Rather, it points to a contradiction, the kind that is ambrosia to Gosho, who characteristically sees in such contradictions unexpected, irrefutable truths—in this case, that when all is said and done, the Ogatas are nevertheless happy.

Interestingly, the most significant character who finds herself caught up in neighborhood solidarity does not even live in the neighborhood and scarcely knows the Ogatas: Yukiko (Seki Chieko), Senko's friend and co-worker at the radio station. Indeed, she does not even appear in Shiina's novel. A daft creature seemingly without a care in the world, she has no compunctions about using her youth and beauty to live off older men. Yet there is something fundamentally innocent about her. It is as if she regards jewels, furs, and Western clothes as the minimal material benefits that a modern Tokyo woman should expect from a relationship. As it happens, she is a good deal more than she seems. This is illustrated when Katsuko appears at the Ogatas' doorstep to reclaim her baby. It is Yukiko who comforts the distraught mother. In doing so, she upholds the generosity of spirit that characterizes the neighborhood.

As previously said, Gosho sought to create a new *shomin-geki* comedy in *Where Chimneys Are Seen*. Yet, in certain respects, he may have overstated the difference between his work in the genre in the 1930s and 1950s. True, he has left behind the flat-out physical farce of the *nansensu* comedies, but he retains the fundamental lesson he learned: how to blend laughter and tears. He also retains favored story devices, such as the adolescent-acting husband and the beset-upon wife, and themes that preoccupied him throughout his career, including the tension between duty and personal desire, the plight of women, and the valorization of individualism. Then there is the matter of the relationship between the *shomin-geki* of *Chimneys* and the 1930s slice-of-life mode as represented by *Burden of Life*. While both films share an emphasis on character development, the latter film is marked by a looser narrative structure that allows for subplots, a delaying of the main storyline, and a more casual feel—in short, a lower dramatic register. By contrast, *Chimneys* is more explicit thematically and has a more pronounced dramatic register. It also exhibits a greater degree of narrative causality (complete with the central symbol of the chimneys), and adheres much more (but not entirely so) to a single storyline. Put differently, *Chimneys* has subplots, that is, narrative threads involving characters who are either not integral to the main action (such as Ryukichi's boss) or who remain peripheral to that action for most of the narrative (such as

Yukiko). Likewise, there is a certain amount of lack of closure in the main story. What, for instance, will happen with Hiroko's job at the bicycle races? She and Ryukichi never actually get around to resolving this particular sticking point. Finally, although *Where Chimneys Are Seen* might lack the "unaffected approach" of slice-of-life comedy that Burch prizes so highly,[11] few commentators would argue that the film lacks a documentary look or fails to capture the feel of ordinary lives and the flavor of the Japanese ethos.

Properly understood, *Where Chimneys Are Seen* is not so much a break from Gosho's earlier *shomin-geki* as a reimagining, reinflecting, and reshaping of many of the same basic ingredients. However, there is no question that it is more socially cognizant than Gosho's earlier comedy. In this regard Shiina's novel is key. After reading *The Good People*, Gosho enlisted Oguni Hideo, best known as one of the writers of Kurosawa's *Ikiru* (1952) and *Shichinin no samurai* (*Seven Samurai*, 1954), to do the adaptation. Oguni's adaptation, however, did not satisfy Gosho because its light tone diverged markedly from Shiina's original. Gosho, therefore, sought Shiina's advice, arranging for him to stay at an inn in Soshigaya for about ten days so that Shiina could add to Oguni's script what he thought might be missing. Since Shiina had no previous scriptwriting experience, Horie Hideo was given the task of in-house consultant and morale booster.[12] According to Horie, Shiina had to work within certain restrictions. He could not exceed the number of settings already planned and he could not alter Oguni's basic structure. Besides adding details here and there to each scene, he deepened the major characterizations, using an antinomous approach to show the opposites in their nature: in Hiroko's case, her sweetness and her canniness; in Ryukichi's, his somewhat mercenary nature and his generosity; and so on. In fact, Shiina took the job so seriously that he stayed up almost all night for the last three days. Even then, he was not entirely satisfied. "Something is missing to make it more realistic," he said, "but I cannot come up with an idea." When Horie suggested that he leave the problem to Gosho, Shiina agreed, recalling one of Gosho's favorite expressions, "Let's work together and share our problems, since your work is as good as mine."[13]

Much has been written about Gosho and Shiina's collaboration. On the surface, the two men could not have seemed more unlike. Gosho was an intuitive artist who celebrated feeling; Shiina was a conceptual thinker, the first proletarian writer in Japan to appear after World War II, an admirer of Dostoyevsky and an existentialist whose view of the world was influenced by Sartre. But as Mark B. Williams has explained, "Portrayals of Shiina as an author depicting no more than the emptiness and despair of existence . . . fall short of the mark, missing the carefully-crafted dichotomy, the hope

beyond despair, the light beyond the darkness."[14] In questioning the meaning of life and looking for how human beings can achieve freedom, Shiina
came to find that people only begin to live through endurance and making
an effort to affect their own destiny. This is exactly what the Ogatas come
to find. Indeed, though this may be an existentialist position, it is virtually
a truism among the Japanese that the two most important parts of one's
spirit are perseverance (*nintai*) and effort (*doryoku*).[15] Gosho and Shiina
shared a common ground, not only on this point but also on others as well.
Just as Gosho saw that life was filled with contradictions and paradoxes and
that often there was no one who could be blamed, Shiina saw the possibility of something positive coming out of something negative, of optimism
emerging from despair, of relationships of love developing through relationships of hate. In short, both men appreciated the beauty and complexity that make up life. But ultimately what mattered most was that "Shiina
also revealed himself to have an ear and memory for the humour of the
man in the street . . . [and] concern for the fate of the common man."[16]
Without this, collaboration would have been impossible.

Even so, the fundamental difference between the two men should not
be minimized. To understand this difference we have only to compare
Gosho's film and Shiina's novel. In the novel, the abandonment of the baby
is testament to the indifference of society, and the Ogatas' cry for help is
less to the world around them than to an indefinable divinity out there in
the void.[17] Stripped of hope, they cannot believe in anything, not even the
laughter of a baby.[18] Shiina's humor is never anything less than bitter. Not
Gosho's. Bittersweet at times, it is unwaveringly compassionate.

Critics have frequently observed that in the *shomin-geki* the allegoriza-
tion of family and daily life often leads to characters being "signs in a system of behaviour before they are psychological individuals."[19] Although
this is sometimes true of Gosho's films, it rarely prevents him from creating
complex, well-rounded characterizations. Such is the case in *Where Chimneys Are Seen*. Consider, for example, his two male protagonists. Ryukichi is
a decent, hard-working man whose basic fears and insecurities surface when
his role as husband and head of the household suddenly changes. Soft-
hearted but in many respects conventional, he expects Hiroko to be open
with him and to obey him. Consequently, when she takes a job behind his
back, he not only feels betrayed but also threatened, protesting that she
knew his earnings when she married him. Then the baby is dumped in
their laps. Frustrated and angry, he blames Hiroko for everything, and dis-
tances himself from her. In a fit of pique and pigheadedness, he even childishly plugs his ears and buries himself inside his futon—shades of the
blocked writer of *The Neighbor's Wife and Mine*. To be sure, his love for her

and the better part of his nature win out, and he begins to help with the baby. But in one way he remains at a loss. When Hiroko, in a moment of despair, confides her innermost fears and feelings, he can only look on in paralyzed silence. When she tries to kill herself, he is no less paralyzed. "I'm weak," he confesses. Having been brought face-to-face with his own inadequacy, made all the more painful by failing the woman he loves, he learns to open his heart. As a result, he grows even closer to Hiroko. He also finds sublime joy in a newly discovered mundane activity: buying baby food.

Kenzo also has a few things to learn, although his kind nature, purity of heart, and love for Senko are beyond reproach. Young and naive, he finds his job as tax collector distasteful because it is at odds with his idealism and desire to do good. As a reminder to live by his principles, he writes himself memos, which he dutifully tacks up on his wall ("Let justice prevail," "Work hard and don't think about Senko," and so forth). It is an endearingly comic activity that suggests he tackles life like a schoolboy trying to master an assignment. Still, he does his best to put his principles into practice. He saves Hiroko's life and takes on the job of searching for Tsukahara to force him to reclaim his baby. However, when the search initially fails, painful reality sets in: putting principles into action is not easy. Exhausted and discouraged, he tells Ryukichi that he doesn't know why he is searching in the first place. "Aren't you doing it for justice?" Ryukichi asks. It remains for Senko to give Kenzo the encouragement he needs to stay the course. However, even after finding Tsukahara, Kenzo discovers that while he may have been true to his principles and to himself, managing to please Senko in the process—hardly a minor consideration—he doesn't understand human nature quite as well as he thinks. When the Ogatas tell him they have decided to keep the baby, he can't believe his ears. "I thought you didn't want the baby," he gasps, then adds, "I spent 750 yen tracking down Tsukahara!"

Even more nuanced and individualized are the two female protagonists, Hiroko and Senko. This is not surprising, given Gosho's feeling for the plight of women. The past has left these women with a solitary spirit that the men in their lives can never fully understand. When Ryukichi asks Hiroko why she never speaks of her first husband, she says that it is because she has forgotten the past and is happy with him. The directness of her answer disarms him; he responds that he is happy, too. And yet he is right to sense that there is something Hiroko holds back in spite of her sweetness of spirit and enormous capacity for love. As she tells him later, when she is exhausted by the baby and terrified that he will leave her, she feels alone, just as she did during the war when she lost all her relatives and scavenged for food to survive. "I felt lower than a dog," she explains, "I was damned." The legacy of the war has her in its grip and refuses to let go. It haunts her in secret and unexpected ways, even in the noise of her neighbors, which reminds her of the bombing. Her happiness threatened, she fears she can depend on only one person: herself. No doubt the past also has much to do with her need to bring in more money, even if by doing so, she risks Ryukichi's displeasure. Her sweetness of spirit is accompanied by tenacity of will, a determination to survive. But when she sees her world falling apart yet another time, her demons get the upper hand, and she is lost in despair. Moments after she is saved from suicide, she sees the stricken look on Ryukichi's face and is filled with shame. "What have I done?" she cries. What she comes to realize is that the past cannot touch her and that she is not alone. This knowledge pulls her back from the abyss.

Like Hiroko, Senko "holds back." When Kenzo presses her about her feelings for him, she explains that she loves him and doesn't love him. But she is far from being the indecisive type. On the contrary, she is an independent, level-headed woman who refuses to be led by emotions, her own or anyone else's. She has cast a cold, unsentimental eye on life, and knows what it is. She also has seen the male-female relationships around her, and they seem a decidedly mixed bag: one good (the Ogatas' marriage), the others bad. In fact, she is outraged when she sees Yukiko's lover slap her. Still, she feels at ease with Kenzo and can even share simple pleasures with him (the most important kind), such as playing with the bobbing head of a toy cow. In her own way she is just as high-minded and principled as he is. She does not approve of Yukiko's behavior, and she will accept nothing less than a man who is worthy of her. When Kenzo reproaches Ryukichi for failing to look for Tsukahara, she challenges him to put his money where his mouth is. When he wants to end the search, she gives him the strength to continue by declaring for the first and only time that she truly loves him. And when he criticizes Tsukahara and Katsuko as "hopeless," she scolds him for passing judgment. Not surprisingly, it is Senko who takes charge when the Ogatas' baby nearly dies. "Isn't anybody going to do anything?" she asks, as the Ogatas look on helplessly. Like Hiroko, she has one lovely moment in which she lets down her guard and speaks her deepest feelings. Quietly, calmly, and without fanfare, she tells Kenzo about how she took care of her brother's baby after he and his wife died. "I loved taking care of it," she confides, "but it died. It made me sad." She then adds, "You wouldn't understand. This is a woman's feeling." We remember this story when she refuses to let the Ogatas' baby die. We also remember that while she tells it, Kenzo, exhausted from looking for Tsukahara, nods off to sleep. Perhaps, as she said, this is a woman's feeling; perhaps this is what she has learned to hold back.

The opening sequence of *Where Chimneys Are Seen* encapsulates the themes, mood, and style of the film. Under the credits appear clouds of billowing smoke, as a moving camera surveys the chimneys of the title from an aerial view. In a series of seven shots the number of chimneys changes in rapid succession: from three in shot one, to four in shot two, to three, two, then finally one in shot three. In shot six the camera quickly pans downs three chimneys to the plant below. This movement is reversed in shot seven as the camera reveals a single chimney. With this shot, scene one begins, with voiceover narration spoken by Ryukichi. "Do you know about our strange chimneys, why they are so famous?" he asks. As he explains how their number seems to change, depending on where one is in relation to them, their number changes once again in staccato fashion. "From my house," he notes, "they look like three, so people around here think that there are only three." A long panning shot of nearly forty seconds follows. Moving from screen right to left, it establishes the spatial relationship between the four chimneys of the power plant, the nearby Arakawa River, and the Ogatas' neighborhood, passing a bleak, marshy landscape and the hill which overlooks the neighborhood and along which a steady stream of people walk, pull carts, and go about their business. This image, typical of Gosho's "poetic" interludes, will recur throughout the film. The camera continues moving until it comes upon a middle-aged woman, whom Ryukichi identifies as his landlady and calls a "religious old hag." In long shot, we see her sweeping the pathway between the two rows of apartments. Then follow three straight set-ups:

1. (medium shot) the landlady interrupts her sweeping to look down at the ground
2. (close-up) a five-yen coin
3. (extreme close-up) the landlady's face as she spots the coin

In shot four, a long shot, she pockets the coin, and heads toward her apartment. A cock crows. It is early morning. As she leaves the frame, not only does the camera resume tracking, but Gosho cuts across the 180-degree axis line, using a type of sudden reverse-shot that the Japanese call a *donden* shot. We now see the action from the opposite direction, until the camera, which is tracking backward, locates the apartment next door to the landlady's: the Ogatas'. Once inside the apartment, the moving camera pauses long enough to focus on Hiroko (two shots), who is brushing Ryukichi's well-worn shoes, and who, he tells us, is a war widow. The second shot is a *donden* shot. In it, Hiroko faces in the opposite direction (left, instead of right) as the camera makes its way to the adjoining room where it continues tracking. There, we get our first glimpse of Ryukichi: his bare feet are sticking out of his futon, followed by a close-up of his face. Needless to say, the fact that Ryukichi is asleep—and snoring—doesn't prevent him from assuming the role of narrator. The camera pauses long enough to scrutinize his face, which enables Gosho once again to use a *donden* shot to shift direction and proceed up the stairs to the second floor. Suddenly, however, Ryukichi remembers that the upstairs renters are still asleep and must not be disturbed. Thus, the moving camera stops midway up the stairs, dollies back down to the first floor, and settles on a steaming kettle. Ryukichi's voiceover comes to an end. Akutagawa Yasushi's jocular score is replaced by the drums and sutras of the landlady and her husband and Western-style music blaring from the radio shop. The story proper has begun.

In the next four scenes—the heart of the sequence—as the noisemaking continues unabated, Gosho not only gives us a palpable sense of the neighborhood's irrepressible vitality but also gets to the most important matter at hand: the juxtaposition of the two central relationships, the Ogatas and their upstairs renters. In the Ogata household Hiroko is serving breakfast. Rattled by the noise, she accidentally drops a dish. "I'm afraid of noise," she apologizes. "It reminds me of the war." Ryukichi, barely taking notice, says, "Don't be silly," as if to reassure her and scold her at the same time. Outside, in a small courtyard, Kenzo and Senko are washing and getting ready for work. "What a racket!" he complains, trying to make conversation. Deflecting his attempt, she sarcastically replies: "At least you don't need an alarm clock." The dynamics of the two relationships having been established, the opening sequence comes to a close.

A model of economy, without a wasted frame or inelegant moment, this sequence of four minutes and fifty seconds has three other notable functions. Thematically, it introduces the central motif of the chimneys and the notion that life involves an ever-changing perspective. Tonally, it introduces the film's two predominant moods: the light, playful feel of comedy, as heard in Akutagawa's music and Ryukichi's narration, and the sober and at times more lyrical feel of drama, as seen in Miura's textured black-and-photography and the physical setting, in particular the steep, expansive hill overlooking the neighborhood. Third, it introduces the hallmarks of Gosho's style: a multiplicity of short shots, striking use of close-ups and extreme close-ups, a mobile camera that sweeps the viewer up in the action, and *donden* shots that keep the narrative flowing seamlessly and visually express the theme of ever-changing perspective from optimal vantage points.[20]

It was Oguni Hideo who, while scouting locations with Miura, hit upon the idea of incorporating the chimneys into the film. They are nowhere to be found in Shiina.[21] Oguni saw these famous landmarks less as symbols of industrial Japan than as the perfect metaphor for the struggles of the characters and their attitude toward life. Hence in the opening sequence he has

The four "phantom chimneys": a perfect metaphor for the characters' attitude toward life. *Where Chimneys Are Seen* (1953).

Ryukichi affectionately call them *obake entotsu*—"phantom or ghostly chimneys." This affection is shared by the other main characters, in particular Kenzo and Hiroko, who frequently pause to marvel at the illusion of their ever-changing number. At one point this illusion prompts Ryukichi to remark that life is very much like these chimneys: "Life is whatever you think it is. It can be sweet or bitter, whichever you are." Not surprisingly, some critics have found this theme prosaic, "hardly a profound insight,"[22] an opinion that fails to take into consideration the implications of the theme, and more importantly what Gosho does with it. As Sato Tadao has noted, the innocence and sense of optimism with which the characters approach the chimneys, and life itself, are exactly the qualities that people needed to effect the new democratic spirit of the postwar era.[23] This will be discussed further later in this chapter.

The unique importance of the chimneys notwithstanding, an appreciation of *Where Chimneys Are Seen* cannot be complete without taking into account the film's many discrete touches, richness of observation, depth of feeling, and incidental pleasures. Consider, for example, Ryukichi's description of his landlady as a "religious old hag." In this segment of four shots, doubtless the most dramatic and interesting shot is the extreme close-up of her spotting a five-yen coin. Wide-eyed in amazement at her good fortune, she is a veritable comic caricature. This is the way Ryukichi sees her, and, caught up in his narration and sharing his point of view, this is the way we see her, too. Yet, even when she is wreaking havoc with her Buddhist sutras, we must wonder why Ryukichi calls her "a hag." (There's no question that she is "religious.") Is it because she is greedy and charges too much rent? (Ryukichi makes a point of saying that he pays 300 yen a month, implying that it is a stiff fee for his humble abode.) Or is it because she has been critical of the Ogatas in the past? This is hinted at in her remark that the abandoned baby is God's way of punishing the Ogatas for being unbelievers. Yet, when the baby takes ill, she immediately goes into action. Offering her noisemaking talents to the Ogatas, she rounds up her group to pray for the baby's recovery—an irresistible reversal that practically guarantees laughter through tears. Moreover, when Katsuko comes for her baby, she watches the tense situation with concern. When the situation is happily resolved, Gosho gives her a close-up that mirrors her extreme close-up of the opening sequence. (Indeed, he devotes the same number of shots to her in both scenes: four.) Only this time there isn't a trace of caricature; instead, she is smiling the broadest possible smile. Has Ryukichi misjudged her, or has her heart softened? Gosho leaves the matter for us to decide. In doing so, he offers us one of the things that represents the *shomin-geki* at its best: the kind of incidental pleasure that only seems incidental, a story within the story that allows the film to breathe, to take in the flavor of life for its own sake, while still playing out larger themes and concerns—in this case, the sweet contradictions inherent in human relationships. One last remark: Is it too much of a stretch to suggest that the look on the landlady's face when she spots the five-yen coin may be something other than greed? After all, a five-yen coin is often given as a gift for good luck. And since "five yen is pronounced '*go-en*,' and '*goen*' means, in this case, 'to have a good relationship with money,' hence 'prosperity,'"[24] might this coin, then, not be a sign of things to come for the neighborhood?

However that may be, before the baby's arrival, life in the neighborhood is essentially good. Apropos of this situation, the mood of the film is by and large comic and lighthearted. The characters are engaged in their routines, have their differences, and enjoy simple pleasures, although the Ogatas are constantly being interrupted when it comes to the one pleasure they would like most to enjoy: making love. After the baby's arrival, however, the mood turns more serious. Comedy at first is blended with pathos and gentle satire; at one point, it is even temporarily abandoned.

At bottom, the situation of two adults at the mercy of an uncooperative child is comic.[25] Gosho's use of piecemeal editing makes the most of this comedy by foregrounding the Ogatas' every microgesture of dismay, exacerbation, and disgust. In the scene in which the Ogatas discover the baby, a series of rapid cuts make their feelings unmistakably clear: a close-up of Ryukichi's bewildered face as he glares at the baby; an extreme close-up of Hiroko as she turns away from it in disgust; and finally an extreme close-up of the baby itself as it cries with impunity. Helpless before the infant's non-negotiable demands, the Ogatas fail utterly to rise to the occasion. And since they hope one day to be parents, Gosho cannot resist poking fun at them.

At the same time Gosho clearly sympathizes with the Ogatas. Indeed, his relentless use of extreme close-ups of the baby arouses a decidedly ambivalent response, even when the baby smiles the biggest, cutest, most winning smile imaginable. Thus, while we want the Ogatas to accept this helpless creature immediately, once it starts to cry and continues crying nonstop, scene after scene without respite, the extreme close-ups become oppressive—as does the less-than-mellifluous sound. We want some distance, if only in the form of an occasional medium shot or some blessed silence. Having been put roughly in the same position as the Ogatas, we realize that their dilemma would test the mettle of anyone, and therefore tend to have more sympathy for them. In short, we may still laugh at their sometimes foolish, even absurd behavior, but we appreciate the situation, which is to say we feel for the Ogatas *and* the baby.[26]

Sound, as noted, is no less important in positioning the audience. In one scene, for example, Ryukichi literally tries to sneak into his house without rousing the baby, who at the moment is miraculously quiet. But no sooner does he step inside the door than the baby, possessing a sixth sense, goes off like a burglar alarm. Understanding Ryukichi's frustration completely, we laugh but at the same are moved, for his every effort to get some peace and quiet is thwarted. An even more effective use of sound occurs when Kenzo returns home one night only to discover the neighborhood in total silence. Conspicuously absent are Buddhist chants, blaring radios, and, most puzzling, the usual howling of the Ogatas' baby. Taken aback, Kenzo stops in his tracks. A master of sound, Gosho recognizes the power of silence. He knows that while the characters, like the viewers, *think* they want an end to the baby's caterwauling, this is not what they want at all if that silence means the baby is seriously ill. Hence we may be amused by Kenzo's reaction to the silence and laugh, but our laughter quickly gives way to concern. The only thing that matters is the baby. And when its fever breaks after a long and agonizing vigil, and it once again begins squalling, like the Ogatas, Kenzo, and Senko, we are immensely grateful and relieved. Perhaps no moment better epitomizes what is meant by "laughter through tears."

Needless to say, there is no possibility for laughter through tears in the darkest sequence of *Where Chimneys Are Seen:* Hiroko's attempted suicide. Stark, near-tragic in its emotional intensity, and ultimately filled with pathos, this sequence has a raw reality and fierce poetry that recalls Italian neorealism in its feel for people and environment. As it opens, Hiroko is trapped in the cramped confines of her apartment, made all the more cramped by her mounting feeling of panic. Bent over the brazier, she warms the baby's milk, but pays no attention to what she is doing. All she can think to do is describe her terrible fears. When she finishes, she vaguely realizes that the milk is burnt and sets it aside. "I'm done with my part," she says to Ryukichi. Moments later she rushes from the house. As if in a trance, she makes her way in the chill autumnal air across the bleak, desolate landscape and into the inky waters of the Arakawa River, pushing through the reeds, determined to drown herself. Helped immeasurably by Miura's harshly textured black-and-white photography, this setting powerfully conveys Hiroko's desperation and sense of isolation and hopelessness. Even after she is rescued, there is nothing pretty or pictorial in Miura's photography; the feel of dampness and chill is palpable. All four characters—Hiroko, Ryukichi, Kenzo, and Senko—are emotionally drained and depleted, and shaken by what has transpired. But tragedy has been averted.

As desperate as Hiroko's situation is, her former husband's lot is even worse. Indeed, in this respect, *Where Chimneys Are Seen* is reminiscent of Vittorio De Sica's *Ladri di biciclette* (*The Bicycle Thief,* 1948). In De Sica's film, we cannot help but feel for Antonio when the bicycle that he depends on for his livelihood is stolen. But when we meet the thief, we see that his circumstances are, if anything, even more dire than those of Antonio. We experience a similar feeling when we meet Tsukahara. Until then, our only concern has been for the Ogatas, whom he has victimized.

Reduced to poverty and living in a makeshift hovel, Tsukahara has become a bottom feeder of society. In large part he has brought misfortune upon himself by gambling away his money, but he also is one of the many who has fallen through the cracks of a society still struggling with the legacy of the war. "I'm really a hopeless failure," he tells Kenzo. It is a pathetic admission that by comparison makes Ryukichi, who calls himself "weak," seem like a tower of strength. As always, Gosho has compassion for all his characters. Tsukahara is no exception. Nevertheless, Gosho does not whitewash the fact that in abandoning his child, Tsukahara has destroyed not only himself but also whatever love Katsuko once had for him.[27]

Indeed, Gosho provides a harrowing portrait of a relationship in which nothing is left but hatred, recrimination, and abuse. By comparison, the Ogatas' marriage is a vision of heavenly bliss, and the problems of Kenzo and Senko mere kid stuff. As a reluctant witness to Tsukahara and Kat-suko's relationship, Kenzo sees firsthand the mass of pain, suffering, hu-miliation, and anger that causes Katsuko to subject Tsukahara to a barrage of insults and strike him repeatedly while he, cowering under her blows, makes no attempt to defend himself. It is as if he believes he deserves this punishment, and much worse. Occasionally, Katsuko glances at Kenzo, aware of his potentially harsh judgment of her. Yet his presence only incites her more. "Take him to the police," she says, adding contemptuously, "He doesn't even care when a woman hits him." She then tells Kenzo that she left Tsukahara only to teach him a lesson. She never imagined he would abandon their baby. Unable to bear the shame, she races off in anger. But unlike Tsukahara, who eventually takes his life, she refuses to succumb to despair. She is a survivor.

Katsuko is even "embraced" by the Ogatas' small, select community when she comes for her child. Granted, at first she is stopped at the en-trance of the Ogatas' apartment and met by a wall of opposition, consist-ing of the couple, Kenzo, Senko, and Yukiko, who is visiting. Hiroko even kneels beside the baby, keeping an eye on Katsuko in case she tries to take back her child by force. A shouting match ensues. Finally, Senko asks Kat-suko how she will be able to support her child, working as she does in a bar. Blocked at every turn and fearing that it may be impossible to take care of her child, she breaks down in tears. "I give up," she exclaims, and rushes from the house. Yukiko, who has been watching the entire proceeding without saying a word, hurries after her, literally colliding with the landlady who happens to step in her way.[28]

What follows is quintessential Gosho. Catching up to Katsuko, Yukiko asks what seems to be a non sequitur: "Do you think I am happy?" Under-standably perplexed, Katsuko replies, "Yes." The contrast between the two women could not be greater or more amusing: Katsuko, clad in a kimono and hobbling along on one geta; Yukiko, attired in a Western-style dress and sporting high heels. Just as Yukiko is about to explain what she means (presumably that Katsuko is not the only one who is unhappy), she notices that Katsuko has only one good geta. The other geta she holds in her hand, its strap broken when she fled from the house. When Katsuko removes her good geta to walk more easily, Yukiko offers her one of her own shoes. At first not knowing whether to laugh or cry, Katsuko accepts it. Of course, she looks patently absurd, dressed in a kimono, sporting a single heel, and hobbling down the road. Yukiko looks no less absurd, hobbling along in her single high heel. Realizing as much, Katsuko returns Yukiko's shoe. "I understand," she says, acknowledging Yukiko's effort to console her. Kat-suko is also capable of generosity. What is more, thanks to Yukiko, she has

Shoeless solidarity: Yukiko (Seki Chieko) consoles the distraught Katsuko (Hanai Ranko). Note the three chimneys in the background. *Where Chimneys Are Seen* (1953).

forgotten her hurt and anger. The scene ends with the two women walking side by side, in shoeless solidarity, as Senko rushes after them with good news: the Ogatas have agreed to hand over the baby. In its mixture of pathos and humor, this scene constitutes a most gratifying and emotionally satisfying demonstration of the compassion and generosity of spirit that Gosho considers typical of ordinary people. Not insignificantly, it also shows that Yukiko shares these values, despite having temporarily abandoned them for material gain.

Like Yukiko's materialism, the plight of Tsukahara and Katsuko and the economic struggle of the Ogatas can be seen as a reflection of 1953 Japan, a country at the crossroads. The Occupation had recently ended, and the process of democratization had brought about a new sense of optimism, but along with this optimism was a mood of uncertainty. In *Where Chimneys Are Seen,* this mood is displaced onto the theme of abandonment, specifically the abandonment of children—a common postwar occurrence. However, it also finds expression in scattered references throughout the film. For example, we learn that the bicycle races is a favorite spot for getting rid of children; we also see a man unable to pay his taxes sarcastically offer Kenzo his child. Abandonment is an ever-present reality that takes different forms: for example, Hiroko's deep-seated fears, Katsuko's repudiation of Tsukahara, and Yukiko's turning her back on a lover in financial straits.

To be sure, the war is fading into the past and there are signs of the "economic miracle" to come, but the society is riddled with contradictions. In one scene Senko and Yukiko meet for lunch at Ueno Park under the statue of Saigo and his dog. Immediately after the war, this site was famous as a gathering place for orphans.[29] Now the orphans are gone, replaced by workers like Senko and Yukiko and visitors taking in the sights and enjoying the hustle and bustle of rebuilding Tokyo. But there are also slums like the one Tsukahara calls home and poor neighborhoods like the Ogatas'. And the chimneys, which overlook both neighborhoods, function not only as a source of delight and hope (as they do for the Ogatas) but also as symbols of the new Japan, which someday may benefit the Ogatas, but can do nothing for Tsukahara. In this new Japan consumerism prevails, changing the surface of modern urban life.[30] In her job as radio announcer, Senko can be heard on loudspeakers everywhere, urging listeners to buy socks and sundry goods at special rates. Hiroko tells a friend that she wants to buy a sewing machine (foreign ones are best, she is told). Like many women, she has been forced by the ideology of consumerism "to earn extra money through low-paying part-time work."[31] By contrast, Yukiko quits her job at the radio station and, with the tacit approval of her parents, takes up with a man who can give her material things quicker, faster, and, presumably, without a hitch. Even the packed stadium at the bicycle races can be seen as a variant of the new consumer mentality: people may or may not have money or leisure time to gamble, but this hardly stops them. Nor does the stigma involved. Thus, Ryukichi's boss shamefacedly asks Hiroko not to tell anyone where she saw him.

And yet, despite the contradictions, there are plenty of reasons for hope. Occupation reforms granted women the vote, called for equality between the sexes, and ended legal authority of the extended family over branch families, leading the way to greater rights for the individual.[32] Of course, some of these reforms proved a double-edged sword for a variety of reasons; nevertheless, they "succeeded in large part because they were headed in the same direction in which forces within Japan were pushing."[33]

Where Chimneys Are Seen has been praised as a film that captures the new democratic spirit. This spirit is most evident in the relationship of the two principal couples, in particular in the emphasis on equality, true affection, and understanding. Granted, Ryukichi may lack the kind of authority he would have had in a traditional patriarchal household, and which he wouldn't mind having from time to time, but then again this is not what he really wants out of marriage. Nor is it anything that Kenzo, as a member of the younger generation, even seems to think about, let alone expect. It may be too much to claim that these men represent a new awareness on the part of the Japanese male; even so, their attitudes are very much in keeping with the new democratic spirit. This spirit is captured in yet another way. Earlier I mentioned that, according to Sato Tadao, there is a direct correlation between the new democracy and the innocence of the main characters. We now need to examine this matter more closely. Sato writes:

> Democratic ideology after the war wished that men begin as infants in order to learn what they hadn't understood, and this is the innocent look on their faces when they look at these famous chimneys. Because of this, although the film develops no political theme, it is nevertheless able to appear as the most pure crystallization of democracy of the postwar period.[34]

One may take issue with Sato's claim that the film "develops no political theme," but he is correct in recognizing the importance of the two couples. In fact, one can take his view a step further and argue that in their idealism, fortitude, and determination, these couples can be said to define postwar endurance—an endurance aptly summed up in the expression that becomes Kenzo and Senko's mantra: "If at first you don't succeed, try, try again." A commonplace, this motto, like the characters' belief that everything depends upon one's point of view—that is, "life is what you make it"—represents common people at their best. Without such people, democracy had little chance to succeed.

Curiously, critics and scholars have paid scant attention to how these qualities of innocence and endurance are intimately bound up with the democratic ideas that were put forward in postwar Japan. In this respect, J. Victor Koschmann's discussion of Maruyama Masao, one of the era's most prominent thinkers, is particularly relevant. Maruyama was drawn to the philosophic ideas of Meiji publicist Fukuzawa Yukichi (1834–1901), and saw that many of Fukuzawa's ideas represented his own thinking, especially the view that human beings "had to intervene subjectively (*shutaiteki ni*) from a position of relative autonomy in order to render the world comprehensible"[35] and that only through play, "the behavior appropriate to man's powerless state," can the human spirit be freed.[36]

Gosho, Oguni, and Shiina may not have been familiar with Maruyama or Fukuzawa as such, but they did not need to be since the issues that engaged the two writers were part of the discourse of the day. Consciously or not, *Where Chimneys Are Seen* tapped into that discourse. As a result, many of its concerns are clearly congruent with the views of Maruyama and

Fukuzawa cited above. Let us look at these views more closely. The first has to do with the need for people to develop the capacity to make judgments in "a historically changing environment."[37] This capacity called for flexibility, composure, and "tireless engagement," as opposed to "passive adaptation and rigid formalism."[38] Put differently, this view states that people need to be fluid, resilient, and open to the demands of each particular circumstance and situation. Above all, they need "to avoid becoming caught in a single perspective."[39] In *Where Chimneys Are Seen,* this view finds its most systematic and eloquent expression in the sense of wonder that the four main characters experience whenever they pause to look at, or talk about, the chimneys. Indeed, the seemingly ever-changing number of chimneys never ceases to amaze and delight them. As such, the chimneys teach a valuable lesson about the world: that nothing is fixed, permanent, or absolute. Although this lesson theoretically can be learned by anyone, if he or she is "open," only the four main characters avail themselves of it. Hence, in one scene Hiroko, instead of going straight home, makes a deliberate detour up the hill overlooking her neighborhood just to get a better look at the chimneys and double check the number. Like Kenzo, Ryukichi, and Senko, she is alive to the world around her, and takes no small pleasure in the "tireless engagement" of testing her own perspective.

That said, it is Maruyama and Fukuzawa's concept of play that bears special relevance to *Where Chimneys Are Seen.* Indeed, this concept holds out an optimistic view of human potential, which, at bottom, is the *raison d'être* of all Gosho's *shomin-geki.* Specifically, Fukuzawa saw play as the antidote to the feeling of powerlessness that defined so much of human experience and rendered human beings like *ujimushi* (small fry). According to Fukuzawa,

> While knowing that human life is but play [*tawamure*], *it is in the nature of a small fry to apply himself to this playing as if it were not play at all but serious . . . work.* Indeed, this is not really the way of small fry at all, but the pride of man alone as the very spirit of all things.[40]

Although by "small fry" Fukuzawa clearly means all humankind, this term is anything but pejorative, and has special resonance when applied to Gosho's film. For it is expressly the small fry—the common people—who are invested with "the very spirit of all things." For them, play provides "the composure and open-mindedness . . . to see beyond the immediate situation,"[41] to constantly step outside "the secure refuge of inertia and attachment" in order keep their own perspective "fluid."[42] Only in this way will they be able to understand their world.[43] In summarizing the essence of

Senko and Kenzo resort to the classic number game, "stone-paper-scissors" (*jankenpon*), to make a decision. *Where Chimneys Are Seen* (1953).

Fukuzawa's philosophy, Maruyama argues that "it is only when the serious-ness of life and the frivolity of life augment and functionalize each other that there can be a truly autonomous and independent spirit."[44] By this he means that there must be a balance between acting as if life were play and acting as if it were serious. Too much of the former would result in "escape or opportunism"; too much of the latter, in a sense of paralysis in the face of "the gravity of it all."[45] Interpreted in this way, Fukuzawa is essentially a humanist who sees humankind as uniquely equipped to grow, progress, and take control of its own destiny. For him, life means opportunity, not in-evitable defeat.

Where Chimneys Are Seen is imbued with Maruyama and Fukuzawa's notion of play. But what form does play take in the film? *Merriam-Webster's Collegiate Dictionary* includes the following definitions of "play": "recre-ational activity; *esp:* the spontaneous activity of children"; "absence of seri-ous or harmful intent"; "a move or series of moves calculated to arouse friendly feelings." Play can also refer to sexual intercourse or "amorous flir-tation."[46] In Gosho's film, play primarily takes the form of "recreational activity," but in terms of Senko and Kenzo's relationship it also carries the additional meaning of "moves calculated to arouse friendly feelings"—

especially on Kenzo's part. Senko and Kenzo's play, in fact, covers a wide range of activities: joking, teasing, bantering, expressing differences of opinion, sharing quiet conversations, and, most interesting of all, literally playing games. This last form is worth commenting on briefly, for Senko and Kenzo are never more serious than when they are "playing." For instance, to find out whether or not Senko loves Kenzo, the couple resorts to the classic number game, "stone-paper-scissors" (*jankenpon*), which often serves as an arbiter.[47] And although, as it turns out, the couple doesn't actually need the game, it provides a convenient way to downplay the importance of this urgent question. The same is true at the end of the film when the couple once again resorts to this game to decide on a different but no less important question. Games, in fact, become a way for the couple to communicate easily, warmly, and affectionately and, in the process, to support one another. Hence the game of balancing a pencil on one end. Senko uses this particular feat as shorthand language to encourage Kenzo "to try, try again." And, indeed, he is encouraged—so much so that when he tries to do it, and cannot, he is not dissuaded in the least. Games have forged the bond between them.

By contrast, the Ogatas' play almost always has to do with "amorous flirtation." It provides balance and ballast for their marriage as they go about the serious demands of daily life. Thus, on one occasion the couple gets sidetracked from eating dinner when Ryukichi compliments Hiroko on her kimono (which is hardly new), prompting her to model it on the spot. Needless to say, dinner is put on hold indefinitely. On another occasion the couple, having retired for the evening, chats before turning out the lights. At one point Hiroko coyly hides under the blanket of her futon, whereupon Ryukichi responds exactly as expected, "making a play" for her. However, once the abandoned baby arrives, all flirtation and lovemaking cease. The Ogatas lose the balance between seriousness and play, regaining it only when the baby recovers. Indeed, they are so happy and relieved that for the first time they engage in an altogether new form of play for them: cooing and making faces as they hover over the baby. In the final scene, they return to more familiar play, or to be more accurate, they plan to do so. Looking at the calendar, Ryukichi whispers something in Hiroko's ear. Evidently, it is a propitious time of the month.

The above forms of play are manifested in the behavior of other characters, as well, but in these instances there is a decided imbalance between seriousness and play. For example, Yukiko's frivolous nature is immediately conveyed by her behavior on the job. While Senko announces specials at the microphone, an obviously bored Yukiko spins a cat around like a top, at first not noticing Senko's signals to stop. The second time we see Yukiko at work, she is hardly playing, but now there is an even greater imbalance between play and seriousness in her life. She is having an affair with her boss, who is angry at her flirtatious manner and slaps her. While she clearly is a victim here, she and her boss have crossed the line, mixing their personal and professional lives. Not long after, she learns that her boss has passed bad checks to pay for the gifts he has given her. Frightened, she leaves him without so much as a word. Seeking Senko's help, she naively tries to dissociate herself from her lover by tossing his gifts aside. But Senko will not let her off the hook so easily. "I don't understand you," she says bluntly, forcing Yukiko to take a long overdue look at herself. In short, it is Senko's tough, no-nonsense friendship that eventually helps Yukiko find the balance between play and seriousness in her life.

There is one last form of imbalance between play and seriousness that figures prominently in Gosho's film, and which *Merriam-Webster's* includes in its entry on "play": gambling.[48] In the case of Ryukichi's boss, gambling seems at best a peccadillo, at worst a guilty pleasure. However, in the case of Tsukahara, gambling is, as we have seen, wholly destructive. It results in a kind of moral inertia, leading this sad, wretched man to "passive adaptation," that is, resignation to his lot and the exact opposite of the process of recuperation and growth that characterizes proper play. In *Where Chimneys Are Seen* there is no better illustration of the need for balance between play and seriousness.

By now it should be evident how Gosho dramatizes his characters' innocence and endurance and how these qualities relate to the climate and discourse of the day. One question, however, remains: What specific implications do these qualities have with regard to democracy in postwar Japan? To answer this question, we need to return to Maruyama Masao. Referring to an article by German sociologist Georg Simmel, Maruyama explains how Simmel takes up Fukuzawa's notion of play and introduces the concept of "sociability," which he defines as "the social counterpart of play."[49] In sociability, "both objective interests and personal egos are suspended, and each participant acts 'as if' all were equal."[50] To be sure, this is exactly what happens in the film's central relationships. But without question sociability receives its most interesting treatment in the scene in which Yukiko comforts Katsuko. Indeed, Yukiko's gesture can be seen as sociability in its purest sense, for in trying to comfort Katsuko, Yukiko means to show that they are equal. Katsuko intuitively understands this, and even seems touched by it, since what is taking place is not only an understanding between two women at the personal level but also a rapprochement, as it were, between two classes. In essence, then, both women comfort and are comforted; both act "'as if' all were equal." Having set aside their own egos and interests, they have acted, without fuss or fanfare, according to an idea that is the cornerstone of democracy.

Although we must be careful not to place too heavy a political burden on *Where Chimneys Are Seen,* we must be equally careful not to minimize its political significance. Put simply, the film is all the better for not being explicit. Democracy, it implies, is both an idea and a constructive process, requiring human beings to interact in such a way as to preserve the autonomy and integrity of each individual. Central to this process is the indefatigable spirit of the *ujimushi* (small fry), which continuously strives to be open and proactive so as to "make the value judgments that can be effective in bringing reality ever closer to an ideal state."[51] In this model for postwar Japan, play is instrumental, and the example of the phantom chimneys and the two women walking side by side, shoelessly, is the epitome of democratic values.

And yet what makes *Where Chimneys Are Seen* memorable—what in Anderson and Richie's words "shows *shomin-geki* at its purest and in the very best postwar form"[52]—is its heartfelt celebration of everyday life as the most authentically human existence, that is, a life not distorted by false values. Indeed, living that life to the fullest, whatever its vicissitudes or disappointments, remains first and foremost Gosho's most fundamental theme. In closing, let us return to a basic shot that recurs throughout the film. An example of Gosho's "poetic interludes," it is a carefully composed shot of the two rows of tenement apartments that make up the Ogatas' neighborhood and the steep hill that rises behind those apartments, spanning the frame—the same hill that Hiroko climbs. Each time Gosho returns to this shot, people can be seen in silhouette crossing this hill, slowly, steadily, without a sound. Occasionally this shot includes a man pulling a large cart. Although this shot in its various transformations serves the narrative by fixing the time of day, and although it may eloquently visualize the truism that life goes on, its real purpose is to concentrate the audience's attention on the image itself. Haiku-like in its compression and succinctness, and clearly meditative in style, it suggests the evanescent and eternal, a specific moment in time that embodies the very nature of lived experience in all its beauty, harshness, and seeming contradictions. At the same time this image crystallizes Gosho's art and demonstrates in yet another way the richness and complexity of his *shomin-geki.*

SIX

An Inn at Osaka *(1954):*
Money, Democracy, and Limited Knowledge

When the Japan Society and the Museum of Modern Art presented a Gosho retrospective of twenty-four films in 1989–90, critic Elliot Stein of *The Village Voice* singled out *An Inn at Osaka* as the "real revelation" of the series.[1] Screened at the 1954 Venice Film Festival, and selected by *Kinema Jumpo* as one of the "Best Ten" of the year, the film has been called "one of the finest of all *shomin-geki*." In it, "everything is incident and character and the calm, very Japanese assurance that things are so bad now that they can only become better."[2]

Based on a novel by Minakami Takitaro, *An Inn at Osaka* is set in the early 1950s in Osaka, the commercial capital of Japan. The central protagonist, Mita Takashi (Sano Shuji), is an insurance company employee in his thirties, who has been transferred from the Tokyo head office for punching his boss in defense of a fellow worker. Having little money, he takes a room in a shabby inn that employs three maids: Otsugi (Kawasaki Hiroko), a middle-aged woman who is scraping together every cent of her meager salary to raise the young son she is separated from; Orika (Mito Mitsuko), a woman in her thirties who is constantly hounded for money by her out-of-work boyfriend; and Oyone (Hidari Sachiko), a wayward teenager who is having a fling with one of the guests. Sympathetic to Otsugi's and Orika's plight, Mita befriends them and tries to help. He also finds himself caught up in the lives of characters outside the inn. These include Omitsu (Anzai Kyoko), a young woman Oyone's age, whose father's illness plunges her into dire poverty; Tawara (Hosokawa Toshio), a college friend, whose idealism and position as company director prove irreconcilable; Imoto (Kitazawa Hyo), a businessman, who takes out a loan from Mita's boss (Tanaka Haruo) to keep his company afloat; and Uwabami (Otowa Nobuko), a smart, sassy, alcoholic geisha, who falls in love with Mita, only to discover that he is in love with a woman he barely knows (Megumi Michiko). Unhappy with his job, Mita realizes that his problems are nothing next to those of the people around him. Powerless, he watches their lives spiral downward. Orika, desperately in need of money, steals from one of the hotel guests and is fired; the innkeeper, unable to pay back a million-yen loan, converts the hotel into a whorehouse rather than lose it; and Otsugi, having no other options, stays on as a prostitute. Matters are no better outside the inn. Mita's boss calls in the loan he made to Imoto, causing Imoto's business to collapse; a scandal ensues, and Imoto commits suicide. When Mita confronts his boss about his part in Imoto's death, he is transferred back to Tokyo. At a farewell dinner he gives for his friends, Mita thanks them for everything they have taught him. "As long as we can laugh at our sorrows," he says, "we have the strength and courage to build a new future." The next day he leaves.

In *An Inn at Osaka,* Gosho continues the re-examination of the *shomin-geki* that he began in *Where Chimneys Are Seen.* Once again, the focus is on the bittersweet, at times tragic lives of ordinary people, and the setting—in this case the inn of the title and its environs—serves as a microcosm of postwar Japan. Structurally, the film interweaves multiple lines of action to tease out the parallels and differences between the lives of the characters. Gosho also fills out the narrative and thematic structure with one of his favorite devices, what Pudovkin called the use of "expressive or plastic objects," that is, props and inanimate materials, which are imbued with meaning. However, the film's most distinctive narrational strategy is its handling of point of view, which makes Mita a rather more complex character than he first appears to be.

Tonally, as might be expected, the film's mood is a mix of laughter and tears, lyricism and realism. Yet for all that, *An Inn at Osaka* is a "deeply sad film."[3] The overall feel is more sober and melancholy than usual in Gosho, and some of the humor is more pungent than lighthearted. Nevertheless, the blend of often diametrically opposed moods *even within the same scene* demonstrates a master at the top of his form. This chapter not only will discuss the above elements—narrational structure, strategies, and mood—but also will pay particular attention to Gosho's striking use of piecemeal editing (there are over 1,000 separate shots) and how it relates to character psychology, behavior, and theme. However, we first need to say a few words about the film's production history and to situate the film in the immediate post-Occupation period.

Gosho first intended to bring Minakami's novel to the screen in 1948, when the newly formed Kinuta Productions invited him to make it his next film, following the completion of *Omokage* (*A Visage to Remember*) for Toho.[4] On the face of it, a collaboration between Gosho and Kinuta Productions seemed ideal, inasmuch as both had been deeply involved in the Toho labor strikes and shared the same basic political views. Kinuta, in fact, was made up of workers fired by the studio during the strikes and awarded monetary compensation to produce their own films. When Gosho and co-writer Yasumi Toshio submitted their completed screenplay, however, there was a problem: Kinuta's production committee was troubled by the character of Mita. Was he a progressive or a reactionary? they asked Gosho. Reportedly this question was debated late into the night, with Gosho repeatedly insisting that Mita was progressive. On his walk home, Gosho is said to have looked up at the star-filled sky, and, struck by its beauty, remarked that *An Inn at Osaka* was no less beautiful, for it was an "upward-looking project" that gave one hope for the future.[5] It is probably no coincidence that Mita echoes this same expression of hope at his farewell party. While this tale may be apocryphal, it, nevertheless, conveys an essential quality of Gosho: a deep personal conviction in the positive and the possible, even in the face of life's tragedies. Today *An Inn at Osaka* is rightly considered to be one of Gosho's most progressive films.[6] At the time, however, Kinuta remained unsatisfied with Gosho's answer and passed on the film. Gosho subsequently formed his own production company, Studio Eight, and several years later returned to *An Inn at Osaka,* its depiction of post-Occupation Japan even more timely and trenchant.

In adapting Minakami's novel, Gosho and Yasumi Toshio made one notable change: they updated the setting from the Taisho era (1912–26) to 1954. This change was not merely for its own sake, but to emphasize the philosophic similarities between the two periods and keep true to the project of Gosho's new *shomin-geki:* concentrating on the contemporary Japanese scene. The Taisho era (known as "Taisho democracy"), like the postwar period, was a time when the development and achievement of the individual self was regarded as the basis for all social reform.[7] This ideal of individualism was of course not new to the Japanese; it had been introduced in the People's Rights Movement of the 1870s and 1880s. However, like nearly all ideals of liberty and individual rights, it was repressed by the militarists during World War II and had to await the democratic reforms enacted by the Occupation. Of these reforms, the most ambitious and far-reaching was the Constitution of 1947, which codified the basic ideals of democracy, establishing equality of the sexes, stressing liberation of women, and promoting "citizen participation in government, labor voice in industry, as well as individual freedom and the eradication of feudalistic practices."[8]

As historians have documented, there was a shift in Occupation policies between 1947 and 1949 "from further reform to economic recovery."[9] This shift was prompted in part by the realization that Japan needed a strong economic base, but also by the developing Cold War and America's anxiety over the spread of communism in East Asia. In this climate America saw a strengthened Japan as an ally and a base for democracy and American military power.[10] Consequently, "the Americans quickly relaxed their severe economic policies and quickly rehabilitated many of Japan's major capitalist powers."[11] This also meant, among other things, replacing previously banned or dismantled *zaibatsu* (oligopolies) with *keiretsu* ("powerful groupings of commercial and industrial enterprises [that] tended to be more horizontal, open, and internally competitive"[12]); suppressing labor unions in their bid for political power; and purging leftists from business and government.[13] While this shift in policy struck many Japanese, especially leftists and radicals, as an ideological contradiction at best and a betrayal of "any genuine 'people's' democracy" at worst,[14] it enabled Japan to enjoy an economic recovery that was already evident in the early 1950s. It also sowed the seeds for the "economic miracle" to come.

Be that as it may, in *An Inn at Osaka,* which takes place roughly two years after the end of the Occupation, there is little sign that Japan's emerging economic recovery or institutionalized democratic values have taken hold or made a difference in most people's lives. Here Tawara, who is at the top of the socioeconomic ladder, is of particular thematic importance. As a company director, who has inherited the business from his father, he not only enjoys certain perks (such as a chauffeur-driven American car), but also has the clout to prevent his good friend Mita from being fired in Tokyo. This last action is merely one instance of Tawara's putting into practice his ideals of justice and humanity. Yet, in spite of his power and position, he finds that he can do nothing to combat the disguised if self-serving nature of his executive board, which insists on giving company profits to preferred shareholders, even though the company is on shaky ground. When Tawara expresses his frustration to Mita, Mita asks why the company union doesn't take action, only to be told that it is too weak to fight. Indeed, in the early 1950s unions "gradually subsided in zeal and importance as workers, like other Japanese [became] increasingly satisfied with the way things [were] going in Japan."[15] Such is the case here where things seem to be going well enough—except for Tawara, who quits his job in disgust. As he tells Mita, "For the company's 100th anniversary, I told the truth." To be sure, during Mita's farewell dinner party, Tawara expresses some small reservation about quitting his job instead of continuing the fight. He even admits that he may have been "defeatist." But he also points out that he now enjoys a freedom he never had before, and can spend more time with his wife and children. He therefore urges Mita to leave his unhappy job. Mita, however, declares that he is more determined than ever to stay in the business world and try to change it. Clearly, this scene elicits a complex response. One is dismayed by Tawara's circumstance, which implies the irreconcilability of individual freedom and economic reality. Put differently, one respects Tawara's decision to do what he feels is right, even as one feels that there is another "right" as well, and that the path Mita has chosen is the only way to make a difference.

The picture is even bleaker at the bottom of the socioeconomic ladder, which includes most of the characters of the film, and where there is even less evidence of Japan's economic recovery or democracy taking hold. Here we see the innkeeper's good-natured, sometimes hard-drinking older brother (Fujiwara Kamatari), and Omitsu, the poverty-stricken young woman on her own, peddling cheap goods to make ends meet. The former specializes in items like soap, razor blades, and sewing equipment, while the latter sells, among other things, a blanket, supposedly American-made, which figures prominently in the dramatic action. Later, when Omitsu can no longer make a living hawking goods, she tries prostitution—but backs away from it immediately, for it is an abyss she refuses to fall into. Otsugi and Orika, however, are not so lucky. By the end of the film, Otsugi is already working as a full-time prostitute, and it appears that Orika will be reduced to the same fate.

Indeed, of all the characters in the film, it is these two maids for whom Gosho clearly feels the greatest compassion. These are women alone, marginalized women outside the traditional family system, who are exploited not only economically but also morally. For them, democracy quite simply does not exist. The world they live in is one where individual freedom and liberation provided women by the 1947 Constitution are denied, and feudalistic practices prevail. Hence the callous innkeeper (Miyoshi Eiko) feels entitled to treat these women as if they have no rights whatsoever. For example, when Orika asks her for financial help, she fobs her off with the threat that she doesn't like having a woman in her hire who has "a man on the string." Likewise, when Otsugi asks for time off to visit her boy, the innkeeper complains that taking time off is uneconomical. Adding insult to injury, she says: "Even animals forget their home." Not surprisingly, the usually meek and docile Otsugi verbally lashes out at her. To be sure, the innkeeper is hardly sympathetic, but for all her insensitivity and cruelty, she is herself a victim of the times—a widow whose years as a geisha are far behind her, and whose horror of being penniless has left her incapable of feeling for others.

Then there is Uwabami, an aging geisha. Like Mita, she seems to straddle the middle and lower rungs of the socioeconomic ladder. That is, she has some money, but is deeply unhappy in her work. Like Otsugi and Orika, with whom she has even more in common, Uwabami knows only too well what it means to be a woman without prospects or worth. Perhaps this is why the notion of democracy is so important to her. For her, democracy seems to be, at the very least, a means to assert her dignity and importance as a person. Indeed, it is from her lips that we hear the only explicit reference to democracy in the film. This comes during a company dinner in which she not only refuses to curb her tongue but also takes Mita's side in confronting his boss over Imoto's suicide. When Mita's boss tells her to shut up because she is showing disrespect for the dinner's guest of honor, the company president, she protests: "I don't care if he is the president. This is a democracy. Say what you feel." Here Uwabami strikes a blow for the ideal of individual freedom, and it is not the only time. Nor does she necessarily need to be sober to do so; after all, her name, Uwabami, is a nickname that means she drinks too much. (Plus, as she proves on more than one occasion, she can drink anyone under the table.) Not surprisingly, she is a bit tipsy when she first pays Mita a visit at the inn. However, she is no less eloquent or impassioned about the true meaning of democracy. "I'm human. So are you. We're just human beings," she declares to Otsugi, who is serving her sake. The message may be lost on Otsugi at the time, but Uwabami's insistence on basic human rights and the bond that she sees existing between women makes her no less progressive than Mita or Tawara. Ironically, the fact that she must insist on this point in the first place shows that the lesson of democracy has yet to be learned. Uwabami, however, is more than willing to do her part in teaching this lesson. Thus, when Orika is fired from the inn and without prospects, she agrees to help her.

Unfortunately, the society Gosho depicts acts on an altogether different principle, controlled as it is by money and "dominated by uncertainty and greed."[16] Meiji writer-philosopher Kitamura Tokoku cautioned that the "ideal of independence, if lived out only on the materialist level of economics, would lead to a struggle between individuals, to social and spiritual isolation, and ultimately to disharmony."[17] Gosho's grandfather put the matter more bluntly. "To have money doesn't mean that you can afford to be cruel to others," he told his young grandson, adding, "To make money is an important thing, but one must stop short of becoming unbalanced about it."[18] Characters in the film speak repeatedly of this "unbalance" and its by-product, the breakdown of trust between people, and the isolation and disharmony that Tokoku describes. As Mita says when he discovers that he has been cheated, "Nowadays everyone lives off everyone else; it's not just Osaka or Tokyo." Beneath this rueful observation is an implicit desire for balance between morality and economics. And out of this desire comes the searing condemnation of an unjust society that can be felt in every frame of the film.

CHARACTER, THEME, AND
NARRATIVE STRUCTURE

As Donald Richie has pointed out, the *shomin-geki* as a mode is character-ized by "a freedom from tight plot and contrived story, which reflected life with a fidelity rare on the screen."[19] While this assertion is true enough, freedom from tight plot is at best a relative thing that varies from filmmaker to filmmaker. In the case of Gosho, we have seen in previous chapters how causal structure was much looser in 1930s films, such as *Burden of Life* and *Woman of the Mist,* than in subsequent *shomin-geki* like *Where Chimneys Are Seen.* The same holds true for *An Inn at Osaka,* where carefully layered plotting in no way precludes an aleatory feel or even at times a loose causal-ity. This is especially so in the opening scenes. Here the emphasis is equally divided between conveying the texture of ordinary life (Mita settles in at the inn, the maids go about their routines, etc.) and establishing the dra-matic through-lines of the story (Mita tells Otsugi and Orika a little about himself and his demotion; he first sees Imoto's daughter, the woman of his dreams, on his way to work; etc.). However, in the lengthy middle section of the film, the emphasis on everyday life gradually gives way to increased dramatic inflection. This section, which opens with Mita and Uwabami's first meeting, concentrates on Mita's developing interactions with the lives around him, and how, one after another, these lives become insupportable and reach a crisis point (climaxing in loss, death, or suicide). It is in this sec-tion that the film is raised to the level of genuine tragedy. In the closing sec-tion, highlighted by two back-to-back dinner parties, drama is foreground-ed until the very last scene, where it is subsumed in an aleatory act and the reassertion of the ordinariness of everyday life.

In *An Inn at Osaka* the characters' lives not only are entwined but also mirror and comment on one another in a continual pattern of parallels and contrasts. This pattern is played out at the level of character and narrative structure. In terms of character, *An Inn at Osaka* demonstrates once again that Gosho's *shomin-geki* is crucially preoccupied with human behavior. Take, for example, Oyone and Omitsu. Both young women are approxi-mately the same age, both are alone in the world, and both fall into prosti-tution. But while Omitsu finds prostitution abhorrent, Oyone in her own capricious way sees it as a good career move, declaring that she doesn't want to be a maid all her life. A product of the times, she has had her first sex-ual experience at fourteen, and, in the words of Orika, is "après-guerre," a

French term "attached to any young person who defied traditional norms."[20] Whether or not Oyone is consciously defying tradition, she certainly is indifferent to it. She makes little effort to conceal her affair with Noro (Tatara Jun), an insufferable dandy. Nor does she think twice about trying to seduce Mita at the same time (when he shows no interest, she blithely dismisses him as "old-fashioned"). By contrast, Omitsu is virtually an emblem of tradition. Unfortunately, she makes a terrible mistake. Desperate to pay back money she owes Mita, she sleeps with Noro. The shame and humiliation of prostituting herself is almost too much to bear. To make matters worse, she is called on the carpet by the innkeeper for whoring in her establishment—a delicious irony since very shortly the inn will exist for just that purpose. In the end Oyone and Omitsu take two different paths—the former sells her body, the latter works at honest if menial jobs. Yet the film, while sympathetic to Omitsu, neither condemns nor condones Oyone, although it occasionally looks at her askance (just as Mita does). Sadly, for these young women—as indeed, for all of the women in the film—principle is a luxury. The best they can hope for is compromise they can live with.

In terms of narrative structure, Gosho employs a variety of strategies. One of these strategies is crosscutting, as in a picnic sequence where Mita, Otsugi, and Orika's friendship, openness, and enjoyment of simple pleasures is contrasted with Oyone and Noro's self-absorption and lovemaking back at the inn. Gosho also makes frequent use of rhyming scenes. Hence the two scenes in which Orika pleads for money, first from the innkeeper (who, not surprisingly, turns her down), and then from Otsugi (who does not); the two scenes in which Otsugi and the innkeeper quarrel over Otsugi's request for time off; and the two dinner-party scenes in the denouement. The film's most distinctive narrative strategy, however, is the way in which Mita is handled as the central consciousness. Specifically, while he is present in the majority of scenes, he is absent from a number of important scenes. The effect of this strategy is to create two discrete but interrelated strands of action, that is, a series of events that Mita observes and takes part in, alongside a series of events he is not privy to. Far from insignificant, this latter series has as much impact on him as the former, for it reveals what he doesn't know, cannot know, but gradually must learn. As viewers, we are privy to both sets of events, and therefore have a decided advantage over Mita. But this does not make us feel superior to him in any way. Quite the opposite, we are prompted to empathize with him even more, for like all of us, he must do the best he can with limited knowledge.

What are these events that Mita does not see? Simply put, they are the behind-the-scenes workings of the inn, the personal problems, the conflicts, the inevitable crises. In particular these events reveal the lives of the maids in the kind of depth and detail that Mita, for much of the film, is only vaguely aware of. He does not see, for example, the innkeeper's bullying of Otsugi and Orika, or the humiliation these two maids must endure when she goes through their belongings searching for Noro's stolen money. Of course, Mita knows a good deal about these two maids' hardships. He has made it his business to know. Yet not fully realizing (until late in the film) how trapped and desperate these women actually are, does he really understand their lives? In short, Mita is forced to learn in bits and pieces and by trial and error, cobbling together what he has seen and what he has only heard about or somehow intuited. Thus, despite his best intentions, he is occasionally prone to misjudgment.

Indeed, as others point out to him, Mita has a good deal to learn about life. In one scene, while preparing his tea, Orika sees a gift Uwabami has left for him: an expensive cloth blanket. Knowing what it signifies, she tells him that Uwabami is in love with him. Gosho's camera cuts to Mita: he says nothing. Then Gosho cuts back to Orika. As if thinking aloud, she says, "You've not suffered like me," while carefully removing a cigarette butt from Mita's ashtray and tucking it away for later. That Mita does not respond to her comment about Uwabami is understandable, but that he seems not to see her pain, while only a few feet away from her, is another matter. Orika is not alone in trying to "teach" Mita. At one point Uwabami tells him that he is like a star (and later she leaves him another gift, a book, appropriately titled *The Stars Look Down*). In one sense, she means to compliment him, to let him know he is a special person (doubly special since she also loves him). Yet her likening him to a star also has a less flattering meaning. A star, after all, is light years away, unreachable, unattainable, and "above it all." Sometimes private to the point of being aloof, Mita is a star in precisely this way. But he is also a "star" in that he is lost in the thrall of an idyllic love (Imoto's daughter) and prefers a dream to reality. (At the farewell dinner, he even refers to this meaning of "star.") The sharpest attack on Mita, however, comes from Omitsu. Having rescued her from the wrath of the innkeeper, who catches her whoring, he tells her, "I didn't know you needed money so badly." He then returns the money she gave him to pay back her debt. However, she refuses to accept the money, and when he keeps pressing it on her, she turns on him. "You really think you're such a good-hearted person, don't you?" she says. He is understandably taken aback by this, not because he considers himself a good person, or even expects thanks, but because he has never imagined his kindness could be met with derision and hostility. Indeed, Omitsu's words cut him to the quick, for they are an implied accusation of self-righteousness and spiritual vanity.

Omitsu (Anzai Kyoko) turns on Mita (Sano Shuji): "You really think you're such a good-hearted person, don't you?" *An Inn at Osaka* (1954).

There is no question that Mita is a good man, a kind, well-meaning man. Still, the film's greatest subtlety might just be the way it problematizes his basic decency, suggesting that this knight has chinks in his shining armor. In holding a part of himself in reserve, he doubtless is trying to protect himself and maintain some distance from the individuals he is helping. While on the one hand, this behavior is perfectly understandable, on the other hand, it can be troubling and perplexing. Indeed, at times the evident ambivalence in his manner and behavior seems to qualify the very help he is giving—hence his occasional, disapproving looks, not to mention the sometimes cutting remarks, as when he greets Uwabami with, "What, not drunk?" At the same time this ambivalence suggests that even a knight in shining armor is prone to blind spots, contradictions, and inconsistencies.

In other words, Mita is only human. As such, he is imperfect and, as he himself comes to realize, he has much to learn. This he graciously admits to his friends at his farewell dinner party when he thanks them for all they taught him. In short, his demotion and transfer to Osaka has turned out to be a good thing. The helper has himself been helped.

Yet the final scene, which immediately follows this farewell dinner party, suggests that there is one last thing Mita does not know—indeed, cannot possibly know. As his train leaves Osaka, he unknowingly passes by Omitsu, whom he had invited to the celebration, but who did not show up. Now, the next morning, we see her salvaging scrap metal below the train tracks and suddenly realize what Mita will never know: that she did not show up because every second of her life is now spent struggling for survival.

Interestingly, Gosho does not cut inside the train to Mita, even though the train stands in metonymic relation to him. Thus the question arises: *Why* doesn't Gosho show us Mita one last time? Is it because Mita is no longer part of the lives he once touched, including Omitsu's? If so, then cutting to him inside the train would have certainly made this point. But obviously, Gosho is interested in something else. Therefore, he foregrounds Omitsu immersed in her work, then cuts to one last image of the train, holding the shot for twenty-eight seconds, which makes it one of the longest shots in the film. Gosho then dissolves from the train to the final shot, a lengthy pan from left to right of Osaka in the distance, its famed commercial quarter (Umeda) nowhere to be seen, only an industrial wasteland dominated by a gray sky and belching smokestacks. This is the reality of Osaka for Omitsu and others like her. In achieving closure, this final scene, then, does not simply wrap up the story. Instead, it subsumes the Mita narrative in a second narrative, that part of "the Osaka story" from which he was always excluded. Now the second narrative takes center stage.

No discussion of narrative and thematic structure in *An Inn at Osaka* would be complete without taking into account two "expressive or plastic objects" that are charged with meaning: a cheap cloth blanket and a treasured French watch. Indeed, with each reappearance these objects shift in meaning, overdetermining the themes of the film. We have already mentioned the blanket in passing; now we must consider it more closely. Actually, there are two blankets in the film. The first is the one Mita has purchased from Omitsu, and which Uwabami examines during her first visit at the inn. She tells Mita (while pulling loose threads from it) that the pattern and mark are good, but that he has been cheated. It is not English-made (read: American-made), even though it is wrapped in an American newspaper. "Now you won't trust Osaka," she says, introducing one of the film's main themes: trust as the basis for solidarity between people. If this bogus blanket signifies the violation of trust in postwar Japan, the blanket that Uwabami gives Mita in a later scene bespeaks not only her love for him but also her determination to restore that trust and prevent him from losing faith in humanity. Like Uwabami, the innkeeper's brother also understands what the bogus blanket means. "It's not good to be cheated; it breaks down trust," he tells Mita. And with that, he takes Mita under his wing, and the two of them track down Omitsu to her shantytown dwelling to confront her. Interestingly, the innkeeper's brother and Omitsu do all of the talking. As Omitsu explains that she too was deceived, and was told the blanket was of good quality, Mita listens quietly, all the while taking in her surroundings and the sounds of a purification rite for her seriously ill father, which is taking place inside her home. With this, any anger he may have felt is dissipated.

There is, however, more to be said about the bogus blanket. Is it mere coincidence that it comes wrapped in an American newspaper? Obviously a ploy to pass off the item as American, the wrapping does the trick, fooling the trusting Mita and Omitsu, but not the shrewd Uwabami. Nor can it be a coincidence that the particular part of the newspaper Gosho has selected is a splashy full-page ad for a Hollywood movie. Setting aside the fact that Gosho, like many Japanese filmmakers, was a lifelong admirer of American films and here is doubtless engaging in a playful homage, this ad nevertheless serves a purpose. Indeed, Gosho takes pains that viewers do not miss the ad. He not only places it conspicuously in the foreground of the frame, but privileges it with a shot/reaction shot, panning across the entire ad from top to bottom, then cutting to Uwabami, who registers a look of bemusement and disbelief. In the process we get a good look at the title and artwork. The film is *The City That Never Sleeps*, a 1953 Republic film noir that has it all: love, murder, adultery, deception, urban angst, and a convoluted plot that features a character who pretends to be "'a mechanical man' in [a] nightclub's display window"[21] and a hero who "has been born again," enabling him and his lover to enjoy "the promise of a new life together."[22] If the ad doesn't quite spell out each and every one of these striking story details, it more than makes up for it by showing the hero and heroine locked in a torrid embrace. It is this image that catches Uwabami's eye, this movieland promise of the triumph of romance, and with it the attendant promise of the lovers' new life together. It is an image that expresses her deepest desire, and if she is skeptical, it is because the narrative of her life is so different that she doesn't quite dare to believe that she and Mita will ever be that couple. Yet dare she does; hence the blanket she sends him.[23]

Finally, there is Mita's French watch. Given to him by his now-deceased uncle, who founded the company Mita works for, it is a gift he treasures. And even though he is down on his luck and cannot afford a decent razor blade when he first arrives in Osaka, he has no thoughts of pawning the watch. This changes, however, the more immersed he becomes in the lives at the inn and the more he feels his own life to be devoid of joy. Interestingly, Gosho does not show us the scene in which Mita sells the watch. Instead, we see him unwrap the chain, which he has obviously kept as a memento, and place it on his desk in his room, the deed now done. Later, he tells Orika that he sold the watch because he wanted to enjoy himself for a change, adding, "I want to use the money well." He then asks her if she needs money. She tells him not to worry about her, suggesting instead that he take her, Otsugi, and Oyone on an outing, for they "want to see the wide open sky." Thus is born the idea for a day of sightseeing and picnicking, one of the few happy times that these characters experience. (Oyone, however, decides to spend her day with Noro.) If one senses that Mita's desire "to use the money well" means more than just enjoying a day of freedom from cares and woes, this impression is reinforced by the last reason he gives for having sold the watch: "One doesn't need old things now, but new things."

What exactly does Mita mean by this cryptic remark? He offers no explanation, but surely he is not alluding simply to the fact that he used part of the money to purchase a new, less expensive watch. More likely, he is thinking about "old things" as old habits, old ways of thinking and doing things—in his case, holding on to his uncle's watch for himself instead of using it to do good. Put differently, the old way was not to share the wealth, but to keep it in the family, as some of the *zaibatsu* (financial and industrial conglomerates) had always done—something Mita is morally unable to do. This, then, is the first meaning of the French watch. Yet it must be remembered that Mita does not give away the complete watch; he keeps the chain. This implies that he does not break ties completely with old ways, that is, with the business world. Nor does he plan to do so. Rather, as he says during his farewell dinner party, he intends to stay in the company and effect positive changes from within. He does not say how he plans to do this; perhaps he does not even know. But already he knows that business must concern itself with "new things." In other words, it must put into practice the egalitarian principles that democratic reform has promised; it must accord people respect and dignity; it must also actively seek to improve their lives. This has been the principle he has operated on in sharing the money from his uncle's watch, although he would be loath to say so. And this, in short, is the second meaning of his uncle's French watch, which now is transformed into a "new thing."

Not surprisingly, one of the greatest enemies of "new things" is Mita's boss. Indeed, with the exception of Uwabami, there is arguably no one in the film who understands Mita better. But here understanding only breeds intense dislike. This small-time branch manager, first of all, envies Mita because of his family connections, even though they profit Mita not a jot. Still, Mita's boss may well imagine that someday they might. What really rankles this petty bureaucrat, however, is that Mita is a man of principle, not to mention a defender of the ordinary man, as he proved in Tokyo. Hence Mita's boss misses no opportunity to publicly chide him or call him an "intellectual" and "socialist" to his face: code words of contempt for anyone daring to stand for "new things." Mita may be an intellectual, but he is no more a socialist than he is a radical. On the contrary, in his own quiet way, and in actions like the pawning of a treasured French watch, he shows what he truly is, and what Gosho rightly claimed him to be: a progressive.

A FILM OF DIVERSE
AND COMPLEX MOODS

By now it should evident that *An Inn at Osaka* is "a deeply sad film," a melancholy social portrait of 1954 Japan, in which money drives everything and democracy remains an unfulfilled promise for many. Gosho's film is a denunciation of this state of things, but this does not mean that he has abandoned his characteristic mood of laughter through tears, his blend of comedy, humor, pathos, sentimentality, lyricism, and realism. Rather, he has blended these elements in unique and interesting ways to evoke the diverse and often complex moods of the film. In this respect alone, *An Inn at Osaka* is one of his consummate achievements.

To fully appreciate the film's blend of diverse and complex moods, we will examine the relationship of lyricism and realism, the role of comedy, the unusual shifts in mood within scenes, and the nature of pathos, sentimentality, and tragedy.

The relationship of lyricism and realism can best be seen in Gosho's handling of the Osaka setting. As noted in previous chapters, Gosho has a penchant for *suikyo* settings, that is, towns and locations near bodies of water. Typically these settings tend to be associated with nature, as in *Dancing Girl of Izu,* where beautiful mountain ranges and crystalline lakes provide ready-made opportunities for pictorialism and lyricism. By contrast, in *An Inn at Osaka,* there is no natural scenery. Indeed, the scenic, tourist Osaka is nowhere to be found; rather, the emphasis by and large is on urban gloom. The inn of the title, in fact, is located a few yards away from one of the city's many watercourses and canals. Here the sound of cargo vessels, tugboats, and other craft forms a constant backdrop for the unfolding human drama. Characteristically, Mita, who tries to see things in the best possible light, comments on the nice view of the river that he has from his room, his way of softening harsh reality. But reality resists such softening. Even scenes that have a possibility for lyricism adhere to social realism, which captures photographic reality, the documentary look of things. Hence the picnic scene. Here Mita, Otsugi, and Orika eat their meal on large stone blocks, pinned in by a wall behind them that obstructs most of the view. Further underscoring this impression of enclosure are two shots in which the three characters walk along the river, a massive wall filling the left half of the frame, towering over their diminutive figures. Needless to say, these settings and images are far from lyrical and ironize the two maids' desire to "see the wide open sky," but at least they do not thwart that desire. And herein lies the special poignancy of the scene, and evidence of Gosho's singular talent. For, no matter how glum or oppressive the setting may be, Mita and the two maids manage to enjoy themselves enormously, talking, laughing, joking, and even teasing one another.

This said, only a few scenes in the film have even a remotely lyrical quality. Indeed, instances of lyricism are mainly confined to isolated, individual shots, the most striking of which is reminiscent of a French Impressionist painting: a lovely deep-focus shot of Oyone and Otsugi doing laundry along the riverbank. Not coincidentally, perhaps, this shot is also the most self-consciously "aesthetic" shot in the film. In the foreground white sheets billow in the breeze on a clothesline that spans the top of the frame, while underneath Oyone and Otsugi carry on with their task, the river behind them. On the opposite bank, downtown Osaka stretches as far into the distance as the eye can see, its streets lined with trees and tall buildings and humming with traffic. On this bright sunny day, the city seems vibrantly alive, and blessedly free from cares. Here, for one of the few times in the film, social realism gives way to an image of undeniable beauty. And although washing women and clotheslines hardly constitute the usual tourist's view, this image conveys a rare and almost idyllic view of "daily life in the city," one that seems to bespeak the secret of true happiness. This image, however, is only fleeting. At the end of the shot, Orika arrives to help with the wash, only to be accosted by her boyfriend demanding money. The idyll is over.

Although the social realist style may be adept at capturing the look and feel of quotidian reality, it has its limits. It cannot easily convey, for example, reality as a nightmarish, surreal experience. Hence Gosho employs an Expressionist style for one of the film's darkest and most ominous scenes: Mita's second visit to Omitsu's home.[24] Prior to this scene, Omitsu had been caught whoring in the inn, refused Mita's offer of help, and attacked him for thinking himself such a good person. Afraid of what she might do in her desperate state, he follows her home, the music on the soundtrack a throbbing, pulsating rhythm that expresses his sense of dread. Finding the outside door open, he steps inside, and asks for her, a pan connecting him to a man across the room slumped in a chair. Mita repeats his question, but the man does not respond. Behind him several baby chicks move in a circle, chirping: an eerie, indeed surrealistic image. Omitsu descends the stairs, a dazed look on her face. Sitting at the foot of the stairs, she says that she found her father dead when she got home. Stunned, Mita looks at her father, who is silhouetted against the background. Then he looks back at Omitsu. With these two looks, he has come to understand the full implication of this tragedy on her life. She walks past Mita, as if only vaguely aware of his presence, and picks up one of the chicks. He leaves her money, but she does not notice. He asks her what she will do. Staring blankly into space, she replies, "Go on living."

This is a powerful, disturbing scene. In it, both Mita and the viewer have been plunged deep into a nightmare of overwhelming loss, death, and helplessness. Abetting this sense of a nightmare is, first of all, cinematographer Ohara Joji's chiaroscuro lighting, which feels right out of film noir, and presents Omitsu's father in two striking silhouette shots that make him as much an emblem of death as a once-living human being.[25] In addition, there is the eerie presence of the chicks. Why they are in the scene in the first place is left deliberately unexplained and unmotivated. Have they just hatched? More to the point, what are they doing in a tailor's home and place of business? But then, when did daylight logic ever apply to dreams or nightmares? Lastly, there is the binary opposition of stillness/motion that pervades the scene, beginning with the obvious figure of the father. Mita in effect seems paralyzed, basically stopping in his tracks at the door and risking only a step or two, if that; Omitsu's few movements—descending the stairs and picking up a chick—have the feel of slow motion, until she, too, finally becomes still. Only the chicks move about, freely, aimlessly, in some kind of mock vigil, their chirping and the ominous music throughout the scene creating a most unsettling effect.

The above scene notwithstanding, *An Inn at Osaka* is not all darkness and tragedy. On the contrary, it occasionally relies on light comedy, which borders on slapstick and makes free use of caricature, satire, and even physical gags. It does so to arouse laughter at the expense of human folly and pretentiousness. Some of this comedy, however, has a markedly pungent edge to it—especially when the characters are self-centered or cruel.

In this regard, there is little to say about one such character, Mita's boss, except that he is an unconscionable lackey and the least sympathetic, developed, or interesting of Gosho's principal satiric targets. The other two targets, to paraphrase Renoir, at least have their reasons: Noro, the inn's resident fop and would-be Lothario, and the penny-pinching innkeeper.[26] Noro, in addition to rivaling Mita's boss as a company lackey, is given to skulking in the hallway to snoop on Mita's activities (he is especially interested in Mita and Uwabami's relationship). The innkeeper, on the other hand, is an admittedly more complicated character, but no less worthy of comic exposure. Her occasional efforts at kindness and consideration, for one thing, are so patently transparent as to be comic and painful at the same time. In one of the film's funniest moments, she is exposed entirely. Here she is complaining to Otsugi about the racket Uwabami is making in Mita's room during a party. Commenting that she never behaved like Uwabami when she was a geisha, she points to a photo of herself in full geisha dress mounted on the wall. In an inspired comic touch, Gosho cuts to the picture, and there is the innkeeper, the most matronly looking geisha imaginable. Then, in a perfectly timed reaction shot, Gosho cuts back to Otsugi's underplayed but devastating assessment. To put it mildly, she is not impressed. One is almost tempted to feel for the innkeeper, given her lack of self-awareness, but her other less-endearing qualities make this difficult to do. By contrast, Noro, smarmy as he may be, at least has enough self-awareness to know that he is considered the office joke. This goes a long way toward explaining his pomposity and pretentiousness, not to mention his need to give the impression that he and Uwabami have been lovers (a lie for which she punishes him).

In fact, although Uwabami is one of the film's most complex and sentient characters, she also is the one who brings the most welcome, uncomplicated comedy to the film. Her refusal to put up with sham, unkindness, and pretension of any kind leads her to dispense quick and ready justice to those characters most deserving. She dumps sake on them. And the characters most deserving are Noro and Mita's boss. In the long run, of course, nothing is changed, but the punishment is still gratifying for both her and the audience, since in the world justice too often is blind. The scenes in which Uwabami finds this novel way to serve sake, however, are never characterized simply by one mood: the comedy invariably is blended with drama. Indeed, what gives *An Inn at Osaka* much of its originality, power, and poignance—and makes it so true to life—are the sudden shifts in mood within the same scene or sequence.

Consider, for example, the sequence in which Mita and Uwabami reach an understanding concerning their relationship. Made up of six scenes, the first five cut back and forth between Mita's and Noro's rooms at the inn, and have to do with the "triangle" involving Uwabami and the two men. In the opening scene, Mita sits at his desk doing translation work (which brings in extra money), when Uwabami barges in. He greets her by remarking that she is sober for a change. This immediately sets the tone of their exchange. She pulls out a bottle, plops it down on his desk, and taunts him with the fact that he loves a woman he does even not know. Taken aback, he counters by saying that Noro told him he met Uwabami in a geisha house—the word "met" obviously being a euphemism. Whether Mita is upset by the unmistakable implications of this supposed meeting because he disapproves of her behavior or because he harbors romantic feelings for her is impossible to tell. Nevertheless, an unperturbed Uwabami heads straight for Noro's room to check out if she ever met the man. In scene two she quickly discovers Noro has been spreading lies. "Does your name mean 'stupid'?" she asks at one point, while agreeing to have a drink. Unable to leave well enough alone, Noro insults her by suggesting that she and Mita are sleeping together. Gosho ends the scene with a close-up of Uwabami pouring Noro a big, tall glass of sake. Scene three cuts back to Mita's room, where he remains at his desk, presumably at work on his translation (or at least pretending to be), while in the background, sounds of shouting, crashing, and banging can be heard from Noro's room next door. Scene four consists of a single shot of Noro and Oyone frantically trying to clean up the havoc Uwabami has wreaked. In scene five, Uwabami returns to Mita's room, which puts an immediate end to the mood of slapstick comedy. Mita remains seated at his desk, his back turned to her. Sitting in the middle of the room, she can feel his icy disapproval. "Am I bothering you?" she asks, in close-up. Gosho cuts to a shot of Mita from her point of view: he does not answer. Then Gosho cuts back to her. This time her close-up is far more tight and extreme than the previous one. "I see," she says, and, gathering up her belongings, she leaves. Only rarely does Gosho use such extreme close-ups. But when he does, his purpose is unmistakable. He means not only to privilege a character's thought or state of mind but also to make viewers feel discomfort, for there is absolutely no distance between them and the character, and no escape from that character's pain.

The mood changes once again in the sixth and final scene of the sequence. Mita rushes after Uwabami, she tells him to leave her alone, and in the one vaguely comic moment, he points out that she lives in the opposite direction. Soon they are walking along the riverbank together, the lights of the tall buildings across the way creating shimmering reflections in the water. The effect is almost romantic, but once again any possibility of lyricism is denied by cutaway images (debris floating down the river, a homeless man nearby trying to keep warm) and by Uwabami's unusual gravity and candor. She confides to Mita that she realizes that she lives a degrading existence. "A geisha's life is pretty well decided," she says bitterly. "It's a worthless life. Get old and die and get thrown out." Baring her soul, she tells him that she wonders why she ever became a geisha in the first place and why she worked so hard; she also tells him about her out-of-work younger brother to whom she sends money each month. "What would happen if I quit?" she asks, half-challenging Mita. "You don't answer." Re-

Uwabami (Otowa Nobuko) realizes that she and Mita can never be more than friends. *An Inn at Osaka* (1954).

alizing what she is really asking, he can only reply, "I like you, but our lives are different." She then says ruefully that she thought their lives were the same, and, of course, she is right. But either he does not see what she means or refuses to understand. Either way, she now knows that she and Mita can never be more than friends. True to character, she also casts off her dark mood, and assumes at least a surface gaiety. A few minutes later, she rushes off, leaving Mita alone with his thoughts.

It is impossible to watch this scene without feeling the pathos of Uwabami's situation—a pathos that is made all the more affecting by her refusal to dwell on grief. As for the sequence itself, suffice it to say that its understatement, its shifts in mood between drama and comedy, and its final resolution in pathos could only be the work of one director.

Pathos, of course, is one of the cornerstones of Gosho's art. For him, as for many Japanese, it assumes special significance. According to literary scholar Makoto Ueda, "The Japanese, when they pursued the truths of life to their ultimate, arrived at pathos."[27] Foremost among these truths was that humankind led "a pitiful existence, bound by passions, measured by time."[28] Ueda goes on to say that "the Japanese single out pathos from all similar emotions. Pathos is not grief, sadness, misery or despair; it is gentler, calmer, more passive and refined."[29] This is certainly borne out in classical Japanese cinema, Gosho's films being no exception.

Pathos, however, can sometimes slip into sentimentality. In *An Inn at Osaka* this almost happens in the series of three scenes involving Otsugi and the innkeeper. In the first scene, during the search for Noro's missing money, Otsugi is forced to display her few meager possessions, including the toy microscope she has bought for her son and which someday she hopes to give him in person. In the second scene, Otsugi shows the innkeeper her son's drawing of a cow as a prelude to asking for time off to visit him. And in the third scene, the innkeeper tries to make amends for refusing Otsugi's request and being cruel, only to end up being even crueler. Anderson and Richie provide an astute analysis of how these scenes manage to avoid "the final plunge" into sentimentality.[30] However, they mistake the order of the scenes, confusing the first scene with the third and most important one. Fortunately, this does not affect their fundamental point: that the "conflict of emotion" that links the three scenes prevents sentimentality and ensures emotional validity.[31] To make Anderson and Richie's point unequivocally clear, let us assume that the third and final scene of the series is scene two, that is, the one in which Otsugi's request for time off is cruelly refused. Here Otsugi has virtually begged and groveled and used her son's drawing to eke out any pity the innkeeper has for her. If this scene had concluded the series, the result almost certainly would have been sentimentality. (Whether this sentimentality is excessive, unjustified, or even necessarily a bad thing is of course an entirely different matter.) The series, however, does not end with this scene. Nor does Otsugi simply take the innkeeper's abuse lying down. On the contrary, she unleashes pent-up fury, and for once refuses to play the victim. The viewer cannot help but realize that she does so at her peril. But to what extent does Otsugi realize the same? More to the point, does she really have a choice between standing up for herself and risking the chance—however unlikely—of getting time off in the future to see her son? It is this "conflict of emotion" that ultimately makes this series of three scenes an example of pathos rather than sentimentality.

However that may be, in its most intense and heartbreaking scene *An Inn at Osaka* goes far beyond pathos and sentimentality and reaches the level of tragedy. In this scene Orika takes money from Mita's wallet, but cannot go through with the act. Trying to return the money, she is caught. Consisting of twenty shots in three minutes, this scene is the emotional and thematic center of the film. In it, Mita is brought irrevocably face-to-face with bitter reality, learning in the most painful and personal way imaginable what the desperate need for money can drive people to do. Mita, however, is not really the focus of the scene. Rather, it is Orika who is the focus, as both victim and victimizer. Indeed, in this scene both Mita and the viewers are made to experience not only Orika's self-debasement, but also to feel that this basically good woman has hit rock bottom. In betraying Mita's friendship, she has betrayed herself as well—all the while forcing herself to do something she clearly abhors. In psychological terms, the power of the scene derives from the agonizing struggle Orika has with her conscience, the revulsion she feels toward the act she is contemplating, and the unbearable sense of shame she suffers after committing the act. Gosho and actress Mito Mitsuko communicate this struggle with such feeling and understanding that it has a lasting, lacerating power. No less remarkable is Gosho's use of sound, camera, and signature piecemeal editing.

Let us examine this scene in detail. Orika's struggle begins with shot three, a two-second close-up of Mita's wallet and several coins lying on his desk. In shot four, a seven-second medium shot, Orika looks at the wallet, clutches nervously at her kimono, then forces herself to turn away. For the moment she has escaped temptation. Shot five is like a pause in a line of music. Fifteen seconds long, it temporarily puts the dramatic action on hold. Here Orika moves away from Mita's desk (at the far left of the frame) and crosses all the way to the right, exiting the frame. Gosho does not follow her, but instead keeps the camera fixed in position at a 90-degree angle on the now empty room. In suspension, we wait for something to happen. We do not wait long. Off-screen sounds indicate that Orika is still in the room; they also imply that she is still thinking, still struggling. When she re-enters screen space, she crosses to the far left, situates herself close to the desk, and tries to concentrate on preparing Mita's tea. But she cannot stop herself from looking in the direction of the wallet, as shot six, a two-second close-up, shows. For all practical purposes, shots seven and eight are the moment of decision. Ten seconds long, shot seven is an extreme close-up that charts Orika's every microgesture, as she looks at the wallet, turns away, then looks again. Even more tightly framed than the extreme close-up of Uwabami, which we discussed earlier, this shot is held for what seems an excruciatingly long duration. Like Uwabami's close-up, it simultaneously creates audience discomfort and empathy, there being no escape from the look of agonized intensity—nay, sheer terror—on Orika's face. In shot eight, which lasts two seconds, she glances towards the open doorway to see if it is safe to make her move. In shot nine, in a marvelous act of self-delusion, she pretends that she is only tidying up Mita's desk, nothing more. But her nerves understandably get the better of her, and she knocks over a glass. Throwing caution to the wind, she snatches up the wallet and rips it open (twelve seconds). In shot ten, she quickly grabs a bill (three seconds).

Mita catches Orika (Mito Mitsuko) stealing from him. *An Inn at Osaka* (1954).

Having stolen the money, Orika hurriedly rises in shot eleven to flee from the room (five seconds). But in her haste, she slips and falls, landing on her bottom. For a split second, we are plunged into black comedy, or so it would seem, but there is no temptation to laugh, for the fall is so patently real (and so patently *not* like a stunt) that we can only gasp, taken as we are by surprise. It is an astonishing moment, this accident that seems an unconscious act of self-punishment. Scrambling to her feet, Orika gets no further than the door. There, in shot twelve, she stops in her tracks, looks at the crumpled bill in her hand, and rushes back to the desk (six seconds). In shot thirteen she frantically tries to straighten out the bill before putting it back in Mita's wallet, but from off-screen Mita calls her name. She lets the bill drop and freezes in place (twelve seconds).

As the above description makes clear, Gosho's editing and shot duration impart a nervous, jagged intensity to the scene. While the shots of two and three seconds in particular convey Orika's overwhelming sense of panic and urgency, the longer shots deal with process, the various steps and stages of her actual behavior. Working in concert with the visuals is Gosho's expressive use of sound. Unlike the first two shots of the scene, which focus on Mita and are accompanied by natural sound, shots three through seven, which center on Orika, are silent except for the brief instance of off-screen sounds in shot five. Interestingly, Orika's extreme close-up in shot seven also begins silently, but after a few seconds, the sounds of boats making their way along the canal insinuate themselves into the shot as a muffled, monotonous rhythm. These sounds—which drone on without any hint of resolving—add yet another layer to the subjective feel of the shot, conveying not only Orika's state of mind but also the relentless insistence of her thoughts. These sounds continue until shot thirteen, when Mita catches Orika in the act. Apropos of this shift in dramatic emphasis, the boat sounds give way to Ikuma Dan's pulsating musical score, which carries over into the next scene.

Thematically, what gives the scene tragic intensity is the dissolution of human bonds, the violation of trust, and the achingly painful self-betrayal. To be sure, there is pathos. How can there not be? For we not only feel for Orika, we share her feelings as well. But the scene does not ask merely for our pity or sympathy. It elicits rather more complex and ever-shifting responses. At first we hope against hope that she will resist temptation; when she does not, we fear for her and do not want her to be caught. Fully aware of the wrong she is doing, we also understand what has brought her to it. If our relationship to Orika is one of involvement and detachment, it is much the same with Mita. In fact, split as we are between these two characters, we occupy a double position in the scene, one that ensures more than simply a "conflict of emotion." Indeed, Anderson and Richie touch on this double position when they point out that beyond the destructive effect of money is "the austere law which slaughters the innocents and which orders Gosho's universe."[32] It is this "austere law" which underpins the scene, determining the shared mood of anguished intensity and melancholy and finally giving the scene tragic implications that go beyond the individual suffering of Orika or Mita. Put simply, in the scene we experience this austere law as terrible waste, the cruel indifference of a materialistic society to the individual—indeed, to its own soul. What deepens both the poignance and tragic implications of the scene is that only a few people seem to care or understand. Mita is one of these people. Indeed, he forgives Orika, giving her the money she could not bring herself to steal. "Take it," he says, without anger. But she cannot. In the penultimate shot, which at twenty-five seconds is the longest in the scene, the two characters remain in the same frame, but are turned away from each other, each trapped in the terrible solitude that has come to define their reality. What has happened is too sad for words. In the closing shot (fifteen seconds), Mita sits at his desk, alone in the room. Tears fill his eyes, and he laments: "Money. Nothing but money. Where did humanity go?" It is an urgent, harrowing question that

Mita's lament: "Where did humanity go?" *An Inn at Osaka* (1954).

cries out for an answer. With that question, the film's darkest scene comes
to a close.

A SENSE OF RELEASE,
A FEELING OF HOPE

While acknowledging darkness and tragedy, *An Inn at Osaka* does not yield
to it. Nor do the six characters who come together at the farewell dinner
party—Mita, Otsugi, Orika, Tawara, Uwabami, and the innkeeper's
brother. Here the mood of laughter through tears reasserts itself in the film,
as these friends celebrate the special bond they share. As the innkeeper's
brother says, "Only when we are close can we trust." And as Mita points
out, "As long as we can laugh at our sorrows, we have the strength and
courage to build a new future." The occasion is a time for laughter as they
reminisce, enjoy good food and drink, and find strength in each other's
company. But the occasion is also a time for tears, and is bittersweet at best,
for they also know that it is a farewell, an end. Thus, at one point Uwabami
excuses herself from the festivities, overcome with the realization that this is
the last time she will ever see Mita. When she returns, she joins the others
in song. "What can we do," the lyrics go, "since we cannot control all things
in life?" Yet the characters sing so loudly and passionately that the song

somehow gives a sense of release, and with that release a feeling of hope. To be sure, the characters' circumstances remain much the same, but typical of Gosho, their "outlook has changed and there is even room for optimism."[33] Still, we cannot know for sure what lies ahead for any of the characters. Indeed, throughout the scene Gosho cuts to the unoccupied place set for Omitsu to remind us of that fact. We especially wonder about Mita. Will he find a better life in Tokyo? Will his renewed commitment to social justice find more fertile soil there? Gosho, of course, offers no answers. But that does not matter, for in the end *An Inn at Osaka* has done its job: it has touched and moved us, and prompted us to thought. An extraordinary film, it neither flinches from difficult truths nor fabricates a roseate picture of the way things are. Instead, it sees life as it is, and, like its characters, embraces life wholeheartedly. It is this quality that makes the film much more than a depiction of Japanese society in the early 1950s.

SEVEN

Growing Up *(1955):*
Adapting the Meiji-mono,
Reconfiguring the Shomin-geki

The closing scene of *Takekurabe* (*Growing Up,* 1955), Gosho's adaptation of Higuchi Ichiyo's classic novella of doomed adolescent love, is justly famous. In it, Midori, a thirteen-year-old girl about to begin her life as a prostitute, pauses in her journey to take one last look at the iris blossom she holds in her hand. Left at her doorstep by the boy she loves, the flower declares the love he has been too shy to speak. But now it is too late. Their lives have taken different paths, and they will never see each other again. Realizing that the innocent days of childhood are over, Midori tosses the iris blossom aside, and continues on her way.

It is not hard to imagine what drew Gosho to Ichiyo's tale. Its story of star-crossed young love recalls other of his films, most notably *Dancing Girl of Izu* (1933); its affectionate depiction of the lives and customs of common people is congruent with his own *shomin-geki;* and its sympathy for the plight of women mirrors his lifelong preoccupation with the theme. In discussing the film, Gosho has this to say:

> The feelings about poor people that are found in *Takekurabe* are also communicated in *Osaka no yado* [*An Inn at Osaka*]. Naturally, the period in which *Takekurabe* is set [the Meiji period] stands out as old times where the position of women is still low, but Ichiyo subtly conveys a strong desire for liberation of women in this period. The screenplay [by Yasumi Toshio] emphasizes these two themes. My aim was to communicate to the audience the love of the author for common people and her desire for the liberation of women.[1]

One of Gosho's rare period pieces, *Growing Up* is an outstanding example of the *Meiji-mono,* films set in the Meiji period (1868–1912). A popular subgenre of the 1930s which reemerged in the early 1950s, the *Meiji-*

mono, like its progenitor, the postwar *jidai-geki* (period film), allowed audiences to escape into a more assuring and less complicated past. No matter that precious few films in this subgenre were actually "nostalgic," except perhaps in their loving evocation of period atmosphere. Mostly, the *Meiji-mono* afforded Gosho and other directors the opportunity to engage in the discourse of the day, using the far-from-utopian past to point out that certain things in postwar Japanese society had not really changed all that much. This discourse centered on a number of nagging social and political issues: Japan's "single-minded pursuit of economic growth,"[2] her rampant material consumption, her mixed feelings about having her fate tied to America,[3] and her still unanswered need to create new life-spaces for women, which would free them from centuries-old binding to the family.[4] Underlying these issues was the sense that newly gained freedoms during the Occupation had not translated into real individualism, genuine liberation, or participatory democracy.[5] Not surprisingly, many Japanese saw strong parallels with the Meiji restoration, which promised social change, but failed to deliver.[6] The *Meiji-mono* tapped into this atmosphere of frustration and anxiety. It underscored the fact that although personal freedom was less subject to the severe limitations of the Meiji period, Japan was still a highly controlled society.[7] While seminal films like Imai Tadashi's *Nigorie* (*Muddy Waters,* 1953) and Toyoda Shiro's *Gan* (*Wild Geese,* a.k.a. *The Mistress,* 1953) dealt specifically with the struggle of women against confinement, they also had broader relevance, for no one was exempt from "the pressure to conform to expectations."[8] *Muddy Waters* in particular may have been of special interest to Gosho. The winner of the *Kinema Jumpo* "Best One" in 1953—over the formidable competition of *Tokyo Story, Ugetsu,* and Gosho's *Where Chimneys Are Seen*—this highly regarded critical and commercial success was based on three stories by none other than Ichiyo. Was it Imai's film that recommended Ichiyo to Gosho? Perhaps so. In any event, Gosho certainly knew that *Growing Up* was one of the enduring masterworks of Japanese literature. And no doubt he was also quick to realize that Ichiyo's novella afforded him the chance not only to combine his interest in literature with his interest in the *Meiji-mono,* but also to continue his reconfiguring of the *shomin-geki.*

Set in Yoshiwara, the licensed quarter of Tokyo in 1895, Ichiyo's novella has to do with the changing relationships of five youngsters over a span of four or five months: Midori, whose sister is the most popular prostitute of the quarter; Shinnyo, the son of a Buddhist priest, on whom Midori has a crush; Sangoro, the son of a poor rickshaw driver, who finds himself caught between two neighborhood gangs; and the rival leaders of the gangs, Chokichi, a fireman's son, and Shotaro, heir to a pawnshop. Although still children, these characters "are poised on the edge of adulthood, when they will perforce lose their spontaneity and their lives take their preordained courses."⁹ Of these characters, Midori, a winsome, extroverted girl, compels the reader's greatest attention. Leading a life of ignorant bliss, she fills her days attending school, playing games with her girlfriends, visiting her famous sister, and engaging in an on-again, off-again flirtation with Shinnyo, who is unable to deal with his feelings. At first the only discordant notes in Midori's world are the insults and injuries she suffers at the hands of Chokichi and his gang, a situation she finds even more intolerable since she mistakenly believes that Shinnyo is part of the gang. Only gradually does she become aware of her destiny and come to accept it. Forced into prostitution, she bids farewell to all of her dreams.

Gosho's seventy-ninth film, *Growing Up* was an independent production made on a tight budget, and released by Shin Toho, which was itself experiencing financial trouble. Not having the backing of a major studio, Gosho was faced with a number of difficulties.¹⁰ Without a property department to fall back on, he could not, for instance, render the look of a Meiji home with appropriate period decor. Budgetary constraints also prevented him from hiring enough extras to recreate the color and vivacity of the Yoshiwara quarter. In the view of prominent Gosho scholar Mizutani Kenji, the film was therefore unable to describe the ambiance adequately.¹¹ Few viewers, however, are likely to find the film deficient in atmosphere or production values, for Gosho has more than compensated for the limitations he experienced. For one thing, he was unusually attentive to *mise-en-scène*. As Anderson and Richie have explained, he personally visited fifty temples while working with art director Kubo Kazuo on the one used in the film.¹² Moreover, "during one of the scenes it is said that he himself polished the wooden floor until it acquired precisely the sheen that he felt was needed."¹³ One disappointment he expressly noted was that he was unable to use as many long shots as he would have liked because of the restrictions of space—indeed, the set was built beside a high school in Kyoto. Even so, he had other resources. Assisted by his longtime collaborator, cinematographer Ohara Joji, he used lighting to render depth and chiaroscuro, even spraying a reconstructed corridor to give it a darker, more "period" look.¹⁴ Always the perfectionist, Gosho worked just as assiduously on every other aspect of the film as well, for he realized that capturing the Meiji period involved more than reproducing pictorial elements; it required nothing less than achieving psychological density, creating the period, as it were, from inside out.

Upon its release, *Growing Up* was unjustly criticized by some as being less interested in presenting a cinematic version of Ichiyo's original than in

Young lovers Midori (Misora Hibari) and Shinnyo (Kitahara Takashi), and the cherry blossom episode. *Growing Up* (1955).

promoting the acting career of Misora Hibari, one of Japan's all-time popular singers.[15] Not surprisingly, these same critics had few kind words for Misora's performance. In fact, she makes a touching, thoroughly credible Midori. The film was also faulted for being "overliterary."[16] To be sure, Gosho and scenarist Yasumi Toshio took pains to retain the essence of Ichiyo's novella, but they also made radical changes.[17] For one thing, Midori and Shinnyo's platonic love is no longer the central focus, but serves as a point of departure, enabling Gosho to interweave the love story with the stories of three other women. This was the structural pattern that Gosho and Yasumi employed to powerful effect in *An Inn at Osaka* so as to counterpoint the lives of its major women characters and to explore themes that held particular relevance in 1950s Japan: money as the sole arbiter of value and worth, the still-lowly status of women, the contradictions inherent in social views and practice, the stripping away of humanity. Thus regarded, *An Inn at Osaka* and *Growing Up* emerge as companion pieces.

While the Midori-Shinnyo story is not the film's sole focus, it suffers no diminution of power. On the contrary, it is enriched by the addition of new incidents and the fleshing out of others that are only sketched in or alluded to in the original. As an example of the latter, consider the scene in which Midori asks Shinnyo (Kitahara Takashi) to pick her a cherry blossom that is on a branch out of her reach. In the novella, not wanting to look foolish in front of his friends, he simply reaches for the nearest branch and tosses the torn-off flower coldly at her. In the film, with his friends nowhere in sight, he is much more gallant, leaping to grab the branch and flower, but falling and scraping his hand in the process. Only when Midori tries to tend the wound does he get flustered and hurl the flower to the ground. Unlike Shinnyo's character in the novella, who does "his best to feign indifference" toward her,[18] in the film Shinnyo even greets her with a smile. In the end he may turn rude, but he is not shackled by the opinions of others, nor does he come across as the weakling Ichiyo describes. He simply is confused by his feelings. Moreover, as we shall see, the film actually deepens Shinnyo's character.

Like this scene, the new incidents that Gosho and Yasumi create by and large expound on the somewhat comic, somewhat painful misunderstandings that characterize Midori and Shinnyo's relationship. In one such incident, no sooner do the two make up after the rift described above than Midori asks, "Shall we be friends?" Suddenly embarrassed, Shinnyo sharply replies, "No." Angry and hurt, Midori storms off and returns home, promptly flinging the cherry blossom he gave her to the floor. In these moments, we are very much on familiar ground in Gosho's world. We laugh because we understand the vagaries of young love perfectly, but we also are touched because we recognize that the couple's mixture of innocence and awkwardness will be replaced in adulthood by experience. Equally touching is a short scene that has no counterpart in the novella. In it, Midori appears outside the temple where Shinnyo lives in the hope of catching a glimpse of him. It is a gesture that betrays her continuing affection for him, in spite of what seems to be his cruel and perplexing behavior. The scene is also indicative of the film's deepening tone of sadness and melancholy, which ultimately leaves no room for laughter.

Where Gosho's film radically departs from Ichiyo's original story, however, is in the depiction of three women characters barely mentioned in the story. Caught in the same trap as Midori, and providing vivid counterpoint to her, these women constitute three generations of feminine tragedy: Omaki (Kishi Keiko), Midori's sister, who is at the height of her career as an *oiran* (prostitute);[19] Ohana (Ichinomiya Atsuko), Shinnyo's half-sister, who has been sold into concubinage; and Okichi (Isuzu Yamada), an aging, once-famous prostitute, who now manages a small shop, takes in sewing, and lives in the past. As might be expected, the filmmakers found the germ of their characters in the novella. Omaki, for example, is clearly inspired by the following line: "Midori knew nothing of Omaki's sorrows and struggles."[20] Omaki's three scenes in the film poignantly dramatize these sorrows and struggles, but they also delineate her compassionate nature and love for Midori, whom she tries to warn about the sordid reality of an *oiran*'s life. Thus, in her last, brief appearance in the film, Omaki reads the announcement of Midori's first "appearance" in the bordello, then turns away sadly.

Of the three women contrasted with Midori, Ohana is the most thinly developed; even so, her plight is no less moving or harrowing than that of the others. In the novella, her money-hungry father uses her as bait behind the counter of his shop to attract young male customers and drum up business. Gosho and Yasumi give her a more painful fate. Virtually reduced to silence, in her first scene she dares speak only one word as she tearfully pleads not to be sold: "Father." But her plea falls on deaf ears. Only Shinnyo comes to her defense, but in vain. "To be a woman is sad," she tells him in a subsequent scene, and so it is for her and for Midori, whom she sees as equally unfortunate. In an even later scene, desperately unhappy, she returns home, having fled from her master and his abusive wife. She begs her father to take her in, but he adamantly refuses. He even personally returns her to her owner. Thus, in the end Ohana's story is not only a study of female oppression but also a condemnation of the patriarchal family system.

Without question, Gosho and Yasumi are at their most inspired in the creation of Okichi, the debauched ex-prostitute who has seen better days and now sees only too clearly Midori's future. Indeed, the film achieves a mood of tragedy,[21] thanks in no small part to Yamada Isuzu's fearsome, intense performance and the harsh, unsentimental portrayal of Okichi's character and her chilling vision of life. Barely mentioned in the original, and left nameless, Okichi probably was suggested by a brief passage that refers to a shopkeeper's wife who once had "a professional name in a cheap house."[22] This passage also notes that "something in her manner tells of her past, and she is a great influence on all of the children."[23] In the film, Okichi is unmarried. However, as said earlier, she runs a small shop. She also has worked as a prostitute (in the most famous brothel of the quarter) and has a decided, if somewhat ambiguous, influence on Midori and her friends. In fact, the importance of Okichi's character is such that she receives nearly as much screen time as Midori.

To this list of three women, we may add a fourth: Shinnyo's mother (Shinobu Setsuko). Overlooked in past discussions, she is neither a prostitute nor a concubine; nonetheless, her circumstance has its own special brand of pain and suffering. Not only is she a second wife, she also has been elevated above her class through marriage, a privilege that comes at a price: living in a state of perpetual insecurity. Having even less power than women who marry within their class, she dares not challenge her husband (Sasaki Takamaru), except in the most meek and innocuous manner. She certainly cannot plead for Ohana. Thus, she earns Shinnyo's scorn. "You don't care about her because she's not your daughter," he says at one point. In truth, she is caught in the middle as her family unravels. The film may not provide the background to her character that Ichiyo supplies, but it makes clear that the life of impotence and subordination she leads is yet another form of female servitude.[24]

What these four women have in common, and what Midori gradually comes to acquire, is an unblinkered knowledge of the world. It is a world that is vividly encapsulated in the film's major setting: a narrow street dotted with shops and tenement houses, behind which looms an elegant, three-storied brothel. We will see this setting throughout the film, never more dramatically than in the opening and closing shots. Bookending the drama, these shots prompt us to view the lives before us as part of an inevitable, ongoing cycle. The opening four shots set the scene. Bordering the street, along the left side of the frame is a high wood fence and a muddy moat. Over the moat, a drawbridge, wide enough to accommodate only one person at a time, provides the sole shortcut to the other side. In the first three shots, it is evening, the time when the brothel comes to life, when it is lit up with seemingly hundreds of lights. On the balustrade we see kimono-clad beauties. Some are chatting; others watch expectantly as rickshaws arrive, promising a bustling trade. "It is a long way around to the gates of Yoshiwara," a voiceover narration announces. "And what stories this licensed quarter could tell!" The narration is in a woman's voice, suggesting Ichiyo herself, or possibly an *oiran* from the past. Either way, it is a knowing voice, a voice of experience, and it immediately piques our interest. Indeed, the phrase "what stories this licensed quarter could tell" holds out the promise of a certain salaciousness, but that promise is quickly dispelled in the fourth and final shot, a dissolve to morning. Neither the view (the brothel) nor Gosho's camera position (a slightly low angle looking up) has changed from the previous shots, but now in the dull grayness of daylight, the glamour of the past night has all but faded. A date appears on the screen: 1895. We then notice the clock on the brothel's tallest tower, which gives the building a mundane, even ironic function, as if it were the town hall or some other official building. And in a way it is, for the brothel is indeed the most important establishment in the district. Certainly, there is no way to avoid it or overlook its presence. It dominates the view in much the same way that the chimneys in *Where Chimneys Are Seen* dominate Tokyo. As such, it is as much a part of the consciousness of the people in the quarter as the air they breathe.[25]

In fact, this elegant brothel is a site of cultural contradictions. Located in the Daionji district, which was named after a Buddhist temple, the brothel is the most concrete manifestation of what society worships, where love is bought and sold in the pursuit of pleasure or money. In a society where success commands respect, the brothel cannot fail to be respected. Indeed, it becomes an *idée fixe,* seemingly the only thing in life that matters for families like Midori's and Shinnyo's, who barter away their daughters' beauty for "advancement." It is in this sense that Ichiyo can say, with mordant irony, that "there are times when daughters are more valuable than sons."[26]

For Midori, who at first has no inkling of these cultural contradictions, the benefits she receives from her sister's prostitution are impressive, indeed: a comfortable life, plenty of money, nice clothes, agreeable girlfriends, a certain status, and, at least on the surface, respect. Power and prestige are hers, but they are wholly dependent on those who have invested in her future (her parents and master) and those who curry favor for material gain (nearly everyone else). Midori's charmed life is belied by an even more disturbing contradiction. As Ian Buruma cannily points out, prostitutes were the superstars of their day, but they were also at the bottom of society.[27] If Midori fails to understand this, others do not. Hence her treatment at the hands of Chokichi (Hattori Tetsu) and his gang, who hold exactly the same views as the adult world, the only difference being that they have no use for pretense or surface politeness. They are crass, upfront, and cruel. Early in the film, when Midori tries to defend Sangoro (Nakamura Masanori), they lob her with insults, declaring that her money, even her kimono, comes from whoring. In a later scene, their violence against her escalates. Once again, she tries to protect Sangoro. Enraged, Chokichi calls her a whore outright, then hurls his dirty sandal at her, striking her in the face. He will allow no one to defy him or threaten his power, especially the likes of Midori. And in protecting Sangoro, whom he sees as a turncoat and surrogate for Shotaro (Ichikawa Somegoro), his chief rival, Midori is doing just that. Ironically, Sangoro basically shares the world's view of her. As he tells his mother (Mochizuki Yuko), when he is rich, he plans to sample Midori's favors at the brothel. His mother promptly scolds him; nevertheless, his remark suggests the extent of society's inner sundering, the schism that exists between family members, rich and poor, adults and children, male and female, and even friends. In the denouement of the film, before Midori leaves for the brothel, she and Sangoro visit for the last time. "Why must we grow up?" she asks. Baffled by her strange mood, he replies, "I'm looking forward to growing up." He is unable to recognize the desperation she feels, for as a male, even one living in poverty, he has at least a remote possibility to better himself. This possibility does not exist for Midori. For her, "growing up" is spiritual suffocation, a living death.[28]

In Midori's society, power is all. For Chokichi and his gang, power means holding on to their turf through muscle and might. For the adult world, where the stakes are vastly higher, power is money pure and simple. As is well known, Japanese cinema of the 1950s was preoccupied with the uncertainty and greed of the times and the resultant stripping away of humanity. This was a major theme for Naruse in films like *Bangiku* (*Late Chrysanthemums,* 1954); it was no less of a concern for Gosho. Indeed, in *Growing Up,* Gosho picks up where he left off in *An Inn at Osaka.* In that film Mita, the one character who tried to make a difference in people's lives, asked an angry question: "Money. Nothing but money. Where did humanity go?" In *Growing Up* it is Shinnyo who in effect asks that question. Like Mita, he is sensitive, idealistic, and principled, but there the comparison ends, for Shinnyo is only a boy and therefore powerless. Earlier I mentioned that Gosho's film deepens Shinnyo's character. It does so by expanding his role, making him a central figure not just in the love story but also in the subplot involving his sister. And it gives him a strength and integrity that makes him not only admirable but eminently sympathetic. Indeed, he is the only character in the film who expresses outrage at the obsession with money—something that not even the victimized women themselves do. But unable to change his father's mind or his sister's fate, he abandons the world and enters the priesthood. In the end he is defeated; even so, he has served his purpose. As the conscience of the film, he has provided Gosho with a means to stir viewers to rediscover their own consciences,[29] a concern Gosho embraced with renewed vigor and commitment in the postwar period, beginning with *Once More.* In fact, in showing that everyone but Shinnyo accepts things as they are, *Growing Up* offers an even more trenchant portrait of the ways of the world and the all-consuming drive for money.

Consider, for example, Shotaro and his aunt (Mori Kikue). Debt collectors, they have more money than most, but their determination to regain their position as pawnbrokers has hardened them. The aunt is so money-hungry, in fact, that people literally hide from her. "All that woman cares about is money. She'd kill herself for it," says one such person. Nor does much milk of human kindness flow in Shotaro's veins. Despised by Chokichi and his gang for being a smug rich boy, he is, in the words of Shinnyo, "hard on poor people." Hence the scene in which he comes to Sangoro's house to collect. Unable to pay, Sangoro's mother grovels before him. Only Sangoro's quick thinking buys his family some time. Knowing that Shotaro is interested in Midori, he remarks that she is at Okichi's store and offers to bring him to her. Taking the bait, Shotaro postpones collecting the debt until after the upcoming Otori festival—as gracious a gesture as business allows.

In *Growing Up* the power of money is announced in two back-to-back scenes that introduce Shinnyo and his family—scenes that also demonstrate Gosho's striking blend of piecemeal editing, long takes, and formal compositions. In the first scene, which consists of twelve shots in one-and-a-half minutes, Shinnyo confronts his mother about Ohana's fate. As the scene opens, he is alone in the garden, lost in thought, when his mother comes searching for him. Why does he not like to see his father? she wants to know. Evidently, she has been instructed to bring the boy to him. Shinnyo ignores her question and asks where his sister is going, although he already knows. Uncomfortable, his mother explains, "It's your father's idea," to which he replies, "Why do we have to have money?" No doubt the question strikes her as a young boy's naiveté, yet she answers him. "Money is important even for a priest's family," she explains. Then, after trying to soothe his anxieties, she urges him to come to the house quickly. Gosho's visual style perfectly conveys the nature of the relationship between Shinnyo and his mother. Despite the wedge between them, there is love and affection. This is especially evident in shot three, a long take in which Shinnyo's mother comforts him by kneeling at his feet as they speak. Clearly, she understands his feelings about Ohana, and shares them. Perhaps deep down, she also shares his feelings about money. Even so, this is the closest that mother and son will ever be. By contrast, the gulf between them is underscored by seven shot/reaction shots. These shots not only foreground Shinnyo's pain and indignation and his mother's discomfort, but also foreshadow what is a certainty: that in the end she must side with her husband against her son. For this reason alone, the garden setting is ultimately ambiguous. It may be a place of solitude and escape for Shinnyo, and even rapprochement for him and his mother, but it is at best a temporary idyll, as the next scene makes clear.

Consisting of fifteen shots in two minutes and thirty-two seconds, this scene offers an even more pungent view of the effects of money on the family. Taking place inside the house, it finds Shinnyo, screen center, sitting alone in the background while his parents sit in the foreground in a fairly rigid, formal pattern—his mother on screen left, his father on screen right. The emotional distance between parents and son, as well as husband and wife, could not be made more apparent. Adding to this sense of emotional distance, Shinnyo keeps his back to his father for well over half of the scene. All the while, his father lectures him in an effort to impose his will. "Being a priest isn't only praying these days," he says, as he continues to examine his accounts. Recognizing this remark as justification for selling Ohana, Shinnyo turns around and faces him. A series of shot/reaction shots between Shinnyo, his mother, and his father follow. These shots not only underscore the undeniable tension in the air, but reveal each of the character's reactions: Shinnyo's perturbation, his father's intransigence, and his mother's sense of helplessness. The discussion at an impasse, Shinnyo's father sends him to check on a loan and to get him some eels on the way home, charging them to the temple. Eager to be excused, Shinnyo exits the room at the beginning of the scene's most unusual shot: a long take lasting sixty-two seconds. And while he remains off-screen for the duration of the shot, except for a few seconds at the end, he is the sole topic of conversation. Explaining that Shinnyo is upset about Ohana, his mother urges her husband not to be so hard on him. But Shinnyo's father digs in his heels. He insists that it will be an honor to have Ohana become a concubine and adds that it does not matter what Shinnyo thinks. Gosho's long take confers a Mizoguchi-like sense of observation on the scene, maintaining distance from the characters and giving them "breathing room." At the same time this camera strategy, which also has the power to implicate characters, does just that in the case of the father. His manifest lack of family feeling is thoroughly exposed. Indeed, he understands Shinnyo's feelings only too well, but is unwilling to acknowledge them. Instead he reasserts the rightness of his actions. "Things are the way they are," he declares in one of the closing shots, adding, "We have to worry about how to eat." To be sure, he has a point, but he is also a priest with a taste for the good life—hence he craves those eels but has no intention to pay for them. Furthermore, admitting he is wrong would require him to give up the very things he has been so desperately pursuing: money and reputation.

Money has an equally sad and insidious effect on Midori's family, which arguably is even more fragmented and devastated than Shinnyo's. Before the film opens, Midori's parents (Yoshikawa Mitsuko and Nakamura Zeko) have sold her and her sister, but they seem impervious to the consequence of this act. Or perhaps they have come to terms with it, thinking they have done the best for all concerned. Either way, Omaki no longer seems to be in their thoughts, and they appear far more interested in pleasing the brothel master (Yanagi Eijiro) than in considering Midori's feelings. Thus, without realizing it, they have turned their back on natural feeling. Midori comes to understand this, and in saying her good-bye before leaving for the brothel, she tells them to think of her as having died. She then thanks them for their kindness, and promises to pay back the money they have spent on her. These are searing, damning words, doubly so in that they are spoken without a trace of anger or recrimination. But then what good would anger or recrimination do? At this point Midori's parents are no freer to act than she is.

The tragedies that befall the families of Midori and Shinnyo signal a major development in Gosho's *shomin-geki* that began with *An Inn at*

Osaka. Strictly speaking, the *shomin-geki* has to do with contemporary Japanese life, but in *Growing Up,* Gosho looks at the past as if it were the present, as if he were actually filming a story about 1895 in that year. Hence, his emphasis is not on period reconstruction as such, but on bringing to the *Meiji-mono* the lived-in texture, the slice-of-life quality, that is germane to his *shomin-geki.* But how exactly do *Growing Up* and *An Inn at Osaka* constitute a new development in Gosho's *shomin-geki?* Put simply, they introduce into the genre a darker, more intense mood.

Central to the *shomin-geki* as a mode was the family. Even in surrogate form—for example, the inn in *An Inn at Osaka*—it represented society in miniature. (Indeed, the terms *shomin-geki* and "home drama" are often used interchangeably.) In Gosho's films of the 30s, like *Woman of the Mist,* the family was cherished as nurturing, understanding, and confident in its sense of purpose. Members looked out for one another, and the family prided itself on being part of a tightly knit community. In *Women of the Mist,* this particular community was the Shitamachi, which flourished before the war and was made up of merchants and tradespeople. In the early 50s, most notably in *Where Chimneys Are Seen,* Gosho's *shomin-geki* was predicated on the assumption that strength and perseverance could prevail over postwar anomie and hardship. In keeping with this view, the tenement building shared by the two principal couples and their neighbors became an updated variant of the Shitamachi idea. But the family, like other institutions, could not help but be affected by the shifting currents of the 50s—the ever-growing materialism, the uncertain Cold War climate, the changing role of women.[30] Indeed, with the notable exception of Ozu's films, the family could no longer be viewed in sanguine terms or stand firm as a bulwark of moral authority. *An Inn at Osaka* and *Growing Up* take into account these shifting currents, yet manage to preserve those elements that define Gosho's *shomin-geki:* unwavering compassion, pathos, and humor (even when the blend is nowhere near fifty-fifty). As always, Gosho's greatest sympathy goes to his women characters. But he also has a wonderful eye and a deep respect for manners and customs, and effortlessly captures the feel, pulse, and look of daily life in all its variety, from the mercurial passions of the street gangs to the carefully honed restraint of Omaki. Thus, even when he exposes the cruelty, greed, and failings of people, he never treats their lives as small or trivial, but as an irrefutable truth of the human condition.

In *Growing Up* the influence of the *shomin-geki* can also be seen in the narrative structure. Consider, for instance, the film's opening scenes. More descriptive than dramatic, they introduce us to the street gangs. As has been pointed out, these gangs have very specific roles to play in the narrative; they complicate Midori and Shinnyo's relationship and act out attitudes that society prefers to hide. Still, privileging these gangs in the opening scenes has the effect of delaying the central stories and this, in turn, lends the film immediate documentary flavor. In the fully realized, lived-in mi-lieu that Gosho is creating, these gangs are but the first in a rich panoply of characters who make up the Yoshiwara. And like other characters, they are primarily linked to a specific setting—in this case, the narrow, cluttered streets where they fight, provoke at will, and indulge in displays of bravado. Important as documentary realism is to Gosho, however, the drama proper begins with Shinnyo and his mother's conversation in the garden. As in *An Inn at Osaka* and other Gosho films of the 50s, narrative causality in *Growing Up* is tighter than it was in his 30s films. Even so, the film owes much to "Japan's traditional narrative means, the *suji* [which] emphasizes sequential flow, connection, association."[31] As such, it retains an episodic quality, even as the drama fixes on the individual stories of Omaki, Okichi, Midori, and Ohana and interweaves them. This, of course, was the same narrative strat-egy that enabled Gosho and Yasumi to commingle drama and slice-of-life reality so effectively in *An Inn at Osaka*. Here it is used with equal success.

This narrative strategy is aptly displayed in two of the film's most pow-erful sequences. The first sequence, which consists of five scenes and runs eight minutes and forty-two seconds, occurs in the first third of the film, during late summer, and is paradigmatic of the way that the four main women characters will be associated and connected throughout the story. Correspondingly, the narrative structure underscores a basic theme: that while these women share the same fate, they are alone and isolated in their individual struggle. In tracing out this theme, the first sequence establishes the stage that each woman is at *vis-à-vis* her life as a prostitute: Ohana is about to enter that life; Okichi is well past it; Omaki is at her peak; and Mi-dori remains ignorant that it is her destiny. Hence the following scenes:

1. As Ohana and Shinnyo look on silently, their father chooses material for Ohana's kimono in preparation for her new life. Later Ohana and Shin-nyo have a brief exchange, in which she states that nothing can be done to help her. (Two minutes, twenty seconds; seventeen shots.)
2. While Midori is visiting Omaki, Okichi talks candidly to her girlfriends about her fate. Shinnyo arrives with the material to be used for Ohana's kimono. (Two minutes, five seconds; seventeen shots.)
3. Midori visits Omaki. (Three minutes, four seconds; seventeen shots.)
4. Ohana and Shinnyo continue their discussion about her fate. (Fifty-two seconds; six shots.)
5. On her way back from visiting Omaki, Midori pauses at the front en-trance of the temple where Shinnyo lives. (Seventeen seconds; three shots.)

Midori feels inexplicably drawn to the aging ex-courtesan, Okichi (Yamada Isuzu). *Growing Up* (1955).

What must be noted first about this sequence is that there is some causality at work. Hence, in the first scene Shinnyo is instructed to have a kimono made; in the next scene he carries out this task. Likewise, the action moves ahead chronologically and with clearly marked-out temporal cues. Thus, we learn about Midori's visit in scene two, witness the actual visit in scene three, and catch a glimpse of Midori on her way back in scene five. Also, the conversation that Shinnyo and Ohana begin in scene one is concluded in scene four. Finally, the plot is structured as an intricate nexus of parallel actions that finds each of the four women trapped in similar fates. Reinforcing these actions are stylistic devices, primarily camera movements and eyeline matches.

Although this sequence is not just about Midori, it is built around her. Even in the three scenes in which she is absent (one, two, and four), she is a topic of conversation or referred to indirectly. In scene one, as mentioned, Ohana sees Midori and herself as equally victimized; in scene four, Ohana takes consolation in the fact that it is better to be a concubine than an *oiran*, whereupon Shinnyo repeats the word *oiran* thoughtfully, as if comprehending its relation to Midori for the first time.

Scene two is particularly notable for Midori's absence. In previous scenes, she was always present with her girlfriends in Okichi's shop. Typically, Gosho's framing placed Okichi in the foreground, sewing, fanning herself, stretching her weary limbs, and drinking tea or something stronger, while in the background the girls played various games. Every so often Midori would look Okichi's way, unsettled by an offhand remark, or threatened by her very presence in some vague or intangible way. At any rate, she sensed Okichi's eyes on her, and was inexplicably drawn to this once-famous courtesan, whom she politely calls *obasan* (aunt). Between them was an unspoken secret, a kind of bond.

As might be expected, scene two is as much about Okichi as it is about Midori. In this scene, Gosho's familiar framing—Okichi in the foreground, the girls in the background—accentuates Midori's absence, even as it paradoxically makes her presence more forcefully felt. This said, Okichi speaks more openly than ever, boasting that she has had a lot of men. But it is when she turns her attention to Midori that she reveals herself to be a complex and sympathetic woman. Having noticed that Midori is never without money, and knowing its source, she also knows what these facts portend. Okichi states that she feels sorry for Midori, because the young girl will end up just like her. Thus, she shows more genuine concern for Midori than her own girlfriends. Indeed, she scolds them for taking money from Midori, insisting that Midori shouldn't give them any. In response, they plead, "Don't tell her that." Although Okichi's phlegmatic manner, elongated facial features, and sweat-covered skin make her seem a thoroughly exhausted and decadent figure, she has not lost her humanity. Her feeling for Midori demonstrates as much, as does her rallying to Sangoro's defense in a later scene when he is being brutally beaten by Chokichi. Still, as the end of scene two cautions, we must not sentimentalize Okichi. Here Shinnyo brings her the fabric to make Ohana's kimono. "Then it's decided?" she asks, meaning Ohana's being sold as a mistress. If she feels for Ohana, she does not show it; rather, she seems to accept the situation as a fact of life. After all, Ohana, unlike Midori, is no longer a child. She should know the ways of the world. Okichi's question, however, stuns Shinnyo. Refusing to accept what it implies, he answers abruptly, "I don't know," and rushes off. In short, Okichi's vestiges of humanity notwithstanding, she has been toughened by life. She is a realist.

Scene three is the most evocative in the sequence. Moving and restrained, its power derives from things not spoken and Gosho's skill at psychological observation. Like the previous scene, it contemplates Midori's innocent nature, but in an altogether different setting: the brothel where Omaki works. The scene also gives us our first look at Omaki, and exam-

The madam summons Omaki (Kishi Keiko) to "entertain" waiting customers, while Midori looks on. *Growing Up* (1955).

ines her relationship with Midori. Set in Omaki's room, it begins with Midori pouring herself a soft drink, while admiring her sister, who is dressing to entertain a customer. In the background a steady stream of laughter merges with the sound of samisen music. Sampling her drink, Midori enthusiastically informs Omaki that it is delicious. Omaki smiles, pleased that her younger sister can take delight in such simple things. However, Midori becomes so preoccupied with the drink—shaking the bottle, taking sips from a spoon, and stirring her ice-filled goblet—that she fails to notice Omaki's mood.

The heart of the scene has to do with just this mood. Indeed, in focusing on Omaki's effort to confide in Midori and warn her about her future, it makes striking use of two shots in tandem with carefully placed shot/re-action shots, thus underscoring the theme of "individual isolation/shared fate" that courses through the film. In this segment Omaki and Midori are seated at the kotatsu (warmer), facing each other for the first time in the scene. As a prelude to their conversation, Omaki gives Midori some spending money and invites her to visit during the Otori festival in the fall. This action is conveyed in a two-shot that stresses the sisters' bond and mutual affection. But when Omaki turns to the thoughts that prey on her mind, describing a bad dream she had and expressing the wish that people could stay young forever, Gosho employs a series of shot/reaction shots. These shots foreground not only her sadness and melancholy, but also Midori's well-meaning if inadequate reassurance. In short, the two sisters remain separate and isolated. To be sure, Midori senses that there is something in her sister's strange mood, but she has no way of understanding what Omaki is trying to tell her about an *oiran*'s life. She has even less awareness that Omaki's words apply to her. Realizing that Midori is still too young to understand, Omaki lovingly urges her never to grow old. Then she falls silent. Moments later, the madam appears at the entryway to remind her that her guests are waiting.

Innocent and naive, Midori sees only the glamour of Omaki's life. Earlier, she had boasted to her friends that her sister was so popular that she received a marriage proposal from a socially prominent client, but turned him down because she did not like him. Now as Omaki goes to meet her guests, Midori asks who she will be seeing. "You shouldn't ask," Omaki says, giving her curiosity a rude check. It is the only time Omaki allows her pain to break through to the surface. Then, after stepping into elevated straw sandals, a sign of her status, she makes her way down the long corridor—a shot that Gosho films in real time. Her face a mask, her movements stately and beautifully controlled, she does not so much walk as glide, like a figure from Noh drama. She seems an apparition. Near the end of the shot, Midori steps into the frame, and for a few seconds we watch her observe Omaki. Then Gosho cuts to the closing shot, a medium close-up of Midori's face. Her eyes are fixed in a gaze, her mouth is drawn in a lovely, if faint, smile: clearly she is in awe of Omaki's grace and beauty. But then her face turns thoughtful, as if she has come to realize something. Whatever it may be, her mood has changed, and the scene ends in tantalizing ambiguity. However, there is little ambiguity with regard to Omaki. One recognizes in her behavior a complex of feelings, a desire not just to scream out but to speak. Yet the reality of prostitution is such that it cannot be put into words. For Omaki, it is the unspeakable.

Scenes four and five, the last two in the sequence, may be discussed together. Inextricably linked by camera movement and eyeline matches, they yoke together Midori, Ohana, and Shinnyo in a pattern of separation and longing. This linkage is announced by an eyeline match between the closing shot of scene three and the opening shot of scene four. Here Midori glances off-screen right, which "motivates" a pan from screen left to screen right, leading the eye across a lake to the shore, where Ohana is deep in thought. Immediately, a connection is implied between the two women. Moments later, this connection is reinforced when Ohana explains to Shinnyo that it is better to be a concubine than an *oiran*. Needless to say, she is trying to console herself as much as him, for, like Midori, she has no choice but to accept her fate. Ohana's words, however, provide no real comfort to Shinnyo. Indeed, as previously mentioned, one word in particular gives him pause: *oiran.* He repeats the word pensively, then grows silent and looks away. It is not hard to imagine whom he is thinking about. Gosho's camera follows his glance from screen right to screen left, back across the lake. Then a dissolve brings us into the opening shot of scene five, whereupon the camera reverses direction and pans from left to right, until it comes upon Midori. She is standing outside the temple where Shinnyo lives, having stopped on her way back from her visit with Omaki. Looking intently past the gate, she is oblivious to the fact that she is in the middle of the street until a rickshaw appears out of nowhere. Startled back into reality, she proceeds on her way.

In these two scenes Gosho's expressive combination of camera movements and eyeline matches meshes perfectly with the larger narrative strategies at work to create a subtly moving pathos. Shinnyo and Midori cannot know, for example, that they are in each other's thoughts at the exact same moment, even though they are separated by space and, most of all, by misunderstandings. Indeed, they are ignorant of each other's deepest feelings. By the same token, Ohana's feelings can find no release, except through the allusion to Midori, who will suffer like herself, and through the pathetic fallacy of the flower-covered lake, with which she and Shinnyo are identified. The sense of sadness and longing that pervades this sequence as a whole is even more intensified in the second sequence to be examined.

This sequence, which takes place several months after the first, focuses on the women's radically changed circumstances. Here Ohana, Okichi, and Omaki find themselves facing the certain tragedy of disease, old age, and abandonment. Midori is no less unfortunate. True, she has not yet experienced what the other women have, but for the first time she learns about her destiny.

This sequence, which runs approximately fourteen minutes, consists of the following scenes:

1. Shinnyo and his friends have a falling out over Ohana, who has returned home. (Forty seconds; six shots.)

2. During a tense family confrontation, Shinnyo begs his father not to force Ohana to return to her master. (Two minutes, five seconds; twenty-one shots.)

3. Midori finds Omaki ill. (Three minutes, twenty-three seconds; seventeen shots.)

4. Ohana and her father set off on the journey back to her master. (Twenty-two seconds; three shots.)

5. Shinnyo's mother asks his forgiveness for being unable to help Ohana. (One minute, twenty-two seconds; seven shots.)

6. Okichi explains to Midori what her life as an *oiran* will be like. (Six minutes, six seconds; thirty-nine shots.)

Despite the chronological unfolding of events, this sequence, like the first one, is intricately structured as a pattern of association and connection. Thus, it is threaded with repeated settings and compositions, stylistic play, and allusions not only to other scenes in the sequence but also to the earlier sequence and to scenes across the film. Most importantly, the sequence is characterized by a deepening of psychic tensions and a foregrounding of societal contradictions. To this end Gosho intensifies the atmosphere of sublimation and suppression, leading his audience to empathize even more with the characters. In this atmosphere, characters and viewers alike find themselves trapped in an ever-tightening skein of actions, events, and limited options. Indeed, Gosho makes his audience complicit in the characters' pain and suffering by treating issues that cannot be resolved in the film, issues whose ideological source lies deeply buried within society. It is in this sense, then, that Gosho's film holds a mirror up to viewers, appealing to a deep commonality of feeling and prompting a response that goes beyond anger, sadness, or democratic yearning. Still, it must be emphasized that Gosho never sacrifices the story or its emotional potential. On the contrary, *Growing Up*'s power derives from Gosho's ability to keep both of these elements in balance.

Scene one promptly gets to the business of unmasking societal contradictions and revealing the attendant psychic tensions. While Ohana is inside the house with her parents, trying to describe her ordeal as a mistress, Shinnyo, clearly preoccupied and anxious, remains outside with his friends. In a disastrous attempt to cheer him up, they point out that at the Imadas his sister lives in a nice house and has plenty of money, the implication being, what more could she possibly want? But Shinnyo will have none of this. He accuses them of not understanding, tells them to shut up, and storms off. Like the rest of society, his friends see only the material benefits; considering Ohana's feelings never occurs to them. Ironically, they also are wholly unaware of the contradiction in their stance: they praise Ohana for the very thing they condemn in Midori.

Scene two is even more lacerating in its treatment of social contradictions and psychic tensions. Ohana frantically pleads not to be sent back to the Imada household. When her father remains obstinate, her mother dares to intercede on her behalf. Immediately, she is silenced and ordered to continue working on the hair ornaments that he intends to sell during the up-coming festival. In showing the mother's reaction, Gosho gives us an example of his *découpage* style at its best—concise, expressive, and exact. In the first of two juxtaposed shots we see her face take on the shamed, embarrassed look of a rebuked child; in the second shot, an ornament drops from her hand onto a large pile of finished ornaments. Nothing more needs to be said about this woman's life. As for Ohana's pleading, the outcome is never in doubt. Thus, the scene evokes genuine pathos for her. Yet this scene is not simply about her and her mother's victimization; it is also about a family in disarray and the lack of natural feeling that lies at the heart of this condition. Echoing the scene at the beginning of the film, in which Shinnyo and his parents were locked in confrontation, it even repeats the same framing and composition. Hence Shinnyo's mother appears on screen left, his father on screen right, while Ohana (taking Shinnyo's place) is positioned in the center background. This time, however, the configuration is challenged, first in a figurative way by the attempted intercession of Shinnyo's mother, and later in a literal way by Shinnyo himself. Indeed, Shinnyo suddenly enters the scene and, sitting beside Ohana, defiantly protests that she will die if forced to return to her master. His father answers this challenge by striking him in the face. However, his father's victory here and in scene four, where he personally oversees Ohana's return, is at best pyrrhic. For as scene five makes evident, with Ohana gone and Shinnyo more determined than ever to enter the priesthood, the destruction of the family is complete.

In challenging his father, Shinnyo also introduces the subject that will dominate the rest of the sequence: death. Scene three, in particular, in which Midori and Omaki have their second visit, is permeated with the feeling of death and disease. During the sisters' first visit, Omaki had a slight cough, but Gosho took pains not to call attention to it. Now that cough has worsened, signaling the onset of the same debilitating illness that we later learn Okichi suffers from, consumption. Scene three deals with the implications of that illness, Omaki's protective feelings for Midori, and Midori's evolving character. Indeed, unlike the Midori of the first visit, who seemed preoccupied with her soft drink, this Midori has only one concern: her sister's well being.

As the scene opens, the camera pans from left to right, across a folding screen painted with cherry blossoms, to Midori, who is heating water for Omaki's medicine. The screen is almost certainly not an expensive one, being neither boldly executed nor finely detailed, but it is meant to lend a touch of elegance and beauty to the room, while serving an obvious practical function. Its chief importance, however, is thematic. Put simply, the screen is emblematic of an effort on the part of the brothel to cloak and "aestheticize" its seamier side. This effort, however, is undercut by the combination of Omaki's condition, Midori's concern, and Gosho's visual style. With respect to style, Gosho alternates two-shots, long shots, and shot/reaction shots seamlessly, but it is his use of chiaroscuro lighting that stands out in the scene. Rather than motivate the lighting by connecting it to realistic sources, cinematographer Ohara Joji and Gosho create a pictorial design that subtly changes from long shot to close-up. Indeed, in long shots darkness engulfs the room, except for Omaki and Midori, who are fully lit and centered in the frame. By contrast, in close-ups Omaki is invariably bathed in half-light, half-darkness, as is Midori as the scene progresses. Thus, the lighting gives expression to Omaki's desperate plight, Midori's confusion and concern, and the veritable prison in which the two sisters are trapped.

The scene is distinguished by three carefully placed close-ups of Omaki. The first of these comes at the beginning of the scene, as she tries unsuccessfully to suppress her cough; the second, at the middle, as she tentatively applies makeup before meeting her client; and the third, at the close, when she is alone. Throughout the scene, Omaki is barely able to muster the strength to speak or hold the small cup that contains her medicine. Understandably worried, but still very much the naive child, Midori says that she will inform the madam that Omaki is too ill to work. But Omaki stops her. "It isn't that easy," she explains, finishing her makeup and staring at her image in the mirror. "You'll understand after a while." Moments later, she suddenly breaks into tears. When Midori asks why she is crying, Omaki tenderly replies, "Because you are such a child." Then she adds, "Don't ever grow up. Stay like this always." Of course, she knows this is not possible. Indeed, one of the last things Omaki tells Midori is, "I hope you will never have to drink this," referring to the medicine she can barely tolerate. Later in the film, we remember these words when we see Omaki for the last time. On her way to entertain a client, she pauses to read the announcement of Midori's "debut." Her face betrays almost nothing of what she feels, but we know only too well. Perhaps at that moment, she also realizes that it is only a matter of time before she will be replaced by her own sister as the quarter's most popular *oiran*. If so, she is seeing the future as clearly as she saw her image in the mirror. Foreshadowing her fate, scene three ends with a close-up as she takes a sip of her medicine, pauses, then presses her eyes shut as if to brace herself for what she must do. Still, she neither moves nor rises, at least not immediately, but remains caught in the half-light, half-shadow, that has come to define her. It is a fitting conclusion to one of the film's most poignant scenes.

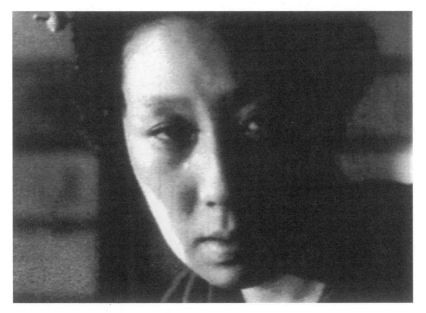

The expression on Okichi's face frightens Midori: "Why are you looking at me this way?" *Growing Up* (1955).

No less poignant is scene six, the last scene of the sequence and the turning point in the film. In this scene Midori finally learns of her destiny. A psychologically complex scene, its pathos is tempered by an ironic tension that is genuinely disturbing.

As the scene opens, Midori arrives at Okichi's store following her visit with Omaki, only to find Okichi drunk and alone in the dark. Bleary-eyed and slumped over the kotatsu, Okichi greets Midori with the remark that her body will not last long and that no medicine can help, only alcohol. Drink, in fact, has loosened her tongue, and she is scary in the scene—as if possessed by a strange and sinister "other." When Midori confides that Omaki is also sick, Okichi says, "Probably Omaki has what I have," and breaks into a bone-chilling cackle. Gosho then employs the most striking and unusual dissolve in the film. In close-up, Okichi abruptly stops laughing, and stares long and hard at Midori. This close-up dissolves into an even tighter close-up as she continues staring, her expression sad, sorrowful, and penetrating. It is the boldest close-up of the film, and is made even more eerie by the off-screen sound of a street vendor hawking his wares to the pulsating beat of a drum. "Why are you looking at me this way?" Midori asks. Never before has she felt so vulnerable or exposed.

Emboldened, Okichi dispenses with any compassion she may feel for Midori. "You're so pretty," she says. "You'll do good in the business." She then proceeds to instruct her on how to carry herself as an *oiran:* "Turn your head this way. And never put your hand on your hip. It makes you round-shouldered." As she demonstrates an *oiran's* artful blend of calculation and coquetry, we catch a glimpse of what she must have been like in her salad days. Midori, however, refuses to listen. Grabbing a ball, she starts bouncing it in childlike defiance to drown out Okichi's words, an action that is touchingly pathetic, for childhood games cannot protect her. Indeed, the film has codified Midori's innocence and irrepressible nature in her body language. That is, she is constantly in motion—from the nervous tapping of her foot in her first scene with Shinnyo to the often exuberant games she plays with her girlfriends. In the present scene, she enjoys the luxury of childhood energy for the last time. From this point on, her body language will become more and more reserved until, like Omaki and the others, she will reach a point of stasis. At this time, however, she cannot be saved even by running out of the store when she sees Shinnyo pass by. For when she returns, as she must, Okichi picks up from where she left off, informing her that when she is an *oiran* she will have to do what she is told, "even if it's Sangoro who comes to see you." Okichi then begins to ruminate on the past. "I thought that men who didn't come to see us were bad," she says, a chilling comment that reveals how she inhered the values of the brothel and unintentionally became complicit in her victimization. Deeply unsettled, Midori says, "Your face makes me frightened." It is at this moment that Okichi's better nature reasserts itself: "You don't understand any of this. I feel sorry for you," she declares. With this, Midori leaves the room; she needs to be by herself. Gosho's camera does not follow her. Instead, it remains behind. Evening descends, the store grows darker, and Okichi lights a lamp. Moments later, Midori reappears, stands over Okichi briefly, then falls into her lap. "What should I do?" she cries out. Okichi gives her the only answer possible: she takes her in her arms and holds her.

By now it must be clear that while Okichi certainly cares about Midori and in the end assumes the role of surrogate mother, she does not act simply out of altruism. Her behavior is a mixture of compassion and cruelty, her gleeful laugh indicative of the pleasure she takes in seeing others share her misery. This is certainly how she sees Omaki. By contrast, her response to Midori is complex. Here is a young girl who has the youth and beauty she has lost. Small wonder, then, that Okichi unleashes her demons on her, until her finer impulses take over and she reclaims her compassion. If Okichi's conflicted nature gives the scene an unexpected tension and edge, Midori's violated innocence gives it poignancy and pathos. In fact, these last two elements are made all the more moving by Gosho's elision of the very scene that would be the centerpiece of most films: Midori's moment of realization. In denying viewers this scene, Gosho not only leaves the scene to their imagination but also rightly puts the emphasis on what Midori will do with the terrible burden and isolation that comes with this realization. For, indeed, as the voiceover narration informs us, "From this day, Midori was a different person. The playful girl was no longer. . . . She had grown up."

The final twenty-five minutes of *Growing Up* focus on this "different person" and the moral strength she finds within herself. While the rest of the quarter is caught up in the Otori festivities, she keeps to her room, seeing few people besides her parents and master, who are busily preparing for her "debut." On one occasion, she is visited by Shotaro, who still hopes to win her affection, but she is too unhappy and preoccupied to pay him much attention. In fact, the visit only exacerbates her anxiety, for when her mother sees the two of them together, she fawns over Shotaro, as if Midori is already entertaining and he is a client. Sickened, Midori curtly dismisses him. After this incident, her relations with her parents grow more distanced and formal, but she never questions the sacrifice they ask her to make in the name of filial piety. To the contrary, in the days leading up to her departure, she moves beyond acceptance of her lot and acquires a certain wisdom and serenity. She is even able to speak the word that neither her parents nor her master can. "I know what an *oiran* is," she says. From that moment on, she holds her head high.

Midori's new maturity is no less evident, and even more touching, in her last meeting with Shinnyo. Looking out of her window during a downpour, she sees him struggling to fix the broken thong on his sandal and tosses him her white lace handkerchief. Lauded as "one of the most moving evocations of adolescence in the literature of any country,"[32] the scene almost certainly had to be included in the film. However, in the original it comes earlier in the narrative, and Midori and Shinnyo, still very innocent, do not speak.[33] By contrast, in the film they have a brief conversation, but now, knowing her fate, Midori keeps her feelings in check, the wooden bars of the window an index to the social constraints placed upon her. Shinnyo keeps his feelings in check as well, knowing that he is destined for the life of a Buddhist priest. With nothing left to be said, Midori closes her window, leaving him to make his repairs. As in the novella, Shinnyo does not pick up the offered handkerchief, but for reasons that are quite different from those of the film. In the novella he is still a confused boy grappling with his feelings; in the film he understands what the handkerchief means. Therefore, when he leaves, he does not look back. Yet Gosho does not end the scene here. Instead he closes with two shots. In the first Midori is seated quietly, her head bowed, her back to the window; in the second, her handkerchief is seen in close-up, still lying on the ground: an object of impossible love.

The handkerchief is exemplary of Gosho's remarkable use of concrete objects. As Donald Richie has explained, in Gosho's films such objects are never reduced to mere symbolic status, but retain their essential reality and urgency; moreover, the emotional context of each object is allowed to speak for itself.[34] To illustrate his point, Richie offers the example of a caged bird that Gosho cuts to at the end of a scene in which Midori's parents do their best to "avoid divulging her precise fate."[35] He goes on to say: "We have noticed this caged bird before; there was even a bit of business around it. Now, however, Gosho makes a comment through cinematic metaphor. Brevity and lack of emphasis restore to the trite symbol much of its original freshness and power, just as in a haiku."[36] As Richie's observation implies, emotional context depends largely upon the meaning that an individual object accrues across the film. In *Growing Up* the most significant objects include flowers, mirrors, and kimonos. Flowers, for example, are first identified with Shinnyo as he reflects in the garden, but their association broadens when Midori asks him to pick her a cherry blossom. Thus, flowers come to signify not just Shinnyo's sensitive nature but also his and Midori's love. As the narrative progresses, flowers acquire more complex and ambiguous signification. We see cherry blossoms adorn the folding screen in Omaki's room—their beauty and innocence now problematized not only by the fact that these particular flowers are traditionally identified with prostitutes of the Yoshiwara,[37] but also by the fact that Omaki herself is a site of contradiction, being both innocent and tainted. In the end, flowers are restored to something of their original meaning when Shinnyo leaves an iris blossom at Midori's door. But, as we shall see momentarily, they are once again problematized by Midori's final act on the drawbridge. In short, an overlay of meanings obtains, and a potentially hackneyed metaphor is redeemed and reinvigorated in the process.

This said, Gosho's art is at its most impressive in the film's ten-minute finale.[38] Here in dramatizing Midori's actual leave-taking, composer Akutagawa Yasushi extends the theme first heard during the main credits into a full-scale passacaglia (a series of variations in 3/4 time with a continuous ground bass), which pulls together the short, ever-changing scenes that cut back and forth from Midori to those who care most deeply about her: Okichi, Omaki, Shinnyo, and Shotaro. In narrative terms, the action is split into different strands, all of which play themselves out, except for the primary one, which focuses on Midori. Likewise, as the music builds to a coda, the dialogue grows more spare, most of it occurring in the first scene where Shotaro and Okichi lament Midori's plight. By the last few scenes, dialogue has fallen away completely, underscoring the fact that anything that needs to be "said" will be said with visuals and music.

And, indeed, such is the case. In its closing moments *Growing Up* goes beyond Gosho's famed laughter through tears and disavows anything remotely akin to sentimentality, romanticism, or transcendence. Midori pauses on the drawbridge that leads to the brothel, and she gives Shinnyo's flower one last look before casting it into the muddy moat below. Neither a gratuitous gesture nor a callous act, it marks the true end of her journey, her acknowledgment that the days of youthful freedom are gone. As she disappears from view, Gosho's camera lingers, then dollies slowly toward the brothel. It is evening and once more the balustrades are filled with kimono-clad beauties and their customers. We cannot help but think that the house, which has long waited for Midori, also waits for countless others like her. A place of shattered dreams and unfulfilled promises, the brothel puts before us the ongoing legacy of the feudal past. The film thus ends as it began; the wheel has come full circle.

EIGHT

The Late 1950s: New Challenges and the Quest to Create

Throughout this study, we have seen how Gosho worked in various genres, experimented with different forms, and tempered his usual mode of laughter through tears, sometimes venturing from it. According to Kakehi Masanori, "he did not like to remain in any one place very long. He always preserved his keen curiosity for new things and all his life, he was embarked on a quest to create."[1] This is certainly true of his work in the late 1950s where he moved beyond the theme of money and commerce that preoccupied *An Inn at Osaka* and *Growing Up*.[2] As Kyoko Hirano reminds us, Gosho "further extended his range" in films like *Banka* (*Elegy of the North*) and continued his "experimental spirit" in *Kiiroi karasu* (*Yellow Crow*, a.k.a. *Behold Thy Son*).[3] In 1957's *Yellow Crow* he filmed in color for the first time; that same year, in *Elegy of the North*, he created a European-style psychological melodrama. And in 1958's *Hotarubi* (*The Fireflies*, a.k.a. *Firefly Light*), he made one of his few *jidai-geki* (period films), which is set in the closing days of the Tokugawa era (1603–1867). Although all three of these films find Gosho striking out in new directions, none of them represents a complete break from his familiar themes and style. In fact, what makes these films fascinating is the way in which they blend the old and the new. *Yellow Crow* thus is very much a characteristic Gosho *shomin-geki*, *The Fireflies* focuses once again on the plight of women, and *Elegy of the North* is a kindred spirit to chamber pieces like 1948's *Omokage* (*A Visage to Remember*) and 1951's *Wakare-gumo* (*Dispersing Clouds*). In this chapter, we will examine each of these three films, focusing primarily on *Elegy of the North*, one of Gosho's most fully realized studies of adult relationships.

YELLOW CROW

Winner of a Golden Globe Award from the Hollywood Foreign Press Association, *Yellow Crow* tells the story of young Kiyoshi (Shidara Koji),

Machiko (Awashima Chikage) introduces Kiyoshi (Shidara Koji) to his father (Ito Yunosuke). *Yellow Crow* (1957).

whose father, Ichiro (Ito Yunosuke), is repatriated from China after eight years. Not having seen his father before, Kiyoshi regards him as an intruder and feels neglected when his mother, Machiko (Awashima Chikage), devotes most of her attention to him and the problems he has readjusting to his job and family life. To make matters worse, Kiyoshi finds that his father has little time for him and is unaffectionate. Following the birth of his sister, Kiyoshi and his father frequently argue. Their relationship further deteriorates when Kiyoshi is accused of injuring a classmate. Angry, Ichiro locks him up in the family's outdoor bomb shelter, where his frantic cries are heard by Yukiko (Tanaka Kinuyo), a kind next-door neighbor, who comes to his rescue. Next day, during an outing with Yukiko and her adopted daughter, Haruko (Yasumura Masako), Kiyoshi finds a wounded baby crow and brings it home. Meanwhile Kiyoshi's teacher, Miss Ashiwara (Kuga Yoshiko), pays his parents a visit to tell them that Kiyoshi's drawings express his unhappiness. Machiko and Ichiro privately agree that they have been too strict. To make amends, Ichiro promises to buy Kiyoshi the kite he has wanted. However, while taking care of his baby sister, Kiyoshi gets in a fight with some classmates, who deliberately overturn the baby's carriage. Upset, Machiko and Ichiro blame him for what has happened. Ichiro even tosses the crow out of the house. Kiyoshi runs away, but, having no place to go, he turns to Yukiko, who once again intercedes for him and urges Ichiro, Machiko, and Kiyoshi to begin anew as a family. Shortly after, Kiyoshi draws a beautiful beach scene filled with bright colors. On New Year's Day, he and his parents go to the seaside, joined by Yukiko and Haruko. There Kiyoshi proudly flies his new kite.

Thematically, *Yellow Crow* has much in common with two other Gosho *shomin-geki* films about a young boy's troubled relationship with his father: 1935's *Burden of Life,* in which Kan-chan suffers in the knowledge that his father never wanted him, and 1962's *Kaachan, kekkon shiroyo* (*Mother, Get Married*), in which young Ichiro makes his way to Tokyo to find his father, whom he has been told is dead. *Yellow Crow*'s chief importance, however, lies in its experimental use of color. At a time when few Japanese films were in color, Gosho and cinematographer Miyajima Yoshio used color to express Kiyoshi's loneliness and sense of isolation. Gosho even consulted experts on the relationship of color and child psychology and incorporated what he learned into the film.[4] Thus Miss Ashiwara, Kiyoshi's teacher, is informed by a colleague, Mr. Murakami (Numata Yoichi), that after the war yellow and black were the only colors used by many lonely children who had a dead or absent father or other family problems. In *Yellow Crow,* Gosho builds a color scheme around these colors. Interestingly, in his autobiography *Waga seishun* (*My Youth,* 1978), Gosho remarks that yellow also happened to be his favorite color and that he had a special fondness for flowers of that color.[5] Perhaps this explains one of the film's most stylish, if flamboyant shots, in which a passing train is virtually dwarfed by yellow flowers looming in the foreground of the frame.

Narratively, *Yellow Crow* is structured in three movements. The first establishes Kiyoshi's basic unhappiness, the second reaches a climax when he runs away from home, and the third concludes with his forging a new relationship with his father. Each of these movements is given expression by one or more of Kiyoshi's drawings.

In the first movement we see Kiyoshi's black and yellow depiction of the Great Buddha. This drawing, which first appears in the opening scene, catches the attention of Miss Ashiwara, who asks Kiyoshi why he uses only these two colors when there are so many different ones to choose from. When he does not answer, she does not press him. "Draw whatever you like," she wisely says. Nevertheless, she is concerned and shows the drawing to Mr. Murakami. Although Kiyoshi's drawing expresses his feelings of loneliness, it also reflects the eight long years of hardship he has experienced during his father's absence.[6] How ironic, then, that Kiyoshi's loneliness only increases with his father's return. Sensing as much, Miss Ashiwara visits his parents in the second movement of the film and shows them the drawing.

Prior to Miss Ashiwara's visit, Kiyoshi completes a second drawing. His most unusual and ambiguous one, it is occasioned by the birth of his baby sister and substitutes the black and yellow color scheme with a red and green one. The drawing makes clear that Kiyoshi is wholly involved in this very special family event. But what else does this drawing "say"? At the risk of reading too much into it, or trying to assign absolute meanings to the colors, it seems safe to say that the drawing suggests a young boy's happy, if ambivalent feelings. The drawing features two human figures. Located on the right is the larger figure. Dominated by a huge green face with a smear of red denoting the lips, it perhaps represents Kiyoshi himself. On the left, suspended in mid-air, is a smaller but full figure with outstretched arms, perhaps representing the baby. If the bright red and green colors express Kiyoshi's happiness over the birth of his baby sister, the disproportionate size of the two figures qualifies that feeling. To be sure, Kiyoshi loves his sister and is never less than gentle and affectionate with her—something viewers see, even if his parents do not. Still, as he confides to Yukiko, he cannot help feeling that baby Miko gets all the attention. Is he envious and jealous? Does he feel pushed aside? Almost certainly. But these are the naturally mixed feelings that any child may have toward a new sibling.

By contrast, there is nothing ambiguous about Kiyoshi's third drawing. Integral to the dramatic action in the film's second movement, it returns to the black and yellow color scheme with a vengeance, and is a direct response to the events leading up to his running away from home, in particular the loss of the baby crow. Upset, Kiyoshi draws the crow as yellow and surrounds it in a wall of black. On the back of the drawing, he writes: "Father, you are a liar. I wish you were dead." With this, all his pent-up emotions and frustrations come to the surface; he means to hurt both of his parents as much as possible. Needless to say, these words are especially crushing for his father, who is filled with such a sense of shame for failing his son that he takes the drawing when Machiko is not looking and examines it in secret. Soon after, he goes in search of Kiyoshi.

When Kiyoshi takes refuge at Yukiko's house, it is left to this caring neighbor to help Machiko and Ichiro understand exactly how he feels. Speaking frankly, she tells Machiko that since Ichiro's return, Kiyoshi has been neglected. "Don't you think it's sad that he has to come to a neighbor's house of instead of his own home?" she asks. She then has Machiko eavesdrop on her conversation with him so that she can hear firsthand what he cannot say to her directly. "Father hates me," he tells Yukiko, who insists, "That's nonsense. He loves you, and is looking for you." But Kiyoshi pleads with Yukiko to adopt him. For the first time Machiko realizes how much in the wrong she and Ichiro have been, and that Kiyoshi has been "perfectly right in rebelling and running away."[7] In short, Gosho comes down on the side of the boy. It is the parents who must change their ways.

Kiyoshi's fourth and final drawing marks the beginning of his new-found happiness and concludes the last movement of the film. Filled with bright reds, oranges, pinks, and greens, this drawing, appropriately enough, is a sunset scene at the seashore. Besides mirroring the closing shot of the outing scene with Kiyoshi, Yukiko, and Haruko, it symbolizes the wish that Kiyoshi makes in the opening of the film: that his returning father take him to Eno Shima, a famous seaside resort. In the film's closing scene Kiyoshi's wish comes true. The subdued shades of browns, greens, yellows, and blacks that have dominated the film are now replaced with the brightest colors imaginable.

Gosho's use of color is by no means his sole accomplishment in *Yellow Crow*. True to its roots in the *shomin-geki,* the film also offers an honest and affecting exploration of a troubled father-son relationship. Gosho and scriptwriters Tateoka Kennosuke and Hasebe Keiji are especially attentive to the interplay of elements that complicates this relationship: the misunderstandings, the missed opportunities, the inability to acknowledge another's feelings, and, of course, the irrefutable bond of blood. The filmmakers also show enormous respect for their characters. Kiyoshi, who is probably no older than ten, is basically an ordinary boy. When he feels particularly unloved by his parents, he retreats into his private world (his "zoo" of small animals), or seeks out surrogate parents (Yukiko and Miss Ashiwara). He also turns sullen, defiant, or clinging and demanding as a baby. Yet, as he proves on more than one occasion, like Kan-chan in *Burden of Life,* he can be unusually sensitive for his years and more mature than his parents. Unlike them, he is willing to forgive.

Wisely, the film refuses to demonize Ichiro. Indeed, it gives him different sides, which makes it possible not only to understand him but also to feel for him, even when he is unbending or obtuse. In his own way, this returning veteran is as isolated as Kiyoshi is, and finds himself in a world he doesn't fit into, either at home or at work (where new business practices only add to his woes). Thus, Gosho frequently photographs him seated alone, his face wracked with uncertainty, guilt, or shame. Basically, he is a good man, and he truly loves his son. But he believes that Kiyoshi is spoiled and needs discipline; therefore, he assumes the role of a traditional patriarch. Unfortunately, this role model is not only outmoded but also forces him to deny his feelings. This is made painfully clear when he confides to Machiko, after a particularly nasty quarrel with Kiyoshi, that he wanted to forgive the boy and get closer to him, but could not find the way. Yet Ichiro is not simply the victim of misguided or thwarted intentions. Self-absorbed, he fails to recognize Kiyoshi's efforts to get closer. Hence when Kiyoshi shows him the clay figures he made at school, Ichiro barely looks at them, mistakes a tiger for a housecat, and says that he should be studying math and science, not art. Moreover, when he is angry or frustrated, Ichiro can be unintentionally cruel, as when he drags Kiyoshi from the house and locks him in the bomb shelter. This hardly seems the same man who once engaged in a friendly game of arm wrestling with this son. In short, Ichiro's failed relationship with Kiyoshi requires Machiko to step in. Determined to do right by her son and save her family, she takes matters into her own hands, paving the way for Ichiro and Kiyoshi's reconciliation.

Unfortunately, as critics have pointed out, this reconciliation happens too quickly. As a result, it is sentimental and unconvincing. It also is disappointing since much of the observation of the father-son relationship is insightful and true. Faltering as it does in the closing section, *Yellow Crow* cannot be deemed one of Gosho's best films. Even so, it merits attention not only for its ambition but also for its achievements—none more so than its experimental use of color to represent psychological states of mind in purely visual terms.

THE FIREFLIES

With *The Fireflies,* Gosho conducted a different kind of experiment, turning his attention to the *jidai-geki* (period film). As Mark Le Fanu points out, this historical drama "cedes nothing to [Mizoguchi,] Gosho's great contemporary[,] either in the rigour of its form or in the encompassing humanity of its content."[8] Based on a novel by Oda Sakunosuke, a prominent writer known for his depiction of the lives of common people, Gosho's film does full justice to the *jidai-geki* while concentrating on how one woman's life is impacted by history. For Gosho, history is not a series of larger-than-life legendary events. Rather, it is a story of human beings and must be told in those terms, on that scale. This applies not only to the film's female protagonist but also to the historic figure Ryoma, whom Gosho transforms "from historical legend to human proportions."[9] Put simply, in *The Fireflies* Gosho refashions the *jidai-geki* into something uniquely his own.

Set in the 1860s, the final years of the Tokugawa Shogunate, *The Fireflies* focuses on Tose (Awashima Chikage), the mistress of the Teradaya, a small inn in the Kyoto suburb of Fushimi. She does not have an easy life. Her husband, Isuke (Ban Junzaburo), is a wastrel who fancies himself a kabuki singer and who is obsessed with cleanliness. Her mother-in-law, Sada (Miyoshi Eiko) dislikes her because of her humble origins (her family are farmers) and because she fears that she will inherit the inn instead of

Sugi, her daughter. Sada's hopes for Sugi, however, are dashed when she runs off with a con artist and leaves her child behind for Tose to take care of. When Sada becomes seriously ill, it is Tose who nurses her. On her deathbed, Sada asks her daughter-in-law's forgiveness. Meanwhile Isuke spends most of his time with a mistress he has taken, forcing Tose to manage the inn by herself. One day a stranger appears in the Teradaya's kitchen. He is Sakamoto Ryoma (Mori Miki), the man who seeks to end the Tokugawa Shogunate and establish a democracy. He tells Tose that he is being hunted by the police and asks for shelter. Over Isuke's objection, she takes him in. Soon she finds herself attracted to Ryoma, but learns that he and her eighteen-year-old adopted daughter, Oryo (Wakao Ayako), have fallen in love. When officials come to the inn looking for Ryoma, Tose helps the couple escape. Later she is paid a visit by Tami, her husband's mistress, who claims to be pregnant with his child. Tose graciously offers to let her live at the inn. But Isuke tells Tose that Tami lied about the pregnancy because she wants the inn for herself. He also explains that he has broken off the relationship. Tose and Isuke reconcile, promising to treat each other better in the future. A few days later they read that Ryoma has been assassinated.

Modeled in part on an actual innkeeper of the Teradaya, who supported anti-Tokugawa patriots, Tose is regarded by Gosho "as no less heroic than Ryoma, notwithstanding her middle-class life, because her acts and her free spirit align her with a struggle for change.[10] Gosho uses a series of flashbacks to establish her character and circumstance. In the first flashback, the evening of Tose and Isuke's wedding, maids at the inn talk about how Tose's mother-in-law does not approve of her. When we first see Tose, she is alone, and in one notably lovely moment, she catches a firefly, cradling it gently in the palm of her hand, before releasing it. Although the firefly can be interpreted in a number of ways, it almost certainly expresses her free spirit, which awaits release. Yet she will find no release in her marriage. Indeed, later that evening, Isuke discovers that the servants have spread the bed without cleaning up first. He throws a temper tantrum. "I can't stand anything but cleanliness," he exclaims, and orders Tose to get a broom and dustpan—hardly the wedding night a new bride might expect. But Tose's spirit cannot be crushed. Intelligent, gracious, and armed with self-knowledge, she measures her life "under the aegis of constancy,"[11] and is resolutely long-suffering. She may be a figure of pathos, but she is never an object of pity.

Still, there is no question that a part of Tose remains unfulfilled. Gosho overdetermines this point by frequently ending scenes with a shot of her alone in the frame, reinforcing her basic loneliness and isolation. He also uses long flashbacks to motivate her feelings and actions in the present. In one flashback she is asked if she minds taking care of Omitsu, Sugi's child, while Sugi goes out and has a good time. She replies that being with Omitsu makes her happy. Here a pattern of behavior is established—Sugi's irresponsibility, Tose's emotional need. This pattern reaches a climax when Sugi later returns and demands that Tose hand over the child she has abandoned. When Omitsu runs to Tose for protection, Sugi drags her away to a boat that she has waiting. Distraught, Tose pleads with Isuke to intervene, but he refuses. She rushes after Sugi, but is too late. Two shots underscore Tose's wrenching pain and the pathos of the situation: a close-up of her against a dark, ominous sky, and a shot of the boat pulling out, with only a small lantern lighting the way. In yet another flashback, Tose witnesses a man being beaten for stealing three eggs to feed himself and a little girl. Taking pity on the pair, she brings them to the inn. There, while tenderly combing the girl's hair, she learns that her father was a doctor killed by rebel forces. Shortly after, she adopts the child, who turns out to be Oryo.

While both of these flashbacks make manifest Tose's desire for a child, the second one sets the stage for the impact that unfolding historic events have on the lives of common people. Indeed, the struggle between Tokugawa loyalists and their opposition soon makes its way to the doorstep of the Teradaya, changing Tose's life forever.

In *The Fireflies* the historical incident that serves as the basis for the story is the "Teradaya incident," in which the Choshu and Satsuma clans convened at the inn in April 1862 to plot their strategy against the Tokuganate. Gosho has stated that he was interested in this incident only insofar as it delineates Tose's character.[12] No doubt this is true; nevertheless, we must be careful not to minimize Gosho's skill in evoking the period or handling action. In fact, this master of the *shomin-geki* proves himself entirely at home in the *jidai-geki*, staging rousing action scenes "as well as his peers."[13] Take, for example, the scene at the inn in which the two clans wait for Arima, one of their leaders, to announce the start of the rebellion. Deeply suspicious of each other, even though they are fighting on the same side, the clans discover a traitor in their midst, and a fight breaks out. In the melee that ensues, the traitor tries to use Arima as a shield, but Arima selflessly urges his followers to plunge their swords through him to get to the traitor—which they do. Immediately, more fighting erupts, and soon blood splatters walls, shoji screens topple, and men drop, dying or wounded. A superbly staged action scene, it elicits exactly the kind of reactions from Isuke and Tose that one might expect. For Isuke, all that matters are the stained walls, which violate his sense of cleanliness. For Tose, all that matters is that a man gave up his life for a cause he believes in. In a later scene she visits Arima's tomb to pay her respects.

By this point in the film, Tose has progressed from being sympathetic to the patriots' cause to allying herself with it. Enter Ryoma. "Feel secure here," she says, granting him asylum. Defending her action, she tells Isuke, "I don't want to sacrifice important people . . . those who benefit this country." Later she learns that Ryoma has one purpose in life—to end poverty, class distinction, and feudalism. The boldness and sweep of his goal stirs her deeply; it is something she could never have imagined as being remotely possible, least of all for women in feudal Japan.

Not surprisingly, Gosho's film is built on the bond between Tose and Ryoma. This bond takes a double form. First, it is an unrequited romance, in which Ryoma is unaware of Tose's love for him; second, it is a drama of two soulmates who speak the same language, politically and emotionally. Soulmates that they are, however, there is one insuperable difference between them. As a man, Ryoma can act directly, whereas Tose can act only indirectly and behind the scenes.[14] Put differently, she must act through Ryoma. Still, her acts are no less bold or revolutionary, or less essential to the patriots' cause than his. In fact, in aiding Ryoma she aids "men of revolutionary dedication to prepare a future liberation of women."[15] Between Ryoma and Tose there is a wonderful intimacy, but this intimacy never would have been possible if Gosho had chosen to portray Ryoma as a larger-than-life historical figure or even the savvy political creator of "furtive intrigues."[16] Instead he depicts Ryoma as a man of the people—indeed, in many ways just an ordinary man. Hence in one scene Ryoma confides to Tose the feelings of loneliness and isolation that go hand-in-hand with his dedication to political change. Here we sense that he is as much a man chosen by destiny as one who has destiny in his hand.

Be that as it may, it is Tose's feelings for Ryoma that engage us most. In one scene she has just drawn his bath and is about to leave when he begins to sing a ditty in praise of people who were "only merchants," but who nonetheless sacrificed their lives for the common good. She stays to listen not only because she shares the song's sentiments, but also because she finds happiness in seeing him take pleasure in simple things. A lovely scene, it allows us to peer into her soul and share her hope that somehow he will provide the means for her to escape her present life.

Unfortunately, this is not meant to be. Hence Gosho's use of mistiming and misunderstanding. Having decided to confess her love to Ryoma, Tose begins by expressing her willingness to leave the Teradaya. Not realizing how she feels about him, he misinterprets her meaning. Compounding this mistake, he says that he wishes to ask her something. Now it is Tose who misunderstands. She thinks he is about to declare his love, when in fact he is about to ask permission to marry Oryo and have her join him. At this point Ryoma and Tose are interrupted—an interruption that we gladly welcome, for we want Tose spared further pain and almost certain embarrassment. As might be expected, at first Tose and Oryo have a falling out over Ryoma, but their bond is too strong to be broken. "We are mother and daughter," Tose declares, urging Oryo to do everything in her power to help Ryoma. Tose has come to understand that it is Oryo whom destiny has chosen to be by Ryoma's side. Her destiny lies elsewhere.

In fact, Tose's destiny lies with Isuke, with whom she reconciles in the closing scenes. Unfortunately, this reconciliation is not entirely convincing. Tose tells Isuke, "Let's just forget everything," adding that she feels lonely without him. "Really?" he asks incredulously, a feeling that viewers are likely to share. Nor does the Isuke we encounter in this scene seem to be the same self-absorbed, absurdly comic fussbudget we have known throughout the film. Now inexplicably sensible, he even promises to give Tose the child she has always wanted. To be sure, Gosho and scriptwriter Yasumi Toshio add a delightful touch when Isuke takes Tose's hand to seal the bargain: he first turns it over and wipes it clean. Thus, we are reminded that the old Isuke has not entirely disappeared. Even so, we wonder what is to become of Tose's free spirit, her desire for release, and her commitment to the struggle for change. Has she given up these dreams? Or are we to believe that the "new" Isuke can help her realize them? Perhaps these nagging questions are part of the reason why some critics find *The Fireflies* to be "very flawed."[17] Yet, its flaws notwithstanding, it has also been deservedly called "not only a great historical movie [but also] one of Gosho's most sympathetic studies of a woman character."[18] Whatever one's view of the film may be, *The Fireflies* occupies a unique place in Gosho's career. Indeed, in this *jidai-geki* he not only undertakes something new but also manages to confirm his art and extend it.

ELEGY OF THE NORTH

Elegy of the North represents a notable departure from *Yellow Crow* and *The Fireflies*. It not only eschews Gosho's usual mood of laughter through tears but also breaks new ground in a way that the other two films do not. Thus, while *Yellow Crow* experimented with color and *The Fireflies* ventured into the *jidai-geki*, *Elegy of the North* refashions a genre that Gosho worked in throughout his career: romantic melodrama. His previous benchmark in the genre was *Once More* (1947), a lavishly mounted celebration of love that served as a political allegory in the immediate postwar period. *Elegy of the North* has far less in common with this film than it does with *Dispersing Clouds* (1951) and *A Visage to Remember* (1948), both of which are intimate psychological studies. A brief comparison with these two films is useful, as is an examination of an equally important source on which *Elegy of the North* draws, European-style storytelling. For many critics, the film ranks among Gosho's finest. As William Johnson has said, "Although *Elegy of the North* (1957) could be described as a triangle of adultery and deception, it goes beyond melodrama to join the small group of films I consider masterpieces."[19]

Based on a bestselling novel by Harada Yasuko, *Elegy of the North* has to do with Hyodo Reiko (Kuga Yoshiko), a restless young woman whose arthritic left arm makes her feel like an outcast. She begins an affair with Katsuragi (Mori Masayuki), an unhappy middle-aged architect whose wife, Akiko (Takamine Mieko), is having an affair with a young medical student (Watanabe Fumio). Intrigued by Akiko, Reiko spies on her; insecure in her relationship with Katsuragi, Reiko taunts him about his wife's infidelity. When he goes away for a month to work in Sapporo, she deliberately strikes up a friendship with Akiko, whom she discovers is filled with remorse over her affair and failing marriage. That Reiko genuinely likes her (and even calls her "Mama") only serves to complicate things. When Katsuragi tells Reiko that he plans to get a divorce, she protests vehemently, but cannot stop herself from seeing him. She even makes a point of visiting Akiko the day he returns from Sapporo, so that she can be "introduced" to him. One day Akiko pays Reiko a visit. When Reiko's grandmother (Urabe Kumeko) accidentally reveals Reiko's affair with Katsuragi, Reiko brazenly admits it is true. Akiko quietly leaves. Following her, Reiko begs forgiveness, but Akiko only smiles and tells her to take good care of herself. Shortly after, Akiko drowns herself. Weeks later, Reiko begins going regularly to Katsuragi's house while he is at work to prepare the meal that Akiko taught her. Once when he returns early, she rushes away, rather than see him. Eventually, he moves to Tokyo, and she resumes her activity in an amateur theatre troupe. En route to a performance, she sees the hotel where she and Katsuragi first made love, and is confronted with the past.

In considering the shaping influences on *Elegy of the North,* we must first look briefly at *A Visage to Remember* and *Dispersing Clouds.* (See the Appendix for a detailed discussion of these films.) The former centers on a triangle involving a woman and the two men who love her, her husband and his former student. In this intimate romantic melodrama, the student and the wife make clear their feelings for each other—he, directly; she, obliquely. However, neither feels free to act on those feelings. In this film Gosho sought to explore the irresolvable tension between propriety, the claims of friendship, and human desire, but felt that he failed to sufficiently probe the characters or material. He fared much better in this regard three years later with *Dispersing Clouds,* which in terms of story and theme has more in common with *Elegy of the North.* Again, a psychological drama in the guise of romantic melodrama, it focuses on a self-centered college girl from Tokyo who falls ill during an outing in the country and is nursed back to health by a dedicated young doctor and a middle-aged woman who works at a local inn. The similarities in story between *Dispersing Clouds* and *Elegy of the North* are readily apparent: the central protagonist of both films is a young woman who needs to be cured spiritually more than physically and who forms a close, if not unambiguous, relationship with an older woman. In addition, she becomes romantically involved with a man who proves to be unattainable. These similarities notwithstanding, *Elegy of the North* has an altogether more intense mood than *Dispersing Clouds,* and is suffused with a bleak melancholy and sense of fatalism lacking in the latter film. Finally, *A Visage to Remember* and *Dispersing Clouds* serve as barometers for the way Gosho progressively refined and shaped his romantic melodrama, not only in *Elegy of the North* but also throughout the rest of his career.

That said, *Elegy of the North* has also been shaped by other influences. As one critic has noted, "The story of the film seems a direct import of some European model."[20] But what exactly is meant by "European model"? The critic offers this explanation:

> In the normal course of Japanese cinematic discourse the focus of the film would centre on the question of the morality of the [adulterous] relationship and the question of the possibility of its success. But in the case of this story, both the attention and sympathy of the writer are given to the feelings and fate of the young woman. Although this was hardly a startling departure in Japanese fiction, its [the film's] popularity is an indication that such a "European-style" story could reach a large Japanese audience.[21]

Understood correctly, this quote states that Gosho's film, like Harada's novel, is "European" in that it depicts sympathetically a character that Japanese film normally would view in moral terms and find wanting. Perhaps so, but there are two problems with this explanation. First, as we shall see, while Gosho never loses sympathy for Reiko, his attitude toward her is far from simple.[22] Second, using sympathy as a measure of what constitutes a "European-style" story is woefully inadequate, especially since sympathy for a female protagonist is "hardly a startling departure in Japanese fiction." In short, a more complete description of "European style" is in order if the term is to have any meaning.

To arrive at that description, we need to recognize that the European "art film" of the late 50s posited a "rational aesthetic" that "chose not to linger on the more sensational aspects of the story or develop the volatile conflicts inherent in the relationship of the [main] characters."[23] In *Elegy of the North* this aesthetic may be seen at work in Gosho's de-emphasis of standard melodramatic rhetoric. Hence the muted confrontation between Reiko and Akiko when the latter learns of the affair and the even more understated parting of Reiko and Katsuragi. Indeed, their parting is not precipitated by a lover's quarrel or even by Akiko's suicide, but rather is a case of two people drifting further and further apart. The rational aesthetic, however, can be best seen in the film as a coming together of the following elements: a mixture of sympathy and detachment in the depiction of character; a privileging of emotion and character psychology over sociological, economic, or political issues; a reluctance to explain or motivate behavior; the use of *mise-en-scène* to communicate inner life; a preoccupation with the theme of obsessive love/compulsive need; and a pervasive sense of alienation.[24]

In examining how these elements refashion Gosho's melodrama, first we will look at how *Elegy of the North* deviates from conventional melodrama by rejecting pat explanations for Reiko's behavior and Akiko and Katsuragi's failed marriage. Next we will focus on how Gosho utilizes the theatre as a metaphor to foreground Reiko's role-playing, structure the dramatic action, and place the viewer in shifting patterns of involvement and detachment. Finally, we will examine how Gosho's use of *mise-en-scène* and his signature analytical editing style express the theme of alienation and impart a surprisingly "modernist" feel to the film.

Although its story is deceptively simple, *Elegy of the North* is intricately structured. As the main credits unfold, we hear the strains of the title song and see wood burning in a fireplace. The camera dollies out, revealing a portrait of a woman above the mantle. Later in the narrative we will return to this setting and learn that it is the Hotel Kohansho, where Reiko and Katsuragi have their first rendezvous. In the final scene we return to this setting once more, but remain outside, as befits a love affair that is now a distant memory. This pattern of repetition and return is key to *Elegy of the North,* and underpins the conceit of lives trapped in an endless cycle of limited options. Scenes are doubled, even tripled (as, for example, Reiko's visits to Katsuragi's office). One Western-style cafe—the unidiomatically named "Coffee Daphne"—serves primarily as a meeting place for Akiko and her lover, Tatsumi, while another cafe—appropriately called "Again"— is identified with Reiko and Katsuragi. Pairings metamorphose in an ever-changing, entangled constellation: Reiko and Katsuragi, Reiko and Akiko, Katsuragi and Akiko, Tatsumi and Akiko, and Reiko and her boyfriend, Mikio (Ishihama Akira). In opposition to this constellation is the film's only stable couple, Reiko's father (Saito Tatsuo) and Mrs. Tanioka (Takasugi Sanae), the widow he plans to marry. Even the roles that the characters assume shift and change. Hence Katsuragi is as much father as lover to Reiko, while Akiko is at once Reiko's rival, mother, and friend. Significantly, these patterns become increasingly complicated as the narrative progresses. To cite one example: the Hotel Kohansho, the signifier of Katsuragi and Reiko's love, is initially contrasted with the Hotel Lotte, the site of Akiko and Tatsumi's single night of passion. But this contrast is problematized when an angry Katsuragi takes Reiko to the Hotel Lotte against her will. "An ideal spot for you," he says, contemptuously.

In *Elegy of the North,* setting and mood are integral to character. The "north" of the title is Hokkaido, Japan's northernmost island, which many Japanese still consider a frontier;[25] the specific location is the southeastern coastal city of Kushiro, which is nearly two hours from Tokyo by air and five hours from Sapporo, the province's largest city, by train.[26] In the film, Segawa Junichi's moody black-and-white photography and Hirata Kanji's smoky, noir-like lighting transform Kushiro into a bleak, isolated place. Subjected to fog and mist blowing in from the ocean and the unceasing moan of a distant foghorn, the city seems as much a state of mind as an actual place. If the overcast daytime skies suggest lives at an impasse, the night scenes, with their empty streets, sharply demarcated pools of light, and elongated shadows, accentuate the dangers of uncontrollable passions, of psyches on the verge of dissolution. During one such night scene, Katsuragi asks Reiko, "Are you afraid to be alone?" No stranger to solitude, she has already asked herself an even more unsettling question. In the opening scene, as she wanders across a desolate volcanic landscape, she ponders: "Am I deformed in both mind and body?" It is the very question that the narrative seeks to answer.

One of Gosho's most provocative and unusual women characters, Reiko is far more rebellious and needy than her closest counterpart, Masako in *Dispersing Clouds.* There is no question that her withered arm makes her feel like an outsider in society. Still, this disability does not "explain" her behavior. Nor does her disability—or her "sharp intelligence," for that matter—necessarily make marriage unlikely, as one critic contends.[27] It certainly poses no problem to Mikio, who is devoted to her, or to Katsuragi, who plans to divorce his wife and marry her. Likewise, her father and grandmother seem less concerned about her arm than her unladylike demeanor, although they may be trying to shift attention elsewhere. However that may be, one suspects that Reiko's problems go beyond her withered arm. This suspicion is reinforced during the talk that she and her father have about marriage. In this rare lighthearted scene he announces that he has found her a marriage prospect, a temple priest. He then pulls out a stack of photographs from inside his suit pocket and begins searching for the candidate in question, apparently not the first one he has brought home. Reiko cannot help but be amused by her father's zeal; nonetheless, she tells him that a priest is not for her. Ever indulgent of his daughter, he does not press the point. But she is not inclined to let him off the hook, and says that the reason he works so hard to find her a husband is because she is disabled. He denies this is so. In a later scene he even says, "Being mother-less has made you a strange girl," implying that his only concern is her un-conventional nature. Whether Reiko believes him either time is unclear. However, during their first talk, she threatens, half-seriously, to come down again with pneumonia, if he persists in matchmaking. To be sure, this scene does not resolve any of the questions surrounding Reiko's disability. But it establishes a pattern that is repeated throughout the film—Reiko is the only character to bring up the subject. Moreover, she never mentions the other "disability" that she refers to in the opening scene: the possibility of being deformed in mind. Nor does she ever broach an equally sensitive subject: the death of her mother when she was a child. Indeed, whenever her grand-mother mentions her mother, Reiko changes the topic.

Reiko, in fact, is something of a contradiction. On the one hand, she evinces the kind of "real and direct feelings" (*jikkan*) that the Japanese ad-mire.[28] Hence her unapologetic declaration: "What I want is not kindness. I want to be loved as fiercely as I love." On the other hand, she can be in-sensitive, cruel, and destructive, never more so than in her role in Akiko's death. Gosho allows no easy response to her, yet he makes sure that she does not lose our sympathy. Thus, most of the film is filtered through her con-sciousness in the form of voiceover narration, frequent shots of her alone, and the privileging of her feelings and emotions in close-ups and reaction shots. No less crucial, she is the most vital character in the film. Indeed, her strengths and weaknesses derive from her vitality, or what one critic aptly calls her "restless energy."[29] Take, for instance, her childlike impetuosity and her utter lack of qualms about asking personal questions. Thus, early in the film, she asks Katsuragi out of the blue, "Are you happy?" Later her ques-tions are far less innocuous, especially those directed at Akiko. "Was yours a love marriage?" she asks at one point. Needless to say, Akiko does not an-swer. In these instances, Reiko's calculating nature cannot be mistaken for childlike innocence. A troubled young woman, she is clearly searching for something. When Katsuragi enters her life, she thinks her search is over.

Immediately attracted to each another, Reiko and Katsuragi have two things in common: loneliness and a desperate need for absolutes. During their first conversation, he tells her that when he was in the army, he visited the ruins of Angkor Vat, the oldest civilization in the Orient, and realized that the houses he builds will never last as long. Katsuragi's remark is revealing. He plainly yearns for something permanent, complete, and absolute, not just in his work as an architect, but in his life. At one time perhaps he sought this fulfillment in his marriage; now he seeks it in his affair with Reiko. Reiko is looking for something no less permanent. Hence her desire to be loved as fiercely as she loves. If Katsuragi and Reiko's absolutism sets them apart from the world they live in, a world that can never realize their expectations, it also leads them to end up inflicting pain on themselves and others.

Like Reiko's character, Katsuragi and Akiko's failed marriage defies easy explanations. Once again, the narrative raises questions, but provides no definitive answers: How did the marriage get to this point? Why does Katsuragi rebuff Akiko's attempts to save it? Doubtless Akiko's adultery has widened the gulf between husband and wife, but it seems to be no more the root cause of their problems than does Katsuragi's adultery. When she asks him, "Why are you so silent?" his only answer is that he wishes they could live happily together, adding, "I share your misery." But this is no answer at all, and the distance between them increases. Katsuragi grows more "strangerlike" (*mizukusai*),[30] and embarks on an affair with Reiko, which only brings about added pain and suffering for all concerned. During their last conversation, Katsuragi even tells Akiko that Reiko is already beyond his reach. It is a curious remark, coming from a character who prides himself on having cultivated an "unruffled temper" to distance himself from feeling. In short, there are no answers to the above questions, only the simple fact that what has been done cannot be undone. Even so, Katsuragi seems needlessly cold and ungenerous. By contrast, Akiko emerges as the film's most bruised and touching character, her efforts to begin anew all for naught. Indeed, her ability to love, care, and suffer remorse touches Reiko profoundly, bringing about a change in this young woman's life.

Perhaps because *Elegy of the North* leaves key questions unanswered, it was even more imperative that Gosho cast the three main roles with actors who brought certain associations from past films. Mori Masayuki excelled in a wide range of roles, including the arrogant samurai in Kurosawa's *Rashomon* (1950) and the bewitched potter who abandons his family in Mizoguchi's *Ugetsu monogatari* (1953). But arguably his most famous role was the worthless lover in Naruse's *Ukigumo* (*Floating Clouds*, 1955), which won him the *Kinema Jumpo* "Best Actor" award and led to other roles as a disillusioned romantic lover.[31] Kuga Yoshiko found success in modern youth films like Naruse's *Furyo shojo* (*Bad Girl*, 1949) and Imai's *Mata au hi made* (*Until the Day We Meet Again*, 1950), where she played independent-minded women in conflict with feudal restrictions.[32] Later in the decade, she played a mellower variation on this role in Ozu's *Higanbana* (*Equinox Flower,* 1958). Like Kuga, Takamine Mieko made her reputation as a modern woman, who was "determined to face the world on her own terms."[33] In films like Yoshimura's *Danryu* (*Warm Current,* 1939) and Gosho's *Once More,* she brought a tremulous sensitivity and quiet dignity to her roles. Together, these actors imbue *Elegy of the North* with a resonance it otherwise would lack.

Earlier I stated that while Gosho's sympathy ultimately remains with Reiko, his attitude toward her is complex. This is borne out in his use of the theatre as a metaphor to delineate her relations with other characters and to place the audience in a position of involvement and detachment. This metaphor is introduced in the opening scenes where the amateur theatre group to which Reiko belongs is rehearsing its latest production.[34] As a member of the crew, Reiko obviously has no chance to do any acting on-stage, but this does not mean that she lacks a flair for drama. She merely saves that flair for real life. Hence her spying on others and indulging in mind games with Katsuragi and Akiko. Her own private kind of theatre, Reiko's game-playing begins innocently enough, but quickly escalates to something disturbing and dangerous, as she progresses from spying to role-playing to wheedling her way into Akiko's life.

Reiko's spying scenes set the stage for the audience's complex interaction with her. At first her eavesdropping amounts to little more than natural curiosity. In one scene she snoops through a crack in the door outside Katsuragi's office to see if he is in. Catching her, he invites her in and they have their first real conversation. In another scene, she is on her way to Katsuragi's house when a couple whom she does not know crosses in front of her. That couple is Akiko and Tatsumi, and their distraught behavior immediately catches her attention. Not about to let this chance encounter go to waste, Reiko follows them, her curiosity having got the better of her. Nevertheless, our sympathy remains with her, even as it extends to the other two characters as well. Indeed, thanks to Gosho's staging, we are granted information that Reiko is denied. Thus, we learn that Tatsumi loves Akiko and wants to speak to Katsuragi, but she will not allow it. For her, the affair is over, and now she is as desperate to end it as Tatsumi is to make it into something more lasting. Reiko hears only the tail end of the conversation, in which Akiko urges Tatsumi to go home. Nor does she see what we as viewers see, for she is hidden a distance away from the lovers—in what is the equivalent of an extreme long shot. By contrast, we face no such spatial barriers, but rather are positioned within the series of shot/reaction shots (mostly medium and close-up in range) that make up the greater part of the scene. As such, we not only hear what the lovers say, but also see the expressions of pain and suffering on their faces. In the process we gain a more complete and accurate understanding of these two people than Reiko does. For Reiko, Akiko and Tatsumi are only objects of curiosity until she sees the family name on the gate outside the house and realizes that the woman she has been watching is Katsuragi's wife. Now she makes certain assumptions: that Akiko is having an affair and that Katsuragi does not know about it. Neither assumption is quite correct. Nevertheless, she has become emotionally invested in these three characters and realizes that her destiny is intertwined with theirs.

In her next encounter with Akiko and Tatsumi, Reiko is not satisfied merely to watch from a distance; she enters their space. The encounter takes place at the Coffee Daphne, where Reiko is seated at the bar having a cup of coffee when the two enter. No sooner do they take a table in a back corner than Reiko moves to a different seat to overhear what they are saying. In a deep-focus shot that includes all three characters, we see that Akiko and Tatsumi are too absorbed in conversation to notice what is going on around them, while Reiko, even though her back is turned to them, is listening intently. Yet listening is not good enough. Thus, she takes one rather long and unguarded look in their direction. Then, observing that the waitress has prepared a tray of coffee for them, Reiko seizes the opportunity and asks if she may take it to their table. In this way she gets her first real look at Akiko. However, what she sees and what we see are two different things. She sees the beautiful face of her rival. We see a plaintive expression on Akiko's face—indeed, as lovely and ambiguous an expression as the *Mona Lisa*'s, whose portrait overlooks the couple's table. We also know, unlike Reiko, that Akiko is still trying to end the affair and let Tatsumi down as gently as possible. Akiko has no idea, of course, who Reiko is or that she is only pretending to be a waitress. Nor does Tatsumi know her identity, although he is immediately suspicious of her. Later in the film, when it turns out that she, not Katsuragi, is his chief rival for Akiko's affections, he even tells her that he always knew she had ulterior motives. Even then, however, his simple decency is no match for her complicated nature and "deformed" mind.

What are we to make of Reiko in this scene at the Coffee Daphne? We no longer can excuse her behavior simply as natural curiosity. Nor can we shake off the nagging feeling that she acts as though being privy to the couple's secrets gives her special rights. Doubtless, she is nosey and presumptuous, but what is most troubling about her role-playing is that she is treading on shaky moral ground and in the end will pay a terrible price. Indeed, shortly after this scene, Reiko grows more audacious in her flirtation with

The first explosion of passion between Katsuragi (Mori Masayuki) and Reiko
(Kuga Yoshiko). *Elegy of the North* (1957).

Katsuragi, as if Akiko's affair has given her tacit permission to do whatever
she likes. In this regard Reiko's chance meeting with Katsuragi at the Again
Bar proves crucial. Not having seen each other since their conversation in
his office, they clearly are pleased to cross paths once more. He even jokingly calls her a burglar, referring to her snooping at his door. Yet their reunion takes a disastrous turn. Reiko's attempt at humor is too barbed: "You
build bars too, so that men can drink and forget their troubles?" And his reaction—telling her that this bar is no place for her—angers and hurts her.
She retaliates with a cruel note: "No one ever scolds me. I'm a free woman.
Hurry back to your 'happy' home, though I doubt your wife is waiting for
you. From the burglar who snooped into your life."

What follows is the first explosion of passion between Katsuragi and
Reiko. He reads the note and leaves the bar without saying a word to her;
she rushes after him. Discussing this scene, Mark Le Fanu finds that Reiko
"throws herself at him as if she had never before held a man."[35] Le Fanu's
observation is shrewd, but the interaction between the two characters is
rather more complex than he suggests. For Katsuragi is just as needy and
sexually attracted to her as she is to him. Still, he greets her sharply: "So you

snooped into my life. A dangerous thing to do," he says, adding that she did so "with a sly smirk." Put on the defensive, she offers a feeble excuse: "I only did this to help." Irritated, she calls him a cuckold. Cutting through all of the talk, he suddenly grabs her by the shoulders, violently shakes her, and presses his hand against her mouth to silence her. Then he kisses her long and hard, while bending her back. (In an insert shot, Gosho cuts to her withered arm, which hangs limp and is dead even to passion.) Freed from his grasp, she wipes the kiss off her lips, but he has turned the tables on her. Her last remaining barrier has been obliterated. The next day, she and Katsuragi reconcile and go to the Hotel Kohansho. Thus begins their affair. Their relationship, however, is never easy, despite their feelings for one another or the moments of happiness they share. Nor, finally, can it survive Akiko's suicide and the differences between them.

The central importance of Reiko and Katsuragi's relationship notwithstanding, it is Reiko and Akiko's relationship that proves to be the most psychologically complex and compelling in the film. This relationship is even more incisively drawn than that of Masako and Osen in *Dispersing Clouds,* another younger woman–older woman friendship. Indeed, in what is almost certainly the major dramatic irony in *Elegy of the North,* Reiko thinks that it is Katsuragi she wants when all along it actually is Akiko—not as a love object or even primarily as a friend, but as the mother she lost in childhood. Of course, this desire is largely unconscious on Reiko's part. Thus, the cruel remarks she directs at Akiko can be viewed not just as examples of displaced childish aggression but as attempts to hide her very real need for Akiko. Given Reiko's behavior, it is not difficult to feel sympathy for Akiko, but our attitude toward Reiko tends to vacillate between sympathy and alienation, involvement and detachment. We are put off by her self-centered behavior, her intrusion in Akiko's life—in short, her unconscionable role-playing, in which she first pretends to be an admirer (who wants to sketch Akiko), then tries to pass herself off as a friend. Yet, by and large we remain sympathetic to Reiko, not only because she has a painfully desperate need to be loved but also because she unknowingly puts herself in a perilous psychological position. Significantly, she crosses the line from *pretending* to be Akiko's friend in order to spy on her life with Katsuragi, to truly *wanting* to be her friend. This change is signaled by the imperceptible shift in terms with which she addresses Akiko. At first she calls her "Madam" or "Oku-san," a term of respect for a married woman, but soon she refers to her simply as "Mama." What Reiko has not foreseen in playing out her game is that she could actually learn to care about Akiko and admire her. When this happens, she finds herself in the untenable position of wanting both Katsuragi and Akiko. In other words, she no longer knows what she wants.

Reiko's dilemma is further complicated by the fact that in her relationship with Akiko she unconsciously enacts a childlike rage against an absent mother. As psychoanalytic studies have shown, the mother has a unique role in the formation of her daughter's psychic and social health. Specifically, in identifying with the mother's "femaleness and femininity," a young girl develops a sense of self.[36] This sense of self has been denied Reiko. Hence her father's charge that she is "strange" and her grandmother's complaint that she is "unladylike." No father or grandmother, however well meaning, can replace Reiko's mother or check her rebellious behavior. That said, when Reiko places Akiko in the maternal role, the result is psychologically a double bind for her. She cannot help resenting Akiko as a rival for Katsuragi's affections or as an unconscious reminder of her lost biological mother. Yet, at the same time she is drawn to certain qualities in Akiko: her deeply caring nature, her capacity for love, her soulfulness and sadness, her physical beauty, and, perhaps most of all, her normality, conventionality, and domesticity—in short, all of the qualities that might be included under the rubric of "femininity." Reiko's love for Akiko is emblematized in Mikio's sketch of her, which Reiko keeps in her room and looks at throughout the film. In fact, this sketch not only captures Akiko's serene and ambiguous beauty, but also invites comparison with the *Mona Lisa* in the Coffee Daphne and the portrait over the mantle in the Hotel Kohansho. Simply stated, Akiko embodies everything that Reiko secretly would like to be, including those things that she has disdained and tried to suppress. Even so, she remains deeply ambivalent about Akiko.

This ambivalence is stunningly visualized in the scene in which Mikio sketches Akiko while Reiko looks on. Having finished the sketch, he tells Akiko about a place where migrating swans can be seen in April. Bored and restless, Reiko sarcastically remarks that Akiko should accompany Mikio to this place since she herself is the queen of the swans. This action is played out in a three-shot that lasts forty seconds. In contrast, the rest of the scene—a tense exchange of nine shot/reaction shots—lasts a total of thirty-nine seconds, and has the impact of successive psychic jabs. In shot two Reiko stands over the seated Akiko and declares that if Akiko were a swan, she would kill her. "I never miss what I take aim at," she says, leveling an imaginary rifle at her at point-blank range. Shot three, a close-up of Akiko's face, captures her discomfort and bewilderment. In shot four, an extreme close-up, Akiko pulls the trigger, then smiles, as if to reassure Akiko that this is just a harmless game after all. Then follows the most dazzling and unexpected shot in the scene: a spectacular image of hundreds of pure white swans rising off a lake. One of the few shots in the film to exemplify high-key lighting—in fact, it is overexposed—shot five represents Reiko's desire to break free from her "deformed" mind and body and to be as beautiful as Akiko. A dissolve leads into shot six, a close-up of Akiko, who smiles demurely at Reiko in what seems to be an attempt to defuse the intensity of the moment. But Reiko's unyielding glare forces Akiko to look away; Reiko has gone too far. This impression is reinforced in shot seven by the look of disapproval on Mikio's face. In shot eight the tense mood that has progressively built up is broken when the phone rings and Akiko excuses herself to answer it. As she rises to leave the room, Reiko lowers her rifle. The scene ends with a brief standoff between her and Mikio. In shot nine, acting as the audience surrogate, he chides her for mistreating Akiko. Naturally, she takes offense.

This disquieting scene is more complex than it appears. At one level, it obviously is an act of psychic violence, in which Reiko plays out the desire to "kill" the mother/rival whom she can never equal in feminine grace or beauty. Indeed, Gosho deliberately overdetermines Akiko's femininity in this scene to underscore Reiko's feelings of resentment and impotence. Thus, he not only has Akiko engage in a traditionally "feminine" activity—crocheting—but he dresses her in an elegant, classically designed dress, complete with a pearl necklace and matching earrings. By contrast, Reiko is in her usual outfit, "the sweater and slacks of the international art movement."[37] And while she bears a striking resemblance to Audrey Hepburn in Stanley Donen's *Funny Face* (1957), next to the stylishly attired, poised Akiko, she seems a bit gawky, even tomboyish. Undoubtedly, she regards herself as the ugly duckling to Akiko's swan. However that may be, it does not excuse her treatment of Akiko, which is cruel and unpleasant to watch. Nonetheless, it would be wrong to see Reiko's behavior simply as an act of barely veiled aggression. It also seems to be a kind of test, an attempt to get a reaction from Akiko and break through the wall of placidity with which she surrounds herself, and which prevents more intimate interaction between her and Reiko. Given this possibility, Reiko's act may be viewed as both the spiteful petulance of a spoiled child and an effort, however misjudged and pathetic, to force Akiko to acknowledge her as her symbolic daughter. This effort, of course, fails miserably, but later the two women do in fact draw closer together and, for a very short time, assume the roles of mother and daughter.

This new phase of Reiko and Akiko's relationship begins when Reiko contracts pneumonia. One night, ill with fever, she shows up at Akiko's doorstep and collapses. Insisting that Reiko stay with her, Akiko nurses her back to health—indeed, she saves her life. In one scene, after Reiko is well enough to return home, Akiko visits her to see how she is doing. By now their relationship has deepened considerably, but Reiko, who is still in-

Reiko brazenly admits her affair to Akiko (Takamine Mieko). *Elegy of the North* (1957).

volved with Katsuragi and trapped in her role-playing, understandably feels unworthy of Akiko's love. "Why are you so nice to me?" she asks. Still, she allows Akiko to tend to her as only a mother might do, combing her hair and braiding it, talking to her about marriage, and even scolding her gently ("You're a bit reckless, but you have your bright side")—something Reiko permits no one else to do. Yet, even at this seemingly harmonic moment, there are undercurrents and intimations, not to mention the inescapable sense that the secrets Reiko is keeping from Akiko will out. Thus, at one point, Akiko notices her portrait beside Reiko's bed. Pleased, she interprets the fact that Reiko keeps it by her side as evidence of the young woman's feelings for her. And, of course, she is right. Yet we also know that Akiko's portrait is only one of two items that Reiko keeps by her side. The other is the book on Angkor Vat, which is metonymic of Katsuragi and which she understandably hides during Akiko's visit. Taken together, these two objects visually convey the conflicting claims of love and loyalty she feels.

Not surprisingly, Reiko admits to her affair with Katsuragi by showing Akiko the Angkor Vat book. No further proof is needed. A powerful scene, it is stylistically a companion piece to the "swan" scene in its use of short, quick shots to express psychological violence. Indeed, no sooner does Reiko's grandmother accidentally reveal the affair than Gosho resorts to six

Shocked by Akiko's suicide, a guilt-ridden Reiko collapses. *Elegy of the North* (1957).

consecutive shot/reaction shots between Reiko and Akiko. In these shots, the two women say nothing; they merely look at each other—Reiko in defiance, Akiko in pain and disbelief. The sheer brazenness of Reiko's behavior is further underscored by an inspired bit of business that Gosho gives her. While a shaken Akiko vacantly turns the pages of the Angkor Vat book, avoiding eye contact with Reiko, Reiko stares intently at her, waiting for her reaction. Reiko even takes slow, deliberate bites from a piece of fruit, an image that is reminiscent of the moment in Alfred Hitchcock's *I Confess* (1952), where the camera singles out a "fat and repulsive woman eating an apple and looking on [a potential mob scene] with an expression of malevolent curiosity."[38] By contrast, Reiko is an attractive young woman, her arthritic arm notwithstanding. Yet the expression on her face is no less an example of "malevolent curiosity." In fact, it is further manifestation of her "deformed" mind. To say that she hurts Akiko is an understatement. But perhaps saddest of all, she hurts herself. Indeed, she throws away any possibility of a relationship with Akiko to exult in a new role: the revenger bent on righting the wrongs she has suffered. However, she quickly learns that this role is hollow and unsatisfying, and one she does not truly want. Rushing after Akiko, she asks forgiveness and begs to be her friend. But the roles of friend and daughter, which before were blurred and tangled, now are shattered. All feeling voided in her, Akiko can only say, "You must take care of yourself. This is a crucial time for you." She then walks away. Reiko has lost her mother not once, but twice.[39]

Akiko's suicide forces Reiko to take a long, hard look at herself. Knowing that her betrayal was a major cause of Akiko's death, she makes the only reparation she can, a symbolic one in which she discovers her true self. As William Johnson notes, most films would have ended with a brief wrap-up after Akiko's suicide, but Gosho continues with a coda, which, "instead of easing the tension . . . increases it."[40] For Johnson, this coda, which consists of two scenes, is an "inspired ending [that] may be *Elegy*'s biggest surprise."[41] In it, Gosho rejects a tragic, downbeat conclusion to show that Reiko can be forgiven for her part in Akiko's death and, in time, can begin a new life. In the first scene Reiko goes regularly to Akiko and Katsuragi's home while he is at work. There, she prepares the special meal that Akiko taught her. For her, these visits are both a gesture of profound respect for Akiko and a form of communion with her. This is especially true of her last visit. Here she begins preparations for the meal by asking Akiko's permission to wear her apron. Then suddenly she bursts into copious tears. "Oh, Mama, forgive me!" she cries out. With this act of remorse, Reiko attains forgiveness.

One of the first things we notice in this scene is Reiko's attire. Her trademark slacks and sweater have been replaced, for the first and only time, by a skirt and blouse, and by Akiko's apron. This change in dress, along with Reiko's preparation of Akiko's meal, would seem to suggest that she intends to replace Akiko. But this is not the case. Indeed, she wants nothing more to do with Katsuragi. Hence when he comes home early one afternoon, she hides from him, then runs away. This said, at first there is something disconcerting about Reiko's new attire and sudden embrace of domesticity; they seem to imply that Reiko must be punished for her former behavior and made to conform. Such a regressive stance, however, would be shockingly un-Gosholike. A far more plausible reading of the scene would be to view it as a powerful illustration of what might be called "Akiko's legacy." Put differently, thanks to Akiko's love and nurturing, Reiko has begun to accept those aspects of conventionality and domesticity in herself that previously she denied. In so doing, she has taken her first steps toward healing, toward achieving the kind of psychic and social health that is a mother's unique gift to her daughter. She also has regained Akiko as her symbolic mother.

However, as the closing scene makes manifest, the process of healing is never complete. While traveling with the theatre troupe, Reiko sights the Hotel Kohansho and is confronted by the past. Feeling dizzy, she asks the driver to stop the truck, whereupon the troupe, in a show of communal solidarity, immediately tends to her. One individual even jokingly declaims, "My black magic will fix you," and places an oversized leaf on her head. A few minutes later, much to his amazement, Reiko tells him, "It really helps." The crisis past, the troupe continues on its way, as Reiko takes one last look in the direction of the hotel. Although this scene is deceptively light, even whimsical in tone, it leads us to wonder what Reiko means when she says, "It really helps." Ostensibly, she is of course referring to her dizziness, but almost certainly she is thinking of her deepest feelings. To be sure, none of the troupe, not even Mikio, knows the significance of the hotel, or how it triggers a plethora of memories and emotions. But that does not matter. The troupe has come to Reiko's aid, and she has graciously accepted it. If they have not "cured" her of the past, they have at least "helped," and this is not nothing. Perhaps their black magic has even achieved something akin to what anthropologist Takie Sugiyama Lebra talks about when she writes: "For the Japanese, truth is associated with what might be called mental exorcism, whereby one is supposed to eradicate all the inner pollutions that are clouding the true self."[42] In this condition, the self comes into "perfect harmony" with the social good and the community.[43] It is unlikely that Reiko has eradicated "all" of her inner pollutions or achieved "perfect" harmony with others. Thus, she is not completely cured, and probably never will be. Even so, she has made a difficult and painful journey since Akiko's death. She not only has discovered her true self but also has overcome the deformity of the mind that has long "polluted" her.

In concluding our discussion of *Elegy of the North,* we need to examine one final matter: how Gosho uses *mise-en-scène,* in conjunction with his signature piecemeal editing style, to express the theme of alienation, and how in the process he further refashions melodrama and extends his range by evoking the mood and feeling of "modernism."

Nowhere does Gosho's synthesis of *mise-en-scène* and piecemeal editing better convey his characters' sense of alienation than in an early scene in which Akiko and Tatsumi try to sort out their relationship. In this scene, which runs two minutes and thirty-four seconds and consists of fourteen shots, setting itself is a metaphor of the couple's tense interaction. The setting is a marsh, a gray, desolate landscape, bordered by a span of mist-enshrouded trees in the background and boasting only one distinct feature, a wooden-truss railroad bridge. Dominating the setting, this bridge, with its framework of four triangular beams, creates an impression of strength and stability that serves as counterpoint to the fragility and tentativeness of Akiko and Tatsumi's relationship. Trying to end their affair, Akiko explains that she feels guilt over Tatsumi's neglect of his medical studies and begs him to return to Tokyo. She also confides that what hurts her most is Kat-suragi's silence. Not wanting to lose her, Tatsumi replies that he too suffers and that he loves her. Trapped in an irresolvable dilemma, the lovers can neither continue the relationship nor break it off. "There is no solution for us," she says, mournfully. And so they continue to meet, for being to-gether—even under these circumstances—is preferable to loss or loneliness.

The first two shots strikingly announce this impossible state of affairs. In the first, an extreme long shot, we see the couple walk toward the bridge, dwarfed by the vastness of the space around them. Shot two is even more expressive. A centripetal composition in which the camera views the bridge and railroad tracks at a 90-degree angle, it steers our eye into the deepest reaches of the frame, using the tracks as the key element of this vanishing-point perspective. In this nearly perfect symmetrical composition, Tatsumi and Akiko walk together yet remain at a distance from each other, he on the left, she on the right—the tracks between them. This paradigmatic shot vi-sually encapsulates the central dynamic of the couple's relationship: their coming together, only to pull away.

This dynamic is most dramatically played out in shots three through ten, which comprise the middle section of the scene. Of these shots, all but one are alternating shots that find Akiko and Tatsumi each confined in sep-arate spaces, their backs turned to the camera or to each other, their eyes meeting only briefly, the expressions on their faces invariably anguished. In the first two shots, shots three and four, the camera gazes objectively on each character in succession, maintaining a certain distance. This, in turn, invites viewers to do the same. Here we observe Akiko and Tatsumi rather than identify with them. By contrast, the remaining shots, shot eight ex-cepted, are shot/reaction shots, that is, subjective shots that render what the character sees. Here the distance between viewer and character is greatly re-duced, and consequently, we are able to feel empathy and sympathy. As the scene progresses, we become even more involved with these two characters.

In this scene composition and editing work hand-in-hand to convey the couple's feelings of estrangement. As noted above, one way that Gosho's compositions reify psychological and emotional space is by placing Akiko and Tatsumi in separate frames. Another way is through the remarkable use of two-shots. Hence shot eight, a simple, yet elegant and implicative com-position. In it, Gosho shoots past Akiko in the right foreground of the frame to Tatsumi in the center background. Turning to face her, Tatsumi briefly speaks, then walks left, almost out of the frame. As Akiko takes a few, tentative steps toward him, Gosho subtly reframes. Drawing near Tat-sumi, Akiko stops, careful to leave some distance between them. She then continues to plead with him, but he keeps his back to her. Only at the end

Alienated lovers: Akiko and Tatsumi (Watanabe Fumio). *Elegy of the North* (1957).

of the shot when he can no longer remain silent does he turn to face her. Although the two characters share the same space in this shot, they do not come together in any meaningful way. If anything, they grow emotionally further apart. Moreover, despite his initial placement in the background of the frame, it is Tatsumi who remains the psychologically dominant character. It is he who must be appealed to, he who has the power to reject that appeal. Equally important, this shot expresses Akiko and Tatsumi's estrangement from each other, not only in spatial terms but also in temporal terms. Twenty-nine seconds long, the shot seems even longer because it is surrounded by shots of much shorter duration, which range from two to six seconds. It also is the only shot in the scene that plays out in real time. In shots nine and ten Gosho reverts to the shot/reaction shot pattern. Once again, the tempo changes and the characters are confined in separate spaces. The impasse has deepened.

The last section of the scene (shots eleven through fourteen) is the most formally arresting. Here Gosho calls attention to his visual style while maintaining illusionism. That is, he incorporates a self-reflexive element without any loss of intensity or involvement in the story world. In shots eleven and twelve Akiko ruefully turns away from Tatsumi and stares at the water below. At this point in the narrative, we read these shots as an expression of her sadness and sense of futility—in short, an apt pathetic fallacy. But ret-rospectively these shots acquire an altogether different meaning, foreshad-owing Akiko's suicide by drowning. Indeed, these may be the very waters in which she dies. A dissolve leads into shot thirteen, an extreme long shot of the bridge from across the marsh, creating a radical perceptual shift in the visual field. This shot in effect puts the action on hold, inviting reflection on what has already transpired. Significantly, it also frames Akiko and Tat-sumi in separate triangular beams of the bridge—an unmistakable image of isolation and entrapment. In the fourteenth and final shot, a medium-long shot, Gosho returns to the now-familiar 90-degree perspective of the bridge. We see Tatsumi standing alone; seconds later, Akiko steps into the frame and approaches him to make one last appeal. Rejecting it, he pulls her to him in an awkward embrace, but she frees herself and walks away. Tatsumi watches briefly, then follows at a discreet distance. Nothing has been re-solved. The scene comes to a close.

One of the most impressive achievements of this scene is the supple-ness of Gosho's piecemeal cutting style. While some of the shots are short, quick shots that typically define this style, the rhythm of the scene feels de-liberate and measured, its early *adagio* pace yielding to the carefully con-structed *largo* of the last three shots, which range from thirteen to forty-one seconds in duration. As we have seen, however, the scene's tempo and mood are not created by shot duration alone, but rather in combination with the use of setting, composition, and other editing strategies. And while these elements primarily serve to bring a psychological intensity to Akiko and Tatsumi's doomed relationship, they also call attention to themselves, deep-ening the melodrama, refashioning it, and going beyond it. Indeed, they in-fuse the scene with a feeling of world weariness, an indefinable grief, which is at once larger and more far-reaching than the lovers' feelings of alien-ation, and which paves the way for the even more profound sense of alien-ation experienced by Katsuragi and Reiko. In this respect Gosho's use of composition, setting, and editing calls to mind the modernist aesthetic of films of the 60s, especially Antonioni's trilogy, *L'Avventura* (1960), *La Notte* (1961), and *L'Eclisse* (*The Eclipse*, 1962).[44] Gosho, however, is no mod-ernist. For one thing, he does not hold the view that "our accustomed ways of making sense are no longer reliable, our received assumptions of the world no longer adequate."[45] For another, he does not subvert or reject "character" or "plot," two cornerstones of traditional storytelling. Nor does he share the modernist's skepticism about the ability to know the self. Nonetheless, in the above scene in *Elegy of the North*, and other scenes as well, his unique conjoining of subject matter and stylistic features has much in common with this aesthetic. No doubt this conjoining is, in large part, the result of his desire to probe human psychology in the most vivid cinematic terms possible. But obviously he also wanted the audience to experience the various rhythms of his characters' inner lives—none more so than the lingering sense of paralysis.

This said, although the above scene epitomizes the film's darker mood, that mood is not the final one, anymore than the theme of alienation is the totality of Gosho's concerns. This is made unmistakably clear in the coda, in which Reiko attains forgiveness and begins a new life. For Gosho, a classical humanist who believes in the possibilities of the awakened soul, human beings can find a purpose simply in the act of living, and through that sense of purpose can bring direction to their lives and the lives of others. In *Where Chimneys Are Seen* he espoused the view that life is what we make it; in *An Inn at Osaka,* that regardless of what life has in store for us, it is the only thing we have. Even in tragedy, as in *Growing Up,* Gosho finds something positive in the human spirit's refusal to be defeated. If in the end, the mood of *Elegy* is bittersweet and tinged with melancholy, it is because Gosho is too much of a realist either to deny the sadness and pain in life or to countenance anything less than hope.

What, finally, can be said of Gosho's experiments in the late 1950s? In *Yellow Crow* he used color to enrich the psychological study of a young boy; in *The Fireflies* he stretched the famously masculine *jidai-geki* genre to examine the heroism of an ordinary woman. These are remarkable, formally innovative achievements. Yet, in the last analysis, *Elegy of the North* seems both the subtlest and most profound of these three films, not to mention the most formally interesting. Here Gosho not only refashions melodrama to produce a trenchant study of adult relationships, but extends his stylistic range as well. For Gosho, the 50s was a glorious decade. With *Where Chimneys Are Seen, An Inn at Osaka,* and *Growing Up* he reached the pinnacle of his career. With *Yellow Crow, The Fireflies,* and, most of all, *Elegy of the North* he proved that the quest to create not only could keep a filmmaker in his mid- to late fifties young but also could result in some of his most thoughtful and innovative work. Throughout the 1960s, Gosho's quest to create would continue unabated.

NINE

Gosho in the 1960s:
Changing Times,
Undiminished Mastery

I n the 1960s, his last decade as an active director, Gosho continued to experiment and extend his range. In the uncharacteristically harsh but stunning *Osorezan no onna* (*An Innocent Witch*, 1965), he chronicled a young woman's short, nasty, and brutish life as a prostitute. In the puppet film, *Meiji haru aki* (*Seasons of the Meiji,* 1968), he told a story about lost love that features a character who looks exactly like Gosho himself in old age. Gosho's quest to create remained as strong as ever, but the industry he had known and helped to shape was changing rapidly. Like other veteran directors, he found it increasingly difficult to work in this new climate.

The changes within the film industry have been well documented elsewhere.[1] Here a brief summary will suffice. In the 1960s television dealt the major studios a severe blow. By 1963, 65 percent of the movie audience owned television sets, and attendance was down by 50 percent from its all-time high in 1958.[2] This trend would continue throughout the next two decades. Television, however, was part of an even larger phenomenon. Until the 1960s the Japanese thought of themselves as a poor nation, but as the economic miracle of modernization took hold and the standard of living increased, the country experienced affluence for the first time. Public attitudes and behavior changed dramatically.[3] According to Sato Tadao, until the end of the 1950s some of the most durable stories in Japanese film had to do with "the poor helping each other out" and "the triumphant survival of the strongest and the most powerful."[4] In the 1960s "altogether rosier ideas became current: 'hard work brings rewards,' for example."[5] Along with these changes, a new wave of young directors emerged. The most influential was Oshima Nagisa, who broke with humanist films of the past, contending that they were hymns to victimization.[6] At the same time, certain genres fell out of favor, unable to accommodate the tastes of the moviegoing generation that was born after the war. The *jidai-geki* gave way to the *yakuza* (gangster) films; sentimental dramas and melodramas, which had long been a Shochiku staple, found new life on television, as female audiences stayed home in droves. Like international films, Japanese film competed with television by giving viewers something the tube could not: more sexually explicit entertainment. Hence the emergence of Nikkatsu Studio's highly profitable *roman poruno* ("soft-porn") genre. Richie points out that 1964 marked a watershed year between the old Japan and "the new economically motivated, transistorized country it had become."[7] Movie studios were forced to retrench quickly, or go bankrupt (indeed, some did). Financial accountability in the form of tight allocations and budgets became the modus operandi. Writers and directors were accorded precious little freedom, control lay in the hands of businessmen, and the producer became the dominant figure, deciding the kinds of pictures that got made and how they were to be made.[8] Only the safest products got the green light. Gosho, like other many other directors, continued to work in this new system as best as he could. But to preserve artistic control, he formed his own independent company, Friend Productions. Even so, he had to depend on the studios to release his films.

In spite of these conditions, Gosho managed to make a dozen films between 1960 and 1968, for the most part alternating between romantic melodramas and *shomin-geki*. As Mark Le Fanu has said, he had lost none of his powers as a filmmaker:

> [I]f I speak especially admiringly of the late films of Gosho it is because they possess a sense of ease that can only have been built up over decades of practice. A late film like *Rebellion of Japan* (black and white, CinemaScope, made a year before Gosho's retirement) demonstrates, it seems to me, an authentic mastery of form and transition: impalpable pauses, rhythms within rhythms, flashes of sky and the weather which sum up a mood—a feat of editing, in short, and economy, which, for refinement, has no parallel in contemporary Western cinema.[9]

True enough, but Gosho's work in this decade was uneven, and some of it was never intended to be much more than well-made commercial entertainment.[10] Take, for example, *Hyakuman-nin no musumetachi* (*A Million Girls,* 1963). Dealing with two sisters (Iwashita Shima and Obata Kinuko), who are rivals in love and who work as tour guides on a sightseeing bus, it was one of a number of Japanese films that had a tie-in with tourist resorts to cover financing costs.[11]

More satisfying and ambitious were the following three *shomin-geki: Kaachan kekkon shiroyo* (*Mother, Get Married,* 1962), *Kaachan to juichi-nin no kodomo* (*Our Wonderful Years,* 1966), and *Onna to misoshiru* (*Woman and Miso Soup,* 1968). In one respect, the first two films were something of a departure for Gosho. Instead of concentrating on ordinary people in the old downtown section of Tokyo, which no longer existed, Gosho turned his attention to country people, celebrating their indomitable life force.[12] *Mother, Get Married,* which is set in a remote fishing village, focuses on the efforts of a single mother (Aratama Michiyo) to raise her boy (Sha Harukuni), choose between two marriage prospects, and contend with her no-good ex-husband. *Our Wonderful Years* is a Ferberesque family saga that is based on the real-life memoirs of a woman who married at age fourteen, reared eleven children, worked the land, and experienced a cornucopia of joys and hardships during forty years of the Showa era (1926–89). An allegory of Japan during this period, it allows "for a nostalgic but not necessarily rosy summary of past happenings—in turn implicitly commenting on the changes in society."[13] *Woman and Miso Soup,* Gosho's last *shomin-geki,* is an engaging, if minor, film about a beautiful, hard-working, middle-aged geisha (Ikeuchi Junko), who is admired as much for her miso soup as her virtue. Recognizing a good business venture when she sees it, she buys a van and begins selling soup out of it. Somewhat ironically, this "Ofuna-flavored film"—a warm, sentimental work made for a female audience—was not produced by Shochiku, which specialized in such films, but by Toho, which was best known in the 60s for its marketable comedies and science-fiction films.[14] This irony notwithstanding, *Woman and Miso Soup* provides a respectable farewell for Gosho's work in a genre that he served well.

Gosho's most impressive work of the decade, however, was probably not in the *shomin-geki,* but in romantic melodrama. This chapter will discuss three of his most highly regarded melodramas. In the first two sections we will examine in detail *Ryoju* (*Hunting Rifle,* 1961) and *An Innocent Witch* (1965), devoting a separate section to each film. Our primary focus will be on how Gosho uses the widescreen—which became a standard format in Japanese films in the 50s—to explore familiar themes, such as the plight of women and male-female relationships, and to dramatize the psychological dynamics between his characters.[15] We also will observe how his signature style of analytical *découpage* and the widescreen process work together. In the third and final section we will briefly consider Gosho's last major film, *Utage* (*Rebellion of Japan,* 1967), and offer some concluding remarks on his achievement and his place in Japanese film history and film history as a whole.

HUNTING RIFLE

Hunting Rifle marks Gosho's third and most successful film in what might be called the "Inoue Yasushi trilogy." The first film, *Waga ai* (*When a*

Woman Loves, 1960), which tells the story of an affair between a young woman (Arima Ineko) and a married, middle-aged journalist (Saburi Shin), was faulted for excessive sentimentality.[16] The second film, *Shiroi kiba* (*White Fangs,* 1960), fared no better with the critics. Focusing on an upper-middle-class family after World War II, its criticism of *giri* (duty or obligation) was found to have no basis in the reality of Japanese society, but rather was inspired by foreign films. The result was a distorted and superficial view of the Japanese family and a far cry from Gosho's usual approach.[17] Nor was Gosho himself satisfied with the film. He especially felt that he had made mistakes in casting:

> "I learned from making the movie *Shiroi kiba* that the actresses who play the women in Inoue's works must have strong personalities," he explained. "In this respect I feel comfortable with the casting of the three actresses in *Ryoju.* As the story is about lonely and anxious people who betray each other, suffer from anxiety, seek love and want to be loved but cannot love or be loved, I found it a challenge to depict this kind of human psychology in visual terms. I consider *Ryoju* to be a psychological suspense film."[18]

Critic William Johnson sees *Hunting Rifle* in precisely these terms. Calling it "a tour de force," he goes on to say that given its "continuous undercurrent of tension," it "might be loosely described as a soap opera overhauled by Hitchcock."[19] A tale of adultery and deception, *Hunting Rifle* is based on the 1949 novel that established Inoue's reputation. Intricately structured, it opens with the narrator (an unnamed poet) relating an experience that he had in the Amagi mountains. There he happened upon a hunter, a total stranger. Struck by the man's overwhelming sense of loneliness, he published a poem about him. One day he received a letter from this man, one Misugi Josuke. Enclosed were three other letters as well. These letters make up the greater part of the novel and are written by the three women in Misugi's life: Shoko, his teenage niece, whose mother Saiko has committed suicide; Midori, Misugi's wife, who has lived with the knowledge that he and Saiko have conducted a long-term affair; and finally Saiko herself, who tries to explain to him her true self, which she has never allowed anyone to know. The novel ends with a brief epilogue, in which the narrator ponders what the letters may have meant to Misugi. Primarily an epistolary novel, *Hunting Rifle* has understandably been given a more conventional structure by Gosho and screenwriter Yasumi Toshio, but they are remarkably faithful to Inoue's characters, incidents, and themes.

Told in flashback, *Hunting Rifle* opens with Misugi (Saburi Shin), a wealthy businessman in his late forties, walking through a snow-covered forest, carrying a rifle. He and his wife Midori (Okada Mariko), who is twenty years his junior, live in Ashiya, a fashionable suburb of Osaka and Kobe. Theirs is not a happy marriage. Also living in Ashiya is Midori's cousin and closest friend, Saiko (Yamamoto Fujiko). While her husband, Kadota (Sada Keiji), is studying medicine in Tokyo, Saiko receives a visit from a distraught woman (Otowa Nobuko), who informs her that he is the father of her eight-year-old daughter, Shoko. She leaves the child for Saiko to raise. Stunned by the revelation, Saiko divorces Kadota, even though the affair took place before they were married. One day Midori introduces Saiko to Misugi. The two not only share a passion for art, but also are immediately attracted to each other and begin an affair. Unknown to them, Midori learns about the affair. Eight years pass. On the surface everything seems fine between Misugi, Saiko, and Midori, but the two lovers feel guilty about deceiving her. Meanwhile she deceives them by pretending not to know. Rejected by her husband, she embarks on a life of partying and meaningless affairs. Falling ill, she is hospitalized. When Saiko visits her, she is confronted by Kadota, who is now the director of the hospital. He tells her he still loves her, but she rebuffs him. Later Saiko becomes ill, and Kadota is called to the house. Once again he tries unsuccessfully to reconcile with her. When Midori visits the recovering Saiko, she is startled to see her dressed in the *haori* (outer kimono garment) that she wore on the day Misugi and she began their affair. Midori confesses that she knows everything. Back home, she also tells Misugi and asks for a divorce. Soon after, Saiko learns that Kadota has remarried. Realizing that she still loves him but feeling she has no reason to live, Saiko takes poison. Meanwhile Shoko (Wanibuchi Haruko) reads Saiko's diary and learns the truth about the three adults' relationship. At Saiko's wake, she tells Misugi that all three adults have acted badly. With Saiko gone and Midori about to divorce him, Misugi goes alone to Mount Amagi, presumably to take his life.

Like Inoue, Gosho and Yasumi are less interested in the social background of the characters than in the psychological impact that the central affair has on them. Thus, the focus is more on self-deception and deep-seated loneliness than on adultery and the deception of others. In this respect *Hunting Rifle* is thematically reminiscent of *Elegy of the North*. Generally, critics are of two minds on the film. Some consider it an excellent psychological melodrama; others feel that Gosho's and Inoue's creative aims are simply not compatible.[20] For these critics, Gosho's talent for depicting harmonious human feelings makes him unsuitable for capturing the quality of narcissism and egotism that defines Inoue's lonely and isolated characters. But clearly Gosho found Inoue's work compelling enough to film not one, but three of his novels. Put differently, although Inoue's approach is more "cold" and cerebral than Gosho's, the two artists have certain concerns in common. They share concerns with human suffering and pathos, loneliness and isolation, and compassionate treatment of their characters. Gosho is especially compassionate toward Saiko.

Then there is their shared love of nature and beauty. Translator-scholar Leon Picon has this to say of Inoue: "While separation and isolation strike gloomy chords throughout Inoue's works, it is to the natural and other visual beauty that he inevitably turns for release, comfort and meditation."[21] Gosho conveys Inoue's feelings about such beauty with complete ease and conviction. Hence the scene in which Saiko and Misugi begin their affair. We see them walk along the grounds of the hotel where they are staying, surrounded by trees that are aflame with autumnal colors—fire-red oranges and burnished golds and ambers. These intensely passionate colors carry over into the evening sunset, which the couple observes from the balcony of their room, the colors bathing them in an expressionistic glow. As Misugi says, nature is even more beautiful, since they share it together. In the hands of Gosho and cinematographer Takeno Haruo, natural beauty is not simply external reality, but a manifestation of Misugi and Saiko's inner feelings, their very souls. Gosho does equally well with the even more difficult matter of "visual beauty." This particular form of beauty originally has to do with Misugi's passion for art, specifically the Tang Dynasty vases that he collects. But later he transfers this love of art to Saiko, whom he is unable to see "except in terms of a precious rare object."[22] He even tells her, when he gives her a vase she has admired, that he no longer needs it since he now has her. True to Inoue, Gosho suggests that there is a dark side to Misugi's aestheticism, which prevents him from truly knowing Saiko or recognizing beauty in other forms (as, for example, Midori's love for him). Indeed, he is trapped in his own ego, and, like Saiko and Midori, is fated to a life of loneliness. In Inoue loneliness has nothing to do with an individual's inability to form relationships with others; rather it has to do with the notion that even in the warmest personal relationships something is missing, "complete fulfillment is negated." And why is this so? Because every human being has "a vital inner sphere (in *The Hunting Gun* it is called a small snake) from which other humans are barred."[23] Did Gosho share this belief? To some degree, yes. But, as we shall see, he also tends to soften and romanticize this belief, for unlike Inoue, he could not philosophically accept negation.

Gosho, however, had no trouble accommodating Inoue's style. Indeed, in *Hunting Rifle* he finds the visual equivalent of Inoue's celebrated precision of language and evocation of calm surfaces in his use of widescreen *mise-en-scène* and analytical editing. In terms of composition, he often divides the frame into distinct vertical or horizontal sections to make visible psychological relations—positioning the figure of interest sometimes in the

The breach that cannot be mended: the space between Kadota (Sada Keiji) and Saiko (Yamamoto Fujiko). *Hunting Rifle* (1961).

center of the frame, sometimes to the left or right side. Thus, in the first confrontation scene between Kadota and Saiko, Gosho situates each character at the opposite side of the frame, leaving the center conspicuously empty. Clearly, the breach between husband and wife cannot be mended. Although Gosho typically uses a rich variety of straight cuts, here he relies on fewer insert shots. Instead he uses the moving camera. Often he sets up a scene in long shot, then subtly reframes during dialogue passages. To suggest that the psychological gap between characters is (temporarily) being bridged, he dollies forward to a closer view; at other times he exploits the horizontal dimensions of the frame by using a lateral camera movement, which "happens" upon the characters in private, solitary moments. For example, in one scene we observe Saiko at her desk writing in her diary; in a parallel scene at the end of the film, we see Misugi seated at the same desk, reading her farewell letter. This is but one instance of the stylistic and dramatic rhymes that Gosho creates in the film. Apropos of Inoue's famed calm surface and inner turmoil, Gosho also gives *Hunting Rifle* a studied, deliberate feel. The film resonates with pauses, silences, things unspoken, and the richly varied rhythms that Mark Le Fanu admires. Together, these elements serve to create what Johnson calls Hitchcockian tension and what Gosho describes as psychological suspense.

Following the opening hunting scene, Gosho gives us two scenes that set up "an ingenious time bomb that will explode at the end."[24] In the first scene we learn that Misugi and Midori's (arranged) marriage is in name only. While Misugi is busy cleaning his pipe in the living room of his modern, Western-style home, Midori, looking especially girlish with her hair down, enters with coffee. Gosho's moving camera follows her, enabling the viewer to see the room in its entirety. In long shot, it looks not only spacious, but positively cavernous—all the more so since Midori remains at the far left of the frame, while Misugi (scarcely taking notice of her) keeps to the right. On the wall a few feet from him is a glass-enclosed gun rack with four of his rifles prominently displayed. As for the wall itself, it is almost entirely glass—a combination of picture windows and sliding glass doors, which open out on the surrounding natural setting. In the middle of the room is a table with several vases from the Tang Dynasty (other valuable vases are showcased throughout the room). Behind the table, a row of black metal bars reaches to the ceiling, sectioning off the living room proper from the entranceway in the rear. Hirakawa Totetsu's set makes clear that this room, which looks like a man's den, is unmistakably Misugi's. There is no room for Midori, or any indication of her personality in it. She is an interloper, and she behaves like one.

Tentative, unsure of herself, almost pathetic in her efforts to please, she tries repeatedly to reach Misugi, who barely tolerates her, but is careful to maintain the illusion of civility. "Can I help?" she asks. When he politely declines her offer and takes a seat in another part of the room, she follows and stands over him awkwardly, trying to think of something to say. Noticing one of the vases on the table (in one of Gosho's few insert shots in the scene), she says that she knows nothing about art and asks him to teach her. "It's not a thing to be taught," he replies. Not knowing what to say, she is visibly relieved when she spots a brochure for the Gamagori Hotel on the end table beside him. Picking it up, she remarks that she would like to go there. (Ironically, it is Saiko, not Midori, whom he will take there.) Finally, accepting defeat, she crosses to the opposite side of the room and sits. The series of medium-long shots of the preceding section now give way to a long shot, which once again makes the room seem cavernous and positions Misugi and Midori as far away from each other as possible. At this moment, however, Gosho pulls a mini-surprise. Misugi notices that Midori is holding something and asks what it is. Seizing the opportunity, she explains that it is a photo album of her schooldays and shows it to him. Almost immediately, a photo of Saiko catches his eye, and he asks who she is. For the first time in the scene Gosho gives us close-ups: one of the photo and a second that registers Misugi's reaction. There is no question that he is intrigued, that he has already made a connection with Saiko. Not surprisingly, when he meets her in person, his first words are, "Just as I imagined."

In the next scene we get a much closer look at Saiko. Dressed, as always, in a kimono, she is the epitome of traditional Japanese womanhood. As the scene opens, she is in the garden, picking flowers when the maid announces that a distraught woman is waiting to see her. This woman is Hamako, who has come to tell her about her affair with Kadota and leave her with Shoko, their child. On the soundtrack, a low, barely discernible beat of a drum can be heard, signaling the shattering of Saiko's peace and serenity. Gosho will repeat this sound throughout the film to suggest the tension and anxiety that his characters feel, no matter how poised and controlled they appear to be. Like the preceding scene, this one makes eloquent use of widescreen to emphasize the relationship between people. But here there are far fewer long shots, since there is little surface politeness or illusion of decorum. In fact, the situation is rife with danger. Hamako immediately takes control and pummels Saiko emotionally. To convey the shock and horror that Saiko experiences as she learns about Kadota's betrayal, Gosho photographs her in a series of ever-tighter close-ups and centers her in the frame. By contrast, he photographs Hamako in medium shots and positions her off to the side, reinforcing her mental instability. Trapped, Saiko can find no safe or separate space, although the small table between her and Hamako provides a buffer of sorts. Yet Hamako, in the most startling moment in the scene, tries to obliterate this space as well. Naming Kadota as her lover, she slams her daughter's belongings on the table, emits a piercing cackle, and then suddenly lunges at Saiko. For a split second the scene threatens to erupt into violence. But just as quickly Hamako pulls back, as if remembering something, and begins fidgeting with her hair. "I can't stay here. I have to be at work," she says, as if Saiko has forced her to stay. She then bolts from the room, leaving Shoko to scurry after her, screaming, "Mother!" Although our sympathy in the scene mainly lies with Saiko, we cannot help but be moved by Hamako's evident pain and desperation. "I don't want to suffer anymore," she says to Saiko early on. Indeed, Hamako's pain and suffering presages what awaits Saiko.

As sympathetic as Saiko is, she is hardly perfect. Her uncle (Yanagi Eijiro) tries to dissuade her from divorcing Kadota, but becomes exasperated and calls her "stubborn." In actuality, she is a mystery to herself. Carrying on an affair with her closest friend's husband, she suffers in the constant knowledge of her betrayal. She also is struck by an irrefutable irony: "I couldn't forgive Kadota for what he did. Why was I able to condone my own inconstancy so easily?" Like Misugi and Midori, she is a study in contradiction, selfish and generous, honest and dishonest at the same time. As one might imagine, of all her relationships, the one with Midori is the most complex and interesting, for it involves the greatest degree of deception and the wearying, unceasing effort by both women to maintain the illusion that theirs is a close and enduring friendship. Indeed, once Midori learns of the

Saiko, Midori (Okada Mariko), and the "hidden" vase between them. *Hunting Rifle* (1961).

affair, she sets out on a path of revenge, goading Saiko in numerous small ways, her mien so unfailingly sweet that Saiko can never know for sure whether the barbs are intentional or not. Every one of their encounters is filled with tension and the possibility that Midori will reveal what she knows, that she will let this particular "bomb" explode.

This bomb finally explodes in the scene in which Midori sees Saiko wearing what she bitterly calls "the *haori* of fond memories." However, an earlier scene is no less tense and even more remarkable in its deployment of widescreen. The scene opens with a close-up of the vase that Misugi has given to Saiko. Then the camera dollies back to reveal Midori in the middle of the room, staring at it. She has just arrived at Saiko's home for a visit, and is waiting for her. It is not difficult to guess how she feels. She cannot help but recall pleading with Misugi to teach her about these precious artworks. Now she is faced with what she has long known: that she cannot compete with her rival. It is a case of insult being added to injury. Upon entering the room, Saiko no sooner greets Midori than she steals a glance at the vase, feeling its overwhelming presence and hoping Midori has not noticed it. Of course, neither woman ever mentions the vase, yet it is the single most important thing in the scene. The discomfort Saiko feels, her ineffectual effort to "hide" the vase, and Midori's pretense that she and Saiko are enjoying just a pleasant tête-à-tête—all of these elements are barely contained beneath the surface.

Gosho's widescreen compositions not only convey the psychological dynamics between the two women but also wittily comment on those dynamics. Thus, in an effort to block Midori's view of the vase, Saiko sits between the vase and Midori. As if to underscore the absurdity of this effort, Gosho's camera position, which looks on the room at a 90-degree angle, has Saiko block the vase from the audience's view, as well. Needless to say, this gives the vase even greater prominence. Moreover, by sitting alongside Midori, Saiko puts herself in an awkward social position, for she has to strain to maintain eye contact. To foreground the fact that the emotional distance between these two women could not be greater, Gosho subtly reframes. As a result, they end up being positioned at opposite sides of the frame, although they are only a foot or two apart. Indeed, in an appropriation of Ozu's famed *sojikei* shot, the women remain seated side by side throughout the scene, their bodies facing in the same direction. In Ozu's films this kind of shot presents conversation not as "contradiction and confrontation, but as sympathy."[25] His characters proceed as if they are "speaking about the same kinds of things" and are "in perfect harmony, as if one image."[26] Interestingly, Gosho uses the *sojikei* shot in exactly the opposite way—to show conversation as contradiction, concealment, and the *illusion* of harmony. In fact, Midori is visiting Saiko expressly to torment her. Thus, she shows Saiko some recent snapshots of herself and Misugi in which they look every inch the ideal married couple. At the same time she talks as if she no longer cares about her marriage, explaining that she has two parties to go to later that day. She also matter-of-factly adds that she is neglecting her health. The latter is true enough, but as we see in the next scene, there are no parties, at least not that day. Instead she sits alone in her vast living room, smoking and drinking. She even is reduced to asking the maid to keep her company. Significantly, Gosho juxtaposes this scene with the one in which Misugi proposes marriage to Saiko, only to be turned down on the grounds that "wicked people like us" do not marry. In linking these two scenes, Gosho reinforces the inescapable cycle of loneliness and sadness that marks these three characters' lives.

In the last scene to be examined, the crucial "plastic object" is not a vase, but a rifle—what the usually laconic Misugi describes as "a merciless cold weapon of destruction, a gleaming instrument of death." The tensest scene in the film, it presents the very real threat of physical violence, as the pent-up hostility between Midori and Misugi finally breaks through the surface. As the scene opens, Midori returns home tipsy after a night on the town and finds Misugi cleaning one of his rifles. She pauses in the entranceway behind the area divider, the prisonlike bars closing in on her and spanning the frame. "I'm home," she says, wanly. He barely looks up to greet her.

Then begins the most powerful portion of the scene. Consisting of twenty-four shots in three minutes and twenty-three seconds, it employs widescreen composition and editing to stunning effect. Indeed, Gosho creates a montage of Hitchcockian psychological tension, stretching out time and detailing his characters' every action and gesture. The first half of the scene is pure cinema. It is essentially silent, except for the few words that Midori speaks. (Sound begins in earnest only in shot fourteen, after Misugi pulls the trigger twice—and we hear empty clicks, followed by a drumbeat, which continues to the end.) The action is classically simple: a weary, demoralized Midori takes a seat across the room from Misugi. Gradually she becomes aware of his reflection in the window: he is aiming his rifle directly at her. In the series of shots that follow, Midori's face registers a range of feelings and emotions—from outright fear and hurt to calm resignation to her fate. Misugi's face has a fixed, determined expression. In the first half of the scene he is always centered in the frame, even in the very striking shot in which he is a blur in the background and only the tip of the rifle barrel is in sharp focus and close-up. By contrast, Midori is confined to the left of the frame, the gun rack behind her occupying the right half. Thus, Gosho shows her trapped on both sides by the threat of violence. Most of the shots of Misugi and Midori are medium or close-up. As such, they not only foreground his hatred of her and her own self-hatred, but also the sense of suffocation that both feel—their lives a living hell, their stylish living room, a prison. Clearly, Gosho understands that widescreen can be uniquely effective in showing confinement.

However, this does not mean that Gosho is any less a master at exploiting the full spatial possibilities of widescreen. Indeed, he opens this section of two dozen shots with an establishing shot that places Midori and Misugi at opposite ends of the room. Throughout the scene, he returns to long shots at key moments, most notably in the climactic shot where Midori turns the gun on Misugi and aims it at point-blank range. Taking the gun from her, Misugi leaves her standing in the middle of the room and returns it to the rack. She walks over to him and embraces him (there is no question she still loves him), but he pulls frees from her and takes a seat across the room.

In the penultimate shot of the scene, an emboldened Midori confronts Misugi in a way that she has never done before. Running forty-three seconds, this shot is the most dramatically decisive in the scene. It also is the longest in duration. (By contrast, the shortest is a mere one second, and the average shot duration is approximately eight seconds.) In this shot Midori—having been not only rejected but also symbolically murdered—redefines her relationship with Misugi. Acting as much out of pride as pain and humiliation, she unceremoniously pulls the tie from around his neck, declaring that it doesn't match his outfit. From now on, she says, she will

Misugi (Saburi Shin) takes aim at Midori. *Hunting Rifle* (1961).

Midori's initial reaction. *Hunting Rifle* (1961).

Midori waits for Misugi to pull the trigger. *Hunting Rifle* (1961).

pick his ties. It is the only wifely duty she has left, and she lays claim to it. At the same time, however, she is making clear that from this point on she intends to do exactly as she pleases.

Ultimately, of course, there are no winners in this roundelay of adultery and deceit. In what is perhaps the film's most moving scene, Saiko painfully realizes as much. Having lost Kadota forever, she takes out two photo albums and carefully removes the photos of him. But unable to throw the photos away, she arranges them in a small pile and places them inside one of the albums. Then she takes a small case from a drawer and opens it: it is her wedding ring. She has kept the ring all this time—clearly in hopes of reconciliation, which in the last analysis she herself could not allow. The final legacy of adultery and deceit is found in Saiko's letter to Misugi. Here she explains that the small white serpent she had was "neither love nor hate, but the attachment I had for Kadota." She goes on to say that when she left him, she was lonely, and that when she took Misugi in her arms, she resolved to deceive him and herself as long as she lived. This deceit was her small white serpent—her true inner self. As we might expect, Gosho's Saiko is softer, more "romantic" than Inoue's. Thus, she declares that her behavior was rooted in her love for Kadota. Inoue's character says no such thing. On the contrary, she admits the possibility that her behavior was driven by love or hate (she isn't sure which). However, she finds no consolation in the memory of her love for Kadota. What is interesting is how Gosho is faithful to Inoue's notion of the "small white snake" except in this one detail, a detail that happens to make all the difference. Put simply, Gosho believes in love, and so does Saiko, even in her darkest hour. And Misugi? What finally does he believe in? The ending seems to suggest that Misugi's cold art has engulfed him. As he finishes reading Saiko's letter, Gosho dissolves to a shot of him alone in the snowy landscape of Mount Amagi, carrying a rifle. We are back at the opening scene. In the shot that follows Misugi makes his way up a slope, receding into the distance.

AN INNOCENT WITCH

Gosho's most critically acclaimed film of the 1960s was *An Innocent Witch* (1965). Ranked seventh in *Kinema Jumpo*'s "Best Ten" poll, it is rightly considered to be one of his most powerful works. Set on the Shimokita Peninsula in the northernmost area of Honshu, the film tells a stark and harrowing tale. Oshima Ayako (Yoshimura Jitsuko), a young woman in her teens, lives in a small, impoverished fishing village. Her father, Matsukichi (Yoshida Yoshio), is too ill to work. As a result, her mother, Kikuno (Sugai Kin), sells her to a nearby brothel. There she quickly is stripped of her innocence and illusions. Her first customer is Yamamura Kansuke (Tonoyama Taiji),

The Japan Film Center in Association with The Museum of Modern Art presents

HEINOSUKE GOSHO RETROSPECTIVE

December 1, 1989–March 9, 1990
13 Fridays, 24 Films
at the Japan Society

December 5–14, 1989
7 Films, each screened twice
at The Museum of Modern Art

Program cover for the Gosho retrospective at the Japan Film Center and the Museum of Modern Art in New York: Yoshimura Jitsuko in *An Innocent Witch* (1965). Courtesy of the Japan Society of New York.

a middle-aged man who owns the largest lumber business in town. Soon after, she sleeps with Toda Kanjiro (Terada Minoru), a young male virgin whose innocence attracts her. The two fall in love, but she is shocked to discover that he is Yamamura's adopted son; he, in turn, is shocked to find her having sex with his father. Still, their love prevails, and when he is drafted, he asks her to wait for him. Ayako wants nothing further to do with Yamamura, but he forces her to have sex with him. Suffering a heart attack, he dies. Shortly after, Ayako receives news of Kanjiro's death in China. Once the most popular prostitute in the brothel, she now is an object of scorn and derided as a "man killer." One day she goes to the cemetery to pray at Kanjiro's grave. There she meets Yamamura's oldest son, Kanichi (Kawasaki Keizo). At first their relationship is platonic, but eventually they make love. When he proposes marriage, she accepts, but their happiness is cut short when he is struck by a military truck and killed. Her reputation as a "man killer" thrice confirmed, she is shunned by prostitutes and customers alike. At the brothel madam's urging, she goes to the Osorezan shrine to be exorcised of demons that are thought to possess her. During the ritual, she is struck repeatedly with a cane and dies, a peaceful expression on her face.

Based on Ogawa Hajime's award-winning novel, *Reiba no onna* (*A Woman in a Sacred Place*), the film is set in the Osorezan, a desolate and gloomy wilderness that is one of the three most sacred places in Japan. Local folklore has it that the Osorezan is the entrance to the world of the dead. Each July a festival is held, in which pilgrims come to establish contact with the spirits of deceased family members with the help of old women called *itako*. These women, most of whom are blind, perform a shamanistic ritual that entails the use of trances and objects associated with the particular dead spirit.[27] While this indigenous custom and tradition has been the subject of various plays in underground theatres,[28] it received popular exposure in Uchida Tomu's *Kaiga kaikyo* (*Hunger Straits*, 1964), a crime drama, in which the Osorezan served as a backdrop.

However, it is not custom or tradition that primarily interests Gosho and screenwriter Horie Hideo, but Ayako's tragic life. As Donald Richie points out, in *An Innocent Witch* "a feudal society pushes the girl, played by Jitsuko Yoshimura, into a whorehouse, and a feudal religion kills her when a priest beats her to death trying to exorcise the evil spirits he believes live within her."[29] For Gosho and Horie, Ayako's tragedy is that she internalizes the feudalistic thinking of her society, which promulgates absolute loyalty and subordination of the self. This thinking not only convinces her that she is possessed but also robs her of her individuality and eventually crushes her. In a 1999 talk he gave on the film, Horie recounted how he came to empathize with Ayako. While traveling to the northeastern part of Honshu to scout locations, he and Gosho visited an old house that once was a brothel. "When I walked down the old hallway," he explained, "I felt empathy for Ayako's life. . . . And I still remember the moment when I felt confident that I could write about the world of *An Innocent Witch*."[30] Tellingly, that world also includes the war that Japan was waging in China.

An Innocent Witch is Gosho's darkest work. Its unique mood is evident from the opening scene, with its strange, otherworldly setting and Kikuno's desperate desire to make contact with her deceased daughter. We learn that Ayako died on September 11, 1940, but we have no idea how much time has passed since then. We only know from Kikuno's greeting to the *itako* that this is not her first pilgrimage to the Osorezan. It is as if time has stood still. As the film moves into the long central flashback, which makes up the greater part of the narrative, another date appears on the screen: "Autumn 1938." The year that Ayako entered the brothel, it brings home a brutal fact: that she had barely two more years to live.

In this scene, as in the film as a whole, Gosho uses widescreen boldly. Hence the transitional shot into the flashback. It begins as an intense close-up of Kikuno's face. Then, as ambient sound fades away, the camera pans left, across the entire frame, traversing open, sterile terrain. In this single shot, as we move simultaneously across time and space, Kikuno's consciousness gives way to Ayako's. It is her consciousness that controls the narrative, even when the images are not literally from her point of view.

When we first meet Ayako, she is a young woman whose purity and innocence is associated with nature. Standing in crystal-clear water, fishing, she is vibrant and alive, worlds removed from the spare and austere volcanic landscape of the opening scene or the constrained interiors of the brothel. In the broad horizontal expanse and open frames of the widescreen, the seascape seems Edenic. Ayako is nature's unspoiled child. Thus, en route to the brothel, while Kikuno makes arrangements with the broker who has come to accompany them, she occupies herself by petting a horse, the busy transactions of the adult world of little concern to her. But unspoiled nature is not exactly what the brothel wants. No sooner does Ayako arrive there than the madam (Nakakita Chieko) begins her lessons in brothel etiquette. In a scene that reminds one of something out of Colette, the madam instructs Ayako always to speak politely, coquettishly, seductively. She also tells her never to say "ain't." It is as if the brothel were nothing more than a rather exclusive finishing school. Not surprisingly, Ayako has little idea of the world she is entering. In fact, she is too overwhelmed by its size, splendor, and shiny corridors to think clearly. As she sees it, she has fallen into good fortune. And in a grim sort of way, perhaps she has. For what other options does a woman of her class have? No matter that she is complicit in her own exploitation by agreeing to enter a brothel in the first place, something she has done out of a sense of filial duty and obligation (*giri*). In agreeing to be sold, she has abdicated any right to freedom and happiness. For her, *ninjo* (personal desire) no longer exists.

As always, Gosho brings a fully realized, lived-in texture to his milieu. In *An Innocent Witch* the brothel functions in much the same way as the inn in *An Inn at Osaka*. It is a world unto itself with a unique set of manners and mores. But there is one notable difference: flesh peddling requires all the style, decorum, and overlay of euphemisms it can muster. Thus, human interaction (especially between prostitutes and clients) is sublimated by social ritual, and the crassness and nature of the business are denied. Yet, as we shall see, this facade is forever breaking down or threatening to do so.

A confining and repressive place, the brothel is epitomized in one of the film's most expressive visual motifs: a shot in which the prostitutes are lined up in a narrow entranceway that looks out on the street, an area whose wooden bars make it resemble a cage. Identified with the statues of *maneki-neko* (beckoning cats), the women try to entice passers-by. Able to see and be seen, but physically constrained, they exert what limited power they have by "beckoning," which occasionally means heckling reluctant or un-interested males, but which mostly means being submissive and inviting. Apropos of confinement, this motif is dominated by *hikisoto* shots, in which an open door, window, or some other object is placed between the actor and the camera.[31] Here the wooden bars that span the widescreen frame reinforce the notion that there is no escape.

Gosho's most significant use of this motif is to chart the different phases of Ayako's life in the brothel, in particular the last two, which find her in an ever-deepening depression. In the first of these appearances, she is in a numbed state, haunted by the fear that she is responsible for Yama-mura's death. Yet she is still required to solicit customers. When three men pass by and point her out as Yamamura's killer, adding that she has had his son, too, it is too much for her. Something snaps, and she screams at them, shattering all pretense of brothel decorum. Then, in a transition shot into the next scene, Gosho's camera pans across the frame, past the wooden bars into a close-up as Ayako studies her face in a mirror, trying to determine whether it masks an evil inside. In her final appearance in the cage, she is even more withdrawn. Devastated by yet another death, this time Ka-nichi's, she clings to the cigarette lighter he gave her to pledge his troth. The other prostitutes, however, have no sympathy for her. Infuriated with her for driving away customers, one of them even physically attacks her. From this point on, Ayako's depression and isolation are made worse by the women's insistence that she is possessed.

Of all Ayako's relationships, unquestionably the most important are those with Yamamura and his two sons. In the first of these relationships, Ayako's virginity is sold to Yamamura, a rich, middle-aged businessman whom the brothel fawns over. To convey the grotesque nature of this rela-tionship, Gosho privileges close-ups and extreme close-ups. These close-ups, however, would not be as effective without the scene in which the madam prepares Ayako for her night with Yamamura. Here a finely attired Ayako kneels before a mirror, while the madam puts the finishing touches on her hair and gives her last-minute instructions. Speaking as if everything were being done for Ayako's personal benefit, the madam explains that tonight she is beginning a new life and will become what every woman is destined to be. The madam also takes pains to impress upon her how lucky she is to be favored by Yamamura and tells her to obey him. Then, to stave off the sordid reality of what is about to take place, she invokes the metaphor of marriage. As she does so, she delivers Ayako, the "bride," to the room where Yamamura, the "groom," is waiting, opening the shoji screen just enough for Ayako to be seen, just enough to create the proper ef-fect. An inspired shot, it fixes Ayako at the edge of the frame, her face in profile looking off to the right. Gosho keeps the camera on her throughout the shot, while off-screen the madam and Yamamura briefly converse. "Is the bridegroom ready?" she asks. Neither moving nor speaking, Ayako betrays no emotion. What she is feeling, how much she understands, we can only surmise. But one thing is certain: there is no joy on her face.

The moment Ayako and Yamamura are left alone, any pretense of nuptials is quickly shattered. Yamamura forces her to drink, explaining that it is the custom on the wedding night. Then, eager to get down to business, he pulls her to his side. The violence of his act is reinforced by Gosho's unbalanced composition, which in widescreen seems even more unbalanced, for it leaves the right half of the frame empty and the couple crammed together along the left side. Exposing this encounter for what it is, Gosho employs a series of close-ups and extreme close-ups. Specifically, a tight close-up of Yamamura and Ayako is followed by an even more suffocating close-up, in which he compliments her on what a nice ear she has, then sticks his tongue into it—a stomach-turning metonym of the penetration-to-come. Ayako recoils in disgust. Yet Yamamura remains undeterred. Stroking her repeatedly, he virtually drools. "Charming, very charming," he says. Then he bends her back in a painful-looking embrace. The scene ends with an extraordinary close-up of her face in profile. Unlike her earlier profile shot, this one spans the frame *horizontally*, her face cast downward, her eyes looking vacantly into the void below. Later, after Yamamura has finished with her, the madam checks in on her and finds her weeping inconsolably. "It's foolish to cry," she says. "You're a woman now." Ayako says nothing, but when the madam leaves, she takes her hand and wipes Yamamura's kisses off her lips. Then she walks toward the camera, framed by the bars which border one side of the room. It is a *hikisoto* shot that needs no explanation.

Ironically, Ayako experiences romantic love for the first time with Yamamura's adopted son, Kanjiro. By the time she meets him, in the winter of 1939, she has come to terms with her life in the brothel and has discovered that she enjoys sex. But thanks to her innate decency, she also has remained miraculously unjaded. Indeed, what draws her to Kanjiro is his innocence.

Their first encounter provides a complete contrast with Ayako's sexual initiation by Yamamura. Here she is dominant, their interaction marked by playfulness and affection. She can see immediately that he wants to be coaxed, so she obliges, virtually dragging him upstairs to her room, while gently teasing him. Once they are there, Gosho privileges Kanjiro's nervousness with two subjective shots: an insert shot of an erotic print (*shunga*) on the wall—which gives him pause—followed by a panning shot across two futons that are waiting to be used. Kanjiro's nervousness, however, does not prevent him from grabbing Ayako impulsively, roughly. Breaking free, she scolds him, and laughs at his clumsiness. Only then does it occur to her that this is his first time. In a tender two-shot, as he sits expectantly, she begins to unbutton his shirt, assuring him that she will tell him what to do. In subsequent scenes Gosho uses variations of this two-shot to highlight the relatively few moments of happiness that the couple enjoys.

Not surprisingly, Gosho's widescreen strategy changes dramatically when Kanjiro learns that Ayako is sleeping with Yamamura. Here Gosho reprises the pattern of intense close-ups that he used in the "wedding" scene. Thus, when Kanjiro reveals that he is Yamamura's adopted son, Gosho has Ayako cross the room in close-up, a stunned, sickened expression on her face. No less sickened, Kanjiro (in medium shot) explodes: "The first woman I embrace—my father's woman!" Then to reinforce the shame and revulsion Ayako feels, Gosho cuts to a close-up of her face in profile. A repetition of the shot that concluded the Yamamura scene, it spans the frame horizontally, her head cast downward, her eyes filled with tears. As such, it underscores the fact that Kanjiro's revelation has as violent an impact on her as the rape itself. Unable to look at him, she orders him to leave. The scene does not end here. Seething, Kanjiro slaps her across the face repeatedly, then rushes out. In replaying visual strategies from the Yamamura scene, Gosho does not mean to imply that Kanjiro is like his father. Rather, he means to foreground the diapason of unkind fate that marks Ayako's life.

Violent as this altercation is, it does not end the relationship. When Kanjiro is drafted, he returns to the brothel to tell Ayako, and they reconcile. Gosho expresses their continuing love for each other in a two-shot that echoes the one in their first meeting. At first Ayako and Kanjiro sit at opposite sides of the frame. As they continue talking, little by little, almost imperceptibly, she moves closer toward him until she is by his side. Widescreen is used no less effectively in the next scene, which Mark Le Fanu has called the most passionate in the film.[32] Here Gosho gives his horizontal compositions an altogether different meaning from those in the Yamamura scene. Making love for the last time before Kanjiro departs for China, the couple spans the entire frame. In an act that is unusually realistic, they kiss, a line of spittle connecting their lips as they draw apart. An admittedly novel use of widescreen, this kiss was probably not planned. Nevertheless, Gosho kept it in the film, perhaps because it undercuts one of the brothel's most curious and artificial prohibitions: that kissing between prostitutes and clients is not permitted—a prohibition that has the effect of making a kiss seem an even more intimate act than intercourse. Thus seen, the couple's kiss reclaims lovemaking as a natural expression of feelings rather than a prescribed code of commerce.

In the next sequence, however, Gosho returns to widescreen strategies he deployed during Ayako and Yamamura's first encounter. Here Ayako tries to break off with Yamamura, but he overpowers her and rapes her a second time. In one shot he brutally pulls her to his side, leaving most of the frame empty. Two quick close-ups follow—a shot of her hand clutching the edge of the futon, a shot of her feet pressed against the wall. Yet these close-ups reveal a very different Ayako from the naive innocent of the earlier encounter. No longer passive, she physically defends herself, refusing to be victimized. However, in the end, events conspire to make her even more victimized than before. Yamamura dies in her bed. Soon after, she receives news that Kanjiro killed another soldier in a quarrel over her, then committed suicide. Blamed for this tragedy, she is branded a "pernicious influence" and treated like a pariah.

It is during this time that she meets Kanichi, Kanjiro's half-brother and Yamamura's natural son, and falls in love a second time. The happiest of her relationships, albeit the most psychologically ambiguous, it is enshrouded in an atmosphere of foreboding from the start. Indeed, Kanichi and Ayako first meet in a cemetery. As she places flowers at Kanjiro's grave, Kanichi approaches her, asking if she is from the "Seven Fortunes" brothel. Frightened, she says no and hurries off, a long shot dwarfing both figures in an expanse of tombstones. Here the combination of setting and widescreen achieves a most unsettling effect. In their second meeting, Kanichi confronts Ayako at the brothel about the deaths of his father and brother. Prepared to condemn her, he discovers that she is no monster, but an exploited young woman filled with guilt and remorse. Touched by her plight, he makes a startling proposal: he will visit her regularly, posing as a customer, to prove the rumors wrong. Theirs will be a platonic relationship.

To convey the ambiguity and sense of foreboding that surrounds Ayako and Kanichi's relationship, Gosho privileges diagonal compositions. This strategy is best illustrated in the scene where Kanichi first stays overnight with Ayako. As they lie in their futons, Ayako expresses anxiety about the curse on having sex with a father and son. She is especially uneasy because she senses the undercurrent of desire between herself and Kanichi and does not want to tempt fate. In this scene, diagonals are key. Take, for example, the spatial arrangement of Ayako and Kanichi's futons. Although they are placed next to each other, they are not quite parallel, as would normally be the case. Rather, Kanichi's futon is lined up at a 90-degree angle to the top and bottom of the frame, while Ayako's is positioned at a slightly diagonal angle, the head of her futon extending away from his, the foot almost touching his. In fact, at one point she accidentally touches him and apologizes. As both characters realize, this moment brings the possibility of sex to the surface, but here that possibility is denied for an altogether different kind of intimacy. Thus, slipping her feet inside Kanichi's futon, Ayako confides that she is lonely when he does not visit. Urging her to go home on her vacation, he graciously offers to accompany her. They then link their fingers in *yubi-kiri*, the sign of a promise or pact.

This idyllic moment does not last. Kanichi remarks that there is something "fatal" about Ayako, even "lethal." Cut to the quick, she bursts into tears, his words being too close to the world's opinion of her. Kanichi apologizes, explaining that he was joking (!), and insists that she is "just an ordinary human being, that's all." But this momentary breach suggests the fragility of their relationship and the dangers it faces. Gosho underscores this fact in the scene's two most unusual close-ups, which position Kanichi and Ayako at diagonal angles—his face slanted to the upper right of the frame, hers to the upper left. Like the spatial layout of the futons, these off-angles call attention to themselves, creating a sense of instability and leaving the viewer tense and uneasy.

Appropriately, Gosho saves his most conventional use of widescreen for the couple's one unequivocal moment of happiness: their frolicking on the beach during Ayako's vacation. Echoing Ayako's introduction in the film, this scene gives us the Ayako of old—spontaneous, ebullient, filled with life. Here she runs along the beach, umbrella in hand (until it is whisked away in the wind), urging Kanichi (dressed in suit and tie, no less!) to catch up. Here there is time for horseplay, as the couple splashes in the water and makes a competition out of digging in the sand. There is even time to dream. Thus, Ayako speaks of someday having a house of her own. Gosho's compositions seem to take their cue from the horizon line itself where sand and sea meet; and while the scene is admittedly overdetermined in terms of style and content, that is almost certainly the point, for it constitutes a reprieve from reality as a fantasy of Edenic bliss. For Ayako, this outing is a return to childlike innocence, yet never has she seemed so sensual. This paradox is not lost on Kanichi, who looks admiringly at her body, the pan down her legs representing his point of view.

Back in their room at the inn, the couple finally make love. Initially, Ayako resists: "No! Something will happen," she protests, but Kanichi insists that this is superstition, and she yields to her feelings. Following their lovemaking, a tight close-up of their faces fills the frame. In it, Gosho photographs Ayako exactly straight on, while Kanichi appears in profile, looking off to the right, away from her. At first this composition leads us to think that the characters are too ashamed to look at one another, an impression reinforced by Ayako's blank expression and dire comment: "We're doomed." Kanichi's response, however, corrects this misimpression. "Be my wife," he says. Gosho's camera then slowly reframes, pulling back to a slightly wider view of the couple. "It's like a dream," Ayako declares, weeping for joy and leaning her head on his shoulder. Pledging his troth, Kanichi places his cigarette lighter in the palm of her hand. However, their dream of happiness is tempered by Akutagawa Yasushi's atonal score, which rises on the soundtrack, and the diagonals of the next scene, which make an unwelcome return. In yet another instance of capricious fate, Ayako and Kanichi miss their train, and when he tries to flag down a military truck, he is fatally injured. Now the atmosphere of foreboding takes center stage.

In the closing sequence Ayako is viciously beaten to death by a crazed priest intent on purging her of evil spirits, her sexuality far too threatening to be contained. Undoubtedly the most violent passage in all of Gosho's films, it may strike some viewers as sensationalistic and may even evoke outrage, but that is what it is meant to do, for it is the final, unforgivable act perpetrated on a human being who has been repeatedly brutalized. In an earlier scene, in her proudest moment, Ayako invokes Kanichi's words, protesting, "I'm just an ordinary human being." In this last sequence, however, she rejects these words and accepts society's view of her. It is a sad and frightening thing to see. Saddest of all, only at the moment of death does she experience peace. A serene expression appears on her face. Eerily beautiful, it constitutes the most damning condemnation possible of feudal society.

Ayako's tragedy is given even greater resonance by the parallel with Japan's war in China. During 1938–40, the period that the story covers, the war had escalated into a full-blown conflict. In *An Innocent Witch*, its impact is visible everywhere. When Ayako first arrives at the brothel, soldiers are marching in the street. When she and Kanjiro meet, the war is intensifying and military slogans abound. In fact, the "spirit of attacks," a slogan he mockingly refers to at one point, is clearly inspired by the phrase "spiritual mobilization," which emerged out of the *Kokutai no hongi* (*Principles of the National Polity*), a 1937 educational pamphlet that promoted putting the nation before the self.[33] As part of the mobilization effort to achieve national unity, such slogans marked another step in the military's domination of the country, sealing Japan's fate just as certainly as Ayako's life as a prostitute sealed hers.

Of all the characters in the film, only Kanjiro expresses opposition to the war. Through his eyes, we follow key events of 1939, such as the occupation of Hainan Island to cut off Chiang Kai-shek from foreign help.[34] In-

deed, when Kanjiro is drafted, he not only tells Ayako that common soldiers are merely cannon fodder, but also orders her to write her name on the
Japanese flag—a deliberate act of defiance and desecration. Ayako com-
plies, yet she does not really understand his political views, for what she sees
around her is a country caught up in patriotic fever. By contrast, Kanjiro
sees the harsh reality: the country's willingness to sacrifice young and innocent lives, his own included. Passionate and idealistic, he is too hotheaded
and intemperate to make clear to Ayako that the war affects them in more
ways than just their separation. In short, he is ultimately ineffectual. From
the front he sends a postcard, urging her to "keep the home fires burning."
Doubtless he is being sarcastic, but the point is lost on her. She proudly
shows his note to the madam, who replies, without the least bit of irony,
that keeping the home fires burning is just what the brothel is doing.

In fact, the brothel and the military enjoy a mutually beneficial relationship. This relationship is borne out even in language. Thus, in one
scene three sailors announce their arrival at the brothel, exclaiming, "Full
speed ahead at thirty knots." The implication is hard to miss. If military
language can be used to describe whoring, then what difference is there between what is done in the name of duty and what is done in the brothel? As
if to punctuate this point, Akutagawa gives a snippet of martial-sounding
music a jaunty, airy rhythm.

In this climate of war fever, the military's overweening arrogance cannot be checked. When Kanichi is fatally struck, the driver shouts, "Fool!
Trying to stop a military truck!" and just keeps moving. The loss of individual life means nothing. The scene is even more chilling when one realizes that the driver is almost certainly an ordinary soldier and that most of
these men hail from rural, impoverished areas.[35] As such, they are by and
large the male counterparts of women like Ayako. Indeed, like Ayako, this
driver has internalized society's attitudes, but unlike her, he is so puffed up
with his newly gained status that he has lost his humanity.

As a woman and a prostitute, Ayako has nothing but her humanity.
Unable to express, let alone demand, her rights as a human being, she has
no option but to remain at the bottom of feudal society. Yet we must avoid
the temptation to see her only as a victim of societal oppression. Truth be
told, she does not always makes the best of the few choices she has. Thus,
even if there were no "curse" on having sex with men from the same family,
she might have heeded her best instincts and broken off with Kanjiro and
not become involved with Kanichi in the first place. But in the end her
loneliness, isolation, and need for love prevail—all of which makes her
human. Wisely, Gosho does not sentimentalize Ayako. Rather, he treats her
with compassion and insight, trusting viewers to recognize that ultimately

Hapless lovers Suzuko (Iwashita Shima) and Taté (Nakayama Jin) and the
coup d'état of 1936. *Rebellion of Japan* (1967).

she is more sinned against than sinning. At the same time he implies that
the only real solution to women's oppression is the dismantling of feudalism. Unfortunately, this dismantling will come too late for Ayako.

The closing shot of *An Innocent Witch* is appropriately bleak. The flashback ended, we return to the vast expanse of Osorezan, which we saw at the
beginning. Only now the landscape is even more barren, except for a small
statue and a burnt-out wooden edifice. A fitting epitaph for Ayako's short,
unhappy life, it is also a prophetic image of Japan at the end of the war.

REBELLION OF JAPAN
AND CONCLUDING REMARKS

Based on a novel by Tonegawa Hiroshi and scripted by Horie Hideo, *Utage*
(*Rebellion of Japan* [lit., *The Banquet*], 1967) is Gosho's last major film. It
focuses on the tragic romance between an idealistic young army officer
(Nakayama Jin) and a married woman (Iwashita Shima), and is set against
the backdrop of the failed coup d'état of February 26, 1936. On that date,
a group of young ultrarightist army officers, driven by "a kind of imperial-
ist fundamentalism, obsessed with purity and religious worship of the nation,"[36] assassinated several prominent cabinet members and took over
parts of downtown Tokyo. Their goal was to rid the country of corrupting
Western influence and reinstate direct imperial rule, bringing about a new

"Showa restoration." The emperor, however, suppressed the rebellion and had the leaders executed.

A tale of thwarted love, *Rebellion of Japan* focuses primarily on the single-minded devotion of Suzuko, the heroine, to Taté, one of the officers dedicated to the ultrarightist cause. Suzuko is first drawn to Taté when she overhears him tell her brother, Seiki (Takahashi Masaya), "Once you decide something, see it through." These words kindle her love and nurture her indomitable spirit. Yet from the start her love faces an insurmountable obstacle: Taté's renunciation of all personal ties in the name of the cause. Brokenhearted, Suzuko desperately declares her love for him, but his response is short, succinct, and nonnegotiable. "I love you, too," he says, "but this doesn't mean marriage in our case." Rejected, Suzuko marries Shennosin (Kawabe Kyuzo), a Noh actor. Predictably, their marriage is a failure. Shennosin knows that Suzuko does not love him, and the harder she tries to be a good wife, the more untrusting and distant he becomes. Further complicating matters, Suzuko and Taté find it impossible to make a complete break from one another.

In the film's most intensely romantic scene, Taté accompanies Suzuko home after the two have attended a Noh performance. Caught in an unexpected snowstorm, they wind their way along a narrow path between two rows of houses, the *mise-en-scène* and high camera angle investing the shot with an Ophüls-like aura. Suzuko's geta and socks prove inadequate in the foot of snow that has fallen, and overtaken by cold and exhaustion, she faints. Finding shelter, Taté gently strokes her face and breathes into the palms of her hands to help her regain consciousness. Removing her geta and socks, he massages her foot. "Your foot is numb," he explains. "You'll get frostbite." Then he bends toward her and takes her toes into his mouth. The expression on her face is pure ecstasy. However, just as she and Taté are about to kiss, he pulls away. He will permit himself to embrace her, even to touch her cheek and lips, but nothing more. Needless to say, his denial of his feelings charges an already erotic scene with even greater passion.

Rebellion of Japan, however, does not applaud Taté's denial of feelings. Nor does it approve his eagerness to die, which Suzuko finds incomprehensible and which he is at a loss to explain. On the contrary, the film valorizes Suzuko's life-affirming belief in love as the *raison d'être* of human existence. Expressive close-ups not only privilege this belief and communicate her feelings, but also create an intimate bond between her and the viewer. Essentially the only female character in the film, she stands in marked contrast to the masculine world's suppression and denial of feelings. In that world, all feelings, especially personal ones, are viewed as weaknesses and must be stamped out. Under the circumstance, Taté's rejection of Suzuko is hardly surprising, for he is by and large a product of that environment. Although a commonplace, it is nevertheless true that self-denial, when carried to extremes, can lead to deformation of personality, which, in turn, can fuel the kind of fanaticism that Taté and his fellow officers have fallen prey to.[37] Ultimately, Taté repudiates this fanaticism, but not before he is victimized by it. Indeed, throughout the film, he is engaged in a struggle that he is only dimly aware of. This struggle is evident in his anguished decency, his agonizing rationalizations, and, above all, his unacknowledged need for Suzuko. At base, this struggle is the proverbial conflict between *ninjo* and *giri*.

Rebellion of Japan constitutes one of Gosho's most forceful statements on this conflict. Taté's sense of *giri* (duty) is out of all proportion to *ninjo* (personal desire). As a result, he ends up sacrificing not only his own life but also the lives of those around him. Swept up by the rhetoric of rebellion, he is left with two equally impossible choices: either to take part in the coup d'état or to go to Manchuria. In the event, he chooses the former. But when he and fellow officers burst into the home of a high-ranking government official and assassinate him, Taté is brought face-to-face with reality. Cleaving to her husband's body, the official's wife screams out in a torrent of anger and grief, "Shoot me!" Taté cannot bring himself to do it. Indeed, at that very moment, he sees Suzuko's face before him—an insert shot that represents an appeal to his true nature. At this moment, it is Suzuko's values that win out, yet Taté experiences no sense of release. Instead, in prison, awaiting execution, he is haunted by what might have been. He tells Suzuko, during their last time together, that he regrets not having allowed their love to grow, adding that he was wrong to think that the desire for personal happiness was "effeminate." But by then it is too late for both of them. As he faces a firing squad, Suzuko takes her own life.

At one point in the film, one of the characters says of the ultrarightists, "History will decide if they were right or not." There is no question, of course, that Taté is on the wrong side of history. Yet Gosho fleshes out his character in such a way as to put a human face on history and complicate it. Stated baldly, Taté may be fighting for the wrong cause, but he is still a complex and moral human being. This seeming paradox may be of no concern to history; however, it is vitally important to Gosho, for it underscores the fact that Taté is more than the sum total of his political beliefs. This point is especially significant, given his dogmatic pronouncements. Indeed, his actions speak louder than his words. Thus, he stands by Seiki, when this friend and former classmate is imprisoned for leftist activities. He even defends him when Suzuko, in a rare lapse in understanding, naively laments, "For our country, he's a criminal." Here Taté demonstrates that he is incapable of holding a narrow partisan view of patriotism, and that, despite what he says, human relationships continue to be important to him. This is a side of his character that he may not be aware of, but Gosho makes sure that we do not overlook it. In short, Gosho wants us to recognize that the project of history is to focus only on those sides of an individual's character that translate into public action or political events. As such, any verdict history renders must be incomplete.

Its love story and political theme notwithstanding, *Rebellion of Japan* is also remarkable for its visual style. An amalgam of expressionism, realism, and theatricalism, this style endows the drama with a tragic, romantic intensity. First of all, as in *Once More,* there are numerous expressionistic touches. We have already described one such example: the insert shot of Suzuko at the moment where Taté is faced with killing the official's wife. Equally striking is the shot that announces Suzuko's opening flashback. Here Taté's face is seen in profile superimposed over an image of marching soldiers. This shot not only identifies him as part of the military and as the object of Suzuko's affection, but also hints at the tension between these two roles. Second, there is the matter of "realism." The film's core style, realism shifts from one level to another in its depiction of everydayness. Thus, it ranges in mood and texture from the romantic images of Suzuko and Taté's erotic encounter in the snowstorm to the stark images of Shennosin and Suzuko's marriage in the bare confines of their home.

Finally, there is the third and most intriguing style, theatricalism. A dialectic between film and Noh drama, it works hand-in-hand with Gosho's use of widescreen and Nagaoka Hiroyuki's black-and-white photography. As in *Hunting Rifle* and *An Innocent Witch,* Gosho evinces a keen instinct for the psychological use of space, but here he also seizes upon the opportunities that Noh offers for stylized expression of emotion and makes the most of them.[38] In his introduction of Shennosin, the third member of the romantic triangle, Gosho fills the frame with fiercely beautiful images: a bone-white mask, resembling the face of a young woman (*ko-omote*), lies in a dark-lined container, while Shennosin's stockinged feet enact prescribed, formalistic dance movements. Such scenes function like set pieces, possessing a mysterious, abstract quality, even as they serve to elucidate Shennosin's character. Consider, for example, the sequence in which he forces Suzuko to make love. After the act, Suzuko takes refuge in the bathroom where she washes out her mouth. However, Shennosin sees what she has done and confronts her. His rage spills over into the next scene, which is the most visually dynamic in the film. Laved in darkness, and garbed in full Noh attire, he executes one 360-degree turn after another in succession, at one point briefly disappearing into the blackness. He continues these turns in the next shot, which focuses on his feet. Finally, a mask emerges out of the darkness in extreme close-up, completing two full revolutions as it moves across the frame. Given the abrupt shifts in size and scale, and the absence of markers to indicate shallowness or depth, the effect is one of disjunction, a spectacle of lines, shapes, light, and shadow to be enjoyed as much for its own sake as for its role in the diegesis. Adding to the pleasure is Noh's traditional beat of drums and the strain of a bamboo flute. In short, this scene is, in part, about Noh itself.

But primarily it is about Shennosin's thwarted desires. Only in his art can he hope to attain calm and sublimity and to escape the rage bottled up inside him. Interestingly, we are told that for the first six months of his marriage, he was inspired by Suzuko and not only overcame this rage but greatly improved as an actor. Now, however, his art is suffering. As his critics explain to Suzuko, he dances too intensely and must strive to become more "placid." In this respect the lessons of Noh and life are one and the same. Shennosin may be dedicated and driven, but mastering Noh requires moral discipline—in a word, character. In this quality, Shennosin is sadly lacking. In fact, he is selfish and cruel, and even revels in his cruelty. Thus, he not only rebuffs Suzuko's efforts to get closer to him, but he also humiliates her. Finally, unable to endure this treatment, she tells him that she is leaving. In the middle of a rehearsal, he at first barely acknowledges her presence. Then he suddenly breaks into a paroxysm of frantic Noh-like gestures, mocking her and symbolically lashing out at her behind the guise of his art. In so doing, he throws away his last chance for love, along with any possibility for growth as a person and an artist. Indeed, his art is as out of reach for him as history's commendation is for the ultrarightists. In *Rebellion of Japan,* the sole value that remains untainted is Suzuko's devotion to love. Thus, her suicide must not be seen as an act of defeat or despair, but as the fulfillment of a promise she made to herself long ago—to see her love through to the end. Hers is the ultimate act of integrity.

In effect, the three melodramas discussed in this chapter constitute a meditation on the complex relationship between personal histories and the past and present. In *An Innocent Witch* and *Rebellion of Japan,* Gosho's focus on the impact of the war on the main characters implicitly invites audiences to reflect on the relevance of that event to their own lives, especially at a time of unparalleled economic growth. In *Hunting Rifle,* which is set in the present, Gosho invites reflection on the impact of prosperity itself. On the face of it, his affluent middle-class characters would seem to have everything. Yet they are enclosed in solitude, cut off from their feelings—the very materialism that benefits them is also a cause for concern. Basically decent but jaded, they don't seem to know who they are or what they want. In this regard they are a far cry from the desperately poor, ignorant heroine of *An Innocent Witch,* who struggles just to survive, or the unhappily married woman of *Rebellion of Japan,* who knows what matters in life, but lacks the power to attain it. These three films may not ask us to laugh through tears, or even to laugh at all, but like all of Gosho's melodramas, they are infused with pathos. They compel us to care.

Even so, these films are unlike melodramas of the 1930s and 1940s, such as *Woman of the Mist* and *Once More,* which evince a warmth, intimacy, and solidarity between people, despite societal oppression or calamitous historical events. One finds in these earlier melodramas a more pronounced blend of laughter and tears, humor and pathos, the very ingredients that define the *shomin-geki*—specifically, "Goshoism." This is not to suggest that Gosho's melodramas of the 60s are somehow deficient. Quite the opposite, they demonstrate Gosho's branching out from the *shomin-geki* to deepen and develop the mode of melodrama itself—something he had tried to do as early as 1948 with *A Visage to Remember,* but only fully realized in 1957 with *Elegy of the North.* This said, most of Gosho's films, regardless of genre, are grounded in the *shomin-geki,* and invariably derive their richness and vitality from the mixing of various moods. Thus, whether a film is primarily an example of the *junbungaku* movement (like *Dancing Girl of Izu*), the *jidai-geki* (like *The Fireflies*), or the *Meiji-mono* (like *Growing Up*), it not only embodies this special mix of moods but depicts life's ups and downs, ensuring the requisite laughter through tears.

Gosho's laughter through tears, however, does not remain a static or fixed mood throughout his forty-three-year career. It changes to reflect the times. That is to say, while we may laugh and cry—sometimes literally, sometimes not—we don't always do so for the same reason or to the same degree. For example, in the *shomin* comedies of the 30s, the laughter and tears tend to be in response to a relatively simple and direct situation, whereas in slice-of-life comedies, they tend to be the result of more complex factors. Consequently, our involvement with a community that is turned upside down over a husband's or wife's sleeping habits (the *Bride* and *Groom* films) is quite different from our involvement with a young boy, who is trying to cope with his father's rejection (*Burden of Life*). The same is true of our response to those *shomin-geki* that approach tragedy. Hence *Where Chimneys Are Seen* and *An Inn at Osaka,* two of Gosho's greatest films and the apotheosis of his *shomin-geki.* Moving, richly textured works, they achieve a real sense of pain and urgency, while never losing sight of the exhilarating moments of genuine happiness that also define human experience. Gosho's purpose in making these films was to bring the *shomin-geki* up to date, to accurately depict the lives of the people immediately after the war. Resembling Italian neorealist films like *Bicycle Thief,* these were socially cognizant comedies about survival from a director who was keenly sensitive to the contemporary scene. In these films, and also *Growing Up,* in which the *Meiji-mono* and *shomin-geki* are expertly blended, Gosho was at the peak of his powers and directly confronted the social problems of the day, in particular materialism and the pressures of modernity. Even in the last decade of his career, when his work lost some of its urgency and edge, he produced two films that rank among his best: *Elegy of the North* and *An Innocent Witch.*

At the core of Gosho's work was a realist impulse, albeit dramatically and poetically heightened. He once explained that "the purpose of a film director's life is to describe the real life around him and create works which express the true feelings of human beings." Indeed, his films were integral to the development of realism in the Japanese cinema of the 20s and 30s. To describe real life, however, did not mean simply photographing quotidian reality or depicting a close-knit neighborhood or community. Rather, it meant probing "true feelings," that is, showing the way people behaved with an often-novelistic density. Gosho's realism was also directly linked to his visual style. Following the lead of his mentor, Shimazu Yasujiro, he embraced Lubitsch's analytical editing style, which he made his own. He also was deeply indebted to haiku for its precision, abbreviation, and expression. If Gosho's style remained consistent throughout his career, so too did his principal set of themes: his identification with the individual, his sympathy for the plight of women, and his concern with the socially oppressed and marginalized. No less importantly, Gosho never lost his youthful excitement about film as a medium.

In closing, we need to answer one question: What is Gosho's place in Japanese film history and cinema history? Rather than rehearse what has been said above, or attempt an exhaustive catalogue of his achievements, let us simply focus on the following. First, his films provide a record of a way of Japanese life that no longer exists, of the manners and mores of past eras and now-gone neighborhoods like the Shitamachi of old downtown Tokyo. Second, although his films may be Japanese in detail, they are universal in their ability to speak across time and cultures. Third, his work serves as a site of intersection between Japanese film and international film. Like other directors of his generation, Gosho shaped his style and themes out of a selection of Japanese and foreign norms. For this reason alone, any examination of the influences that national cinemas have exerted on one another throughout film history would do well to consider Gosho. Fourth, and most important, along with directors like Ozu and Mizoguchi, Gosho played a central role in two of Japanese cinema's "Golden Ages," the 1930s and the 1950s. Indeed, he helped to create the classical humanist tradition of Japanese film, which provided the foundation and guiding principle of that cinema and which, by and large, no longer exists. In short, Gosho is essential to any understanding of Japanese film history and cinema history.

The Gosho of this study, then, is the humanist par excellence, the dedicated visual stylist, the active experimenter, the close observer of the Japanese scene, the devotee of American and French film, and the genuine auteur who never stopped working, even after his "retirement." Doubtless, he would be the first to admit that he made too many films, and that too many of them were failures. But, as Billy Wilder once said, a director should be judged on his best work, not his worst work. Like the finest directors, Gosho made his films out of deeply held convictions. He had an unbowed faith in people, yet this did not preclude a clear-eyed view of them or of reality. He realized that people could be cruel, misguided, and hard-hearted; he also knew that life was often filled with loneliness, disappointment, and tragedy. Nonetheless, like his true heroes and heroines, he firmly believed that "Life is what you make it." Finally, for better or worse, Gosho rarely shied away from sentimentality, even when it was excessive, and even when his critics faulted him for it. In *Great Expectations,* Charles Dickens writes: "Heaven knows we need never be ashamed of our tears, for they are rain upon the blinding dust of earth, overlying our hard hearts."[39] It is a statement that Gosho would have embraced proudly and wholeheartedly.

APPENDIX: THREE FILMS

This section briefly examines three films that were only touched on in previous chapters, but warrant fuller consideration: L'Amour (Ramuru/Aibu/Caress/Love, *1933),* Omokage (A Visage to Remember/A Face to Remember/Image, *1948), and* Wakare-gumo (Dispersing Clouds/Drifting Clouds, *1951).*

L'AMOUR (RAMURU/AIBU/ CARESS/LOVE, 1933)

In a village not far from Mount Fuji, Dr. Murata (Arai Jun) runs a small clinic. He lives with his grown daughter, Machiko (Okada Yoshiko), and expects his son, Hideo (Watanabe Tadao), to join him in his practice when he finishes medical studies in Tokyo. As the film opens, Murata is paid a visit by an old friend, Matsuoka (Sakamoto Takeshi), now a famous novelist. He also receives an offer from Yoshika (Kawamura Reikichi), a wealthy but obnoxious businessman, who will build a hospital for Murata in exchange for Machiko's hand in marriage. Murata refuses. He knows Machiko loves Konishi (Kobayashi Tokuji), the local schoolteacher. One day Murata misdiagnoses a case of appendicitis. His confidence shaken, he takes down his shingle over the protests of Machiko, Konishi, and Seikichi (Tani Reiko), his loyal rickshaw driver, saying that he'll put up an even bigger shingle when Hideo returns home, but he does not really believe it. Meanwhile the village turns on him, and the papers get hold of the story. To make matters worse, he gets a letter from Hideo, who claims to be sick in bed, and asks for money and a winter kimono. Upset by her brother's insensitivity, Machiko goes to Tokyo. There she learns that he has no interest in medicine and is cutting classes, drinking heavily, and living with a woman named Setsuko (Oikawa Michiko). "Just as father diagnosed wrongly, he misjudged me," Hideo tells Machiko. However, she discovers that Setsuko truly loves her brother and is trying to reform him. When Murata learns about his son's dissolute life, he suffers a heart attack. Matsuoka intervenes, forcing Hideo to return home to see his gravely ill father. Hideo tells his father that he has never been able to talk to him. "Perhaps my stubbornness made you silent," Murata says, adding: "Live your life the way you want to." Father and son reconcile, and Matsuoka promises Murata to help Hideo become a writer. Recovering from his illness, Murata moves away to begin a new life, and Machiko and Konishi plan to marry.

The last of five films Gosho made in 1933, *L'Amour* (the title is never explained) was one of his favorites among his own pictures.[1] The film is also a favorite with Gosho scholars. John Gillett of the British Film Institute called it "a particularly rich silent, detailed and dense like a novel."[2] David Owens thought that "the presence of the star Yoshiko Okada (herself the daughter of a very prominent Kyushu medical family) transformed the film."[3] William Johnson was impressed by the way in which Gosho "challenges assumptions about what a good narrative film can and should be."[4]

Like other films Gosho made during the 1930s, namely *Burden of Life* and *Woman of the Mist*, *L'Amour* represents a marriage of two often disparate impulses: the *shomin-geki*'s evocation of the unrushed, seemingly unstructured flow of common people's lives and the melodrama's heightening of events. Thus understood, the film's narrative structure can be appreciated for its mastery of design rather than its failure to adhere to a traditionally shaped plot that announces the main action from the start, then develops that action in a systematic, organic fashion. William Johnson instinctively understood that with this strategy Gosho "embraces the sheer messiness of life,"[5] although "messiness" must not be misunderstood as something pejorative but as a way of rendering the larger continuities of life. As Johnson points out, this "messiness" is the result of Gosho's "digressions" from the main plot—that is, Murata's misdiagnosis—so as to include a number of subplots, including Murata's relationship with Matsuoka and his conflict with Yoshika. Johnson sees the most important of these subplots as the one dealing with Hideo's profligate life in Tokyo, and rightly asserts that it "gradually comes to dominate the film."[6] However, it does not do so quite as unexpectedly as Johnson seems to imply. There are hints about this subplot early in the film, namely the references to Murata's hopes for his son and the prominent place that Hideo's picture occupies in Murata's house. Gosho even has Matsuoka look at the photo during his first visit with Murata. Later, the two plots are specifically linked when Hideo remarks that his father misdiagnosed both him and the sick patient.

Gosho conveys the "messiness of life" in yet another way. In the opening scenes he plays with audience expectations *vis-à-vis* melodrama, deliberately muting and upending such expectations. For example, in the scene in which Murata gives schoolchildren a physical exam, Gosho establishes the doctor as kind and devoted (which, indeed, he is), while also encouraging the audience to make other assumptions as well, all of which are based on the fact that he is the film's protagonist. Hence when he is visited by Matsuoka, we at first imagine that Gosho is preparing for an inevitable contrast between the doctor (whose work goes unnoticed by the outside world) and the novelist (whose work is celebrated). Moreover, while Matsuoka is a thoroughly amiable fellow, he also seems somewhat vain. Looking in a mirror, he finds a gray hair and immediately pulls it out; in response, Murata points out that he has nothing but gray hair. There is also a curious scene in the film that has nothing to do with Murata. In this scene Mitsuoka visits his publisher, who remarks that he hopes Mitsuoka will meet his deadline, since his readers are eagerly awaiting his next work. This scene, in fact, is misleading. At first, it seems to imply that Mitsuoka may be suffering from writer's block, or, since he is not exactly forthcoming with his publisher, that perhaps his celebrity outstrips his talent. However, neither of these possibilities turns out to be the case. Nor does the scene serve any other narrative purpose. It exists simply to be enjoyed as an example of the lived-in quality of Gosho's *shomin-geki*.

The most startling way in which Gosho upends audience expectations, however, has to do with Murata's misdiagnosis. We have such complete faith in Murata that when it turns out that he has made a mistake, we are shocked. Murata had previously given instructions to keep the patient warm, but when he checks in on the patient, he finds another doctor on the scene. "Prepare ice bags," this doctor orders, adding that the patient has appendicitis and must be transported to a hospital immediately for an operation. What deliberately misleads us is the young doctor's body language. He rubs his brow and casts suspicious, darting looks (in close-up, no less), prompting us to assume that he is a quack. Added to this, we imagine that since he is a younger, Western-dressed doctor, he is something of a smarty pants and yet another instance of the new pushing out the old. Gosho's reversal of expectation cuts deeply, driving home the point that dedication, compassion, and goodness are not always enough. Deceived by our trust in the very conventions of melodrama, we are brought face-to-face with reality.

Gosho's above use of close-ups should come as no surprise, since the deployment of such shots is an instrumental part of the rhetoric of emotional and psychological insight that constitutes analytical (or piecemeal) editing. Gosho also makes masterful use of composition, lighting, and the moving camera. Murata's realization of the enormity of his misdiagnosis is visualized in a shot worthy of German Expressionism. A canted angle, it shows only part of his face in the lower left of the frame and only a lamppost in the top right; the greater part of the frame it leaves empty. The scene in which Machiko reveals the truth about Hideo to her father uses chiaroscuro to striking effect as she and Murata are largely surrounded by darkness. And Gosho's tracking camera underscores the growing bond between Machiko and Setsuko—a strategy he will repeat in *Where Chimneys Are Seen* to signify another important relationship between two women.

For Johnson, Gosho has a divided self as a filmmaker—hence the sobriquet, Setter and Solver.[7] Setter introduces the problems (the quirks of character, the pursuit of subplots for their own sake, the darker strains and implications of the action—in short, the "messiness" of life), while Solver busily seeks to resolve and control. It is an interesting idea, though frankly it tends to make Gosho seem pat and schematic. Still, it offers a plausible enough explanation for the conflicting impulses of his narrative, the push-pull mechanism that leaves a residue of tension and ambiguity, even when the film ends on a nominally happy note. Like so many of Gosho's works, *L'Amour* concerns itself with the twin struggle of needing to accommodate the demands of society with those of the self. In the end it posits, perhaps somewhat optimistically, that these demands, even in the case of Hideo, can and must be fulfilled. But this optimism is neither facile nor unfelt: for Gosho, it is an act of faith.

OMOKAGE (*A VISAGE TO REMEMBER/ A FACE TO REMEMBER/IMAGE*, 1948)

During his summer holiday, Kawasaki Ryuichi (Ryuzaki Ichiro), a handsome engineer in his late twenties, visits his teacher and mentor, Professor Inagaki (Sugai Ichiro), at his seaside home. There he meets the professor's lovely young wife, Sachiko (Hamada Yuriko), and is unsettled by the striking resemblance she bears to his wife, who died three years earlier. Attracted to Sachiko, he does his best to hide his feelings. The couple, however, senses a deep-seated melancholy in him. Attributing it to the loss of his wife, they urge him to marry their niece, Kaoru (Wakayama Setsuko), but he is not interested. Shortly after, Fumiko (Akagi Ranko), Sachiko's older sister, realizes that Sachiko and Kawasaki have feelings for each other, but she keeps her counsel. One day Kawasaki, Sachiko, and Kaoru go boating when a storm forces them to stay overnight at a hotel. Unable to sleep, Kawasaki takes a walk along the beach where he finds Sachiko, also unable to sleep. He declares his love for her. Frightened by this declaration (and her feelings for him), she takes flight. The professor realizes that something has happened between her and Kawasaki. When he presses her on the matter, she tells him everything. Torn between feelings of jealousy and guilt—he has come to believe that he has robbed Sachiko of her youth—he asks Kawasaki to leave, explaining that no one is to blame, that they have been victims of fate. As Kawasaki departs, there are tears in Sachiko's eyes.

Following the success of *Once More,* Toho invited Gosho to direct another romance. According to Kakehi Masanori, Gosho's assistant director on both of his Toho films, Gosho was given considerable freedom in making *A Visage to Remember,* despite the worsening labor problems at the studio.[8] The story, written by Tateoka Kennosuke, "was scripted according to the director's personally-written blueprint. The inspiration came from his own experiences, hence Gosho's own personal delight was pronounced."[9] Yet, as Kakehi also notes, Gosho was not pleased with the end result: "'If only I could go a bit deeper,' he said, 'As it is, the film's a failure.'"[10]

Perhaps so, but it is an interesting, ambitious failure that represents a decisive move on Gosho's part in the direction of art cinema.[11] As pointed out in the discussion of *Elegy of the North* (1957) in chapter 8, the aesthetic he embraced involved de-emphasizing "the most sensational aspects of the story" and "volatile" character conflicts.[12] Indeed, *A Visage to Remember* is very much a chamber piece, a psychological study of three characters cast in the form of a romantic triangle. Like the characters themselves, we never know for sure to what degree Kawasaki is attracted to Sachiko for her own sake or as a stand-in for his dead wife, Akiko. Ultimately, this distinction hardly seems to matter. This point is evocatively brought home in the scene in which Kawasaki dreams of his wife. (Or is he dreaming of Sachiko? Actress Hamada Yuriko plays both women). In this dream, Kawasaki's nocturnal visitor calls out his name, then takes his hand in hers. "What a cold hand," she remarks, as she sits beside him. She then offers him a cigarette. Moments later, he awakens. "Akiko, Mrs. Inagaki," he calls out in the dark, making a conscious connection between the two women. To his amazement, he finds that he is holding a cigarette.

Although dramatically restrained, *A Visage to Remember* is stylistically of a piece with the sumptuous *Once More* and, like that film, is a meditation on memory, loss, and isolation. Photographed by Kizuka Seiichi, *A Visage to Remember* makes extensive use of superimposed images, voiceovers, and expressionistic lighting to convey the thoughts, fantasies, and recollections that haunt the characters and lie buried in their hearts. For example, when Kawasaki thinks of his dead wife, he envisages her at the piano, teaching him the only tune he knows how to play—the lush romantic melody that serves as the film's main theme. In fact, the first time we see her, she is in silhouette, until soft light gradually reveals her face. For Kawasaki, she is both a shadow and a powerful essence. No less powerful are words, although they tend to be tantalizingly ambiguous. Hence the seemingly innocuous phrase, "I trust you," which the characters often repeat, or the troubling, paradoxical adage, "Lovers spoiled by happiness aren't always happy," which prompts the professor to reflect on his "happy" marriage and the age difference between him and his wife (he is fifty; she is twenty-eight).

In this meditation on memory, loss, and isolation, setting is of paramount importance. The film is set in a resort area on the coast of Hozo, which boasts a long, sandy beach with rocks and boulders and is dotted with Western-style hotels and vacation homes. Even though few Japanese today would consider this setting posh, it exudes a sense of privilege and luxury that early postwar audiences facing poverty and deprivation could only dream of.[13] Here the war seems ages past and worlds removed, and even the single overt reference to it startles, perhaps deliberately. As might be expected, luxury is synonymous with Western style and fashion. The Inagakis' residence is a thoroughly Westernized dwelling, complete with a piano located at the bottom of the stairs in a large, spacious living room. Similarly, most of the characters wear Western dress. In the opening scene, for example, Kaoru is smartly done up in a tennis outfit (white blouse, matching short skirt, and even a white ribbon in her hair), while Kawasaki is suitably dashing in white Bermuda slacks. By contrast, Sachiko wears a kimono throughout most of the film (indicative of her role as a traditional wife, the role in which she feels safest). Only once does she change into Western clothing, but it is an altogether singular moment.

Joining Kawasaki and Kaoru for a swim at the latter's insistence, Sachiko puts on a suit that makes no effort to conceal her womanly beauty. Nor is she reluctant to show off her skill as a swimmer (she dives into the water from atop a rock and wins a "race" against Kawasaki). Needless to say, this scene does not exist to demonstrate Sachiko's previously unsuspected athletic ability, but instead to reveal her pent-up energy (sexual and otherwise) and the mutual physical attraction between her and Kawasaki. In this lovers' idyll, outsiders are not wanted; therefore, Gosho makes a point of keeping Kaoru largely out of view. Likewise, as Sachiko and Kawasaki swim side-by-side, Gosho replaces ambient sound with a full orchestral love theme, charging the scene with undeniable eroticism. Small wonder that when the professor shows up and observes his wife and friend together, he immediately senses this eroticism, and is disturbed by it. In effect he has seen his wife for the first time.

Still, nothing is quite what it appears to be, and by the end of the film ambiguities multiply. Kawasaki, now guilt-ridden for having declared his love to Sachiko and having betrayed the professor, apologizes to both. The professor graciously shares part of the blame. Sachiko, however, refuses to accept the apology, no doubt because it represents a denial of Kawasaki's feelings for her. Indeed, what are we to make of his explanation that his love for her was motivated by envy toward her and the professor's happiness and by guilt over his treatment of his dead wife? At best this seems only partially true, an attempt to undo the emotional damage he has caused. But can the damage be undone? The complex closing scene leaves this question unanswered. While Kawasaki boards the bus that will take him away, the professor and Sachiko retire to their living room. The professor picks up the book that Kawasaki has given him, entitled *Of a Happy Life,* and briefly scrutinizes it. He then looks at Sachiko. A dolly-shot from his point of view reveals that her back is turned to him. Gosho then cuts to her face—to show us what the professor cannot see, what she does not want him to see. There are tears in her eyes, and in voiceover she hears Fumiko's words, "He won't be back." Moments later, as if remembering her duty or acknowledging her feelings for her husband, she is by his side, offering him a cigarette and fanning him as he falls asleep in his chair. Nothing is simple: she loves this man, who has stood by her, taken her in his arms, and comforted her when she felt most tempted and terrified. But she also loves the man who has brought passion into her life. Why, then, does she cry? Perhaps because in losing Kawasaki, she has also accepted the fact that a "happy" marriage is not always happy.

Finally, although Gosho felt that he had not probed his material sufficiently, *A Visage to Remember*'s chief flaw is its unnecessary repetition and occasional overexplicitness. Too much time, for example, is devoted to establishing the Inagakis' happy marriage and to stressing their age difference. In this respect Dr. Horie (Ryu Chishu), Inagaki's friend and peer, seems to be on hand just to applaud the professor's virility. Still, *A Visage to Remember* continues to fascinate long after it is over, not only because of its unusual setting but also because of its insights on the individual's complicity with society to tamp down and suppress the self.

WAKARE-GUMO (DISPERSING CLOUDS/ DRIFTING CLOUDS, 1951)

Five women classmates from a college in Tokyo are on the first stretch of a walking tour when one of them, Fujimura Masako (Sawamura Keiko), falls ill at a railway station. Osen (Kawasaki Hiroko), a middle-aged maid from a nearby inn, takes her in and nurses her, assisted by Dr. Minami (Numata Yoichi), a young physician who diagnoses her illness as a mild case of pneumonia. With Masako in good hands and needing ten days to recuperate, her classmates continue their tour. Masako's recovery, however, is hampered by her spoiled and immature nature and her determination to punish the world for the loss of her mother. Initially, she is condescending toward

Osen and Minami and cruel to her stepmother, Tamae (Fukuda Taeko), who arrives to take her back to Tokyo. However, Osen's and Minami's kindness gradually leads her to open her heart to others, including her stepmother. By the time she is almost fully recovered, she also has developed romantic feelings for Minami, and on one occasion even assists with patients. Dedicated to his work, he does not return her interest. When her father, Ryohei (Mitsuda Ken), visits her on the way home from a business trip, he realizes that she has changed and is ready to return with him. At the railway station, Minami and Osen see father and daughter off. There Masako expressly thanks Osen, who has loved her like the daughter she lost. Giving Osen a memento she has long cherished from her deceased mother, Masako says simply, "I don't need it anymore." After the train departs, Minami and Osen talk briefly. Neither mentions that it is unlikely they will ever see Masako again.

Dispersing Clouds was the first film Gosho made after his break with Toho Studio. Three years had passed since *A Visage to Remember,* and like a number of other filmmakers who had been branded as Communists during the labor strikes, Gosho formed his own independent company, Studio Eight Productions. It was one of the first such companies in Japan. *Dispersing Clouds,* which was shot entirely on location (in Shinshu) on a very small budget, had no stars, except for Kawasaki Hiroko, then past the peak of her career.[14] In fact, Gosho's name was emphasized in the advertising, rather than the names of the actors. And while the film ended up making stars of Sawamura Keiko and Numata Yoichi,[15] it was less of a commercial success than it was a *succès d'estime.* Even so, this "fable"[16] expertly accommodates Gosho's *shomin-geki* and his talent for depicting complex women characters.

At base, *Dispersing Clouds* is about Masako's spiritual and psychological growth, what Mark Le Fanu has aptly described as "the awakening of happiness in an individual human soul."[17] Like her classmates, Masako is naive, inexperienced, and self-absorbed. But whereas they are carefree, uncomplicated, and endearingly self-dramatizing—at one point, for example, they proclaim that "youth is hard, such a burden!" with scarcely a hint of irony —she is complex, troubled, and in dire need of help. (In this respect, she clearly anticipates the similarly troubled Reiko in *Elegy of the North.*)

To her credit, Masako never deludes herself. She readily admits that she is "selfish and spoiled and restless." In other words, she wants to change, but change would be impossible without Minami's and Osen's tolerance and guidance and the rural setting that brings calm and serenity to her soul. As so often in Gosho, setting is key. In one scene Masako, thinking herself in love with Minami, follows him to an outlying village where she ends up helping him treat a group of women and children. There he introduces her to Dr. Koga, who, like himself, left Tokyo and came to the region to help the underprivileged. Koga has built the first school; Minami plans to build the first clinic. The surrounding mountains and trees give the setting a bucolic feel, but as Minami warns Masako, "Life in Tokyo in no way prepares you for life here where people don't even have electricity." Moved by what she has seen, Masako pleads with Minami to "teach" her, to allow her to be part of his work. Her request recalls *Once More,* in which Akiko, the bourgeois heroine, similarly entreats the idealistic doctor she has grown to love. But there is a difference. The doctor of *Once More* accepts Akiko's request; Minami, on the other hand, refuses to coddle his would-be protégée or permit her to indulge herself by playing the heroine. Calling her "a handful," he explains that dedication and self-sacrifice do not solve one's problems, and that she must solve her problems first. His insistence on this point not only underscores his steadfast idealism but also effectively defines his and Masako's relationship.

It is Osen and Masako's relationship, however, that gives *Dispersing Clouds* its special poignancy and power. Osen's ability to help Masako, even when she resists, is evident from the start. Hence when Masako refuses to unbutton her blouse for the doctor to examine her, Osen has only to gently say, "Young lady," and Masako obeys. In time Masako grows to trust Osen, and they become as close as mother and daughter. Osen, however, can be as firm as Minami. When Masako treats her stepmother shamefully (and clearly hates herself for doing so), Osen does not hesitate to scold her. "If I were your mother, I'd slap your face," she says. "Slap it!" Masako answers back, but Osen refuses to play the young woman's game, teaching her a lesson that has far more sting than any slap.

What makes Masako and Osen's relationship especially complex is that it is based on mutual need. In fact, Masako's recognition that Osen needs her solidifies the bond between them, and this, in turn, enables Osen to help her even more. Thus, when Osen confides that she left Tokyo to find peace of mind after losing her daughter, her words have the effect of curbing Masako's egotism and chastening her pride. Realizing that she is not the only person in pain, Masako takes another step toward maturity. What Osen does not say is that she found peace of mind only when Masako entered her life. Hence the added poignancy of their inevitable parting. At the railway station, as the two women say their good-byes, Masako gives Osen a spoon from her mother that she has treasured; it is the greatest sign of love Masako can offer. She then moves on, her whole life ahead of her. We need no longer worry about her. But what is to become of Osen? Of all the characters in the film, she alone evokes pathos. Earlier in the film Gosho gives her a scene by herself, in which she looks at the gloves Masako has sewn for her and realizes that she has lost her daughter not once, but twice.[18] Only Minami seems to understand her situation, and at the railway station, he tells her to take care of her health. On the surface this remark is an amenity, but in actuality it is an expression of concern. Osen has changed Masako's life; now she must change her own. Otherwise, she will consign herself to a life without illusions.

As moving as Osen's plight is, *Dispersing Clouds* never succumbs to unwanted sentimentality, thanks to Gosho's introduction of humor. In one of the film's running gags a young man is so besotted by Masako (he dubs her his "Mona Lisa") that he pursues her relentlessly just to snap her picture. His efforts come to naught. Then there is the comic subplot dealing with the innkeeper's wife (Okamura Ayako) and her spoiled daughter (Kurata Mayumi). Self-centered, dishonest, and distrustful of each other, they represent a travesty of what a mother-daughter relationship should be. As such, they provide the perfect foil for Osen and Masako.

Like Gosho's best films, *Dispersing Clouds* contains moments of intimacy that seem to come out of nowhere and take one's breath away. No one who has seen the film is likely to forget the most startling of these moments: Masako's massaging of her father's feet by treading on them. As Mark Le Fanu remarks, "Why should this be so sensual? It has the sweetness and directness of the best sort of naturalism."[19] True, but it also is a charged and risky moment, for it shows a father and daughter talking for the first time, and giving to one another for the first time, in a way that very few directors would have dared—and fewer still could have pulled off.

NOTES

INTRODUCTION

1. In the 1950s the following Gosho films were seen abroad: *Entotsu no mieru basho* (*Where Chimneys Are Seen/Four Chimneys*, 1953), *Osaka no yado* (*An Inn at Osaka*, 1954), *Takekurabe* (*Growing Up*, 1955), and *Kiiroi karasu* (*Yellow Crow/Behold Thy Son*, 1957). The first two films also showed at European festivals. Apparently, Gosho's first film to play theatrically in the United States was the now-lost *Hito no yo no sugata* (*A Daughter of Two Fathers/The Situation of the Human World*, 1928). Starring Tanaka Kinuyo, it featured a live performance by a *katsuben* or *benshi* (a narrator of silent films) and shared a double bill with Harry Langdon's *Soldier Man* (1926). It was reviewed by Mordaunt Hall in the *New York Times* on March 12, 1929. See the Filmography for further details.

In the 1980s, renewed interest in the history of Japanese film gained international attention for Gosho. A few of his 30s films were included in the touring package "Before *Rashomon:* Japanese Film Treasures of the 30's and 40's." There were also retrospectives exclusively devoted to him: at La Cinémathèque Française (1984–85), the National Film Theatre in London (March 1986), the Tenth Hong Kong International Film Festival (1986), and at the Museum of Modern Art and Japan Film Center (1989–90), among others. In addition, a retrospective of his films was the main event at the twentieth edition of Verona's International Film Week, April 6–12, 1989.

2. David Thomson, *A Biographical Dictionary of Film*, 3d ed. (New York: Alfred A. Knopf, 1994), 297.

3. Liz-Anne Bawden, ed., *The Oxford Companion to Film* (New York and London: Oxford University Press, 1976), 297. For an accurate description of Gosho's work, see Horie Hideo, "Gosho Heinosuke to sono kaiwai: Ikiru koto wa hitosuji ga yoshi" ("Gosho Heinosuke and His Milieu: Living One's Life to the Fullest"), *Gosho Heinosuke tokushu*, Eiga Kozo (*Special Issue on Gosho Heinosuke*, Film Lectures) (Tokyo: Gendai Engeki Kyodai Foundation, March 1987). Horie points out that Gosho was "a prolific director and [that] his works are categorized in a wide range of genres. . . . He was described as 'The Master of Women's Pictures,' 'The Master of Lyrical Films,' and 'The Master of *Shomin-geki*' in advertising catch phrases. Each title, however, merely describes one side of Gosho; none captures his essence as a director" (29).

4. Bawden, *The Oxford Companion*, 298.

5. Sato Tadao, "Le Point de vue sur les cheminées fantômes" ("The Point of View on the Phantom Chimneys"), trans. from Japanese into French by Patrick de Vos and Cecile Sakai, in Hiroko Govaers, ed., *Le Cinéma japonais de ses origines à nos jours* (*Japanese Cinema from Its Origins to Our Day*), Part 2 (Paris: La Cinémathèque Française/La Fondation du Japon, 1984), 73.

6. However, in 1977 Gosho directed a thirty-minute documentary entitled *Waga machi Mishima* (*My Town Mishima*). See the Filmography.

7. Gosho is usually credited with having made ninety-nine feature films, but after careful and repeated examination, I have found the number to be ninety-seven. However, if *Shindo* (*The New Road*), the 1936 film that was made in two parts and released separately, is counted as *two* films rather than one, this brings the total number of features to ninety-eight. If Gosho's 1977 short feature, *Waga machi Mishima* (*My Town Mishima*), is also added to the list, the number climbs to ninety-nine. It should also be pointed out that some titles credited to Gosho in various filmographies turn out to be either the works of other directors, or in one case a film that Gosho planned, but never actually made. See the Filmography for details.

Gosho's surviving films can be found at the Kawakita Memorial Film Institute and the National Film Center in Tokyo. (In Japan, Gosho's films are increasingly finding their way to video and DVD; unfortunately, in the West, his films remain unavailable.)

8. Gosho even tried his hand at black comedy in *Yoku* (*Avarice/Half a Loaf,* 1958), a vehicle for actor Ban Junzaburo, which Shochiku (Kyoto) asked him to direct. The story deals with a doctor who is researching the formula for eternal life. However, he runs into a snag: he discovers that he cannot use the reproductive organs of dogs, cats, or even raccoon dogs (*tanuki*), which are famed in popular legend for their oversized scrotums. Only the human penis and testicles will do. Admittedly racy for its time, the story was a satire on the loss of authority that many Japanese men experienced after the war. It also offered plenty of opportunity for broad comedy and slapstick. Not surprisingly, Gosho balanced the satire and black comedy with his characteristic respect for human feeling. See "*Yoku* (*Avarice*)," in *Gosho Heinosuke kantoku tokushu* (*Special Issue on Director Gosho Heinosuke*), Vol. 21 (Tokyo: Film Center of the Tokyo National Museum of Modern Art, 1974), 36.

As noted above, *Yoku* was made at Shochiku (Kyoto), one of the studio's main production facilities, along with Shochiku (Kamata) and Shochiku (Ofuna) in the Tokyo area. However, when Shochiku built the studio at Ofuna in 1936, the one at Kamata was closed.

9. Kyoko Hirano, "Heinosuke Gosho," in *The International Dictionary of Films and Filmmakers,* vol. 2: *Directors/Filmmakers,* ed. Christopher Lyon (Chicago: St. James Press, 1984), 226.

10. Donald Richie, *The Japanese Movie,* rev. ed. (Tokyo, New York, and San Francisco: Kodansha International, 1982), 38.

11. However, we at least have the screenplay for *The Village Bride.* It is published in *Kinema Jumpo, Nihon eiga daihyo shinario zenshu 5* (*A Collection of Representative Japanese Screenplays,* no. 5) (September 1958); and *Kinema Jumpo, Nihon eiga shinario koten zenshu, Dai ikkan* (*A Collection of Classical Japanese Screenplays*), vol. 1 (December 1965). The problem of lost Japanese films, however, goes far beyond Gosho. As Donald Richie has said: "Except for a few known titles, there is little fully extant from the period of 1897 to 1917 and only somewhat more from 1918 to 1945. The 1923 earthquake, the 1945 fire-bombing of the major cities, the postwar Allied Occupation torching of banned films, and the later indifference of the industry itself have meant the destruction of ninety percent of all Japanese films made before 1945" (*A Hundred Years of Japanese Film: A Concise History, with a Selective Guide to Videos and DVDs* [Tokyo, New York, and London: Kodansha International, 2001], 12).

12. Kakehi Masanori, "Gosho Heinosuke no sekai: Gosho Heinosuke no entotsu no mieru basho o megutte" ("The World of Gosho Heinosuke: About His Work *Where*

Chimneys Are Seen"), *Nihon eiga o yomu: paionia tachi no isan* (*Reading Japanese Film: Heritage of the Pioneers*) (Tokyo: Dagereo shuppan, 1984), 125.

13. Quoted in Kakehi, "Gosho Heinosuke no sekai," 127. This passage originally appears at the beginning of Gosho's book *Waga seishun* (*My Youth*) (Tokyo: Nagata shobo, 1978), 7–8.

14. Anderson and Richie, *The Japanese Film*, 196.

15. "Gosho Heinosuke," in *World Film Directors*, vol. 1: *1890–1945*, ed. John Wakeman (New York: H. W. Wilson, 1987), 401. Anderson and Richie state that Shimazu "provided the first and some say the only cinematic influence on Gosho's style" (*The Japanese Film: Art and Industry*, expanded ed. [Princeton, N.J.: Princeton University Press, 1982], 356).

16. Donald Richie, *Japanese Cinema: Film Style and National Character* (Garden City, N.Y.: Anchor/Doubleday, 1971), 21.

17. Ibid., 22. For a fuller discussion of Shimazu and *Our Neighbor, Miss Yae*, see Sazaki Masaaki, "'Tonari no Yae-chan' o meguru geki sekai no hensen: Shimazu Yasujiro ron" ("About Shimazu Yasujiro and His Film *Our Neighbor Miss Yae*"), *Nihon eiga to modanizumu: 1920–1930* (*Japanese Film and Modernism: 1920–1930*), ed. Iwamoto Kenji (Tokyo: Libroport, 1991), 164–87.

18. Noël Burch, however, sees Shimazu's style as a "pale imitation" of Western-style *découpage* practices (in *To the Distant Observer: Form and Meaning in the Japanese Cinema*, rev. ed., ed. Annette Michelson [Berkeley: University of California Press, 1979], 258).

19. Horie, "Gosho Heinosuke to sono kaiwai: Ikiru koto wa hitosuji ga yoshi," 31.

20. Quoted in Horie, "Gosho Heinosuke to sono kaiwai: Ikiru koto wa hitosuji ga yoshi," 30–31.

21. David Bordwell, *Ozu and the Poetics of Cinema* (London: British Film Institute; Princeton, N.J.: Princeton University Press, 1988), 144.

22. Wakeman, *World Film Directors*, 402.

23. John Gillett, "Heinosuke Gosho," *Film Dope* (April 1980): 31.

24. Donald Richie, *A Hundred Years of Japanese Film*, 50. For an invaluable discussion of the relationship between Japanese and Western filmmaking norms, see Donald Kirihara's chapter, "The International Film Culture of Japan," in *Patterns of Time: Mizoguchi and the 1930s* (Madison: University of Wisconsin Press, 1992), 39–57.

25. Kakehi Masanori, "Reminiscences of Gosho, " in *Heinosuke Gosho*, program of the Tenth Hong Kong International Film Festival, presented by the Urban Council, 1986, 8.

26. Sato Tadao, "Le Point de vue sur les cheminées fantômes," 72.

27. Interestingly, Sato claims that Gosho, like all human beings, was himself not without contradictions and that he surmounted these contradictions in sentiment and humor, which—along with feeling—are the three cornerstones of his work (see "Le Point de vue sur les cheminées fantômes," 72).

28. Wakeman, *World Film Directors*, 404.

29. John Gillett, "Heinosuke Gosho: A Pattern of Living," National Film Theatre Programme Booklet, March 1986, 2. Also see Hubert Niogret, "Heinosuke Gosho et la maîtrise du découpage" ("Heinosuke Gosho and the Mastery of *Découpage*"), *Positif* 313 (March 1987): 37–41.

30. Indeed, however remote the possibility, lost films do occasionally show up. In a letter to the author, dated June 26, 2002, Ohba Masatoshi, the chief curator of the National Film Center in Tokyo, wrote that in 1999 two Gosho titles were discovered at a

Russian film archive. The first was *Goju no to* (*The Five-Storied Pagoda,* 1944), which contained almost the complete footage. This is especially good news since the print at the National Film Center is very poor and missing many scenes. In fact, this print runs only thirty-six minutes. (According to the late Shimizu Akira, the film originally ran nearly seventy minutes.) The second film that was found is *Shinsetsu* (*New Snow,* 1942). Unfortunately, it was not the complete film, only some missing parts. Still, it gives us more of an impression of what the film looked like. And that alone is cause for celebration.

1. GOSHO AND *SHOMIN* COMEDY IN THE 1930s

1. David Bordwell in *Ozu and the Poetics of Cinema* (London: British Film Institute; Princeton, N.J.: Princeton University Press, 1982), 164, discusses this matter in relation to Ozu's work, but it also holds true for Gosho.

2. Noël Burch, *To the Distant Observer: Form and Meaning in the Japanese Cinema,* rev. ed., ed. Annette Michelson (Berkeley and Los Angeles: University of California Press, 1979), 152. For further information on the *shomin-geki,* see Max Tessier's "Au fil des saison: de cinéma 'intimiste' et 'familial'" ("In the Course of the Seasons: 'Intimate' and 'Familial' Cinema"), in *Images du cinéma japonais* (*Images of Japanese Cinema*) (Paris: Henri Veyrier, 1981), 47–67, 60, 64; Arthur Nolletti, Jr., "Ozu's *Tokyo Story* and the 'Recasting' of McCarey's *Make Way for Tomorrow,*" in *Tokyo Story,* ed. David Desser, Cambridge Film Handbooks (New York: Cambridge University Press, 1997), 50, n. 3; and Joseph L. Anderson and Donald Richie, *The Japanese Film: Art and Industry,* expanded ed. (Princeton, N.J.: Princeton University Press, 1982), 450–51.

3. Donald Richie, *Japanese Cinema: An Introduction* (Hong Kong, Oxford, and New York: Oxford University Press, 1990), 11.

4. Osanari Kaoru, co-director of *Souls on the Road,* also was an important figure in Shingeki. An advocate of modern European drama, which he translated into Japanese, he founded the *Jiju Gekijo* (Free Theater) in the early 1920s.

5. Donald Richie, *Japanese Cinema: Film Style and National Character* (Garden City, N.Y.: Anchor, 1971), 23.

6. Tessier, *Images du cinéma japonais,* 49.

7. Arne Svensson, *Japan: An Illustrated Guide* (London and New York: Zwemmer/Barnes, 1971), 122.

8. See, e.g., Burch, *To the Distant Observer,* 259–60.

9. Tadao Sato, *Currents in Japanese Cinema: Essays by Tadao Sato,* trans. Gregory Barrett (Tokyo: Kodansha International, 1982), 139.

10. Burch, *To the Distant Observer,* 259–60.

11. Ibid., 287.

12. Ibid., 259.

13. Ibid.

14. Sato Tadao, "Le Point de vue sur les cheminées fantômes" ("Point of View on the Phantom Chimneys"), trans. from Japanese into French by Patrick de Vos and Cecile Sakai, in *Le Cinéma japonais de ses origines à nos jours* (*Japanese Cinema from Its Origins to Our Day*), Part 2 (Paris: La Cinémathèque Française/La Fondation du Japon, 1984), 72.

15. For additional information on Kido's policies during his tenure at Shochiku, consult Kido Shiro, *Nihon eiga den: eiga seisakusha no kiroku* (*The Story of Japanese Film: A Film Producer's Record*) (Tokyo: Bungei shunju-sha, 1956). For a history of the

studio, see *Shochiku kyujunen shi* (*A Ninety-Year History of Shochiku Studio*) (Tokyo: Shochiku kabushiki kaisha, 1985).

16. Anderson and Richie, *The Japanese Film: Art and Industry,* 101.

17. Ibid., 53.

18. David Owens, "Introduction," in "Before *Rashomon:* Japanese Film Treasures of the 30's and 40's," program, Museum of Fine Arts, Boston/The Japan Society of New York, 1985, n.p.

19. In *Ozu and the Poetics of Cinema,* David Bordwell points out that nonsense comedy was in fact particularly influenced by Harold Lloyd (18). In Gosho's nonsense comedies, the director even has actor Kobayashi Tokuji don Lloyd's famous trademark, horn-rimmed glasses.

20. In his essay, "Eiga haiyu no seikatsu to kyoyo" ("The Life and Education of Movie Actresses and Actors"), director Itami Mansaku speaks for many Japanese directors when he describes that what they loved best about American films was the energy, the fast pace, and the sense of optimism (quoted in Sato, *Currents in Japanese Cinema,* 34). For the influence of American films on Japanese directors, also see Audie Bock, "Ozu Reconsidered," *Film Criticism* 8, no. 1 (Fall 1983): 50–53; Tadao Sato, "The Comedy of Ozu and Chaplin: A Study in Contrast," *Wide Angle* 3, no. 2 (1979): 50–53; and Yamamoto Kikuo's *Nihon eiga ni okeru gaikoku eiga no eikyo: hikaku eigashi kenkyu* (*The Influence of Foreign Films on Japanese Cinema: Research in Comparative Film History*) (Tokyo: Waseda Daigaku shuppan, 1983) (see esp. the chapters on slapstick, Lloyd, and Chaplin, 279–342).

21. Kakehi Masanori, "Gosho Heinosuke no sekai: Gosho Heinosuke no entotsu no mieru basho o megutte" ("The World of Gosho Heinosuke: About His Work *Where Chimneys Are Seen*"), in *Nihon eiga o yomu: paionia tachi no isan* (*Reading Japanese Film: Heritage of the Pioneers*) (Tokyo: Dagereo shuppan, 1984), 130.

22. Tessier, *Images du cinéma japonais,* 57.

23. Quoted in Donald W. McCaffrey, *Four Great Comedians: Chaplin, Lloyd, Keaton, Langdon* (London: Zwemmer, 1968), 56.

24. Iwamoto Kenji, "Sound in Early Japanese Talkies," in *Reframing Japanese Cinema: Authorship, Genre, History,* ed. Arthur Nolletti, Jr. and David Desser (Bloomington and Indianapolis: Indiana University Press, 1992), 312–27. Also, as film critic Iijima Tadashi has said, Gosho "remained within cinematic traditions and borrowed none from the stage. . . . He knew from the start that film must always be a film and must not attempt to be recorded theatre" (quoted in Anderson and Richie, "The Films of Heinosuke Gosho," *Sight and Sound* 26, no. 2 [Autumn 1956]: 78). Elaborating on this view, Richard N. Tucker, in *Japan: Film Image* (London: Studio Vista, 1973), points out that Gosho's sparse use of dialogue not only enabled the narrative to move "at a more economic level," but also privileged the nonverbal communication between the characters, bringing a greater sense of reality to the action (19).

25. Anderson and Richie, "The Films of Heinosuke Gosho," 78. It is also worth emphasizing here that since no recording or dubbing facilities existed at the time Gosho made *The Neighbor's Wife and Mine,* all of the sounds (dialogue, sound effects, and music) had to be recorded during shooting.

26. Another of Gosho's male protagonists who shares this habit of writing himself memos is Kenzo (Akutagawa Hiroshi), the young tax collector in *Where Chimneys Are Seen.*

27. Tadao Sato, "Tokyo on Film," trans. Larry Greenberg, *East-West Film Journal* 2, no. 2 (June 1988): 3.

28. Japanese audiences, however, would be primed to interpret the antics of Komura and his buddies in another way: as socially acceptable behavior, in fact, as a ritual of sorts specifically designed to allow one to let off a little steam. Here the concepts of *honne* and *tatemae* apply. As Ian Buruma explains in *Behind the Mask: On Sexual Demons, Sacred Mothers, Transvestites, Gangsters, Drifters, and Other Japanese Cultural Heroes* (New York: Pantheon Books, 1984), *honne* is "the private feeling or opinion, which, in normal circumstances, remains hidden or suppressed" (221). Opposite is *tatemae,* "the façade, the public posture, the way things ought to be" (221). Interestingly, such adolescent male behavior as drinking and dancing in one's underwear, according to Buruma, is actually a form of *tatemae* in the long run, for it allows emotions to be vented without threatening "outward harmony" (221). In short, this kind of behavior is a way of encouraging people to act out their private feelings and fantasies in a permissible, monitored format. Social order, then, is protected and preserved in this simultaneous act of allowance and containment.

29. Donald Richie, *Ozu* (Berkeley: University of California Press, 1974), 150.

30. See Buruma's chapter, "The Eternal Mother," in *Behind the Mask,* 18–37, for a witty and informative discussion of the complex relationship of mother and child in Japanese society.

31. For a concise overview of this period of Japanese history, see W. G. Beasley, *The Rise of Modern Japan* (New York: St. Martin's Press, 1990), 176–212; and W. Scott Morton, *Japan: Its History and Culture* (New York: McGraw-Hill, 1984), 179–200. Here we can offer only the following brief summary: Beginning in the late 1920s, the military was pushing Japan further to the right and directing its ire against party politicians, liberal intellectuals, and any other group it thought to be responsible for the country's economic woes. Ultranationalistic (and in part even fanatic), the military condemned the liberal trend of the 1920s, which it regarded as one of the principal causes of Japan's moral decline. Of course, one of the chief characteristics of this liberal trend was the embracing of things Western, including democracy. Intent on pursuing what it euphemistically called *kyoson-kyoei* ("coexistence and co-prosperity"), Japan saw its mission to rule over much of Asia, beginning with Manchuria. The rest, as the saying goes, is history. As the military became more powerful, restraints were imposed and censorship in various forms increased. Film directors, for their part, risked censorship for being critical of the social system or introducing "British-American" ideas into their films. As Anderson and Richie point out in *The Japanese Film: Art and Industry,* 128–29, the Home Ministry laid down increasingly strict codes, with which filmmakers were expected to comply. By 1935 there was already a strong sense of repression in the air, with Western-style individualism especially suspect and under fire. In 1940, even the description of personal happiness on the screen was not exempt from watchful eyes. For Gosho and filmmakers like him, making films under these conditions proved well nigh impossible. See chapter 4 on *Once More* for further detail.

32. Quoted in the program note for *Burden of Life* in "Before *Rashomon*: Japanese Film Treasures of the 30's and 40's," n.p.

33. Ibid.

34. Burch, *To the Distant Observer,* 259.

35. See, e.g., Tessier, *Images du cinéma japonais,* 57.

36. In fact, the groom is played by Saburi Shin, who, in the official credits for the film, is listed as "*chusoi,*" first lieutenant. In the film, however, he is dressed in civilian clothes, which makes this sole reference to current political events oblique at best. See "*Jinsei no onimotsu* (*Burden of Life*)," in *Gosho Heinosuke kantoku tokushu* (*Special Issue*

on *Director Gosho Heinosuke),* vol. 21 (Tokyo: Film Center of the Tokyo National Museum of Modern Art, 1974), 17.

37. Anderson and Richie, *The Japanese Film: Art and Industry,* 355.

38. Bordwell, 34–35.

39. Saito, in fact, became Shochiku's archetypal salaryman. His most famous role is probably the father in Ozu's *Umarete wa mita keredo* (*I Was Born, but . . .* , 1932).

2. *DANCING GIRL OF IZU* (1933)
AND THE *JUNBUNGAKU* MOVEMENT

1. Horie Hideo, "Gosho Heinosuke to sono kaiwai: Ikiru koto wa hitosuji ga yoshi" ("Gosho Heinosuke and His Milieu: Living One's Life to the Fullest"), *Gosho Heinosuke tokushu,* Eiga Kozo (*Special Issue on Gosho Heinosuke,* Film Lectures) (Tokyo: Gendai Engeki Kyodai Foundation, March 1987), 32.

2. Ibid.

3. Keiko I. McDonald, "A Lyrical Novella Revamped: Gosho's *Izu Dancer,*" in *From Book to Screen: Modern Japanese Literature in Film.* (Armonk, N.Y., and London: East Gate Book/M. E. Sharpe, 2000), 85.

4. The first-person novel, the *shishosetsu,* is chiefly associated with Japanese naturalism and writers like Kunikida Doppo (1871–1908), Tokuda Shusei (1871–1943), and Shimazaki Toson (1872–1908). It was an often autobiographical, confessional mode that was especially prevalent during the 1930s (Donald Richie, *The Japanese Movie,* rev. ed. [Tokyo: Kodansha International, 1982]), 49).

5. Makoto Ueda, *Modern Japanese Writers and the Nature of Literature* (Stanford, Calif.: Stanford University Press, 1976), 177.

6. *Far Eastern Literature in the Twentieth Century: A Guide,* rev. ed., ed. Leonard S. Klein (Harpenden, Herts, U.K.: Oldcastle, 1988), 104.

7. Keiko I. McDonald, "Popular Film," in *Handbook of Japanese Popular Culture,* ed. Richard Gid Powers and Hidetoshi Kato (New York, Westport, Conn., and London: Greenwood Press, 1989), 107.

8. Yasunari Kawabata, *The Izu Dancer and Other Stories,* trans. Edward Seidensticker (Rutland, Vt. and Tokyo: Charles E. Tuttle, 1983), 21.

9. Ibid., 11.

10. Ibid., 26.

11. See McDonald, "A Lyrical Novella Revamped," 17–45; and Joseph L. Anderson and Donald Richie, *The Japanese Film: Art and Industry,* expanded ed. (Princeton, N.J.: Princeton University Press, 1982), 21–34.

12. Eric Cazdyn, *The Flash of Capital: Film and Geopolitics in Japan* (Durham, N.C. and London: Duke University Press, 2002), 90, 106. For a somewhat different version of Cazdyn's discussion, see his essay, "The Ends of Adaptation: Kon Ichikawa and the Politics of Cinematization," in *Kon Ichikawa,* ed. James Quandt (Toronto: Cinematheque Ontario, 2001), 221–35.

13. Specifically, with regard to the *eiga-ka* movement in the mid-1930s, Cazdyn contends that it "corresponded to the most significant ideological return to 'origins' that modern Japan had yet to experience" (90). These origins were as follows: national/racial origins of the Japanese people, origins of economic production, and cultural origins (90). In discussing *Dancing Girl of Izu* I tend to see the connection between film adaptation and national discourse in more direct economic and political terms.

14. "*Dancing Girl of Isu (Isu no odoriko),*" in *Heinosuke Gosho,* program of the Tenth Hong Kong International Film Festival, presented by the Urban Council, 1986, 22.

15. Ibid.

16. Fujita Motohiko, as quoted in McDonald, "A Lyrical Novella Revamped," 17.

17. McDonald, "A Lyrical Novella Revamped," 85.

18. Ibid., 15.

19. "*Dancing Girl of Isu,*" in *Heinosuke Gosho,* the Tenth Hong Kong International Film Festival, 22.

20. Ibid.

21. McDonald, "A Lyrical Novella Revamped," 91. These familiar rhetorical devices of melodrama are a central part of McDonald's close analysis of *Dancing Girl of Izu.* For more information on melodrama, see Thomas Elsaesser, "Tales of Sound and Fury: Observations on the Family Melodrama," *Monogram,* no. 4 (1972): 2–15; reprinted in *Home is Where the Heart Is: Studies in Melodrama and the Woman's Film,* ed. Christine Gledhill (London: British Film Institute, 1987), 43–69; and Christine Gledhill, "Rethinking Genre," *Reinventing Film Studies,* ed. Christine Gledhill and Linda Williams (London: Arnold, 2000), 221–43. Two useful English-language essays on Japanese film melodrama and how it relates to a melodramatic aesthetic as defined in the West are Mitsuhiro Yoshimoto, "Melodrama, Postmodernism, and the Japanese Cinema," *East-West Film Journal* 5, no. 1, Special Issue on Melodrama and Cinema (January 1991): 28–55; and Joseph A. Murphy, "Approaching Japanese Melodrama," *East-West Film Journal* 7, no. 2 (July 1993): 1–38. Murphy's essay is particularly worthwhile. It brings into "a position of dialogue" (14) Gledhill's insistence on the role of women in melodrama both as spectator and subject, and Yoshimoto's view that the study of melodrama must take into account "the fundamental difference between the positions of Japan and the United States as subjects of modernity" (32). For a Japanese-language consideration of Japanese film melodrama, see Murakawa Hide, "Shochiku merodorama no kindaika" ("Modernization of Film Melodrama in Shochiku Film Company"), *Nihon eiga to modanizumu: 1920–1930 (Japanese Film and Modernism: 1920–1930),* ed. Iwamoto Kenji (Tokyo: Libroport, 1991): 188–99.

22. Miriam Silverberg, "Constructing A New Cultural History of Prewar Japan," in *Japan in the World,* ed. Masao Miyoshi and H. D. Harootunian (Durham, N.C. and London: Duke University Press, 1993), 120.

23. Richie, *The Japanese Movie,* 38–39.

24. McDonald, "A Lyrical Novella Revamped," 92.

25. Kawabata, *The Izu Dancer,* 26.

26. Christena Turner, "The Spirit of Productivity: Workplace Discourse on Culture and Economics in Japan," in *Japan in the World,* ed. Masao Miyoshi and H. D. Harootunian (Durham, N.C. and London: Duke University Press, 1993), 149.

27. McDonald, "A Lyrical Novella Revamped," 93.

28. Jean-Claude Courdy, *The Japanese: Everyday Life in the Empire of the Rising Sun,* trans. from the French by Raymond Rosenthal (New York: Harper and Row, 1984), 17.

29. McDonald, "A Lyrical Novella Revamped," 93.

30. Gosho's stylistic flourishes merit further comment. One such example is his practice of super-inscription (i.e., superimposing a title over the image), which Noël Burch praises highly in *To the Distant Observer* (Berkeley and Los Angeles: University of California Press, 1979), 121. For Burch, these inscriptions are "extra-diegetic." But

since they serve to communicate the emotional state or feelings of the characters, especially Kaoru, it might be argued that they actually occupy something of a middle ground between diegetic and extra-diegetic. Another striking example of Gosho's stylistic flourishes is his idiosyncratic use of the pan. His panning is not so fast as a swish pan, but it certainly moves fast enough, and at times even unsteadily, its energy and tempo inseparable from the content. In one instance in *Dancing Girl of Izu* Gosho pans from a policeman cycling off in one direction to Kubota entering the village in the opposite direction. Here Gosho seems to be underscoring the fact that his characters' lives intersect. As I point out in my discussion, he also uses crosscutting as a structural device throughout the film to make this same point. Basically, Gosho's fast pans feel like stylistic embellishment, his way of showing the sheer delight he takes in filmmaking itself. The most unusual example of his stylistic flourishes is his use of two freeze frames in the banquet scene. Donald Kirihara, in *Patterns of Time: Mizoguchi and the 1930s* (Madison: University of Wisconsin Press, 1992), rightly sees this usage as "potentially more transgressive" than Gosho's practice of super-inscriptions (63). These freeze frames take place when Eikichi, in an effort to humor a drunken guest, plays a samurai warrior named Sawasho and leaps about, swinging a sword. Virtually a parody of kabuki's *mie* ("frozen poses"), these shots only add to the comedy of the scene, emphasizing Eikichi's lack of coordination and skill. The audience I saw the film with at the Harvard Film Archive in spring of 1990 not only found the scene amusing but also laughed uproariously at the two freeze frames. But what exactly was the audience laughing at: Eikichi's lack of coordination, or the use of the freeze frame technique itself? Eikichi seems to be deliberately embarrassing himself to handle a boor—and thus may be exaggerating his lack of coordination and skill for just this purpose. As for the freeze frames, they may well be a distancing device to put the comedy, as it were, in quotation marks. For a fuller discussion of Gosho's style, see chapter 3 on *Oboroyo no onna* (*Woman of the Mist*, 1936). For a thoughtful overview of Japanese film style during the prewar period, see David Bordwell, "Visual Style in Japanese Cinema, 1925–1945," *Film History: An International Journal* 7, no. 1 (Spring 1995): 5–31.

31. Mary Ann Doane, *The Desire to Desire: The Woman's Film of the 1940s* (Bloomington and Indianapolis: Indiana University Press, 1987), 67.

32. McDonald, "A Lyrical Novella Revamped," 96.

33. Kobayashi Tokuji, who plays Eikichi, was a regular in Gosho's films. He starred in the director's first film, *Nanto no haru* (*Spring in Southern Islands*) in 1925 and made his last appearance in a Gosho film in the 1959 *Karatachi nikki* (*Journal of the Orange Flower*). Often cast in the role of a well-meaning but ineffectual man, he was either an idler (*Burden of Life*), someone in need of a good woman's guidance (*The Bride Talks in Her Sleep* and *The Groom Talks in His Sleep*), or just an ordinary person struggling to get ahead. For example, in *L'Amour* (1933), he is a country schoolteacher, who, in his own words, "almost passed my high school teacher exam." The "almost" says it all. Nevertheless, the heroine recognizes his many virtues and chooses him over a wealthy suitor. Frequently paired with Tanaka Kinuyo, his Eikichi in *Dancing Girl of Izu* is a self-admitted spendthrift, but he is also a man choked with self-disappointment and the knowledge that he is one of life's plodders, someone ill-equipped to deal with the world around him. Still, much of the time, he seems carefree, as if he were trying to put the best face on everything. Kobayashi never lets us know for sure. Rather, he gives us hints that more is going on than meets the eye, as when Eikichi remarks that he and his wife recently lost their baby. Mostly, however, Kobayashi shows us Eikichi's strengths and weaknesses: his naivete, his sometimes-faulty judgment, his love for Kaoru, and his in-

nate openness and kindness. Needless to say, his strengths outweigh his weaknesses, and earn him Mizuhara's friendship and our affection.

34. McDonald, "A Lyrical Novella Revamped," 96.

35. Ibid.

36. Ibid., 97.

37. Although Tanaka's most famous collaboration was with Mizoguchi, she also enjoyed a long and successful association with Gosho. It began in 1926 with *Machi no hitobito* (*Town People*) and continued with sixteen more films between 1926 and 1936, including *Mura no hanayome* (*The Village Bride*, 1928), *Madamu to nyobo* (*The Neighbor's Wife and Mine*, 1931), and *Izu no odoriko* (*Dancing Girl of Izu*, 1933). Born near Osaka, Tanaka still had her Kansai accent when she made *The Neighbor's Wife and Mine*. This added flavor to the landmark "talkie." Tanaka and Gosho's collaboration continued well into the 1950s. For the record: in Ichikawa's 1987 *Eiga joyu* (*Film Actress*), which deals with Tanaka's life, Tanaka (played by Yoshinaga Sayuri) and Gosho (Nakai Kiichi) are seen in a re-creation of the 1927 film shoot of *Hazukashii yume* (*Embarrassing Dreams*).

38. "*Dancing Girl of Isu*," in *Heinosuke Gosho*, program of the Tenth Hong Kong International Film Festival, 22.

39. Ibid.

3. *WOMAN OF THE MIST* (1936)

1. Joseph L. Anderson and Donald Richie, *The Japanese Film: Art and Industry*, expanded ed. (Princeton, N.J.: Princeton University Press, 1982), 355.

2. Anderson and Richie, "The Films of Heinosuke Gosho," *Sight and Sound* 26, no. 2 (Autumn 1956): 78.

3. See *Kinema Jumpo, Nihon eiga daihyo shinario zenshu 3* (*A Collection of Representative Japanese Screenplays*, no. 3), in *Kinema Jumpo* (May 1958); and *Kinema jumpo, Nihon eiga shinario koten zenshu, Dai 3 kan* (*A Collection of Classical Japanese Screenplays*, vol. 3) in *Kinema Jumpo* (April 1966).

4. The title *Oboroyo no onna* is difficult to translate into English since there is no equivalent word for *Oboroyo*, which in Japanese means something like "the night of a hazy moon." Thus, the film has various English titles: *Woman of Pale Night, A Woman of the Misty Moonlight, Woman of the Mist*, and even *Moonlit Night Lady*. Of these, *Woman of the Mist* is the most frequently used.

5. Tadao Sato, "Tokyo on Film," trans. Larry Greenberg, *East-West Film Journal* 2, no. 2 (June 1988): 2.

6. Ibid.

7. In crediting himself for the original story idea, Gosho uses the name "Goshotei," his signature as a haiku writer. Also worth noting is that Gosho based Iida Choko's character on one of his relatives and that the actual screenplay was written by Ikeda Tadao, one of Shochiku's leading writers and an expert at describing the Shitamachi scene. See *Gosho Heinosuke kantoku tokushu* (*Special Issue on Director Gosho Heinosuke*), vol. 21 (Tokyo: Film Center of the Tokyo National Museum of Modern Art, 1974), 18.

8. Noël Burch, *To the Distant Observer* (Berkeley: University of California Press, 1979), 287.

9. Harold G. Henderson, *An Introduction to Haiku* (New York: Doubleday, 1958), 1–8.

10. Quoted in Kakehi Masanori, "Gosho Heinosuke no sekai: Gosho Heinosuke no entotsu no mieru basho o megutte" ("The World of Gosho Heinosuke: About His Work *Where Chimneys Are Seen*"), in *Nihon eiga o yomu: paionia tachi no isan* (*Reading Japanese Film: Heritage of the Pioneers*) (Tokyo: Dagereo shuppan, 1984), 125. Also see Kakehi, "Reminiscences of Gosho," in *Heinosuke Gosho,* program of the Tenth Hong Kong International Film Festival, presented by the Urban Council, 1986, 8.

11. Claude Chidamian, *Bonsai: Miniature Trees* (New York and Princeton, N.J.: D. Van Nostrand, 1955), 12.

12. The term "plastic material" was coined by Russian director and theorist Vsevolod I. Pudovkin, who believed that visually expressive objects and images "could communicate emotions and ideas more effectively than any other cinematic tool" (quoted in Gerald Mast and Bruce F. Kawin, *A Short History of the Movies,* 6th ed. [Boston: Allyn and Bacon, 1996], 189). "Plastic material" is also known by other terms, e.g., "pictorial symbols" and "concrete objects." Gosho makes use of this tool throughout his career. Hence the chimneys in *Where Chimneys Are Seen* and the bird cage in *Growing Up,* to cite just two of his most famous examples.

13. During the Gosho workshop that I conducted at the University of Hawaii Summer Session on June 4, 1990, Shimizu Akira of the Kawakita Memorial Film Institute/Japan Film Library Council pointed out that today Teruko would probably have an abortion. But no such possibility existed in the 1930s, because abortion was illegal. For the past five decades, however, abortions have been legal in Japan, and can be obtained for medical or economic reasons under Article 14 of Japan's Eugenic Protection Law. This change is reflected in Gosho's 1956 film *Aru yo futatabi* (*Twice on a Certain Night*), in which the heroine (Otowa Nobuko) has an abortion chiefly because her husband (Sano Shuji) is out of work.

14. This reference to China is the only specific allusion to the war Japan was waging there. This war and the establishment of the puppet regime of Manchukuo earned Japan worldwide condemnation in the 30s, but as Donald Keene notes, "for the Japanese who participated in the colonization of Manchuria, life was immeasurably better than it had been at home" (*Dawn to the West: Japanese Literature of the Modern Era—Fiction* [New York: Holt, Rinehart and Winston, 1984], 858). References to China as a place to find work appear in films as late as Ozu's *Todake no kyodai* (*Brothers and Sisters of the Toda Family,* 1941). See David Bordwell, *Ozu and the Poetics of Cinema* (London: British Film Institute; Princeton, N.J.: Princeton University Press, 1988), 282.

15. Anderson and Richie, *The Japanese Film,* 102.

16. In the last part of the film, questions also arise as to the exact nature of Bunkichi's feelings for Teruko. In the scene in which he visits her on her deathbed, and again in the scenes of her wake, he is genuinely grief-stricken, and even weeps. At first we imagine that this is because he has come to admire her, and thus cannot help being moved when she suddenly takes ill and dies so young, a victim of unkind fate. Yet Gosho continually foregrounds Bunkichi in these scenes, showing us his deep and abiding sorrow, and often in close-up. Thus, these feelings begin to seem ambiguous, all the more so when we recall that he has known Teruko in the past—in a relationship that is itself ambiguous. Nothing is made of these ambiguities; indeed, they are not even acknowledged in the film. Still, we cannot help but wonder: Was Bunkichi once in love with Teruko? Is he still? Only he, Gosho, and writer Ikeda Tadao know for sure.

17. Anderson and Richie, *The Japanese Film,* 356.

18. In fact, *The Song of the Flower Basket* was released on January 14, in conjunction with the live-in servants' holiday called "Yabuiri," on January 15. Since this holi-

day followed New Year's Day, film studios anticipated brisk business at the box office. Certainly Shochiku had good reason to be optimistic, since the film was a sweet-natured love story that was rich in old downtown atmosphere and starred popular players (Tanaka Kinuyo, Sano Shuji, and Kawamura Reikichi). After the war, January 15 became a national holiday known as "Coming of Age Day." See "*Hanagako no uta (The Song of the Flower Basket),*" in *Gosho Heinosuke kantoku tokushu (Special Issue on Director Gosho Heinosuke)*, 19.

4. *ONCE MORE* (1947) AND GOSHO'S ROMANTICISM IN THE EARLY OCCUPATION PERIOD

1. Horie Hideo, "Gosho Heinosuke to sono kaiwai: Ikiru koto wa hitosuji ga yoshi" ("Gosho Heinosuke and His Milieu: Living One's Life to the Fullest"), *Gosho Heinosuke tokushu,* Eiga Kozo (*Special Issue on Gosho Heinosuke,* Film Lectures) (Tokyo: Gendai Engeki Kyodai Foundation, March 1987), 28.

2. Quoted in Joseph L. Anderson and Donald Richie, "The Films of Heinosuke Gosho," *Sight and Sound* 26, no. 2 (Autumn 1956): 77, 80.

3. Mark Le Fanu, "To Love Is to Suffer: Reflections on the Later Films of Heinosuke Gosho," *Sight and Sound* 55, no. 3 (Summer 1986): 198.

4. Joseph L. Anderson and Donald Richie, *The Japanese Film: Art and Industry,* expanded ed. (Princeton, N.J.: Princeton University Press, 1982), 356.

5. Shimizu Akira, "Nihon ni okeru senso to eiga" ("War and Cinema in Japan"), in *Nichibei eiga sen: Paru Haba gojushunen (Media Wars Then and Now: Pearl Harbor Fiftieth Anniversary)*, Yamagata International Documentary Festival, October 7–10, 1991 (Tokyo: Cinematrix, 1991), 5–50. The essays in this informative anthology are published in Japanese and English. See also *Japan/America Film Wars: WWII Propaganda and Its Cultural Contexts,* ed. Abe Mark Nornes and Fukushima Yukio (New York: Harwood, 1994), 7–58.

6. "Heinosuke Gosho," in *World Film Directors,* vol. 1, *1890–1945,* ed. John Wakeman (New York: H. W. Wilson Company, 1987), 403.

7. Ibid.

8. Sato Tadao, interview by author, National Film Center, Tokyo, April 15, 1985.

9. Kakehi Masanori, "Gosho Heinosuke no sekai: Gosho Heinosuke no entotsu no mieru basho o megutte" ("The World of Gosho Heinosuke: About His Work *Where Chimneys Are Seen*"), in *Nihon eiga o yomu: paionia tachi no isan (Reading Japanese Film: Heritage of the Pioneers)* (Tokyo: Dagereo shuppan, 1984), 133.

10. Kyoko Hirano, "Japan," in *World Cinema since 1945,* ed. William Luhr (New York: Ungar Publishing Co., 1987), 380.

11. Kyoko Hirano, *Mr. Smith Goes to Tokyo: Japanese Cinema under the American Occupation, 1945–1952* (Washington, D.C. and London: Smithsonian Institution Press, 1992), 75, 242.

12. For further discussion of the immediate postwar period, see W. Scott Morton, *Japan: Its History and Culture* (New York: McGraw-Hill, 1984), 201–9.

13. Fujita Motohiko, *Nihon eiga gendai-shi II: Showa nijunendai (Modern History of Japanese Cinema,* vol. 2: *1945–1955)* (Tokyo: Kashin-sha, 1977), 47–48.

14. Kakehi, "Gosho Heinosuke no sekai," 120.

15. Morton, *Japan: Its History and Culture,* 205.

16. Hirano, *World Cinema since 1945,* 382.

17. Kakehi, "Gosho Heinosuke no sekai," 133.

18. Horie, "Gosho Heinosuke to sono kaiwai," 29.

19. Quoted in Kakehi, "Gosho Heinosuke no sekai," 133.

20. "Heinosuke Gosho," 403.

21. Gosho Heinosuke, "Romanshugi no igi enshitsuka no tachibakara" ("The Significance of Romanticism in Movies—From the Director's Point of View"), *Eiga Tenbo (Film Review)* 11, no. 3 (1946): 33.

22. Ibid., 32.

23. Donald Keene, *Dawn to the West: Japanese Literature of the Modern Era—Fiction* (New York: Holt, Rinehart, and Winston, 1984), 186.

24. Ibid., 187.

25. Quoted in Keene, *Dawn to the West,* 195. For analyses of Tokoku's ideas on social and spiritual harmony, see Francis Mathy, "Kitamura Tokoku: Essays on the Inner Life," *Monumenta Nipponica* 19, nos. 1–2 (1964): 66–110; and Janet A. Walker, *The Japanese Novel of the Meiji Period and the Idea of Individualism* (Princeton, N.J.: Princeton University Press, 1979), 69–74.

26. Ibid., 199.

27. Gosho, "Romanshugi no igi enshitsuka no tachibakara" ("Significance of Romanticism"), 32.

28. Ibid.

29. Ibid.

30. Ibid., 33.

31. Ibid.

32. Ibid.

33. Ibid.

34. Ibid., 32.

35. "*Once More (Ima hitotabino),*" in *Heinosuke Gosho,* program of the Tenth Hong Kong International Film Festival, presented by the Urban Council, 1986, 27. First published in *Eiga shijo besuto 200 shiriizu: Nihon eiga (200 Classics of Japanese Cinema: The Great Films of the World/Japan)* (Tokyo: Kinema Jumpo, May 30, 1982), 158–59.

36. Ibid., 27.

37. Uekusa Keinosuke, *Keredo yoake ni: waga seishun no Kurosawa Akira (After Dawn—Memories of Kurosawa Akira in My Youth)* (Tokyo: Bungei shunju-sha, 1985), 7–12.

38. "*Once More,*" *Gosho,* 27. For an overview of Takami's work, see Keene, *Dawn to the West,* 871–78.

39. Fujita, *Nihon eiga gendai-shi,* 50.

40. Ibid., 49–51. *No Regrets for Our Youth* is based on the 1933 incident in which Prof. Takigawa Yukitoki was forced to resign from Kyoto University because of his alleged Communist thought. For detailed discussions of the film, see Donald Richie, *The Films of Akira Kurosawa* (Berkeley and Los Angeles: University of California Press, 1970), 36–42; and Hirano, *Mr. Smith Goes to Tokyo,* 179–204.

41. Hirano, *Mr. Smith Goes to Tokyo,* 194.

42. *Currents in Japanese Cinema,* trans. Gregory Barrett (Tokyo: Kodansha International, 1982), 32. The extent of *Seventh Heaven*'s influence on Japanese film is well detailed by Yamamoto Kikuo in *Nihon eiga ni okeru gaikoku eiga no eikyo: hikaku eigashi kenkyu (The Influence of Foreign Films on Japanese Cinema: Research in Comparative Film History)* (Tokyo: Waseda Daigaku shuppan, 1983), 460–67. Yamamoto cites

reviews of the film in the October 21, 1927 issue of *Kinema Jumpo* that highly recommend it, praising its script, art direction, soft-focus photography, and use of the moving camera. The scene of Chico's going off to war is singled out as particularly memorable. It is noted that audiences were deeply touched throughout the film, and that they laughed and cried. As an example of the film's influence, Yamamoto cites specific allusions to Chico and Diane in the Japanese silent film, *Hafu no minato.* At one point the heroine talks about the "Chico type." Later, another character remarks, "I wonder where Janet Gaynor is," only to be answered in an intertitle: "Here's Janet Gaynor" (462). Even Ozu paid homage to the Borzage film. See David Bordwell, *Ozu and the Poetics of Cinema* (London: British Film Institute; Princeton, N.J.: Princeton University Press, 1988), 72.

43. However, two other American films with which *Once More* has points in common are McCarey's *Love Affair* (1939) and LeRoy's *Waterloo Bridge* (1940). In fact, LeRoy's film, like *Once More,* opens with its male protagonist returning to the spot where he and his love met before the war, then proceeds into an extended flashback. Anderson and Richie note that LeRoy's film was an influence on Shochiku's postwar smash hit, *Kimi no na wa* (*What Is Your Name?* 1953) [*The Japanese Film,* 260–61], but I have not been able to find anything that suggests it was an influence on Gosho.

Once More also echoes other films and filmmakers, although this does not necessarily mean that any influence is involved. For instance, *Once More* evokes the lush, virtuoso lighting and photography of 1940 Cukor melodramas like *A Woman's Face* (1941) and *Keeper of the Flame* (1942). A notable example is Nogami and Akiko's meeting at the gallery where Sakon's paintings are on exhibit. Here the two characters, both dressed in black, are at times basically silhouetted against the background or only back-lit or side-lit. At other times—as in close-ups that reveal the feelings they are trying to hide—they are lit by a soft key light, their faces partly in shadow—like Joan Crawford's scarred face in Cukor's 1941 film. Occasionally, *Once More* also reminds one of Sirk. A case in point is Sakon's visit to Nogami at the dam site. As Sakon grows more and more distraught, he becomes convinced that he can paint again, and rushes out to the dam's narrow walkway, calling out Akiko's name. Low-angle shots and the acceleration of the cutting tempo convey his out-of-control behavior—he races to the forefront of the frame, shot after shot, as if he will plunge either off the screen or, as it turns out, to his death. Here melodramatic excess is the perfect objective correlative for the character's loss of control. Gosho may not be as baroque as Sirk—we need only think of Marylee's frenetic dance during her father's heart attack in *Written on the Wind* (1956)—but he too understands the kind of excess that melodrama sometimes requires.

44. Gosho, "Romanshugi no igi enshitsuka no tachibakara" ("Significance of Romanticism"), 33.

45. Elaine Showalter, "Representing Ophelia: Women, Madness, and the Responsibilities of Feminist Criticism," in *Hamlet* by William Shakespeare, ed. Susanne L. Wofford (Boston and New York: Bedford Books/St. Martin's Press, 1994), 224.

46. Ibid., 225, 228.

47. Quoted in Showalter, 228.

48. Robert Bresson, "Appendix: Interview," by Ian Cameron, *The Films of Robert Bresson* (New York: Praeger, 1969), 135.

49. For a discussion of the *tateyaku* see Sato, *Currents in Japanese Cinema,* 15–30.

50. Uekusa told me in an April 16, 1985 interview at the National Film Center in Tokyo that Hara Setsuko was originally chosen to play Akiko, but did not because of the Toho strike. Takamine, who had first gained attention in Yoshimura's *Danryu*

(*Warm Current,* 1939), was therefore borrowed from Shochiku. According to Uekusa, both he and Gosho were a little bit in love with her throughout the shooting.

51. "*Once More,*" in *Gosho,* 27.

52. "*A Visage to Remember* (*Omokage*)," in *Gosho,* 29.

5. *WHERE CHIMNEYS ARE SEEN* (1953)

1. Kyoko Hirano, *Mr. Smith Goes to Tokyo: Japanese Cinema under the American Occupation, 1945–1952* (Washington, D.C. and London: Smithsonian Institution Press, 1992), 254. For an account of the independent movement, see Hirano, *Mr. Smith Goes to Tokyo,* 252–57; and Joseph L. Anderson and Donald Richie, *The Japanese Film: Art and Industry,* expanded ed. (Princeton, N.J.: Princeton University Press, 1982), 237–38. For Gosho's role in this movement, see Kakehi Masanori, "Gosho Heinosuke no sekai: Gosho Heinosuke no entotsu no mieru basho o megutte" ("The World of Gosho Heinosuke: About His Work *Where Chimneys Are Seen*"), in *Nihon eiga o yomu: paionia tachi no isan* (*Reading Japanese Film: Heritage of the Pioneers*) (Tokyo: Dagereo shuppan, 1986), 135.

2. Joseph L. Anderson and Donald Richie, "The Films of Heinosuke Gosho," *Sight and Sound* 26, no. 2 (Autumn 1956): 80.

3. Mark Le Fanu, "To Love Is to Suffer: Reflections on the Later Films of Heinosuke Gosho," *Sight and Sound* 55, no. 3 (Summer 1986): 201.

4. "*Asa no hamon* (*Morning Conflicts*)," in *Gosho Heinosuke Kantoku tokushu* (*Special Issue on Director Gosho Heinosuke*), vol. 21 (Tokyo: Film Center of the Tokyo National Museum of Modern Art, 1974), 26.

5. Horie Hideo, "Gosho Heinosuke to sono kaiwai: Ikiru koto wa hitosuji ga yoshi" ("Gosho Heinosuke and His Milieu: Living One's Life to the Fullest"), *Gosho Heinosuke tokushu,* Eiga Kozo (*Special Issue on Gosho Heinosuke,* Film Lectures) (Tokyo: Gendai Engeki Kyodai Foundation, March 1987), 29.

6. "*The Cock Crows Twice* (*Niwatori wa futatabi naku*)," in *Heinosuke Gosho,* program of the Tenth Hong Kong International Film Festival, presented by the Urban Council, 1986, 37.

7. Quoted in Kakehi, "Gosho Heinosuke no sekai," 137.

8. See, e.g., Anderson and Richie, *The Japanese Film,* 196; and Georges Sadoul, *Dictionary of Films,* trans., ed., and updated by Peter Morris (Berkeley and Los Angeles: University of California Press, 1972), 103. Gosho's best-loved film in Japan, *Where Chimneys Are Seen,* also placed among the top ten in the annual *Kinema Jumpo* poll. On the whole, the film was greeted as a "revelation for Western audiences whose knowledge of Japanese cinema had previously been limited to samurai films" ("Heinosuke Gosho," in *World Film Directors,* vol. 1, *1890–1945,* ed. John Wakeman [New York: H. W. Wilson, 1987], 404). However, there was at least one dissenting voice, which complained that the film "lacked the intensity and penetration of earlier pix from Tokyo, notably 'Rashomon'" (Harold Myers, "Two US Pix in 1st 10 at Berlin Fest; Riots Curtain 'Window' into West," *Variety,* July 1, 1953, 2, 25). This was exactly the attitude that led Japanese distributors to believe that films about modern Japanese life could not be appreciated in the West. Hence, it was not until the 1970s and 1980s that Western audiences got a look at the work of Ozu, Naruse, and Gosho.

9. Anderson and Richie, "Films of Heinosuke Gosho," 81.

10. Sato Tadao, "Le Point de vue sur les cheminées fantômes" ("The Point of View on the Phantom Chimneys"), trans. from Japanese into French by Patrick de Vos and

Cecil Sakai. in *Le Cinéma japonais de ses origines à nos jours* (*Japanese Cinema from Its Origins to Our Day*), Part 2 (Paris: La Cinémathèque Française/La Fondation du Japon, 1984), 75.

11. Noël Burch, *To the Distant Observer: Form and Meaning in the Japanese Cinema* (Berkeley and Los Angeles: University of California Press, 1979), 287. Also see the discussion of Gosho's *shomin-geki* in chapter 1.

12. Horie, in fact, worked on twenty-nine of Gosho's films and wrote scripts for seven of them. For additional information on Gosho and Horie's association, see chapter 9, n. 30.

13. Quoted in Horie, "Gosho Heinosuke to sono kaiwai," 35.

14. Mark B. Williams, "Shiina Rinzo," in *Japanese Fiction Writers Since World War II: Dictionary of Literary Biography,* vol. 182, ed. Van C. Gessel (Detroit, Washington, D.C., and London: A Bruccoli Clark Layman Book/Gale Research, 1997), 206.

15. Christena Turner, "The Spirit of Productivity: Workplace Discourse on Culture and Economics in Japan," in *Japan in the World,* ed. Masao Miyoshi and H. D. Harootunian (Durham, N.C. and London: Duke University Press, 1993), 146.

16. "*The Cock Crows Twice,*" *Gosho,* 37. After *Where Chimneys Are Seen,* Gosho and Shiina collaborated twice more, both in 1954: on *Ai to shi to tanima* (*The Valley between Love and Death*), based on Shiina's novel of the same name, and on *The Cock Crows Twice.* Shiina received sole screenplay credit for both films. *The Valley between Love and Death* deals with a detective (Akutagawa Hiroshi), who is hired by a suspicious husband to follow his wife, only to become involved with a doctor (Tsushima Keiko) and the family she is attending—all of whom, like postwar Japan, are caught between love and death. The film was a critical failure, but Gosho and Shiina worked together a third time on *The Cock Crows Twice,* which was generally considered more successful. This drama has to do with three young women who make a suicide pact, but acquire a better understanding of themselves and life in general when they meet a team of oil prospectors. Gosho's hope to collaborate with Shiina again did not work out, most likely because Shiina was heavily invested in his own career as a novelist and playwright. (He died in 1973.) However, in 1956, Gosho filmed *Aru yo futatabi* (*Twice on a Certain Night*), which he and Hasebe Keiji freely adapted from Shiina's story, "Tsuma no shisso" ("A Missing Wife"). Regarded as something of a companion piece to *Where Chimneys Are Seen,* this film has to do with a beaten-down, unemployed man (Sano Shuji) and his optimistic, hard-working wife (Otowa Nobuko), who think they understand each other, but do not. At first, this realization makes them uneasy; nevertheless, like the Ogatas in *Where Chimneys Are Seen,* they are still able to live optimistically ("*Aru yo futatabi* [*Twice on a Certain Night*]," in *Gosho Heinosuke Kantoku tokushu* [*Special Issue on Director Gosho Heinosuke*], 32).

17. Sato, "Le Point de vue," 74.

18. Ibid.

19. Burch, *To the Distant Observer,* 203.

20. For further discussion of *donden* cuts, see Bordwell, *Ozu and the Poetics of Cinema* (London: British Film Institute. Princeton, N.J.: Princeton University Press, 1988), 91–92, and Sato, *Currents in Japanese Cinema: Essays by Tadao Sato,* trans. Gregory Barrett (Tokyo: Kodansha International, 1982), 189.

21. Horie, "Gosho Heinosuke to sono kaiwai," 33–34. According to Horie, it was also Oguni who suggested the film's title.

22. See "*Where Chimneys Are Seen* (*Entotsu no mieru basho*)," *Gosho,* 33. A different complaint is voiced by Burch, who finds the chimney symbol "curiously obtrusive" (287).

23. Sato, "Le Point de vue," 76.

24. John Condon and Keisuke Karata, *In Search of What's Japanese about Japan* (Tokyo: Shufunotomo, 1974), 37.

25. Also consult my discussion in "*Where Chimneys Are Seen,*" in *Magill's Survey of Cinema: Foreign Language Films,* ed. Frank N. Magill, vol. 7, TAL–Z (Englewood Cliffs, N.J.: Salem Press, 1985), 3363–64.

26. As Kyoko Hirano perceptively observes, Gosho uses not only close-ups effectively but also long shots and long takes. To illustrate her point, she describes the sequence photographed from a train window, in which Kenzo notices (and comments upon) the ever-changing number of chimneys. She writes: "The fluidly vibrating image of the chimneys as the scenery swiftly passes is visually refreshing" ("*Entotsu no mieru basho,*" in *The International Dictionary of Films and Filmmakers,* vol. 1, *Films,* ed. Christopher Lyon [Chicago: St. James Press, 1984], 143).

27. Katsuko's status in the film is by no means clear. Critics have described her as "Tsukahara's mistress" (Sato, "Le Point de vue," 73), Tsukahara's "second wife" (*Eiga shijo besuto 200 shiriizu: Nihon eiga* [*200 Classics of Japanese Cinema: The Great Films of the World/Japan*] [Tokyo: Kinema Jumpo, May 30, 1982], 210–11), Tsukahara's "estranged wife" ("*Where Chimneys Are Seen,*" *Gosho,* 32), and "a woman he lives with" (Arne Svensson, *Japan* [London and New York: Zwemmer/Barnes, 1971], 17). One anonymous source even lists her as Tsukahara's "divorced wife." In cast listings she is given the family name "Ishibashi," but nowhere in the film is this name mentioned. Further complicating the issue is her remark to Kenzo when they meet. "I'm just an acquaintance," she says, referring to Tsukahara. Obviously, this isn't the case. Most likely what she intends to convey here is her anger and disgust at Tsukahara, and to dissociate herself from him as much as possible. Although she and Tsukahara are probably not married, they have lived together long enough to have a child. For all practical purposes, they have a common law marriage.

28. This collision is one of the many examples of "accidents" or "miscues" that occur in the film and which find characters slipping, tripping, falling, or bumping into each other. Most often these accidents are not integral to the dramatic action and thus take the viewer by surprise. To my knowledge, no critic or commentator has discussed these accidents. Since at the most basic level, they intrigue as behavioral details, they warrant attention. These accidents or miscues come across as aleatory happenings, and lend an improvisatory feel to the film, as if they are no part of Gosho's carefully planned design of blocking and choreography. As such, they contribute to the film's documentary, slice-of-life quality, underscoring the fact that life is occasionally messy (usually at the most inopportune times) and not always in one's control. Hence, in the scene when Hiroko attempts suicide, Ryukichi inadvertently slips and falls—an altogether curious and "realistic" behavioral detail that somehow manages to intensify the tragic mood. However, these accidents or miscues by and large have a comic tincture and even offer wry comment on character relationships. For example, in one scene, Hiroko is trying to put away some clothes, including Ryukichi's overcoat. Since he is sitting on it, she politely says, "Excuse me," to get his attention. When he doesn't move, she simply pulls it out from under him. However, she pulls with such force that she loses her balance and almost falls over backwards. Ryukichi notices none of this. All told, these accidents and miscues deepen the realist impulse of Gosho's *shomin-geki,* creating the impression that the viewer is seeing not only ordinary people but also activity that normally would not be permitted to intrude upon carefully wrought illusion.

29. Bordwell, *Ozu and the Poetics of Cinema,* 301.

30. In noting that "the consumerist ideology . . . was present in urban culture since at least the 1920s" (48), Bordwell makes this intriguing observation about postwar consumerism in Japan: "the desire to possess them [material goods] becomes at once a source of humor and a substitute for unresolved social conflicts" (49).

31. Ibid., 48.

32. Consult Bordwell, *Ozu and the Poetics of Cinema,* 36–37; Hirano, *Mr. Smith Goes to Tokyo,* 182; and W. Scott Morton, *Japan: Its History and Culture* (New York: McGraw-Hill, 1984), 203–206.

33. Edwin O. Reischauer, *The Japanese Today: Changes and Continuity* (Cambridge, Mass. and London: Belknap Press/Harvard University Press, 1988), 109.

34. Sato, "Le Point du vue," 76.

35. J. Victor Koschmann, "Maruyama Masao and the Incomplete Project of Modernity," *Postmodernism and Japan,* ed. Masao Miyoshi and H. D. Harootunian (Durham, N.C. and London: Duke University Press, 1989), 128.

36. Ibid., 130, 134.

37. Ibid., 129.

38. Ibid.

39. Ibid., 128.

40. Ibid., 130. (Italics are in the original quote.)

41. Ibid., 131.

42. Ibid., 133.

43. Ibid.

44. Ibid., 131.

45. Ibid.

46. *Merriam-Webster's Collegiate Dictionary,* 10th ed. (Springfield, Mass.: Merriam-Webster, 1995), 892. For fuller explanations of the concepts of "play" discussed in this chapter, see the entry in *The Oxford English Dictionary,* 2d ed., vol. 9, *Ow–Poisant,* prepared by J. A. Simpson and E. S. C. Weiner (Oxford: Clarendon Press, 1989), esp. 1011–15.

47. *Discover Japan: Words, Customs and Concepts,* vol. 1 (Tokyo and New York: Kodansha International, 1982), 170–71.

48. *Merriam-Webster's Collegiate Dictionary,* 10th ed., 892.

49. Quoted in Koschmann, "Maruyama Masao and the Incomplete Project of Modernity," 132.

50. Ibid.

51. Ibid., 136.

52. Anderson and Richie, *The Japanese Film,* 196.

6. *AN INN AT OSAKA* (1954)

1. Elliot Stein, "The Greatest *Shomin-geki* on Earth," *The Village Voice,* December 12, 1989, 109.

2. Donald Richie, *The Japanese Movie,* rev. ed. (Tokyo, New York, and San Francisco: Kodansha International, 1982), 112.

3. Adam Garbicz and Jacek Klinowski, *Cinema, The Magic Vehicle: A Guide to Its Achievement,* vol. 2, *The Cinema in the Fifties* (New York: Schocken Books, 1983), 231.

4. Novelist Minakami Takitaro was one of the leading authors of *Mita Bungaku,* the literary magazine of Keio University. Not coincidentally, Gosho was a graduate of the university and doubtless was familiar with much of Minakami's work.

5. Kakehi Masanori, "Gosho Heinosuke no sekai: Gosho Heinosuke no entotsu no mieru basho o megutte" ("The World of Gosho Heinosuke: About His Work *Where Chimneys Are Seen*"), in *Nihon eiga o yomu: paionia tachi no isan* (*Reading Japanese Film: Heritage of the Pioneers*) (Tokyo: Dagereo shuppan, 1984), 135.

6. Max Tessier, *Images du cinéma japonais* (Paris: Henri Veyrier, 1981), 64.

7. Tomi Suzuki, *Narrating the Self: Fictions of Japanese Modernity* (Stanford, Calif.: Stanford University Press, 1996), 52.

8. Joseph L. Anderson and Donald Richie, as quoted in Audie Bock, *Japanese Film Directors* (New York: Kodansha International, 1978), 138.

9. Edwin O. Reischauer, *The Japanese Today: Change and Continuity* (Cambridge, Mass. and London: Belknap Press/Harvard University Press, 1977), 110.

10. Ibid.

11. Kyoko Hirano, *Mr. Smith Goes to Tokyo: Under the American Occupation, 1945–52* (Washington, D.C. and London: Smithsonian Institution Press, 1992), 261.

12. John W. Dower, *Embracing Defeat: Japan in the Wake of World War II* (New York: New Press/W. W. Norton, 1999), 545.

13. Hirano, *Mr. Smith Goes to Tokyo,* 205–40; Dower, *Embracing Defeat,* 255–73.

14. Dower, *Embracing Defeat,* 269.

15. Reischauer, *The Japanese Today,* 282.

16. Garbicz and Klinowski, *Cinema, The Magic Vehicle,* 2:231.

17. Janet A. Walker, *The Japanese Novel of the Meiji Period and the Idea of Individualism* (Princeton, N.J.: Princeton University Press, 1979), 71.

18. Joseph L. Anderson and Donald Richie, "The Films of Heinosuke Gosho," *Sight and Sound* 26, no. 2 (Autumn 1956): 80.

19. Richie, *The Japanese Movie,* 111.

20. Dower, *Embracing Defeat,* 154.

21. Alain Silver and Elizabeth Ward, eds., *Film Noir: An Encyclopedic Reference to the American Style,* rev. and expanded ed. (Woodstock, N.Y.: Overlook Press, 1988), 60.

22. Ibid.

23. Interestingly, the first time Gosho shows us the newspaper in which the bogus blanket is wrapped, we see only the names of the film's two stars: Fred MacMurray and Vera Hruba Ralston. The next time we see the newspaper we are given a good look at the film's title, *The City That Never Sleeps.* However, since MacMurray and Ralston are not the stars of this particular Republic opus but another one, the 1952 *Fair Wind to Java,* we can only assume that both films were playing in Osaka at the time, or that we have discovered a continuity error. Either way, Gosho's film suffers no harm. After all, *Fair Wind to Java* is also an example of Hollywood adventure and romance, its story having to do with "a sailor with a mutinous crew [who] seeks a South Sea treasure." See Leslie Halliwell, *Halliwell's Film Guide: To Over 10,000 Films,* 2d ed. (New York: Charles Scribner's Sons, 1980), 337.

24. Perhaps this scene also shows the influence of French Poetic Realism. Indeed, Max Tessier sees the tone of Gosho's film as akin to the Poetic Realism of Carné or Duvivier in its pessimistic view of life (*Images du cinéma japonais,* 64). Tessier's view is especially intriguing in light of Gosho's expressed admiration for French films of the 1930s, in particular those of Duvivier. See chapter 4 on *Once More.*

25. In their 1956 *Sight and Sound* article on Gosho, Anderson and Richie point out that Ohara Joji's photography in the film "has been called the best ever seen in a Japanese film" (81). Even today, its rich and atmospheric evocation of a by-gone Osaka remains impressive.

26. Perhaps Gosho's version of Renoir's famous quote is to be found in his 1962 *Kaachan, kekkon shiroyo* (*Mother, Get Married*), when a boy's teacher tells him, "Very few people are really bad."

27. Makoto Ueda, *Literary and Art Theories in Japan* (Cleveland: The Press of Case Western Reserve University, 1967), 222.

28. Ibid.

29. Ibid., 227.

30. Anderson and Richie, "The Films of Heinosuke Gosho," 80.

31. Ibid.

32. Ibid., 81.

33. Ibid., 80.

7. GROWING UP (1955)

1. Quoted in Mizutani Kenji, "Film d'autore e condizioni produttive: 'Takekurabe' di Gosho" ("Film Author and Production Conditions: Gosho's *Takekurabe*"), trans. into Italian by Aldo Tollini and Ueda Hatsumi, in *Schermi Giapponesi: La Fin-zione e il sentimento* (*Japanese Screens: Fiction and Feeling*) (Venice: Marsilio Editori, 1984), 63.

2. John W. Dower, *Embracing Defeat: Japan in the Wake of World War II* (New York: New Press/W. W. Norton, 1999), 564.

3. Ibid., 526, 542–45, 557–64.

4. S. N. Eisenstadt, *Japanese Civilization: A Comparative View* (Chicago and London: University of Chicago Press, 1966), 148.

5. Dower, *Embracing Defeat*, 525–28; and Eisenstadt, *Japanese Civilization*, 95–105.

6. Ian Buruma, *Behind the Mask* (New York: Pantheon Books, 1984), 96.

7. Ibid., 97.

8. Ibid.

9. J. Thomas Rimer, *A Reader's Guide to Japanese Literature: From the Eighth Century to the Present* (Tokyo and New York: Kodansha International, 1988), 110.

10. Mizutani, "Film d'autore e condizioni produttive," 59–60.

11. Ibid., 60.

12. Joseph Anderson and Donald Richie, "The Films of Heinosuke Gosho," *Sight and Sound* 26, no. 2 (Autumn 1956): 81.

13. Ibid.

14. Mizutani, "Film d'autore e condizioni produttive," 60.

15. See, e.g., "*Growing Up* (*Takekurabe*)," in *Heinosuke Gosho,* program of the Tenth Hong Kong International Film Festival, presented by the Urban Council, 1986, 38–39. Also see Dower, who, citing Japanese historian Takahashi Nobuo, has this to say about Misora Hibari: "From 1949 on, the prevailing mood in music and lyrics [in Japan] was one of wandering, loneliness, resignation, and a nostalgia that spilled over into inconsolable longing. The charismatic symbol of this bittersweet emotionalism was the precocious Misora Hibari, born in 1937, who rocketed to fame singing boogie-woogie, but became the exemplary voice of a 'native' sentimentalism before the occupation drew to a close" (*Embracing Defeat,* 527). Dower sums up her importance as follows: "Hibari (her stage name) was the preeminent female vocalist of postwar Japan until her death in 1989—her charisma, if not her style, comparable to that of Judy Garland or Edith Piaf" (*Embracing Defeat,* 643, n. 5).

16. Joseph L. Anderson and Donald Richie, *The Japanese Film: Art and Industry,* expanded ed. (Princeton, N.J.: Princeton University Press, 1983), 279.

17. Yasumi Toshio was a specialist in adapting *junbungaku* literature to the screen. Although he is best known for his collaboration with Toyoda Shiro, he and Gosho worked together on seven films, beginning with *An Inn at Osaka* (which they co-wrote), followed by *Growing Up, Banka* (*Elegy of the North,* 1957; written with Yuki Shigeko), *Hotarubi* (*The Fireflies,* 1958), *Waga ai* (*When A Woman Loves,* 1959), *Ryoju* (*Hunting Rifle,* 1961), and *Aijo no keifu* (*Love's Family Tree,* 1961).

18. Higuchi Ichiyo, "Growing Up," in *Modern Japanese Literature,* ed. Donald Keene (New York: Grove Press, 1960), 87. All subsequent references to Ichiyo's story are from this translation by Edward Seidensticker.

19. According to Nicholas Bornoff in *Pink Samurai: Love, Marriage and Sex in Contemporary Japan* (New York: Pocket Books, 1991), "Courtesans throughout the pleasure quarters always addressed their seniors as *oiran,* which originally meant 'rare flower.' In the late eighteenth century, the term came to be used as a general name for the cream of the crop" (190).

20. Ichiyo, "Growing Up," 90.

21. Janet A. Walker, "The Cinematic Art of Higuchi Ichiyo's *Takekurabe* (Comparing Heights, 1895–1896)," in *Word and Image in Japanese Cinema,* ed. Dennis Washburn and Carole Cavanaugh (Cambridge and New York: Cambridge University Press, 2001), 58, n. 38.

22. Ichiyo, "Growing Up," 71.

23. Ibid.

24. Shinnyo's mother is not the only woman in Gosho's films to be elevated in class through marriage. So too are Tose, the innkeeper in *The Fireflies,* and Akiko, the heroine in *Twice on a Certain Night* (1956). All three women are steadfastly loyal to husbands who are not always worthy of them. And while all three women are unhappy to varying degrees, that unhappiness is essentially rooted in class difference.

25. In this regard it is worth noting that the word "takekurabe" is often translated into English as "comparing heights" or "comparison of heights." As Rimer points out, in naming her story "takekurabe," Ichiyo is alluding to a Noh play by Zeami, in which children "compare" their growth by making marks on the side of a well (*A Reader's Guide to Japanese Literature,* 110). However, the phrase "comparison of heights" also has another meaning in Gosho's film. It underscores the geographical, as well as psychological, relationship between the brothel above and the rows of shops and houses below.

26. Ichiyo, "Growing Up," 89.

27. Buruma, *Behind the Mask,* 81.

28. Movie audiences of 1955 could not have missed the parallels between the plight of Gosho's Meiji-era prostitutes and that of prostitutes in the postwar period. Indeed, in this period, as Nicholas Bornoff explains, the plight of the prostitute remained largely unchanged, universal suffrage notwithstanding (*Pink Samurai,* 220). By the 1950s, opposition to legalized prostitution was mounting, and films like *Growing Up* and, most famously, Mizoguchi's *Akasen chitai* (*Street of Shame,* 1956), became part of the national discourse. In 1956, the Prostitution Prevention Law was passed—at the time when some 260,000 women worked in 50,000 licensed brothels across the country (*Pink Samurai,* 220).

29. Mizutani, "Film d'autore e condizioni produttive," 64.

30. For further discussion of the family and "home drama," see Tadao Sato, *Currents in Japanese Cinema,* trans. Gregory Barrett (Tokyo: Kodansha International, 1982), 124–44.

31. Donald Richie, *A Hundred Years of Japanese Film: A Concise History with a Selective Guide to Videos and DVDs* (Tokyo, New York, and London: Kodansha International, 2001), 123.

32. Rimer, *A Reader's Guide to Japanese Literature,* 110.

33. For an eloquent analysis of this scene in the novella, and how Ichiyo anticipates cinematic techniques, see Walker.

34. Richie, *A Hundred Years of Japanese Cinema,* 136.

35. Ibid., 50.

36. Ibid.

37. See Bornoff, *Pink Samurai,* 188.

38. According to Donald Richie, when the film was reissued in 1959, over half-an-hour was removed (*Japanese Cinema* [Garden City, N.Y.: Anchor Books/Doubleday, 1971], 122). In a letter to the author, 29 November 2001, Richie wrote: "though all references list the length at 95 minutes, that is the length of the re-release. . . . The original was longer and the splendid coda at the end (with the music turning into a passacaglia) was longer and much more impressive. I have no idea what became of the outtakes. It was cut to make room on a double bill." One further point should be noted: in its original version, *Growing Up* was composed of over 1,000 shots, even more than *An Inn at Osaka.* By comparison, American films at the time averaged between three hundred and seven hundred shots (Richie, *A Hundred Years of Japanese Film,* 49).

8. THE LATE 1950S

1. Kakehi Masanori, "Reminiscences of Gosho," in *Heinosuke Gosho,* program of the Tenth Hong Kong International Film Festival, presented by the Urban Council, 1986, 11.

2. In fact, Gosho followed *Growing Up* with seven more films in the 1950s. The first four of these were co-productions between Shochiku and Kabuki-za Eiga, one of the drama/acting troupes that emerged after the brief period of independent productions came to an end in the mid-50s. The last three were made by Shochiku. During this period, the market was dominated by the six major studios, and increasing commercialization was brought to bear on directors. Nevertheless, Gosho and other established directors still managed to experiment, bring genres up to date, and create worthwhile films. For a detailed discussion of this period, see Joseph L. Anderson and Donald Richie, *The Japanese Film: Art and Industry,* expanded ed. (Princeton, N.J.: Princeton University Press, 1982), 258–96.

3. Kyoko Hirano, "Heinosuke Gosho," *The International Dictionary of Films and Filmmakers,* vol. 2, *Directors/Filmmakers,* ed. Christopher Lyon (Chicago: St. James Press, 1984), 226.

4. Gosho Heinosuke, *Waga seishun* (*My Youth*) (Tokyo: Nagata shobo, 1978), 96.

5. Ibid., 97.

6. Some sources give the number of years of Ichiro's sojourn in China as ten, e.g., Ronald Bergan and Robyn Karney, *The Holt Foreign Film Guide* (New York: Henry Holt, 1988), 61. Other sources say fifteen, e.g., *Gosho Heinosuke kantoku tokushu* (*Special Issue on Director Gosho Heinosuke*), vol. 21 (Tokyo: Film Center of the Tokyo National Museum of Modern Art, 1974), 33, and the program notes on the Shochiku

video edition of the film (SHV Best Selection, n.d.). The film, however, specifically states that he has been away for eight years.

7. Donald Richie, *Japanese Cinema: Film Style and National Character* (New York: Anchor Books/Doubleday, 1971), 123.

8. Mark Le Fanu, "To Love Is to Suffer: Reflections on the Later Films of Heinosuke Gosho," *Sight and Sound* 55, no. 3 (Summer 1986): 202.

9. Joan Mellen, *The Waves at Genji's Door: Japan through Its Cinema* (New York: Pantheon Books, 1976), 65.

10. Ibid., 66.

11. Le Fanu, "To Love Is to Suffer," 200.

12. Mellen, *The Waves at Genji's Door*, 65, n. 12.

13. John Gillett, "Heinosuke Gosho: A Pattern for Living," National Film Theatre Programme Booklet, March 1986, 7. Concurring with this view, David Shipman says of *The Fireflies:* "It also proves that Gosho, usually considered a miniaturist, was the equal of any in the handling of action sequences" (*The Story of Cinema: A Complete Narrative History from the Beginnings to the Present* [New York: St. Martin's Press], 968).

14. Mellen, *The Waves at Genji's Door*, 66.

15. Ibid.

16. Jean-Pierre Lehmann, *The Roots of Modern Japan* (New York: St. Martin's Press, 1982), 152.

17. Anderson and Richie, *The Japanese Film*, 458.

18. Gillett, "Heinosuke Gosho: A Pattern for Living," 7.

19. William Johnson, "The Splitting Image: The Contrary Canon of Heinosuke Gosho," *Film Comment* 27, no. 1 (January–February 1991): 78.

20. "*Elegy of the North* (*Banka*)," in *Heinosuke Gosho,* program of the Tenth Hong Kong International Film Festival, presented by the Urban Council, 1986, 41.

21. Ibid.

22. In fact, the matter of where Gosho's sympathy lies in the film has elicited various critical responses. Mark Le Fanu, for example, maintains that the "really deep sympathy" of the film lies not with Reiko, the "troubled" young modernist, but with Akiko, who like other "traditional" women in Gosho's films, is "shown in [her] unhappiness as understanding what essentially belongs to [her]" ("To Love Is to Suffer," 200).

23. "*A Visage to Remember* (*Omokage*)," in *Heinosuke Gosho,* program of the Tenth Hong Kong International Film Festival, presented by the Urban Council, 1986, 29.

24. For a discussion of international art cinema, see David Bordwell, "Art-Cinema Narration," *Narration in the Fiction Film* (Madison: University of Wisconsin Press, 1985), 205–33.

25. Boye De Mente, *Passport's Japanese Almanac* (Lincolnwood, Ill.: Passport Books/National Textbook, 1987), 124.

26. *Baedeker's Japan* (Englewood Cliffs, N.J.: Spectrum/Prentice-Hall, [n.d.]), 177.

27. Johnson, "The Splitting Image," 78,

28. Takie Sugiyama Lebra, *Japanese Patterns of Behavior* (Honolulu: An East-West Center Book/University of Hawaii Press, 1976), 160.

29. Johnson, "The Splitting Image," 78.

30. According to Lebra, "To show inhibition and reserve in an intimate situation may even be disapproved as *mizukusai*" (*Japanese Patterns of Behavior,* 116). This being the case, Katsuragi's treatment of his wife is perhaps even crueler than an outright expression of anger.

31. Kyoko Hirano, "Mori, Masayuki," *The International Dictionary of Films and Filmmakers,* vol. 3, *Actors and Actresses,* ed. James Vinson (Chicago and London: St. James Press, 1986), 456–57; and Stuart Galbraith IV, *The Japanese Filmography: A Complete Reference to 209 Filmmakers and the Over 1,250 Films Released in the United States, 1900 through 1994* (Jefferson, N.C. and London: McFarland, 1996), 46.

32. Anderson and Richie, *The Japanese Film,* 193–94, 294.

33. Keiko I. McDonald, *From Book to Screen: Modern Japanese Literature in Film* (Armonk, N.Y. and London: An East Gate Book/M. E. Sharpe, 2000), 40.

34. The play in question is Chekhov's *The Sea Gull*—which in Japanese is titled *Kamome.* At first glance, this play would seem to have little relevance to the themes or concerns of the film, apart from introducing theatre as metaphor. Yet there is at least one other parallel between these two works that is worth considering. It has to do with the nature of Reiko and her colleagues' level of self-awareness. In this respect the rehearsal we witness is instructive. Singularly lackluster, it finds the actors reading their lines without feeling. And while Gosho clearly has affection for the theatre company and makes them a warm and amiable group, he also shows that they are out of their depth and too young and inexperienced to understand, much less project, the longing and sweet sadness of Chekhov's characters. Consequently, it comes as no surprise that the play flops or that the headline of the newspaper review reads, "Amateur play, *The Sea Gull* lacks a delicate touch." No less surprising perhaps is Reiko's reaction. She shrugs off the review, not even bothering to read past the headline. Does she recognize that in some ways—in her passion for life, her determination to give everything for love—she is like Chekhov's Nina, the symbolic sea gull of the title? Does she see something of Katsuragi in Trigorin, the middle-aged novelist Nina gives herself to? Probably not, but by the end of the film, like Nina, she will have learned a great deal about herself and life. Whether her colleagues have done the same Gosho and his writers never tell us.

35. Le Fanu, 201.

36. Coppélia Kahn, "The Absent Mother in *King Lear,*" in Donald E. Hall, *Literary and Cultural Theory: From Basic Principles to Advanced Applications* (Boston and New York: Houghton Mifflin, 2001), 119.

37. Le Fanu, "To Love Is to Suffer," 200.

38. François Truffaut, *Hitchcock* (New York: Simon and Schuster, 1966), 153.

39. Interestingly, Reiko and Akiko's relationship has some similarities with another love-hate relationship between a spoiled young woman and a staid older woman, which leads to the latter's suicide. This relationship is key to Françoise Sagan's novella, *Bonjour Tristesse,* which won the Prix des Critiques in 1954. Whether author Harada Yasuko was familiar with Sagan's novella or inspired by it is not known. Preminger's film starring Jean Seberg and Deborah Kerr was not released until 1958, by which time Gosho's film had already finished its run. But it is interesting to contemplate the possibility (even if highly unlikely) that Preminger somehow managed to see Gosho's film.

40. Johnson, "The Splitting Image," 78.

41. Ibid.

42. Lebra, *Japanese Patterns of Behavior,* 161.

43. Ibid., 162.

44. Johnson points out another connection between Gosho and Antonioni: "Occasionally a subplot usurps a main plot, as in the 1933 *L'Amour,* which anticipates Antonioni's *L'Avventura* by a quarter-century" ("The Splitting Image," 75).

45. Gilberto Perez, *The Material Ghost: Films and Their Medium* (Baltimore and London: Johns Hopkins University Press, 1998), 369.

9. GOSHO IN THE 1960S

1. See, e.g., Joseph L. Anderson and Donald Richie, *The Japanese Film: Art and Industry,* expanded ed. (Princeton, N.J.: Princeton University Press, 1985), 439–77; David Desser, *Eros plus Massacre: An Introduction to the Japanese New Wave Cinema* (Bloomington and Indianapolis: Indiana University Press, 1988), 1–38; Tony Rayns, "Run at Your Own Pace," *Eiga: 25 Years of Japanese Cinema* (Edinburgh: Edinburgh International Film Festival, 1984), 8–9; Noël Burch, "Nagisa Oshima and Japanese Cinema in the 60s," *Cinema: A Critical Dictionary: The Major Filmmakers,* ed. Richard Roud, vol. 2, *Kinugasa to Zanussi* (Norwich, UK: Martin Secker and Warburg, 1980), 735–43; Keiko McDonald, "Japan," *The Asian Film Industry,* ed. John A. Lent (Austin: University of Texas Press, 1990), 34–60; Tadao Sato, *Currents in Japanese Cinema* (Tokyo: Kodansha International, 1982), 208–47; and "Enter the New Generation," from "Shinkyu kotai: gekido no jidai" ("Shifting from the Old to the New: A Turbulent Period"), in *Nihon eiga 80-nen shoshi* (*A Journal of 80 Years of Japanese Film*), trans. into English by Suga Shinko and Tony Rayns for *Eiga: 25 Years of Japanese Cinema,* 10–11.

2. McDonald, "Japan," *The Asian Film Industry,* 37.

3. Richie, "Terminal Essay," *The Japanese Film: Art and Industry,* 457; and Tadao Sato, "Enter the New Generation,"10.

4. Sato, "Enter the New Generation," 10.

5. Ibid.

6. Max Tessier, "Oshima Nagisa, or The Battered Energy of Desire," *Reframing Japanese Cinema: Authorship, Genre, History,* ed. Arthur Nolletti, Jr. and David Desser (Bloomington and Indianapolis: Indiana University Press, 1992), 70–78.

7. Richie, "Terminal Essay," *The Japanese Film: Art and Industry,* 460.

8. Ibid., 457.

9. Mark Le Fanu, "To Love Is to Suffer: Reflections on the Later Films of Heinosuke Gosho," *Sight and Sound* 55, no. 3 (Summer 1986): 198.

10. Unfortunately, Gosho also took on projects that did not suit him. Even so, as his critics acknowledged, he always made each film with great enthusiasm. See *"Aijo no keifu* (*Love's Family Tree*)," in *Gosho Heinosuke kantoku tokushu* (*Special Issue on Director Gosho Heinosuke*), vol. 21 (Tokyo: Film Center of the Tokyo National Museum of Modern Art, 1974), 43.

11. *"Hyakuman-nin no musumetachi* (*A Million Girls*)," in *Gosho Heinosuke kantoku tokushu* (*Special Issue on Director Gosho Heinosuke*), vol. 21 (Tokyo: Film Center of the Tokyo National Museum of Modern Art, 1974), 45.

12. *"Kaachan kekkon shiroyo* (*Mother, Get Married*)," in *Gosho Heinosuke kantoku tokushu* (*Special Issue on Director Gosho Heinosuke*), vol. 21 (Tokyo: Film Center of the Tokyo National Museum of Modern Art, 1974), 44.

13. David Shipman, *The Story of Cinema: A Complete Narrative History from the Beginnings to the Present* (New York: St. Martin's Press, 1982), 968.

14. McDonald, "Japan," *The Asian Film Industry,* 37.

15. A still-relevant introduction to widescreen aesthetics can be found in Karel Reisz and Gavin Millar, *The Technique of Film Editing,* enlarged ed. (New York: Hastings House/Communication Arts Books, 1968), 279–96. For a comprehensive study of the historical, technical, economic, and aesthetic aspects of widescreen, see John Belton, *Widescreen Cinema* (Cambridge, Mass. and London: Harvard University Press,

1992). For an insightful analysis into widescreen usage in Japanese film, see Cynthia Contreras, "Kobayashi's Widescreen Aesthetic," *Cinematic Landscapes: Observations on the Visual Arts and Cinema of China and Japan,* ed. Linda C. Ehrlich and David Desser (Austin: University of Texas Press, 1994), 241–61.

16. See, e.g., Peter Grilli, "Theatrical Films," in *Japan in Film: A Comprehensive Annotated Catalogue of Documentary and Theatrical Films on Japan Available in the United States,* ed. Peter Grilli (New York: Japan Society, 1984), 105. Also consult Ronald Bergan and Robyn Karney, *The Holt Foreign Film Guide* (New York: Henry Holt and Company, 1988), who give the film this decidedly left-handed compliment: "This is a full-blooded weepie romance, backed by a lush Western-style score that would do justice to Hollywood. However, within its genre, it's a superior piece of film-making in every department" (611).

17. "*Shiroi kiba* (*White Fangs*)," in *Gosho Heinosuke kantoku tokushu* (*Special Issue on Director Gosho Heinosuke*), vol. 21 (Tokyo: Film Center of the Tokyo National Museum of Modern Art, 1974), 40.

18. Quoted in "*Ryoju* (*Hunting Rifle*)," in *Gosho Heinosuke kantoku tokushu* (*Special Issue on Director Gosho Heinosuke*), vol. 21 (Tokyo: Film Center of the Tokyo National Museum of Modern Art, 1974), 41.

19. William Johnson, "The Splitting Image: The Contrary Canon of Heinosuke Gosho," *Film Comment* 27, no. 1 (January–February 1991): 77.

20. For example, John Gillett calls the film "a rich emotional drama" ("Heinosuke Gosho: A Pattern of Living," National Film Theatre Programme Booklet, March 1986, 6). For a less favorable view, see "*Ryoju* (*Hunting Rifle*)," in *Gosho Heinosuke kantoku tokushu* (*Special Issue on Director Gosho Heinosuke*), vol. 21 (Tokyo: Film Center of the Tokyo National Museum of Modern Art, 1974), 41.

21. Leon Picon, trans., *Yasushi Inoue, The Counterfeiter and Other Stories* (Rutland, Vt. and Tokyo: Charles E. Tuttle, 1965), 7.

22. Mark Le Fanu, "To Love Is to Suffer," 199.

23. Sadamichi Yokoo and Sanford Goldstein, "Introduction," *Yasushi Inoue, The Hunting Gun,* trans. Yokoo and Goldstein (Rutland, Vt. and Tokyo: Charles E. Tuttle, 1988), 5.

24. Johnson, "The Splitting Image," 77.

25. Tadao Sato, "From the Art of Yasujiro Ozu," trans. Goro Iri, in *Wide Angle* 1, no. 4 (1977): 47.

26. Ibid.

27. *Baedeker's Japan* (Englewood Cliffs, N.J.: Spectrum/Prentice-Hall, [n.d.]), 92.

28. "*Osorezan no onna* (*An Innocent Witch*)," in *Gosho Heinosuke kantoku tokushu* (*Special Issue on Director Gosho Heinosuke*), vol. 21 (Tokyo: Film Center of the Tokyo National Museum of Modern Art, 1974), 46.

29. Donald Richie, *Japanese Cinema: Film Style and National Character* (New York: Anchor Books/Doubleday, 1974), 123.

30. Horie Hideo, "*Osorezan no onna* ni tsuite" ("On *An Innocent Witch*"), Introduction to screening of film in Matsuyama-shi, Shikoku, August, 1999. As Horie explained in a letter to the author dated May 20, 1993, helping Gosho scout locations was a way of making sure that the two collaborators shared the same ideas about the film. Hunting for locations, however, was only one of Horie's responsibilities on a Gosho film. In fact, he participated in the moviemaking process from the planning stage, working closely with the producers, cameramen, and art directors. His main responsibility, however, was writing the screenplay. Here Gosho gave him complete free-

dom; he "never poked his nose" into the writing process or made any special requests. During the actual shooting, Gosho requested Horie to be on the set in case any problems or circumstances arose that necessitated reviewing or reworking parts of the screenplay. Horie also was invited to sit in on the rushes during the editing stage. Finally, in the case of the making of *An Innocent Witch,* Horie points out that the set design preceded the writing of the script, a reversal of the usual production process. This change, however, was critical for the film, which required that Horie know the specific settings, so as consider the characters' psychological makeup and behavior, and the effect that the different settings (and changing scenes) had on these characters.

31. According to Donald Richie, "Notes for a Study of Shohei Imamura," in *Shohei Imamura,* ed. James Quandt (Toronto: Cinematheque Ontario Monographs, 1997), the director sees his shots as falling into two categories: *hikisoto* (from the outside) and *hikuichi* (from the inside). Unlike the former category, the latter is "a conventional shot, the camera inside the room or area with the actors" (40). Our discussion of Gosho makes use of the *hikisoto* shot only.

32. Mark Le Fanu, "To Love Is to Suffer," 201.

33. W. G. Beasley, *The Rise of Modern Japan* (New York: St. Martin's Press, 1990), 187.

34. Ibid., 196.

35. Edwin O. Reischauer, in *The Japanese Today: Change and Continuity* (Cambridge, Mass. and London: Belknap Press/Harvard University Press, 1988), comments: "The ultrarightists tended to champion the impoverished peasantry, who provided the bulk of the soldiers, and to excoriate the privileged classes of rich businessmen and powerful politicians" (99). Also see Paul F. Langer, in *Japan: Yesterday and Today,* Contemporary Civilizations Series (New York: Holt, Rinehart and Winston, 1966), 96–100.

36. Ian Buruma, *Inventing Japan: 1853–1964* (New York: Modern Library, 2003), 99.

37. While she does not discuss *Rebellion of Japan* as such, Joan Mellen examines this point in detail in *The Waves at Genji's Door: Japan through Its Cinema* (New York: Pantheon, 1976), 167–200.

38. Although Gosho combines Noh and film with elegance and virtuosity in *Rebellion of Japan,* combining these two modes was hardly unique to him. See Keiko I. McDonald, *Japanese Classical Theater in Films* (London and Toronto: Associated University Presses, 1994), 125–44. It should also be mentioned that Mishima had appropriated Noh to depict a love story and the theme of the February 26, 1936 coup d' état in *Yukoku* (*The Rite of Love and Death,* 1964), the adaptation of his short story, "Patriotism." For further information, see "*Utage* (*Rebellion of Japan*)," in *Gosho Heinosuke kantoku tokushu* (*Special Issue on Director Gosho Heinosuke*), vol. 21 (Tokyo: Film Center of the Tokyo National Museum of Modern Art, 1974) , 48; and Dean McWilliams, "The Ritual Cinema of Yukio Mishima," *Wide Angle* 1, no. 4 (1977): 28–33.

39. Charles Dickens, *Great Expectations,* with an introduction by Stanley Weintraub (New York: Signet Classic/Penguin Putnam, 1998), 160.

APPENDIX

1. Joseph Anderson and Donald Richie, "The Films of Heinosuke Gosho," *Sight and Sound* 26, no. 2 (Autumn 1956): 78.

2. John Gillett, "Heinosuke Gosho," *Film Dope* (April 1980), 31.

3. David Owens, "Before *Rashomon*: Japanese Film Treasures of the 30's and 40's," program, Museum of Fine Arts, Boston/The Japan Society of New York, 1985, n.p.

4. William Johnson, "The Splitting Image: The Contrary Canon of Heinosuke Gosho," *Film Comment* 27, no. 1 (January–February 1991): 74.

5. Ibid.

6. Ibid., 76.

7. Ibid., 74–78.

8. Kakehi Masanori, "Reminiscences of Gosho, " in *Heinosuke Gosho*, program of the Tenth Hong Kong International Film Festival, presented by the Urban Council, 1986, 7.

9. Ibid.

10. Quoted in Kakehi, 7.

11. "*A Visage to Remember (Omokage)*," in *Heinosuke Gosho*, program of the Tenth Hong Kong International Film Festival, presented by the Urban Council, 1986, 29.

12. Ibid.

13. Ibid.

14. "*Wakare-gumo (Dispersing Clouds)*," in *Gosho Heinosuke kantoku tokushu (Special Issue on Director Gosho Heinosuke)* (Tokyo: Film Center of the Tokyo National Museum of Modern Art, 1974), 25.

15. Ibid.

16. Mark Le Fanu, "To Love Is to Suffer: Reflections on the Later Films of Heinosuke Gosho," *Sight and Sound* 55, no. 3 (Summer 1986): 201.

17. Ibid.

18. In his autobiography, *Waga seishun (My Youth)*, Gosho makes special mention of Kawasaki Hiroko's fine acting in this scene and how she was a down-to-earth actress with a special talent for playing common people. He notes that they made twelve films together, the best of which were *Tengoku ni musubu koi (Love Requited in Heaven,* 1932), *Dispersing Clouds,* and *An Inn at Osaka* (226).

19. Le Fanu, "To Love Is to Suffer," 201.

FILMOGRAPHY:
GOSHO HEINOSUKE

1902: Born Gosho Heiuemon on February 1 in Tokyo. Later changed named to the more modern-sounding "Heinosuke." **1921:** Graduated from Keio University (School of Commerce). **1923:** Joined Shochiku (Kamata) Studio; apprenticed under Shimazu Yasujiro, the founder of the *shomin-geki* (drama of the everyday lives of common people). **1925:** Made directorial debut with *Nanto no haru* (*Spring in Southern Islands*). **1927:** First attracted attention with *Sabishiki ranbomono* (*The Lonely Roughneck*). **1928:** Enjoyed major critical and commercial success with *Mura no hanayome* (*The Village Bride*). **1928–31:** Career suffered a slump, which ended with *Madamu to nyobo* (*The Neighbor's Wife and Mine*), Japan's first successful "talkie." **1933–37:** Continued work in the *shomin-geki* with *Jinsei no onimotsu* (*Burden of Life*), *Oboroyo no onna* (*Woman of the Mist*), etc.; helped to found the *junbungaku* ("pure literature") movement with *Izu no odoriko* (*Dancing Girl of Izu*), *Ikitoshi ikerumono* (*Everything That Lives*), etc. **1937:** Contracted tuberculosis and did not film again until *Bokuseki* (*Wooden Head*) in 1940. **1941:** Left Shochiku (Ofuna) Studio for Daiei Studio. **1945:** Returned to Shochiku (Ofuna). **1946:** Joined Toho Studio to direct *Ima hitotabino* (*Once More*). **1948:** Left Toho after labor dispute, in which he took an active role. **1951:** Established Studio Eight Productions, one of the first independent companies; made two of his most celebrated films, *Entotsu no mieru basho* (*Where Chimneys Are Seen,* 1953) and *Osaka no yado* (*An Inn at Osaka,* 1954). **1954:** Dissolution of Studio Eight; worked for various studios, including Shin Toho, Nikkatsu, Kabuki-za, Shochiku (Kyoto). **1964:** Succeeded Ozu as president of the Japanese Association of Film Directors; held this position until 1975; dealt with difficult issues such as directors' copyrights. Also director of the Japanese Haiku Art Association. **1968:** "Retired" after completion of puppet film, *Meiji haru aki* (*Seasons of the Meiji*); wrote for television. **1977:** Filmed documentary, *Waga machi Mishima* (*My Town Mishima*). **1978:** Publication of *Waga seishun* (*My Youth*), an autobiography that also included essays and haiku. **1981:** Died May 1, at the age of seventy-nine.

Honors: Eleven films ranked among *Kinema Jumpo* Best Films of the Year. **1941:** Received Shiji Ho sho Order of the Japanese Government. **1947:** Mainichi Film Prize, Japan, for *Once More;* Kun Yon-to Asahi Shoju sho Order of the Japanese Government. **1953:** International Peace Prize, Berlin Film Festival, for *Where*

Chimneys Are Seen. **1958:** Catholic (ICFC) Prize at the San Sebastian Film Festival for *Ari no machi no Maria* (*Maria of the Ant Village*); Golden Globe Award of the Hollywood Foreign Press Association for *Kiiroi karasu* (*Yellow Crow*). **1960:** Golden Harvest Awards for color cinematography and sound recording at the Fourth Film Festival in Asia for *Waga ai* (*When a Woman Loves*). **1968:** *Seasons of the Meiji* ranked #7 of the Ten Best Kinejun Cultural Films.

NOTES ON THIS FILMOGRAPHY

This filmography has been compiled from the following sources: John Gillett's entry on Gosho in *Film Dope* (April 1980): 30–31; the Gosho filmography in *Nihon eiga o yomu: paionia tachi no isan* (*Reading Japanese Film: Heritage of the Pioneers*), 115–16; the Gosho listings in *Firumu senta shozo eiga mokuroku: Nihongeki eiga—Tokyo kokuritsu kindai bijutsukan* (*Film Center Archive Catalog: Japanese Films—The Tokyo National Museum of Modern Art* [1986]); Horie Hideo's *Gosho Heinosuke to watakushi* (*Gosho Heinosuke and I*), 103–34; Kyoko Hirano's entry on Gosho in *The International Dictionary of Films and Filmmakers, Vol. 2: Directors/Filmmakers,* 225; and the production credits of individual films. However, the principal source was *Gosho Heinosuke kantoku tokushu* (*Special Issue on Director Gosho Heinosuke*), Vol. 21 of the National Film Center in Tokyo (1974).

Some Gosho filmographies list the following films: *Tokyo koshinkyoko* (*Tokyo March,* 1927), *Daishinrin* (*The Big Forest,* 1930), *Tokyo no gassho* (*Tokyo Chorus,* 1931), and *Inochi uruwashi* (*Life Is Beautiful,* 1951). *Tokyo March* is almost certainly Mizoguchi's 1929 film of the same name; *Daishinrin,* although a planned Gosho project at Shochiku (Kamata), was never made; *Tokyo Chorus* is a celebrated Ozu work; and *Life Is Beautiful* was directed by Oba Hideo.

Following the Japanese title for each film is its most common English title. If a film is known by more than one English title, these titles are separated by a slash.

Running times are included for extant films. This information is unavailable for films that no longer survive.

All of the films listed before 1931 are silent; all subsequent films are sound films, unless otherwise indicated.

Japanese *kanji* characters and syllabic writing can often be transliterated in different ways. As a result, proper names can take various forms. For example, the family names of the leading players of *Shinjoseikan* (*A New Kind of Woman,* 1929) have been rendered in English as Tatsuta (or Takita) Shizue and Yamanouchi (or Yamauchi) Hikaru. In such instances I have followed the most common English rendering. However, an even greater difficulty is to be found in the case of one of Gosho's cinematographers for *Nanto no haru* (*Spring in Southern Islands,* 1925).

His family name is Kuwajima, but his first name could be either Subaru or Noboru. I have used Subaru, but followed it with a question mark to indicate that this name cannot be confirmed.

I have indicated the Gosho titles that are on videocassettes (VHS) or DVD (region 2 only). However, by the time this book is published, some of these titles may be out of print or no longer available for purchase. It is also possible that new titles may be on the market. None of the films listed below has English subtitles.

FEATURE FILMS

1925

Nanto no haru (Spring in Southern Islands)
Production Company: Shochiku (Kamata)
Original Screenplay: Gosho Heinosuke
Photography: Kuwajima Subaru (?) and Miura Mitsuo
Cast: Oshimoto Eiji, Kobayashi Tokuji, Matsui Chieko, Mimura Chiyoko
Released April 2. (No extant prints)
This film has an island setting and is a love story between a student from Tokyo and local girl, marking the first time that cinematographer Miura Mitsuo and Gosho worked together.

Sora wa haretari (The Sky Is Clear/No Clouds in the Sky)
Production Company: Shochiku (Kamata)
Screenplay: Noda Kogo
Photography: Miura Mitsuo
Cast: Oshimoto Eiji, Furukawa Toshitaka, Hayashi Chitose
Released May 31. (No extant prints.)
The first film to show the hallmarks of Gosho's analytical editing style.

Otoko-gokoro (Man's Heart)
Production Company: Shochiku (Kamata)
Screenplay: Gosho Heinosuke
Photography: Tanabe Kenji
Cast: Shimada Yoshichi, Okada Sotaro, Tsukuba Yukiko
Released August 21. (No extant prints.)

Seishun (Youth)
Production Company: Shochiku (Kamata)
Original Story Idea: Kido Shiro
Screenplay: Gosho Heinosuke
Photography: Miura Mitsuo
Cast: Arai Jun, Hayashi Chitose, Matsui Chieko
Released November 6. (No extant prints.)

Tosei tamatebako (The Magnificent Pearl Box/A Casket for Living)
Production Company: Shochiku (Kamata)
Original Story and Screenplay: Kitamura Komatsu
Photography: Tanabe Kenji
Cast: Kobayashi Tokuji, Kofujita Shoichi, Futaba Kumiko
Released December 17. (No extant prints.)
Gosho's spirit of tomfoolery and experimentation with photography got him in trouble with the Shochiku front office, and he was put on probation for one year.

1926

Machi no hitobito (Town People)
Production Company: Shochiku (Kamata)
Original Story and Screenplay: Kitamura Komatsu
Photography: Uchida Hitoshi
Cast: Tanabe Wakao, Matsui Chieko, Tanaka Kinuyo, Iida Choko, Akita Shinichi
Released February 20. (No extant prints.)
This was Tanaka Kinuyo's first appearance in a Gosho film.

Hatsukoi (First Love)
Production Company: Shochiku (Kamata)
Screenplay: Gosho Heinosuke
Photography: Uchida Hitoshi
Cast: Mita Eiji, Yakumo Emiko, Kumoi Tsuruko, Takeda Haruo
Released March 26. (No extant prints.)

Honryu (A Rapid Stream)
Production Company: Shochiku (Kamata)
Original Story: Miyake Yasuko
Screenplay: Yoshida Takezo
Photography: Uchida Hitoshi
Cast: Azuma Eiko, Akita Shinichi, Oshimoto Eiji, Tanaka Kinuyo, Iida Choko
Released April 15. (No extant prints.)

Haha-yo koishi (Mother's Love/Mother, I Miss You)
Production Company: Shochiku (Kamata)
Original Story and Screenplay: Mizushima Ayame
Photography: Uchida Hitoshi
Cast: Arai Jun, Yakumo Emiko, Akita Shinichi
Released May 23. (No extant prints.)

Musume (A Daughter)
Production Company: Shochiku (Kamata)
Screenplay: Gosho Heinosuke
Photography: Uchida Hitoshi

Cast: Hayashi Chitose, Yakumo Emiko, Nara Shinyo, Saito Tatsuo
Released July 1. (No extant prints.)

Kaeranu sasabue (No Return/Bamboo Leaf Flute of No Return)
Production Company: Shochiku (Kamata)
Screenplay: Tsukuda Chiaki
Photography: Miura Mitsuo
Cast: Yakumo Emiko, Akita Shinichi, Ogawa Kunimatsu
Released August 5. (No extant prints.)

Itoshi no wagako (My Loving Child/My Beloved Child)
Production Company: Shochiku (Kamata)
Original Story: Mizushima Ayame
Screenplay: Gosho Heinosuke
Photography: Miura Mitsuo
Cast: Harumi Kiyoko, Takeda Haruo, Takao Mitsuko
Released September 21. (No extant prints.)

Kanojo (Girl Friend/She)
Production Company: Shochiku (Kamata)
Original Story and Screenplay: Gosho Heinosuke
Photography: Miura Mitsuo
Cast: Yakumo Emiko, Ogawa Kunimatsu, Tanaka Kinuyo, Iida Choko
Released December 31. (No extant prints.)

1927

Sabishiki ranbomono (The Lonely Roughneck/Lonely Hoodlum)
Production Company: Shochiku (Kamata)
Original Story and Screenplay: Muraoka Yoshio
Photography: Miura Mitsuo
Cast: Arai Jun, Kofujita Shoichi, Kume Junko, Kobayashi Tokuji, Iida Choko
Released February 25. (No extant prints.)
The film that established Gosho as an important talent.

Hazukashii yume (Embarrassing Dreams/Intimate Dream/Shameful Dream)
Production Company: Shochiku (Kamata)
Original Story: Momozono Kyota
Screenplay: Fushimi Akira
Photography: Miura Mitsuo
Cast: Tanaka Kinuyo, Yakumo Emiko, Kunijima Soichi
Released April 8. (No extant prints.)

Karakuri musume (Tricky Girl)
Production Company: Shochiku (Kamata)
Original Story: Gosho Heinosuke

Screenplay: Fushimi Akira
Photography: Miura Mitsuo
Cast: Watanabe Atsushi, Hoshi Hikaru, Yakumo Emiko, Futaba Kaoru
Released June 15. (No extant prints.)
Ranked #6 in *Kinema Jumpo* Best Ten list. The film's mixture of comedy and drama irked Sergei Eisenstein (see Joseph L. Anderson and Donald Richie, *The Japanese Film: Art and Industry,* expanded ed. [Princeton, N.J.: Princeton University Press, 1982], 67).

Shojo no shi (Death of a Virgin/Death of a Maiden)
Production Company: Shochiku (Kamata)
Original Story: Gosho Heinosuke
Screenplay: Noda Kogo
Photography: Miura Mitsuo
Cast: Nara Shinyo, Sasaki Kiyono, Matsui Junko
Released July 22. (No extant prints.)

Okame (Moon-faced/A Plain Woman)
Production Company: Shochiku (Kamata)
Screenplay: Gosho Heinosuke
Photography: Miura Mitsuo
Cast: Iida Choko, Azuma Eiko, Hoshi Hikaru
Released October 26. (No extant prints.)

1928

Suki nareba koso (Because I Love/If You Like It)
Production Company: Shochiku (Kamata)
Original Story: Gosho Heinosuke
Screenplay: Noda Kogo
Photography: Miura Mitsuo
Cast: Ogawa Kunimatsu, Kume Junko, Ishiyama Ryuji, Yoshikawa Mitsuko
Released January 10. (No extant prints.)

Mura no hanayome (The Village Bride)
Production Company: Shochiku (Kamata)
Original Story: Momozono Kyota
Screenplay: Fushimi Akira
Photography: Miura Mitsuo
Cast: Yakumo Emiko, Tanaka Kinuyo, Ishiyama Ryuji
Released January 27 (No extant prints.)
Ranked #6 in *Kinema Jumpo* Best Ten list. Considered Gosho's finest work in this period, this film was in part inspired by the illness of his younger brother. The screenplay is published in *Kinema Jumpo, Nihon eiga daihyo shinario zenshu* 5

(*A Collection of Representative Japanese Screenplays, No. 5,* September 1958), and in *Kinema Jumpo, Nihon eiga shinario koten zenshu, Dai ikkan* (A *Collection of Classical Japanese Screenplays, Vol. 1,* December 1965).

Doraku goshinan (Debauchery Is Wrong/Guidance to the Indulgent)
Production Company: Shochiku (Kamata)
Original Story: Gosho Heinosuke
Screenplay: Fushimi Akira
Photography: Miura Mitsuo
Cast: Yoshikawa Eiran, Watanabe Atsushi, Kume Junko
Released April 24. (No extant prints.)

Kami e no michi (The Way to God/Road to God)
Production Company: Shochiku (Kamata)
Original Story and Screenplay: Mizushima Ayame
Photography: Nomura Ko
Cast: Takao Mitsuko, Mizushiro Kuniko, Yuki Ichiro, Kawahara Kanji
Released June 8. (No extant prints.)

Hito no yo no sugata (A Daughter of Two Fathers/Man's Worldly Appearance/ The Situation of the Human World)
Production Company: Shochiku (Kamata)
Story: Tamura Heizaburo
Screenplay: Noda Kogo and Fushimi Akira
Photography: Nomura Ko
Cast: Inoue Masao, Fujino Hideo, Tanaka Kinuyo, Watanabe Atsushi
Released June 26. (No extant prints.)
A young girl found as a waif by one man is claimed by her real father. Probably the first Gosho film to be shown theatrically in the United States, it was reviewed by Mordaunt Hall in the *New York Times* on March 12, 1929, 26. Hall's main interest was in the performance of Higuchi Kinoshoki, the *benshi,* and the film as an illustration of Japanese customs.

Gaito no kishi (Knight of the Street)
Production Company: Shochiku (Kamata)
Original Story: Iketsu Yutaro
Screenplay: Takeda Akira
Photography: Nomura Ko
Cast: Yamanouchi Hikaru, Fujino Hideo, Yakumo Emiko
Released October 18. (No extant prints.)

1929

Yoru no mesuneko (Cat of the Night)
Production Company: Shochiku (Kamata)

Screenplay: Yumaki Sanpei
Photography: Nagai Shinichi
Cast: Yokoo Tomio, Yakumo Emiko, Okada Sotaro
Released February 9. (No extant prints.)

Shinjoseikan (A New Kind of Woman)
Production Company: Shochiku (Kamata)
Original Story: Kikuchi Kan
Screenplay: Noda Kogo
Photography: Miura Mitsuo
Cast: Tatsuta Shizue, Watanabe Atsushi, Tanaka Kinuyo, Yuki Ichiro, Yamanouchi
  Hikaru
Released June 14. (No extant prints.)

Oyaji to sono ko (Father and His Child/Father and His Son)
Production Company: Shochiku (Kamata)
Screenplay: Yumaki Sanpei
Photography: Miura Mitsuo
Cast: Takeda Haruo, Saito Tatsuo, Hyodo Shizue, Okamura Fumiko
Released September 13. (No extant prints.)

Ukiyo-buro (The Bath Harem/Bath of the Transitory World)
Production Company: Shochiku (Kamata)
Screenplay: Gosho Heinosuke
Photography: Miura Mitsuo
Cast: Watanabe Atsushi, Iida Choko, Hyodo Shizue, Yoshikawa Mitsuko
Released September 26. (No extant prints.)

Jonetsu no ichiya (One Night of Passion/A Night of Passion)
Production Company: Shochiku (Kamata)
Original Story: Gosho Heinosuke
Screenplay: Noda Kogo
Photography: Miura Mitsuo
Cast: Inoue Masao, Yakumo Emiko, Okada Sotaro, Iida Choko
Released December 16. (No extant prints.)

1930

Dokushin-sha goyojin (Bachelors Beware)
Production Company: Shochiku (Kamata)
Original Story: Gosho Heinosuke
Screenplay: Fushimi Akira
Photography: Miura Mitsuo
Cast: Seki Tokio, Arai Jun, Kawasaki Hiroko
Released February 1. (No extant prints.)

Dai-Tokyo no ikkaku (A Corner of Great Tokyo)
Production Company: Shochiku (Kamata)
Screenplay: Fushimi Akira
Additional dialogue (intertitles): Gosho Heinosuke
Photography: Miura Mitsuo
Cast: Saito Tatsuo, Takamine Hideko, Arai Jun, Tatsuta Shizue
Released March 28. (No extant prints.)

Hohoemu jinsei (A Smiling Life)
Production Company: Shochiku (Kamata)
Screenplay: Oda Takashi
Photography: Miura Mitsuo
Cast: Kinuyo Tanaka, Watanabe Atsushi, Yamanouchi Hikaru, Okamura Fumiko
Released May 24. (No extant prints.)

Onna-yo! Kimi no na o kegasu nakare (Woman, Don't Make Your Name Dirty/ Women, Don't Shame Your Names)
Production Company: Shochiku (Kamata)
Screenplay: Kitamura Komatsu
Photography: Miura Mitsuo
Cast: Yoshikawa Mitsuko, Matsui Junko, Oikawa Michiko, Arai Jun
Released August 15. (No extant prints.)

Shojo nyuyo (Virgin Wanted)
Production Company: Shochiku (Kamata)
Original Story: Kobune Katsuji
Screenplay: Kitamura Komatsu
Photography: Miura Mitsuo
Cast: Ogura Shigeru, Yoshitani Hisao, Hara Junko, Kawasaki Hiroko, Yoshikawa Mitsuko
Released August 22. (No extant prints.)

Kinuyo monogatari (Story of Kinuyo)
Production Company: Shochiku (Kamata)
Original Story: Tatsumi Yonesaburo
Screenplay: Noda Kogo
Photography: Miura Mitsuo
Cast: Tanaka Kinuyo, Hanaoka Kikuko, Fujino Hideo, Yoshikawa Mitsuko
Released October 10. (No extant prints.)

Aiyoku no ki (Record of Love and Desire/Desire of Night)
Production Company: Shochiku (Kamata)
Screenplay: Fushimi Akira
Photography: Miura Mitsuo
Cast: Yamanouchi Hikaru, Yuki Ichiro, Tanaka Kinuyo
Released November 10. (No extant prints.)

1931

Jokyu aishi (Sad Story of a Barmaid)
Production Company: Shochiku (Kamata)
Original Story: Yanai Takao
Screenplay: Yoshida Hyakusuke
Photography: Miura Mitsuo
Cast: Yuki Ichiro, Tatsuta Shizue, Hanaoka Kikuko, Yokoo Dekao, Watanabe Atsushi
Released January 22. (No extant prints.)

Yoru hiraku (Blooming at Night/Open at Night)
Production Company: Shochiku (Kamata)
Screenplay: Fushimi Akira
Photography: Miura Mitsuo
Cast: Yamanouchi Hikaru, Iida Choko, Shimada Yoshichi, Yanagi Sakuko
Released March 6. (No extant prints.)

Madamu to nyobo (The Neighbor's Wife and Mine/Madame and Wife), 57 minutes
Production Company: Shochiku (Kamata)
Screenplay: Kitamura Komatsu (gags by Fushimi Akira)
Photography: Mizutani Shiko, Hoshino Akira, and Yamada Yoshio
Art Direction: Wakita Yoneichi
Sound recording: Tsuchihashi Takeo and Tsuchihashi Haruo (a.k.a. Dobashi Haruo)
Cast: Watanabe Atsushi, Tanaka Kinuyo, Ichimura Mitsuko, Date Satoko, Inoue Yukiko, Yokoo Dekao, Kobayashi Tokuji, Sakamoto Takeshi, Himori Shinichi
Released August 1. Print at Film Center of National Museum of Art, Tokyo. On VHS Shochiku: SHV Best Selection. Named "Best One" in *Kinema Jumpo* annual polling. Considered Japan's first successful "talkie." The screenplay is published in *Shinario 1: Shinario sakka kyokai hen,* in *Nihon shinario taikei* (*A Historical Collection of Japanese Screenplays, Vol. 1* [Maruyon purodakushon, 1973–79]); *Kinema Jumpo, Nihon eiga shinario koten zenshu, Dai 2 kan* (*A Collection of Classical Japanese Screenplays, Vol. 2,* February 1966); and *Kinema Jumpo, Nihon eiga daihyo shinario zenshu 1* (*A Collection of Representative Japanese Screenplays, No. 1,* January 1958).

Shima no ratai jiken (Island of Naked Scandal)
Production Company: Shochiku (Kamata)
Screenplay: Fushimi Akira
Photography: Sugimoto Shojiro
Cast: Hanaoka Kikuko, Saito Tatsuo, Seki Tokio
Released September 11. Silent. (No extant prints.)

Gutei kenkei (Silly Younger Brother and Clever Elder Brother)
Production Company: Shochiku (Kamata)
Screenplay: Yanai Takao and Gosho Heinosuke
Photography: Ohara Joji
Cast: Kobayashi Tokuji, Minakami Sachiko, Wakamizu Kinuko, Hanaoka Kikuko, Iida Choko
Released October 8. Silent. (No extant prints.)
Gosho's first film with cinematographer Ohara Joji.

Wakaki hi no kangeki (Memories of Young Days/The Deep Emotion of One's Youth/Excitement of a Young Day)
Production Company: Shochiku (Kamata)
Screenplay: Kitamura Komatsu
Photography: Mizutani Shiko and Ohara Joji
Cast: Kawasaki Hiroko, Takiguchi Shintaro, Yamanouchi Hikaru
Released December 31.
Gosho's first sound film after *Madamu to nyobo*. (No extant prints.)

1932

Niisan no baka (My Stupid Brother/You Are Stupid, My Brother)
Production Company: Shochiku (Kamata)
Screenplay: Kitamura Komatsu
Photography: Ohara Joji
Cast: Takeuchi Ryoichi, Tanaka Kinuyo, Yamanouchi Hikaru, Sawa Ranko, Kawamura Reikichi
Released April 1. Part sound film. (No extant prints.)

Ginza no yanagi (Willows of Ginza/A Willow Tree in the Ginza)
Production Company: Shochiku (Kamata)
Original Story: Saijo Yaso
Screenplay: Fushimi Akira
Photography: Ohara Joji
Cast: Tanaka Kinuyo, Takeuchi Ryoichi, Yuki Ichiro, Tsukuba Yukiko, Kawamura Reikichi
Released April 22. Sound. (No extant prints.)

Tengoku ni musubu koi (Love Requited in Heaven/Heaven Linked with Love/Lovers in the Beyond)
Production Company: Shochiku (Kamata)
Screenplay: Fushimi Akira
Photography: Ohara Joji
Cast: Takeuchi Ryoichi, Kawasaki Hiroko, Katsuragi Ayako, Wakamizu Kinuko, Takamine Hideko
Released June 10. (No extant prints.)

Satsueijo romansu: renai annai (Romance at the Studio: Guidance to Love/A Studio Romance)
Production Company: Shochiku (Kamata)
Screenplay: Kitamura Komatsu
Photography: Ohara Joji
Cast: Takeuchi Ryoichi, Tanaka Kinuyo, Murase Sachiko, Egawa Ureo
Released July 15. (No extant prints.)

Hototogisu (A Cuckoo)
Production Company: Shochiku (Kamata)
Original Story: Tokutomi Roka
Screenplay: Kitamura Komatsu
Photography: Ohara Joji
Cast: Hayashi Chojiro, Kawasaki Hiroko, Aizome Yumeko, Takeuchi Ryoichi, Takamine Hideko, Kawamura Reikichi
Released September 15. (No extant prints.)

Koi no Tokyo (Love in Tokyo)
Production Company: Shochiku (Kamata)
Screenplay: Fushimi Akira
Cast: Takeuchi Ryoichi, Takiguchi Shintaro, Tanaka Kinuyo, Yakumo Emiko
Released September 30. (No extant prints.)

1933

Hanayome no negoto (The Bride Talks in Her Sleep/Sleeping Words of the Bride), 55 minutes
Production Company: Shochiku (Kamata)
Screenplay: Fushimi Akira, from the novel by Yuyama Tosaku
Photography: Ohara Joji
Sound Recording: Tsuchihashi Haruo and Hashimoto Motomu
Cast: Kobayashi Tokuji, Tanaka Kinuyo, Egawa Ureo, Saito Tatsuo, Oyama Kenji, Aizome Yumeko, Sakamoto Takeshi
Released January 14. (Print at National Film Center, Tokyo.)

Izu no odoriko (Dancing Girl of Izu), 93 minutes
Production Company: Shochiku (Kamata)
Screenplay: Fushimi Akira, from the novella by Kawabata Yasunari
Photography: Ohara Joji
Art Direction: Kisu Ko
Costume Design: Shinozaki Umeka
Cast: Tanaka Kinuyo, Ohinata Den, Wakamizu Kinuko, Kobayashi Tokuji, Takamatsu Eiko, Hyodo Shizue, Arai Jun, Takeuchi Ryoichi, Kawamura Reikichi, Mizushima Ryotaro, Iida Choko, Sakamoto Takeshi

Released: February 2. Silent. (Print at National Film Center, Tokyo; unsubtitled print at Museum of Modern Art, New York.) On VHS Shochiku: SHV Best Selection. The screenplay is published in *Kinema Jumpo, Nihon eiga shinario koten zenshu, Dai 2 kan* (*A Collection of Classical Japanese Screenplays, Vol. 2,* February 1966).

Jukyu no haru (The Nineteenth Spring/Spring of a Nineteen-Year-Old)
Production Company: Shochiku (Kamata)
Screenplay: Fushimi Akira
Photography: Ohara Joji
Cast: Fushimi Nobuko, Takeuchi Ryoichi, Yamanouchi Hikaru, Mizukubo Sumiko, Kobayashi Tokuji, Takamine Hideko
Released May 18. (No extant prints.)

Shojo-yo sayonara (Virgin, Goodbye/Goodbye, My Girl)
Production Company: Shochiku (Kamata)
Screenplay: Fushimi Akira
Photography: Ohara Joji
Cast: Fushimi Nobuko, Okada Yoshiko, Ohinata Den, Kobayashi Tokuji
Released June 30. (No extant prints.)

L'Amour (Ramuru/Aibu/Caress/Love), 93 minutes
Production Company: Shochiku (Kamata)
Screenplay: Fushimi Akira
Photography: Ohara Joji
Cast: Okada Yoshiko, Arai Jun, Watanabe Tadao, Oikawa Michiko, Kobayashi Tokuji, Sakamoto Takeshi, Iida Choko, Tani Reiko, Kawamura Reikichi, Takamatsu Eiko
Released November 9. Silent. (Print at National Film Center, Tokyo.)

1934

Onna to umaretakaranya (Now That I Was Born a Woman/When You're Born to Be a Woman)
Production Company: Shochiku (Kamata)
Screenplay: Fushimi Akira
Photography: Ohara Joji
Cast: Iida Choko, Saito Tatsuo, Mizukubo Sumiko, Takamine Hideko
Released January 7. (No extant prints.)

Sakura ondo (Sakura Dance/Cherry Blossom Chorus)
Production Company: Shochiku (Kamata)
Screenplay: Fushimi Akira
Photography: Ohara Joji
Cast: Bando Kotaro, Tanaka Kinuyo, Kawasaki Hiroko, Ohinata Den, Iida Choko
Released April 15. (No extant prints.)

Ikitoshi ikerumono (Everything That Lives/The Living/In the Name of All the Living)
Production Company: Shochiku (Kamata)
Screenplay: Fushimi Akira, based on the novel by Yamamoto Yuzo
Photography: Sugimoto Shojiro
Cast: Ohinata Den, Hanamura Chiematsu, Kawasaki Hiroko, Sakamoto Takeshi, Arai Jun, Takamatsu Eiko, Iida Choko, Tokkan Kozo, Saito Tatsuo, Tani Reiko, Kobayashi Tokuji, Oyama Kenji, Kawamura Reikichi, Yoshikawa Mitsuko, Shinobu Setsuko
Released November 15. (No extant prints.)
Named #3 in *Kinema Jumpo* Best Ten list. The screenplay is published in *Kinema Jumpo, Nihon eiga daihyo shinario zenshu 3* (*A Collection of Representative Japanese Screenplays, No. 3*, May 1958) and in *Nihon eiga shinario koten zenshu, Dai 3 kan* (*A Collection of Classical Japanese Screenplays, Vol. 3*, April 1966).

1935

Hanamuko no negoto (The Groom Talks in His Sleep/The Bridegroom Talks in His Sleep/Sleeping Words of the Bridegroom), 74 minutes
Production Company: Shochiku (Kamata)
Screenplay: Fushimi Akira
Photography: Ohara Joji
Sound: Seo Yoshizaburo
Cast: Hayashi Chojiro, Kawasaki Hiroko, Saito Tatsuo, Kobayashi Tokuji, Shinobu Setsuko, Tokkan Kozo, Takamatsu Eiko, Mizushima Ryotaro
Released: January 13. (Print at National Film Center, Tokyo.)

Hidari uchiwa (Good Financial Situation/Left-handed Fan/A Life of Luxury)
Production Company: Shochiku (Kamata)
Screenplay: Fushimi Akira
Photography: Ohara Joji
Cast: Saito Tatsuo, Takasugi Sanae, Ohinata Den, Sakamoto Takeshi
Released March 15. (No extant prints.)

Fukeyo koikaze (Breezes of Love)
Production Company: Shochiku (Kamata)
Screenplay: Kitamura Komatsu
Photography: Ohara Joji
Cast: Ogasawara Shojiro, Kozakura Yoko, Shinobu Setsuko
Released September 12. (No extant prints.)

Akogare (Yearning/Longing)
Production Company: Shochiku (Kamata)
Original Story: Tsukamoto Yasushi
Screenplay: Ikeda Tadao

Photography: Ohara Joji
Cast: Takasugi Sanae, Izumo Yaeko, Saburi Shin
Released October 1. (No extant prints.)

Jinsei no onimotsu (Burden of Life), 66 minutes
Production Company: Shochiku (Kamata)
Screenplay: Fushimi Akira
Photography: Ohara Joji
Sound: Tsuchihashi Haruo (listed as Dobashi Haruo in the credits)
Art Direction: Gosho Fukunosuke
Music: Horiuchi Keizo
Editing: Shibuya Minoru
Cast: Saito Tatsuo, Yoshikawa Mitsuko, Hayama Masao, Tanaka Kinuyo, Tsubouchi
  Yoshiko, Kobayashi Tokuji, Miyake Kuniko, Iida Choko, Tani Reiko, Saburi
  Shin, Abe Shozaburo, Sakamoto Takeshi, Arai Jun, Oyama Kenji, Kozakura Yoko
Released December 10. (Print at National Film Center, Tokyo.) On VHS Shoch-
  iku: SHV Best Selection.
Ranked #6 in *Kinema Jumpo* Best Ten list. The screenplay is published in *Shinario
  1: Shinario sakka kyokai hen* in *Nihon shinario taikei* (*A Historical Collection of
  Japanese Screenplays, No. 1,* Maruyon purodakushon, 1973–79) and in *Kinema
  Jumpo, Nihon eiga daihyo shinario zenshu 6* (*A Collection of Representative Japan-
  ese Screenplays, No. 6,* November 1958).

1936

Okusama shakuyosho (A Married Lady Borrows Money)
Production Company: Shochiku (Kamata)
Screenplay: Noda Koga and Ikeda Tadao
Photography: Ohara Joji
Cast: Iizuka Toshiko, Konoe Toshiaki, Sakamoto Takeshi, Miyake Kuniko
Released January 15. (No extant prints.)

**Oboroyo no onna (Woman of the Mist/Woman of a Misty Moonlight/Woman
  of Pale Night/Moonlit Night Lady)**, 108 minutes
Production Company: Shochiku (Ofuna)
Screenplay: Ikeda Tadao, from an original idea by Gosho-Tei (Gosho)
Photography: Ohara Joji
Art Direction: Kanasu Takashi
Music: Horiuchi Keizo
Assistant Directors: Shibuya Minoru and Arikawa Iseo
Cast: Iizuka Toshiko, Tokudaiji Shin, Iida Choko, Sakamoto Takeshi, Yoshikawa
  Mitsuko, Okamura Ayako, Saburi Shin, Ryu Chishu, Kobayashi Tokuji
Released May 14. (Print at National Film Center, Tokyo.) On VHS Shochiku:
  SHV Best Selection.

Shindo (The New Road/The New Way), Part I, 64 minutes; **Part II,** 68 minutes
Production Company: Shochiku (Ofuna)
Screenplay: Noda Koga and Gosho, from Kikuchi Kan's serial novel, *Higashi-nihon daimainichi*
Photography: Ohara Joji
Sound: Dobashi Takeo
Art Direction: Gosho Fukunosuke
Music: Fukuda Yukihiko (harp: Shino Shizue; solo: Matsuura Chieko)
Special Effects: Saito Rokusaburo
Assistant Directors: Kameyama Matsutaro, Nakamura Kiyoji, Kusuda Hiroyuki
Cast: Tanaka Kinuyo, Kawasaki Hiroko, Sano Shuji, Uehara Ken, Saburi Shin, Kuwano Michiko, Takamine Hideko, Saito Tatsuo, Yoshikawa Mitsuko, Okamura Ayako, Yamanouchi Hikaru, Oyama Kenji, Ryu Chishu, Tani Reiko, Izumo Yaeko, Wada Toyoko, Morikawa Masami, Shinobu Setsuko
The script of this love story became longer and more involved until it became a two-part movie. Part One released November 13; Part Two released December 2. (Prints at National Film Center, Tokyo.) On VHS Shochiku: SHV Best Selection.

1937

Hanakago no uta (Song of the Flower Basket), 69 minutes
Production Company: Shochiku (Ofuna)
Original Story: Iwasaki Fumitaka
Screenplay: Noda Kogo
Adaptation: Gosho Heinosuke
Photography: Saito Masao and Shigehara Hideo
Art Direction: Wakita Yoneichi
Music: Kubota Kohei
Sound: Dobashi Takeo
Editing: Shibuya Minoru
Cast: Tanaka Kinuyo, Kawamura Reikichi, Takamine Hideko, Sano Shuji, Ryu Chishu, Okamura Ayako, Tokudaiji Shin, Izumo Yaeko, Tani Reiko, Miyake Kuniko, Sakamoto Takeshi, Yoshikawa Mitsuko, Saito Tatsuo
Released January 14. On VHS Shochiku: SHV Best Selection. While making this film, Gosho contracted tuberculosis and did not direct again for three years. (Print at National Film Center, Tokyo.)

1940

Bokuseki (Wooden Head/Wood and Stone), 124 minutes
Production Company: Shochiku (Ofuna)
Screenplay: Fushimi Akira, from a novel by Funabashi Seiichi
Photography: Saito Masao
Art Direction: Kanasu Takashi

Music: Fukuda Yukihiko
Cast: Natsukawa Daijiro, Kogure Michiyo, Akagi Ranko, Yamanouchi Hikaru, Kawamura Reikichi, Tani Reiko, Sakamoto Takeshi, Okamura Ayako, Kobayashi Tokuji, Ryu Chishu, Izumo Yaeko
Released August 1. (Print at National Film Center, Tokyo.) On VHS Shochiku: SHV Best Selection.
Ranked #10 in *Kinema Jumpo* Best Ten list.

1942

Shinsetsu (New Snow)
Production Company: Daiei
Original Story: Fujisawa Tsuneo
Screenplay: Tateoka Kennosuke and Gosho Heinosuke
Photography: Okana Kaoru
Music: Kubota Kohei
Cast: Mizushima Michitaro, Tsukioka Yumeji, Mihato Mari
Released October 1. (A few extant scenes at National Film Center, Tokyo.) Ranked #6 in *Kinema Jumpo* Best Ten list. According to Donald Richie, Gosho "took a script which was intended to be a national-policy drama about a soldier giving up his love for the greater love of country, and turned it into a nicely sentimental melodrama which only happened to occur during wartime" (*The Japanese Movie*, rev. ed [Tokyo and New York: Kodansha, 1982], 68).

1944

Goju no to (The Five-Storied Pagoda), 36 minutes [original running time: approximately 70 minutes]
Production Company: Daiei
Screenplay: Kawaguchi Matsutaro, from the Koda Rohan novel
Photography: Aisaka Soichi
Cast: Hanayagi Shotaro, Mori Masako, Aizome Yumeko, Oya Ichijiro, Yanagi Eijiro, Yamada Masao
Released August 17. (Print at National Film Center, Tokyo.)
The screenplay is on file among Gosho's personal papers at the National Film Center, Tokyo, along with a 53-page booklet of hand-drawn special photographic effects needed for the film. An almost complete print of the film was found in a Russian archive in 1999. Prior to this, the only extant print was poor, had scenes missing, and ran only 36 minutes.

1945

Izu no musumetachi (The Girls of Izu), 72 minutes
Production Company: Shochiku (Ofuna)
Screenplay: Ikeda Tadao

Photography: Ikukata Toshio and Nishikawa Tei

Cast: Saburi Shin, Miura Mitsuko, Kuwano Michiko, Kawamura Reikichi, Sakamoto Takeshi, Ryu Chishu, Izumo Yaeko

Released August 30. (Print at National Film Center, Tokyo.) On VHS Shochiku: SHV Best Selection.

1947

Ima hitotabino (Once More), 118 minutes

Production Company: Toho

Producer: Ito Motohiko

Screenplay: Uekusa Keinosuke, from the novel by Takami Jun

Photography: Miura Mitsuo

Lighting: Onuma Masaki

Art Direction: Matsuyama Takashi

Music: Hattori Ryoichi

Editing: Nagazawa Yoshiki

Assistant Direction: Kakehi Masanori, Horie Hideo, Hasebe Keiji

Cast: Ryuzaki Ichiro, Takamine Mieko, Tanaka Haruo, Kono Akitake, Kitazawa Hyo, Tanima Sayuri, Nakakita Chieko

Released April 1. (Print at National Film Center, Tokyo.) On Toho VHS (TND 1541).

Ranked #3 in *Kinema Jumpo* Best Ten list.

1948

Omokage (A Visage to Remember/A Face to Remember/Image), 93 minutes

Production Company: Toho

Producer: Ide Toshiro

Screenplay: Tateoka Kennosuke based on an original idea by Gosho Heinosuke

Photography: Kizuka Seiichi

Assistant Direction: Kakehi Masanori

Cast: Hamada Yuriko, Sugai Ichiro, Ryuzaki Ichiro, Akagi Ranko, Wakayama Setsuko, Izumo Yaeko, Ryu Chishu

Released April 4. (Print at National Film Center, Tokyo.)

1951

Wakare-gumo (Dispersing Clouds/Drifting Clouds), 110 minutes

Production Company: Studio Eight Productions and Shin Toho

Producer: Hirao Ikuji

Screenplay: Tateoka Kennosuke, Tanaka Sumie, and Gosho Heinosuke

Photography: Miura Mitsuo

Music: Saito Ichiro

Art Direction: Kubo Kazuo

Cast: Sawamura Keiko, Numata Yoichi, Kawasaki Hiroko, Mitsuda Ken, Fukuda Taeko, Okamura Ayako, Nakamura Zeko, Kurata Mayumi, Seki Hiroko, Tanima Sayuri

Released November 23. (Print at National Film Center, Tokyo.)

First film made by Gosho's independent production company.

1952

Asa no hamon (Morning Conflicts), 103 minutes

Production Company: Studio Eight Productions and Shin Toho

Producer: Hirao Ikuji

Screenplay: Tateoka Kennosuke, from the Takami Jun novel of same name published serially in *Asahi Shimbun*

Photography: Miura Mitsuo

Music: Saito Ichiro

Cast: Takamine Hideko, Uehara Ken, Kagawa Kyoko, Ikebe Ryo, Okada Eiji, Sawamura Keiko, Tanaka Haruo, Urabe Kumeko, Saito Tatsuo, Miyake Kuniko, Numata Yoichi, Yoshikawa Mitsuko, Takada Minoru

Released May 1. (Print at National Film Center, Tokyo.)

1953

Entotsu no mieru basho (Where Chimneys Are Seen/Four Chimneys/Three Chimneys), 108 minutes

Production Company: Studio Eight Productions and Shin Toho

Producer: Uchiyama Yoshishige

Screenplay: Oguni Hideo, from the Shiina Rinzo novel *Mujakina hitobito* (*The Good People/The Innocent People*)

Photography: Miura Mitsuo

Sound: Dogen Yuji

Art Direction: Shimogawara Tomoo

Music: Akutagawa Yasushi

Editing: Nagata Nobu

Assistant Direction: Miwa Akira

Cast: Tanaka Kinuyo, Uehara Ken, Takamine Hideko, Akutagawa Hiroshi, Seki Chieko, Tanaka Haruo, Hanai Ranko, Miyoshi Eiko, Nakamura Zeko, Sakamoto Takeshi

Released March 5. (Print at National Film Center, Tokyo.) On VHS, Kinema Club (Tokyo); on DVD in the Shin Toho Masterpieces Collection—Box 7 (Region 2; Imagica/Esummokku).

Ranked #4 in *Kinema Jumpo* Best Ten list. The screenplay is published in *Shinario 2: Shinario sakka kyokai hen* in *Nihon shinario taikei* (*A Historical Collection of Classical Japanese Screenplays, No. 2,* Maruyon purodakushon, 1973–79); and in *Shinario sakka kyokai,* in *Nenkan daihyo shinario shu* (*A Collection of Best Screenplays,* Mikasa shobo, 1953).

1954

Osaka no yado (An Inn at Osaka), 121 minutes
Production Company: Studio Eight Productions and Shin Toho
Screenplay: Yasumi Toshio and Gosho Heinosuke, based on the novel by Minakami
Takitaro
Script Supervision: Kubota Mantaro
Photography: Ohara Joji
Art Direction: Matsuyama Takashi
Music: Dan Ikuma
Cast: Sano Shuji, Otowa Nobuko, Kawasaki Hiroko, Mito Mitsuko, Hidari Sach-
iko, Hosokawa Toshio, Anzai Kyoko, Megumi Michiko, Miyoshi Eiko, Fuji-
wara Kamatari, Tanaka Haruo, Tatara Jun, Kitazawa Hyo, Nakamura Akira
Released April 20. (Print at National Film Center, Tokyo.) On VHS, Kinema Club
(Tokyo).
Ranked #10 in *Kinema Jumpo* Best Ten list. The screenplay is published in *Shinario*
sakka kyokai, in *Nenkan daihyo shinario shu* (*A Collection of Best Screenplays,*
Mikasa shobo, 1954).

Ai to shi no tanima (The Valley between Love and Death), 117 minutes
Production Company: Nikkatsu
Screenplay: Shiina Rinzo
Photography: Ohara Joji
Art Direction: Matsuyama Takashi
Music: Akutagawa Yasushi
Cast: Tsushima Keiko, Akutagawa Hiroshi, Takasugi Sanae, Otowa Nobuko, Ito
Yunosuke, Nakamura Zeko, Anzai Kyoko, Tatara Jun
Released September 21. (Print at Kawakita Memorial Film Institute, Tokyo.) The
screenplay is published in *Nihon shinario bungaku zenshu 10: Shiina Rinzo, Abe*
Kobo shu (*A Collection of Japanese Screenplays from Literature, Vol. 10: Shiina*
Rinzo and Abe Kobo, Riron sha, 1955–56).

Niwatori wa futatabi naku (The Cock Crows Twice), 118 minutes
Production Company: Shin Toho
Producer: Uchiyama Yoshishige
Screenplay: Shiina Rinzo
Photography: Ohara Joji
Art Direction: Shimogawara Tomoo
Music: Mayuzumi Toshiro
Cast: Sano Shuji, Minakaze Yoko, Satake Akio, Watanabe Atsushi, Hidari Sachiko,
Sakamoto Takeshi, Nakamura Zeko, Kozono Yoko, Ito Yunosuke, Miyoshi
Eiko, Tono Eijiro, Iida Choko
Released November 30. (Print at National Film Center, Tokyo.) The screenplay is
published in *Nihon shinario bungaku zenshu 10: Shiina Rinzo and Abe Kobo shu*

(*A Collection of Japanese Screenplays from Literature, Vol. 10: Shiina Rinzo and Abe Kobo,* Riron sha, 1955–56).

1955

Takekurabe (Growing Up/Comparison of Heights/Daughters of Yoshiwara/ Adolescence), 95 minutes
Production Company: Shin Toho
Producers: Fukushima Tsujin, Sugiwara Sadao, Hata Ippei
Screenplay: Yasumi Toshio, based on the novella by Higuchi Ichiyo
Photography: Ohara Joji
Art Direction: Kubo Kazuo
Music: Akutagawa Yasushi
Cast: Misora Hibari, Kishi Keiko, Yamada Isuzu, Kitahara Takashi, Ichikawa Some-goro, Nakamura Zeko, Yoshikawa Mitsuko, Sakamoto Takeshi, Yanagi Eijiro, Mochizuki Yuko, Sasaki Takamura, Shinobu Setsuko, Ichinomiya Atsuko, Nakamura Masanori, Hattori Tetsu, Mori Kikue, Iida Choko
Released August 28. (Print at National Film Center, Tokyo.) On Pyramid Video (VHS).

1956

Aru yo futatabi (Twice on a Certain Night), 99 minutes
Production Company: Kabuki-za Eiga Productions/Shochiku
Producer: Uchiyama Yoshishige
Screenplay: Hasebe Keiji and Gosho, based on Shiina Rinzo's short story, "Tsuma no shisso" ("A Missing Wife")
Photography: Miyajima Yoshio
Art Direction: Kubo Kazuo
Music: Akutagawa Yasushi
Cast: Sano Shuji, Otowa Nobuko, Nozoe Hitomi, Kitahara Takashi, Ichikawa Ko-bai, Sakamoto Takeshi, Sengoku Noriko, Wakayama Setsuko, Hirata Naoko, Urabe Kumeko, Tatara Jun, Hoshi Hikaru, Nakamura Zeko
Released June 8. (Print at National Film Center, Tokyo.)

1957

Kiiroi karasu (Yellow Crow/Behold Thy Son), 104 minutes
Production Company: Kabuki-za Eiga Productions/Shochiku
Screenplay: Tateoka Kennosuke and Hasebe Keiji
Dialogue Director: Yuki Shigeko
Photography (*color*): Miyajima Yoshio
Music: Akutagawa Yasushi
Cast: Awashima Chikage, Ito Yunosuke, Shidara Koji, Tanaka Kinuyo, Kuga Yoshiko, Tatara Jun, Iida Choko, Yasumura Masako, Nakamura Zeko, Takahara Toshio, Numata Yoichi

Released February 28. (Print at National Film Center, Tokyo.) On Shochiku Video: SHV Best Selection.
Gosho's first color film.

Banka (Elegy of the North/Banka Elegy/Dirge), 128 minutes
Production Company: Kabuki-za Eiga Productions/Shochiku
Producers: Kaga Jiro and Uchiyama Yoshishige
Screenplay: Yasumi Toshio and Yuki Shigeko, based on the novel by Harada Yasuko, published serially in *Hokkaido Literature*
Photography: Segawa Junichi
Lighting: Hirata Kanji
Music: Akutagawa Yasushi; song "Banka" sung by Koshiji Fubuki
Assistant Director: Horie Hideo
Cast: Kuga Yoshiko, Mori Masayuki, Takamine Mieko, Ishihama Akira, Watanabe Fumio, Saito Tatsuo, Nakamura Zeko, Urabe Kumeko, Takasugi Sanae, Kaga Chikako, Nakazato Etsuko, Takasaki Atsuo, Matsuyama Teru, Inagaki Yasushi, Takasaki Hajime
Released September 1. (Print at National Film Center, Tokyo; English subtitled print at Pacific Film Archive, Berkeley, California.) On Shochiku Home Video.

1958

Hotarubi (The Fireflies/Firefly Light/Firefly), 123 minutes
Production Company: Kabuki-za Eiga Productions/Shochiku
Producers: Kaga Jiro and Uchiyama Yoshishige
Screenplay: Yasumi Toshio, based on a novel by Oda Sakunosuke
Photography: Miyajima Yoshio
Art Direction: Hirakawa Totetsu
Music: Akutagawa Yasushi
Cast: Awashima Chikage, Ban Junzaburo, Mori Miki, Wakao Ayako, Miyoshi Eiko, Mizuhara Machiko, Suga Fujio, Sawamura Sadako, Ishii Tomiko, Tono Eijiro, Nakamura Zeko
Released March 18. (Print at National Film Center, Tokyo.)

Yoku (Avarice/Half a Loaf /Desire), 106 minutes
Production Company: Shochiku (Kyoto)
Producer: Sugiyama Shigeki
Production Planner: Nanri Konparu
Original: Ozaki Shiro
Screenplay: Inomata Katsuto and Hasebe Keiji
Photography (black-and-white, widescreen): Takeno Haruo
Art Direction: Hirakawa Totetsu
Music: Akutagawa Yasushi
Cast: Ban Junzaburo, Mikuni Rentaro, Morishige Hisaya, Todoroki Yukiko, Fuji Manami, Suga Fujio, Ishiguro Katsuya, Chida Koreya, Seki Chieko
Released: June 24. (Print at National Film Center, Tokyo.)

Ari no machi no Maria (Maria of the Ant Village), 110 minutes
Production Company: Kabuki-za Eiga Productions/Shochiku
Producer: Kaga Jiro
Screenplay: Hasebe Keiji, from the novel by Matsui Toro
Photography (color, widescreen): Takeno Haruo
Art Direction: Hirakawa Totetsu
Music: Akutagawa Yasushi
Cast: Chino Kakuko, Nanbara Shinji, Saito Tatsuo, Sano Shuji, Maruyama Aki-hiro, Natsukawa Shizue, Mizuhara Machiko, Hoshi Hikaru, Nakamura Zeko, Nagata Yasushi
Released December 7. (Print at National Film Center, Tokyo.)

1959

Karatachi nikki (Journal of the Orange Flower), 119 minutes
Production Company: Shochiku (Ofuna)
Producers: Kaga Jiro and Masuda Sayo
Screenplay: Shindo Kaneto
Photography (black-and-white, widescreen): Miyajima Yoshio
Art Direction: Hirakawa Totetsu
Music: Akutagawa Yasushi
Cast: Takachiho Hizuru, Tamura Takahiro, Shimakura Chiyoko, Mizuhara Mach-iko, Kobayashi Tokuji, Yoshikawa Mitsuko
Released April 14. (Print at National Film Center, Tokyo.)

1960

Waga ai (When a Woman Loves), 97 minutes
Production Company: Shochiku (Kyoto)
Producer: Sakai Zengo
Screenplay: Yasumi Toshio, based on the novel by Inoue Yasushi
Photography (color, widescreen): Takeno Haruo
Sound: Hattori Masuo
Art Direction: Hirakawa Totetsu
Music: Akutagawa Yasushi
Editing: Sagara Hisashi
Cast: Arima Ineko, Saburi Shin, Tanami Yatsuko, Otowa Nobuko, Higashiyama Chieko, Nakamura Zeko, Takahashi Toyo
Released January 3. (Print at National Film Center, Tokyo.)
Screened at the 1961 Stratford Film Festival in Ontario.

Shiroi kiba (White Fangs), 96 minutes
Production Company: Shochiku (Kyoto)
Screenplay: Horie Hideo and Hasebe Keiji based on a novel by Inoue Yasushi
Photography (color, widescreen): Takeno Haruo

Art Direction: Hirakawa Totetsu
Music: Akutagawa Yasushi
Cast: Saburi Shin, Todoroki Yukiko, Katsuragi Yoko, Maki Noriko, Mikami Shin-ichiro, Minahara Hiroji, Tatara Jun, Satake Akio
Released June 11. (Print at National Film Center, Tokyo.)

1961

Ryoju (Hunting Rifle), 98 minutes
Production Company: Ryoju Productions/Shochiku
Producers: Tsukimori Sennosuke and Sano Hiroshi
Screenplay: Yasumi Toshio, based on the novel by Inoue Yasushi
Photography (color, widescreen): Takeno Haruo
Art Direction: Hirakawa Totestu
Music: Akutagawa Yasushi
Cast: Yamamoto Fujiko, Saburi Shin, Okada Mariko, Sada Keiji, Otowa Nobuko, Wanibuchi Haruko, Yanagi Eijiro, Taura Masami, Minami Mie
Released January 3. (Print at National Film Center, Tokyo; English subtitled print at Pacific Film Archive, Berkeley, California.) On Shochiku Video: SHV Best Selection.

Kumo ga chigireru toki (As the Clouds Scatter), 93 minutes
Production Company: Shochiku (Kyoto)
Producers: Tsukimori Sennosuke and Gosho Heinosuke
Original Story: Tamiya Torahiko
Screenplay: Shindo Kaneto
Photography (color, widescreen): Takeno Haruo
Music: Akutagawa Yasushi
Cast: Sada Keiji, Arima Ineko, Nakadai Tatsuya, Baisho Chieko, Ito Yunosuke, Hidaka Sumiko, Nakamura Zeko
Released July 9. (Print at National Film Center, Tokyo.) On Shochiku Video: SHV Best Selection.

Aijo no keifu (Love's Family Tree/Record of Love), 106 minutes
Production Company: Shochiku (Ofuna)
Producers: Tsukimori Sennosuke and Gosho Heinosuke
Screenplay: Yasumi Toshio, based on the novel by Enchi Fumiko
Photography (color, widescreen): Kizuka Seiichi
Art Direction: Hirakawa Totetsu
Music: Akutagawa Yasushi
Cast: Okada Mariko, Mihashi Tatsuya, Kuwano Miyuki, Munakata Katsumi, Takamine Mieko, Yamamura So, Otowa Nobuko, Sonoi Keisuke, Maki Noriko, Tonoyama Taiji, Sengoku Noriko
Released November 22. (Print at National Film Center, Tokyo.)

1962

Kaachan kekkon shiroyo (Mother, Get Married), 98 minutes
Production Company: Shochiku (Ofuna)
Producers: Shirai Masao and Sakai Zengo
Screenplay: Horie Hideo and Gosho Heinosuke, based on the novel by Dan Kazuo
Photography (*black-and-white, widescreen*)*:* Narushima Toichiro
Art Direction: Kumaya Masao
Music: Akutagawa Yasushi
Editing: Saito Masao
Cast: Aratama Michiyo, Sha Harukuni, Tamura Takahiro, Ban Junzaburo, Tsu-
gawa Masahiko, Baisho Chieko, Nakamura Zeko, Hana Hajime, Hidaka Su-
miko, Aoyagi Mami, Nagata Yasushi, Takahashi Toyo, Aoyama Hiroshi, Naka-
yama Chinatsu
Released September 1. (Print at National Film Center, Tokyo.)

1963

Hyakuman-nin no musumetachi (A Million Girls), 96 minutes
Production Company: Shochiku (Ofuna)
Producer: Shirai Masao
Screenplay: Hisato Eijiro and Gosho Heinosuke
Photography (*color, widescreen*): Shinomura Sozaburo
Art Direction: Hamada Tatsuo
Music: Akutagawa Yasushi
Cast: Iwashita Shima, Obata Kinuko, Yoshida Teruo, Maki Noriko, Tsugawa Masa-
hiko, Ryu Chishu, Otowa Nobuko, Nakamura Masako, Morozumi Keijiro
Released September 20. (Print at National Film Center, Tokyo.)

1965

**Osorezan no onna (An Innocent Witch/Woman of Osorezan/A Woman of the
Osore Mountains)**, 98 minutes
Production Company: Friend Productions and Shochiku
Producer: Shimazu Kiyoshi
Screenplay: Horie Hideo, based on a novel by Ogawa Hajime
Photography (*black-and-white, widescreen*)*:* Shinomura Sozaburo
Art Direction: Hirakawa Totetsu
Music: Akutagawa Yasushi
Cast: Yoshimura Jitsuko, Terada Minoru, Kawasaki Keizo, Tonoyama Taiji, Sugai
Kin, Yoshida Yoshio, Tono Eijiro, Nakakita Chieko, Ito Sachiko, Tominaga
Misako, Ishii Tomiko, Urabe Kumeko, Nakamura Zeko, Morozumi Keijiro,
Tabu Kenzo
Released October 30. (Print at National Film Center, Tokyo.)
Ranked #7 in *Kinema Jumpo* Best Ten list.

1966

Kaachan to juichi-nin no kodomo (Our Wonderful Years/Mother and Eleven Children), 106 minutes
Production Company: Shochiku
Producer: Shimada Akihiko
Screenplay: Horie Hideo, based on the novel by Yoshida Tora
Photography (color, widescreen): Nagaoka Hiroyuki
Art Direction: Hamada Tatsuo
Music: Saito Ichiro
Cast: Hidari Sachiko, Atsumi Kiyoshi, Baisho Chieko, Tamura Masakazu, Kuga Yoshiko, Hidari Tokie, Toake Yukiyo, Mitsuda Ken, Nakamura Zeko
Released October 1. (Print at National Film Center, Tokyo.)

1967

Utage (Rebellion of Japan/Banquet), 100 minutes
Production Company: Shochiku
Producer: Shimada Akihiko
Screenplay: Horie Hideo, based on the novel by Tonegawa Hiroshi
Photography (black-and-white, widescreen): Nagaoka Hiroyuki
Art Direction: Hamada Tatsuo
Music: Saito Ichiro
Cast: Iwashita Shima, Nakayama Jin, Kawabe Kyuzo, Takahashi Masaya, Fujima Murasaki, Shindo Eitaro, Hayase Kumi, Tamura Takahiro, Higashi Emiko, Sengoku Noriko, Okada Eiji
Released January 14. (Print at National Film Center, Tokyo.) On Shochiku Home Video.

1968

Onna to misoshiru (Woman and Miso Soup/Woman and Bean Soup), 97 minutes
Production Company: Toho
Producers: Sato Ichiro and Shiino Hideyuki
Screenplay: Ide Toshiro, based on the novel by Hiraiwa Yumie (*Gensaku*) and TV series
Photography (color, widescreen): Murai Hiroshi
Music: Saito Ichiro
Cast: Ikeuchi Junko, Nagayama Aiko, Kawasaki Keizo, Tanaka Kunie, Sato Kei, Tamura Masakazu, Kitamura Kazuo, Ishii Tomiko, Sakura Kyomi, Nagayama Aiko, Nakamura Zeko, Tono Eijiro
Released February 14. (Print at National Film Center, Tokyo.)

Meiji haru aki (Seasons of the Meiji/A Girl of the Meiji Period/Four Seasons of the Meiji Period), 73 minutes
Production Company: Hakubutsukan Meiji-mura
Producers: Taniguchi Yoshiro and Tsuchikawa Moto
Screenplay: Horie Hideo, based on an original idea by Ando Tsuruo
Puppet Play: Takeda Ningyo-za
Photography (*color*)*:* Shinomura Sozaburo
Art Direction: Hirakawa Totetsu
Music: Yamashita Takeo
Singing: Frank Nagai
Singing/ Recitation: Miyagi Mariko
Released in August. (Print at National Film Center, Tokyo.)
Puppet film.

SHORT FEATURE (DOCUMENTARY)

1977

Waga machi Mishima (My Town Mishima), 30 minutes
Production Company: Mishima Citizen Salon Productions
Screenplay: Horie Hideo
Photography: Sato Masamichi
Music: Watanabe Zenji
Editing: Horie Sadoko
Assistant Director: Yamaoka Shuichi
Narrator: Kuga Yoshiko
Cast: Children in Mishima City
Gosho lived in Mishima during the last years of his life.

SELECTED BIBLIOGRAPHY

Anderson, Joseph L., and Donald Richie. "The Films of Heinosuke Gosho." *Sight and Sound* 26, no. 2 (Autumn 1956): 77–81.

———. *The Japanese Film: Art and Industry.* Expanded ed. Princeton, N.J.: Princeton University Press, 1982.

Beasley, W. G. *The Rise of Modern Japan.* New York: St. Martin's Press, 1990.

Bock, Audie. *Japanese Film Directors.* New York: Kodansha International, 1978.

Bordwell, David. *Narration in the Fiction Film.* Madison: University of Wisconsin Press, 1985.

———. *Ozu and the Poetics of Cinema.* London: British Film Institute; Princeton, N.J.: Princeton University Press, 1979.

———. "Visual Style in Japanese Cinema, 1925–1945." *Film History: An International Journal* 7, no. 1 (Spring 1995): 5–31.

Bornoff, Nicholas. *Pink Samurai: Love, Marriage and Sex in Contemporary Japan.* New York: Pocket Books, 1991.

Buehrer, Beverley Bare. "*Where Chimneys Are Seen* (1953)." In *Japanese Films: A Filmography and Commentary, 1921–1989.* Jefferson, N.C., and London: McFarland, 1990, 69–72.

Burch, Noël. *To the Distant Observer: Form and Meaning in the Japanese Cinema.* Rev. ed., ed. Annette Michelson. Berkeley and Los Angeles: University of California Press, 1979.

Buruma, Ian. *Behind the Mask: On Sexual Demons, Sacred Mothers, Transvestites, Gangsters, Drifters, and Other Japanese Cultural Heroes.* New York: Pantheon, 1984.

———. *Inventing Japan: 1853–1964.* New York: Modern Library Edition, 2003.

Cazdyn, Eric. *The Flash of Capital: Film and Geopolitics in Japan.* Durham, N.C., and London: Duke University Press, 2002.

Christopher, Robert C. *The Japanese Mind.* New York: Fawcett Columbine, 1983.

Courdy, Jean-Claude. *The Japanese: Everyday Life in the Empire of the Rising Sun.* Trans. Raymond Rosenthal. New York: Harper and Row, 1984.

Desser, David. *Eros plus Massacre: An Introduction to the Japanese New Wave Cinema.* Bloomington and Indianapolis: Indiana University Press, 1988.

Doane, Mary Ann. *The Desire to Desire: The Woman's Film of the 1940s.* Bloomington and Indianapolis: Indiana University Press, 1987.

Dower, John W. *Embracing Defeat: Japan in the Wake of World War II.* New York: New Press/W. W. Norton, 1999.

Eiga shijo besuto 200 shiriizu: Nihon eiga (*200 Classics of Japanese Cinema: The Great Films of the World/Japan*). Tokyo: Kinema Jumpo, May 30, 1982.

Eisenstadt, S. N. *Japanese Civilization: A Comparative View.* Chicago and London: University of Chicago Press, 1996.

Firumu Senta (Film Center), ed. *Gosho Heinosuke kantoku (Special Issue on Director Gosho Heinosuke).* Vol. 21. Tokyo: Film Center of the Tokyo National Museum of Modern Art, 1974.

Fujita Motohiko. *Nihon eiga gendai-shi II: Showa nijunendai (Modern History of Japanese Cinema,* Vol. 2, *1945–1955).* Tokyo: Kashin-sha, 1977.

Galbraith, Stuart, IV. *The Japanese Filmography: A Complete Reference to 200 Filmmakers and Over 1,250 Films Released in the United States, 1900 through 1994.* Jefferson, N.C., and London: McFarland, 1996.

Garbicz, Adam, and Jacek Klinowski. *Cinema, The Magic Vehicle: A Guide to Its Achievement.* Vol. 2: *The Cinema in the Fifties.* New York: Schocken Books, 1983.

Gillett, John. "Coca Cola and the Golden Pavilion." *Sight and Sound* 39, no. 3 (Summer 1970): 153–56.

———. "Heinosuke Gosho: A Pattern of Living." National Film Theatre Programme Booklet, March 1986, 3–7.

———. "Heinosuke Gosho." *Film Dope* (April 1980): 30–31.

———. "Japanese Notebook." *Sight and Sound* 41, no.1 (Winter 1972–73): 27–30.

Gosho Heinosuke. "Jisakau o kataru" ("Gosho Talks about His Films"). *Kinema Jumpo,* no. 101 (October 1954): 31–41.

———. "Romanshugi no igi enshitsuka no tachibakara" ("The Significance of Romanticism in Movies—From a Director's Point of View"). *Eiga Tenbo (Film Review)* 11, no. 3 (1946): 32–33.

———. *Waga seishun (My Youth).* Tokyo: Nagata shobo, 1978.

Govaers, Hiroko, ed. *Le cinéma japonais de ses origines à nos jours (Japanese Cinema from Its Origins to Our Day).* Parts 1–3. Paris: La Cinémathèque Française/La Fondation du Japon, 1984.

"Heinosuke Gosho." In *World Film Directors,* ed. John Wakeman. Vol. 1, *1890–1945.* New York: H. W. Wilson Company, 1987, 401–406.

Hirano, Kyoko. "*Entotsu no mieru basho (Where Chimneys Are Seen).*" In *The International Dictionary of Films and Filmmakers,* ed. Christopher Lyon. Vol. 1, *Films.* Chicago: St. James Press, 1984, 142–43.

———. "Heinosuke Gosho." *The International Dictionary of Films and Filmmakers.* Vol. 2, *Directors/Filmmakers,* 224–26.

———. "Japan." *World Cinema since 1945,* ed. William Luhr. New York: Ungar Publishing, 1987, 380–423.

———. *Mr. Smith Goes to Tokyo: Japanese Cinema under the American Occupation, 1945–1952.* Washington, D.C., and London: Smithsonian Institution Press, 1992.

Horie Hideo. "Gosho Heinosuke to sono kaiwai: Ikiru koto wa hitosuji ga yoshi" ("Gosho Heinosuke and His Milieu: Living One's Life to the Fullest"). *Gosho Heinosuke tokushu,* Eiga Kozo *(Special Issue on Gosho Heinosuke,* Film Lectures). Tokyo: Gendai Engeki Kyodai Foundation, March 1987, 28–35.

———. Letter to the Author. May 20, 1993.

———. "*Osorezan no onna* ni tsuite" ("On *An Innocent Witch*"). Film Lecture. Matsuyama-shi, Shikoku, August 1999.

Horie Hideo, ed. *Gosho Heinosuke to watakushi* (*Gosho Heinosuke and I*). Vol. 243. Tokyo: Foundation in Memory of Gosho Heinosuke, May 1, 1983.

Inoue Yasushi. *The Hunting Gun*. Trans. Sadamichi Yokoo and Sanford Goldstein. Rutland, Vt., and Tokyo: Charles E. Tuttle, 1988.

Iwamoto Kenji. "Sound in Early Japanese Talkies." Trans. Lisa Spalding. *Reframing Japanese Cinema: Authorship, Genre, History,* ed. Arthur Nolletti, Jr. and David Desser. Bloomington and Indianapolis: Indiana University Press, 1992, 312–27.

———, ed. *Nihon eiga to modanizumu: 1920–1930* (*Japanese Film and Modernism: 1920–1930*). Tokyo: Libroport, 1991.

Johnson, William. "The Splitting Image: The Contrary Canon of Heinosuke Gosho." *Film Comment* 27, no. 1 (January–February 1991): 74–78.

Kakehi Masanori. "Gosho Heinosuke no sekai: Gosho Heinosuke no entotsu no mieru basho" ("The World of Gosho Heinosuke: About His Work *Where Chimneys Are Seen*"). In *Nihon eiga o yomu: paionia tachi no isan* (*Reading Japanese Film: Heritage of the Pioneers*). Tokyo: Dagereo shuppan, 1984, 115–38.

———. "Reminiscences of Gosho." In *Heinosuke Gosho,* program of the Tenth Hong Kong International Film Festival, presented by the Urban Council, 1986, 1–44.

Kasza, Gregory J. *The State and Mass Media in Japan, 1918–1945.* Berkeley and Los Angeles: University of California Press, 1988.

Kawabata Yasunari. *The Izu Dancer and Other Stories.* Trans. Edward Seidensticker. Rutland, Vt. and Tokyo: Charles E. Tuttle, 1983.

Keene, Donald. *Dawn to the West: Japanese Literature of the Modern Era—Fiction.* New York: Holt, Rinehart, and Winston, 1984.

Kido Shiro. *Nihon eiga den: eiga seisakusha no kiroku* (*The Story of Japanese Film: A Film Producer's Record*). Tokyo: Bungei shunju-sha, 1956.

Kinema Jumpo. *Nihon eiga daihyo shinario zenshu* (*A Collection of Representative Japanese Screenplays*). Tokyo: Kinema Jumpo sha, 1958.

Kinema Jumpo. *Nihon eiga shinario koten zenshu* (*A Collection of Classical Japanese Screenplays*). Tokyo: Kinema Jumpo sha, 1965–66.

Kirihara, Donald. *Patterns of Time: Mizoguchi and the 1930s.* Madison: University of Wisconsin Press, 1992.

Koschmann, J. Victor. "Maruyama Masao and the Incomplete Project of Modernity." *Postmodernism and Japan,* ed. Masao Miyoshi and H. D. Harootunian. Durham, N.C., and London: Duke University Press, 1989, 123–41.

Lebra, Takie Sugiyama. *Japanese Patterns of Behavior.* Honolulu: University of Hawaii Press, 1976.

Le Fanu, Mark. "To Love Is to Suffer: Reflections on the Later Films of Heinosuke Gosho." *Sight and Sound* 55, no. 3 (Summer 1986): 198–202.

Lehmann, Jean-Pierre. *The Roots of Modern Japan.* New York: St. Martin's Press, 1982.

McDonald, Keiko I. "A Lyrical Novella Revamped: Gosho's *Izu Dancer* (1933)." In *From Book to Screen: Modern Japanese Literature in Film.* Armonk, New York, and London: East Gate/M. E. Sharpe, 2000, 85–98.

———. "Japan." In *The Asian Film Industry,* ed. John A. Lent. Austin: University of Texas Press, 34–60.

———. *Japanese Classical Theater in Films.* London and Toronto: Associated University Presses, 1994.

Mellen, Joan. *The Waves at Genji's Door: Japan through Its Cinema*. New York: Pantheon, 1976.

Mizutani Kenji. *Eiga kantoku: Gosho Heinosuke* (*The Film Director: Gosho Heinosuke*). Tokyo: Nagata shobo, 1977.

———. "Film d'autore e condizioni produttive: 'Takekurabe' di Gosho" ("Film Author and Production Conditions: Gosho's *Takekurabe*"). Translated into Italian by Aldo Tollini and Ueda Hatsumi. In *Schermi Giapponesi: La Finzione e il Sentimento* (*The Japanese Screen: Fiction and Feeling*). Venice: Marsilio Editori, 1984, 59–64.

———. *Gosho Heinosuke kenkyu noto* (*Research Booklet on Gosho Heinosuke*). Tokyo: Gosho Heinosuke kenkyu noto kanko iinkai, 1972.

Morton, W. Scott. *Japan: Its History and Culture*. New York: McGraw-Hill, 1984.

Murakawa Hide. "Shochiku merodorama no kindaika" ("Modernization of Film Melodrama in Shochiku Film Company"). In *Nihon eiga to modanizumu: 1920–1930* (*Japanese Film and Modernism: 1920–1930*). Tokyo: Libroport, 1991, 188–99.

Murphy, Joseph A. "Approaching Japanese Melodrama." *East-West Journal* 7, no. 2 (July 1993): 1–38.

Nakane, Chie. *Japanese Society*. Berkeley and Los Angeles: University of California Press, 1972.

Niogret, Hubert. "Heinosuke Gosho et la maîtrise du découpage" ("Heinosuke Gosho and the Mastery of *Découpage*"). *Positif* 313 (March 1987): 37–41.

Nolletti, Arthur, Jr. "Homage to Heinosuke Gosho." In Program, Heinosuke Gosho Retrospective, presented by the Japan Film Center in Association with the Museum of Modern Art, December 1, 1989–March 9, 1990.

———. "*Once More* and Gosho's Romanticism in the Early Occupation Period." In *Word and Image in Japanese Cinema*, ed. Dennis Washburn and Carole Cavanaugh. New York: Cambridge University Press, 2001, 59–88.

———. "*Where Chimneys Are Seen*." In *Magill's Survey of Cinema: Foreign Language Films*, ed. Frank Magill. Vol. 7, TAL–Z. Englewood Cliffs, N.J.: Salem Press, 1985, 3360–65.

———. "*Woman of the Mist* and Gosho in the 1930s." *Reframing Japanese Cinema: Authorship, Genre, History*, ed. Arthur Nolletti, Jr. and David Desser. Bloomington and Indianapolis: Indiana University Press, 1992, 3–32.

Ohba, Masatoshi. Letter to the Author. June 26, 2002.

Owens, David. "Before *Rashomon*: Japanese Film Treasures of the 30's and 40's." In Program, Museum of Fine Arts, Boston/ Japan Society of New York, 1985, n.p.

Perez, Gilberto. *The Material Ghost: Films and Their Medium*. Baltimore and London: Johns Hopkins University Press, 1998.

Rayns, Tony, ed. *Eiga: 25 Years of Japanese Cinema*. Edinburgh: Edinburgh International Film Festival, 1984.

Reischauer, Edwin O. *The Japanese Today: Change and Continuity*. Cambridge, Mass. and London: Belknap Press of Harvard University Press, 1988.

Richie, Donald. *Japanese Cinema: An Introduction*. Hong Kong, Oxford, and New York: Oxford University Press, 1990.

———. *Japanese Cinema: Film Style and National Character*. Garden City, N.Y.: Anchor/Doubleday, 1971.

————. *The Japanese Movie*. Rev. ed. Tokyo, New York, and San Francisco: Kodansha International, 1982.

————. Letter to the Author. November 29, 2001.

————. *One Hundred Years of Japanese Film: A Concise History, with a Selective Guide to Videos and DVDs*. Tokyo, New York, and London: Kodansha International, 2001.

Rimer, J. Thomas. *A Reader's Guide to Japanese Literature: From the Eighth Century to the Present*. Tokyo and New York: Kodansha International, 1988.

Sato Tadao. *Currents in Japanese Cinema*. Trans. Gregory Barrett. Tokyo: Kodansha International, 1982.

————. Interview with the Author. Tokyo, April 15, 1985.

————. "Le Point de vue sur les cheminées fantômes" ("The Point of View on the Phantom Chimneys"). In Hiroko Govaers, ed., *Le Cinéma japonais de ses origines à nos jours* (*Japanese Cinema from Its Origins to Our Day*). Translated from Japanese into French by Patrick de Vos and Cecile Sakai. Part 2. Paris: La Cinémathèque Française/La Fondation du Japon, 1984, 71–77.

————. *Obake entotsu no sekai. Eiga kantoku Gosho Heinosuke no hito no shigoto* (*The World of Phantom Chimneys: The Movie Director Gosho Heinosuke, the Man and His Work*). Tokyo: Noberu shobo, 1977.

————. "Tokyo on Film." Trans. Larry Greenberg. *East-West Film Journal* 2, no. 2 (June 1988): 1–12.

Shimizu Akira. "Nihon ni okeru senso to eiga" ("War and Cinema in Japan"). *Nichibei eiga sen: Paru Haba gojushuen* (*Media Wars Then and Now: Pearl Harbor Fiftieth Anniversary*). Yamagata International Documentary Festival, October 7–10, 1991, (Tokyo: Cinematrix, 1991), 5–50.

Shinario sakka kyokai hen, Nihon shinario taikei (*A Historical Collection of Japanese Screenplays*). Tokyo: Maruyon purodakushon, 1973–79.

Shipman, David. *The Story of Cinema: A Complete Narrative History from the Beginnings to the Present*. New York: St. Martin's Press, 1982.

Silverberg, Miriam. "Constructing A New Cultural History of Prewar Japan." In *Japan in the World*, ed. Masao Miyoshi and H. D. Harootunian. Durham, N.C., and London: Duke University Press, 1993, 115–43.

Stein, Elliott. "The Greatest *Shomin-geki* on Earth." *The Village Voice*, December 12, 1989, 109.

Suzuki, Tomi. *Narrating the Self: Fictions of Japanese Modernity*. Stanford, Calif.: Stanford University Press, 1996.

Svensson, Arne. *Japan*. London and New York: Zwemmer/Barnes, 1971.

Tessier, Max. *Images de cinéma japonais* (*Images of Japanese Cinema*). Paris: Henri Veyrier, 1981.

————. "Oshima Nagisa, or The Battered Energy of Desire." *Reframing Japanese Cinema: Authorship, Genre, History*, ed. Arthur Nolletti, Jr. and David Desser. Bloomington and Indianapolis: Indiana University Press, 1992, 69–90.

Tucker, Richard N. *Japan: Film Image*. London: Studio Vista, 1973.

Turner, Christena. "The Spirit of Productivity: Workplace Discourse on Culture and Economics in Japan." *Japan in the World*, ed. Masao Miyoshi and H. D. Harootunian. Durham, N.C., and London: Duke University Press, 1993, 144–59.

Ueda, Makoto. *Literary and Art Theories in Japan.* Cleveland: The Press of Case Western Reserve University, 1967.

———. *Modern Japanese Writers and the Nature of Literature.* Stanford, Calif.: Stanford University Press, 1976.

Uekusa Keinosuke. Interview with the Author. Tokyo, April 16, 1985.

———. *Keredo yoake ni—Waga seishun no Kurosawa Akira (After Dawn—Memories of Kurosawa Akira in My Youth).* Tokyo: Bungei shunju-sha, 1985.

Walker, Janet A. "The Cinematic Art of Higuchi Ichiyo's *Takekurabe* (Comparing Heights), 1895–1896." In *Word and Image in Japanese Cinema,* ed. Dennis Washburn and Carole Cavanaugh. New York: Cambridge University Press, 2001, 36–58.

———. *The Japanese Novel of the Meiji Period and the Idea of Individualism.* Princeton, N.J.: Princeton University Press, 1979.

Yamamoto Kikuo. *Nihon eiga ni okeru gaikoku eiga no eikyo—hikaku eigashi kenkyu (The Influence of Foreign Films on Japanese Cinema: Research in Comparative Film History).* Tokyo: Waseda Daigaku shuppan, 1983.

Yoshimoto, Mitsuhiro. "Melodrama, Postmodernism, and the Japanese Cinema." *East-West Film Journal* 5, no. 1 (January 1991): 28–55.

INDEX

Italicized page numbers indicate illustrations. Titles of films by Gosho are indicated with asterisks.

ARTHUR NOLLETTI, JR., is Professor of English at Framingham State College. He is editor of *The Films of Fred Zinnemann,* co-editor of *Reframing Japanese Cinema* (Indiana University Press, 1992), and author of numerous articles on film.